World Economic and Financial Surveys

WORLD ECONOMIC OUTLOOK
October 2009

Sustaining the Recovery

International Monetary Fund

©2009 International Monetary Fund

Production: IMF Multimedia Services Division
Cover and Design: Luisa Menjivar and Jorge Salazar
Composition: Julio Prego

Cataloging-in-Publication Data

World economic outlook (International Monetary Fund)
  World economic outlook : a survey by the staff of the International Monetary
Fund. — Washington, DC : International Monetary Fund, 1980–
  v. ; 28 cm. — (1981–1984: Occasional paper / International Monetary Fund,
0251-6365). — (1986– : World economic and financial surveys, 0256-6877)

Semiannual.
Has occasional updates, 1984–

  1. Economic history, 1971–1990 — Periodicals. 2. Economic history, 1990–
— Periodicals. I. International Monetary Fund. II. Series: Occasional paper
(International Monetary Fund). III. Series: World economic and financial
surveys.

HC10.W7979   84-640155   338.5'443'09048—dc19
                                                            AACR2 MARC-S
ISBN 978-1-58906-807-0

Please send orders to:
International Monetary Fund, Publication Services
700 19th Street, N.W., Washington, D.C. 20431, U.S.A.
Tel.: (202) 623-7430   Fax: (202) 623-7201
E-mail: publications@imf.org
www.imfbookstore.org

FSC © **Mixed Sources**
Product group from well-managed
forests, controlled sources and
recycled wood or fiber
www.fsc.org Cert no. SW-COC-002142
© 1996 Forest Stewardship Council

CONTENTS

Tables

Figures

ASSUMPTIONS AND CONVENTIONS

A number of assumptions have been adopted for the projections presented in the *World Economic Outlook*. It has been assumed that real effective exchange rates will remain constant at their average levels during July 30–August 27, 2009, except for the currencies participating in the European exchange rate mechanism II (ERM II), which are assumed to remain constant in nominal terms relative to the euro; that established policies of national authorities will be maintained (for specific assumptions about fiscal and monetary policies for selected economies, see Box A1); that the average price of oil will be $61.53 a barrel in 2009 and $76.50 a barrel in 2010, and will remain unchanged in real terms over the medium term; that the six-month London interbank offered rate (LIBOR) on U.S. dollar deposits will average 1.2 percent in 2009 and 1.4 percent in 2010; that the three-month euro deposit rate will average 1.2 percent in 2009 and 1.6 percent in 2010; and that the six-month Japanese yen deposit rate will yield an average of 0.7 percent in 2009 and 0.6 percent in 2010. These are, of course, working hypotheses rather than forecasts, and the uncertainties surrounding them add to the margin of error that would in any event be involved in the projections. The estimates and projections are based on statistical information available through mid-September 2009.

The following conventions are used throughout the *World Economic Outlook:*

. . .   to indicate that data are not available or not applicable;

—   between years or months (for example, 2006–07 or January–June) to indicate the years or months covered, including the beginning and ending years or months;

/   between years or months (for example, 2006/07) to indicate a fiscal or financial year.

"Billion" means a thousand million; "trillion" means a thousand billion.

"Basis points" refer to hundredths of 1 percentage point (for example, 25 basis points are equivalent to ¼ of 1 percentage point).

In figures and tables, shaded areas indicate IMF staff projections.

If no source is listed on tables and figures, data are drawn from the World Economic Outlook (WEO) database.

When countries are not listed alphabetically, they are ordered on the basis of economic size.

Minor discrepancies between sums of constituent figures and totals shown reflect rounding.

As used in this report, the term "country" does not in all cases refer to a territorial entity that is a state as understood by international law and practice. As used here, the term also covers some territorial entities that are not states but for which statistical data are maintained on a separate and independent basis.

FURTHER INFORMATION AND DATA

This version of the *World Economic Outlook* is available in full on the IMF's website, www.imf.org. Accompanying it on the website is a larger compilation of data from the WEO database than is included in the report itself, including files containing the series most frequently requested by readers. These files may be downloaded for use in a variety of software packages.

Inquiries about the content of the *World Economic Outlook* and the WEO database should be sent by mail, e-mail, or fax (telephone inquiries cannot be accepted) to

World Economic Studies Division
Research Department
International Monetary Fund
700 19th Street, N.W.
Washington, D.C. 20431, U.S.A.
www.imf.org/weoforum   Fax: (202) 623-6343

PREFACE

The analysis and projections contained in the *World Economic Outlook* are integral elements of the IMF's surveillance of economic developments and policies in its member countries, of developments in international financial markets, and of the global economic system. The survey of prospects and policies is the product of a comprehensive interdepartmental review of world economic developments, which draws primarily on information the IMF staff gathers through its consultations with member countries. These consultations are carried out in particular by the IMF's area departments—namely, the African Department, Asia and Pacific Department, European Department, Middle East and Central Asia Department, and Western Hemisphere Department—together with the Strategy, Policy, and Review Department; the Monetary and Capital Markets Department; and the Fiscal Affairs Department.

The analysis in this report was coordinated in the Research Department under the general direction of Olivier Blanchard, Economic Counsellor and Director of Research. The project was directed by Jörg Decressin, Division Chief, Research Department.

The primary contributors to this report are Abdul Abiad, Ravi Balakrishnan, Petya Koeva Brooks, Stephan Danninger, Antonio Fatás, Prakash Kannan, Daniel Leigh, Pau Rabanal, Alasdair Scott, Marco Terrones, and Irina Tytell. Toh Kuan, Gavin Asdorian, Stephanie Denis, Angela Espiritu, Murad Omoev, Andy Salazar, Min Kyu Song, Ercument Tulun, and Jessie Yang provided research assistance. Mahnaz Hemmati and Emory Oakes managed the database and the computer systems. Jemille Colon, Tita Gunio, Shanti Karunaratne, Patricia Medina, and Sheila Tomilloso Igcasenza were responsible for word processing. Julio Prego provided graphics support. Other contributors include Irena Asmundson, Kevin Cheng, Nese Erbil, Deniz Igan, Thomas Helbling, Armine Khachatryan, Heejin Kim, Prakash Loungani, Shaun Roache, Jair Rodriguez, Marina Rousset, and Mika Saito. Charles Collyns and David Romer of the Research Department provided advice and encouragement. Jordi Galí was an external consultant, and Linda Griffin Kean of the External Relations Department edited the manuscript and coordinated the production of the publication.

The analysis has benefited from comments and suggestions by staff from other IMF departments, as well as by Executive Directors following their discussion of the report on September 16, 2009. However, both projections and policy considerations are those of the IMF staff and should not be attributed to Executive Directors or to their national authorities.

The Recovery Has Started, and the Challenge Is to Sustain It

The global economy is expanding again, and financial conditions have improved markedly. It will still take some time, however, until the outlook for employment improves significantly.

Emerging and developing economies are further ahead on the road to recovery, led by a resurgence in Asia—in general, emerging economies have withstood the financial turmoil much better than expected based on past experience, which reflects improved policy frameworks. However, gains in activity are now being seen more broadly, including in the major advanced economies. Financial market sentiment and risk appetite have rebounded, banks have raised capital and wholesale funding markets have reopened, and emerging market risks have eased.

The triggers for this rebound are strong public policies across advanced and emerging economies that, together with measures deployed by the IMF at the international level, have allayed concerns about systemic financial collapse, supported demand, and all but eliminated fears of a global depression. These fears had contributed to the steepest drop in global activity and trade since World War II. Central banks reacted quickly with exceptionally large interest rate cuts as well as unconventional measures to inject liquidity and sustain credit. Governments launched major fiscal stimulus programs, while assessing their banks with stress tests and supporting them with guarantees and capital injections. And the IMF made use of its enhanced lending capacity and more flexible facilities to help emerging and developing economies cope with the risks associated with the crisis. Together, these measures reduced uncertainty and increased confidence.

But complacency must be avoided. Despite these advances, the pace of recovery is expected to be slow and, for quite some time, insufficient to decrease unemployment. Also, poverty could increase significantly in a number of developing economies where real GDP per capita is contracting in 2009 for the first time in a decade. Activity may pick up quickly in the short term. Yet the forces that are driving the current rebound are partly temporary in nature, including major fiscal stimulus, central banks' support for credit markets, and restocking following exceptionally large cutbacks in production and drawdowns of inventories. These forces will diminish during the course of 2010.

A further key constraint on the pace of recovery will be limits on credit availability. Bank deleveraging will constrain the supply of bank credit for the remainder of 2009 and into 2010 in both the United States and Europe, where credit supply is even more bank-dependent. Bank balance sheets have benefited from capital-raising efforts and positive earnings reports but will remain under pressure as a result of continuing credit deterioration. Our analysis suggests that U.S. banks have recognized somewhat more than half their projected losses from impaired assets through 2010. In Europe, loss recognition is less advanced, reflecting differences in the economic cycle. Although stronger bank earnings are supporting capital levels, they are not expected to fully offset write-downs over the next 18 months. Moreover, steady-state earnings are likely to be lower in the postcrisis environment, and reforms under way to bank regulation are expected to reduce net revenues and result in more costly self-insurance through higher capital and liquidity requirements. Projections for emerging economies assume that capital flows, which took a major hit over the past year, will stabilize or grow moderately. Credit growth will continue to fall or stay at very low levels, and this will hold back investment, with the notable exception of China. Significant credit contraction is generally unlikely, except in parts of emerging Europe and the Commonwealth of Independent States.

Meanwhile, consumption and investment are gaining strength only slowly, held back by the need for balance sheet repair, high excess capacity as well as financing constraints, and rising unemployment, which is expected to peak at over 10 percent of the labor force in advanced economies. Consumption will be particularly weak in advanced economies, especially those that experienced credit booms, housing bubbles, and large current account deficits, such as the United States and the United Kingdom, and in a number of other (especially emerging) European economies. U.S. consumers, in particular, are likely to maintain substantially higher saving rates than before the crisis.

Accordingly, the *World Economic Outlook* projects activity contracting by about 1 percent in 2009 and expanding by about 3 percent in 2010, which is still well below rates achieved before the crisis.

Downside risks remain a concern. The main risk is that private demand in advanced economies remains very weak. If so, policymakers may be confronted with the difficult choice of either maintaining fiscal stimulus, raising issues of debt sustainability, or phasing out the fiscal stimulus, raising the danger of adverse interactions between real activity, the health of the financial sector, and the fiscal situation. However, there is also potential for positive surprises. Specifically, reduced fears about a 1930s-style crash in activity and an accompanying strong rebound in financial market sentiment could drive a larger-than-projected short-term increase in consumption and investment.

Policy Challenges

It is still too early for policymakers to relax their efforts to restore financial sector health and support demand with expansionary macro-economic policies. The challenge is to ensure that continued short-term support does not distort incentives and endanger public balance sheets, with damaging consequences for the medium term. Furthermore, policies must begin to address key medium-term challenges, including the need for reforming financial systems, boosting potential growth, and rebalancing the patterns of global demand.

Notwithstanding already large deficits and rising public debt in many countries, fiscal stimulus needs to be sustained until the recovery is on a firmer footing and may even need to be amplified or extended beyond current plans if downside risks to growth materialize. However, fiscal policy is likely to become increasingly less effective in supporting demand in the absence of reassurances to investors and taxpayers that deficits and debt will eventually be rolled back. This is likely to require major efforts to constrain spending by initiating entitlement reforms and by committing to large reductions in deficits once the recovery is on a solid footing. The credibility of such reductions could usefully be supported with more robust fiscal frameworks, including suitable fiscal rules and strong enforcement mechanisms that help rein in spending pressures when good times return.

The key issues facing monetary policymakers are when to start tightening and how to unwind large central bank balance sheets. Advanced and emerging economies face different challenges. In advanced economies, central banks can (with few exceptions) afford to maintain accommodative conditions for an extended period because inflation is likely to remain subdued as long as output gaps remain wide. Moreover, monetary policy will need to accommodate the impact of the gradual withdrawal of fiscal support. If and when necessary, instruments exist to start tightening monetary conditions even while central bank balance sheets remain much larger than usual. The pace at which the buildup in central bank balance sheets should be unwound depends on progress in normalizing market conditions and the types of interventions in place. Supported by appropriate pricing, short-term liquidity operations are already unwinding naturally as market conditions improve. However, it could take much longer to unwind the buildup in illiquid assets on some central bank balance sheets.

The situation is more varied across emerging economies, but the moment for starting to remove monetary accommodation is likely to materialize sooner than in advanced economies. In some countries, warding off risks for new asset price bubbles may call for greater exchange rate flexibility, to allow monetary policy tightening relative to easy stances in advanced economies.

Policymakers face two major financial sector challenges. The first is to ensure that markets and banks can support economic recovery. This calls especially for renewed efforts to increase bank capital and repair bank balance sheets. So far, only very partial progress has been made on this front. Official stress tests are important instruments through which the condition of banks can be diagnosed in order to design appropriate strategies for the recapitalization and restructuring of viable banks and for the careful resolution of nonviable banks. In addition, exit strategies from public support need to be clearly articulated to help guide markets. Programs need to be phased out gradually, using market-based incentives to encourage reduced reliance on public support. Moreover, clarity on new capital regulation, liquidity risk requirements, provisioning, and accounting standards and, where possible, agreement on resolution strategies are essential for banks to be able to determine how to deploy their resources and which business lines are likely to be profitable in the future.

The second challenge is to put in place financial reforms that forestall a similar crisis in the future. This will require a major overhaul of prudential policies, which must not be jeopardized by growing confidence that the greatest crisis dangers are past, or fears that national competitive advantages might be lost, or concerns that first-best solutions are beyond

reach for technical reasons. Four issues deserve particular attention. First, the perimeter of regulation needs to be broadened and made more flexible, covering all systemically important institutions alongside incentives to preclude further buildups of institutions currently considered "too big or too connected to fail." Second, effective market discipline needs to be encouraged through greater transparency and disclosure and reform of governance in financial institutions. Third, macroprudential frameworks must induce banks to build more buffers—by raising capital and making provisions in good times that can be used in bad times. And, fourth, international collaboration and coordination need to be improved to adequately cope with the challenges posed by cross-border institutions. Looking forward, to avoid a similar crisis, there is a need not just for better rules—through enhanced regulation—but also for adequate enforcement of the rules—through effective supervision—and for prudent behavior by financial institutions—through suitable internal risk-management processes.

Rebalancing Global Demand

Achieving sustained healthy growth over the medium term also depends critically on rebalancing the pattern of global demand. Specifically, many current account surplus economies that have followed export-led growth strategies will need to rely more on domestic demand growth to offset likely subdued domestic demand in deficit economies that have undergone asset price (stock and housing) busts. By the same token, many external deficit countries will need to rely less on domestic demand and more on external demand. This will require significant structural reforms, many of which are also necessary to boost potential output, which has taken a hit as a result of the crisis. Key are measures to repair financial systems, improve corporate governance and financial intermediation, support public investment, and improve social safety nets.

With respect to social policies, rising unemployment will present a major challenge in many advanced economies that must be met with support for incomes, retraining for the jobless, and measures that facilitate wage adjustment in response to shocks. The crisis has also been a setback to poverty-alleviation efforts in many low-income economies, and continued strong donor support will be necessary to safeguard the major progress these countries have made in stabilizing their economies.

Olivier Blanchard
Economic Counsellor

José Viñals
Financial Counsellor

After a deep global recession, economic growth has turned positive, as wide-ranging public intervention has supported demand and lowered uncertainty and systemic risk in financial markets. The recovery is expected to be slow, as financial systems remain impaired, support from public policies will gradually have to be withdrawn, and households in economies that suffered asset price busts will continue to rebuild savings while struggling with high unemployment. The key policy requirements remain to restore financial sector health while maintaining supportive macroeconomic policies until the recovery is on a firm footing. However, policymakers need to begin preparing for an orderly unwinding of extraordinary levels of public intervention.

Global Recession Is Ending, but a Subdued Recovery Lies Ahead

The global economy appears to be expanding again, pulled up by the strong performance of Asian economies and stabilization or modest recovery elsewhere. In the advanced economies, unprecedented public intervention has stabilized activity and has even fostered a return to modest growth in several economies. Emerging and developing economies are generally further ahead on the road to recovery, led by a resurgence in Asia. The recent rebound in commodity prices and supportive policies are helping many of these economies. Many countries in emerging Europe and the Commonwealth of Independent States have been hit particularly hard by the crisis, and developments in these economies are generally lagging those elsewhere.

The pace of recovery is slow, and activity remains far below precrisis levels. The pickup is being led by a rebound in manufacturing and a turn in the inventory cycle, and there are some signs of gradually stabilizing retail sales, returning consumer confidence, and firmer housing markets. As prospects have improved, commodity prices have staged a comeback from lows reached earlier this year, and world trade is beginning to pick up.

The triggers for this rebound are strong public policies across advanced and many emerging economies that have supported demand and all but eliminated fears of a global depression. These fears contributed to the steepest drop in global activity and trade since World War II. Central banks reacted quickly with exceptionally large interest rate cuts as well as unconventional measures to inject liquidity and sustain credit. Governments launched major fiscal stimulus programs while supporting banks with guarantees and capital injections. Together, these measures reduced uncertainty and increased confidence, fostering an improvement in financial conditions, as evidenced by strong rallies across many markets and a rebound of international capital flows. However, the environment remains very challenging for lower-tier borrowers. More generally, as emphasized in the October 2009 *Global Financial Stability Report* (GFSR), the risk of a reversal is a significant market concern, and a number of financial stress indicators remain elevated.

Looking ahead, the policy forces that are driving the current rebound will gradually lose strength, and real and financial forces, although gradually building, remain weak. Specifically, fiscal stimulus will diminish and inventory rebuilding will gradually lose its influence. Meanwhile, consumption and investment are gaining strength only slowly, as financial conditions remain tight in many economies. Thus, after contracting by about 1 percent in 2009, global activity is forecast to expand by about 3 percent in 2010, which is well below the rates achieved before the crisis. These projections reflect modest upward revisions to those in the July 2009 *WEO Update*.

- Advanced economies are projected to expand sluggishly through much of 2010, with unemployment continuing to rise until later in the year. Annual growth in 2010 is projected to be about 1¼ percent, following a contraction of 3½ percent in 2009. The recovery of activity is more clearly evident on a fourth-quarter-over-fourth-quarter basis: from 2009:Q4 to 2010:Q4, real GDP is expected to rise by about 1¾ percent, up from an expansion of about ½ percent (annualized) during the second half of 2009 and a 2 percent contraction in the first half.
- In emerging economies, real GDP growth is forecast to reach almost 5 percent in 2010, up from 1¾ percent in 2009. The rebound is driven by China, India, and a number of other emerging Asian economies. Other emerging economies are staging modest recoveries, supported by policy stimulus and improving global trade and financial conditions.

Downside risks to growth are receding gradually but remain a concern. The main short-term risk is that the recovery will stall. Premature exit from accommodative monetary and fiscal policies seems a significant risk because the policy-induced rebound might be mistaken for the beginning of a strong recovery in private demand. In general, the fragile global economy still seems vulnerable to a range of shocks, including rising oil prices, a virulent return of H1N1 flu, geopolitical events, or resurgent protectionism.

However, short-term risks are not only on the downside, as evidenced by the recent, more-rapid-than-expected improvement in financial conditions. In particular, the policy-induced reduction in fears about a 1930s-style crash in activity and the accompanying strong rebound in financial market sentiment might induce a larger-than-expected surge in consumption and investment across a number of advanced and emerging economies.

Extending the horizon to the medium term, there are other important risks to sustained recovery, mainly in the major advanced economies. On the financial front, a major concern is that continued public skepticism toward what is perceived as bailouts for the very firms considered responsible for the crisis undercuts public support for financial restructuring, thereby paving the way to a prolonged period of stagnation. On the macroeconomic policy front, the greatest risk revolves around deteriorating fiscal positions, including as a result of measures to support the financial sector.

Beyond 2010: Rebalancing the Global Economy

Achieving sustained healthy growth over the medium term will depend critically on addressing the supply disruptions generated by the crisis and rebalancing the global pattern of demand.

Lower Potential Output

Financial firms will need to be restructured and markets repaired to deliver adequate credit for sustained increases in investment and productivity, while labor will need to be redeployed across sectors. Historical evidence presented in Chapter 4 indicates that there were typically large, permanent hits to output in the aftermath of past financial crises, although the extent is difficult to determine and there have been a wide variety of outcomes. The current medium-term output projections are indeed on a much lower path than before the crisis, consistent with a permanent loss of potential output. Investment has already fallen sharply, especially in the economies hit by financial and real estate crises. Together with rising scrap rates, as corporations go bankrupt or restructure, this is reducing effective capital stocks. In addition, unemployment rates are expected to remain at high levels over the medium term in a number of advanced economies.

Demand-Side Rebalancing

To complement efforts to repair the supply side of economies, there must also be adjustments in the pattern of global demand in order to sustain a strong recovery. Specifically, many economies that have followed export-led growth strategies and have run current account surpluses will need to rely more on domestic demand and imports. This will help offset subdued domestic demand in economies that have typically run current account deficits and have experienced asset price (stock or housing) busts, including the United States, the United Kingdom, parts of the euro area, and many emerging European economies. To accommodate the shifts on the demand side, there will need to be changes on the supply side as well. This will require action on many fronts, including measures to repair financial systems, improve corporate governance and financial intermediation, support public investment, and reform social safety nets to lower precautionary saving. Even with a strong commitment by all countries to reform along these and other lines, however, this process of rebalancing global demand will be a drawn-out process and will need to be supported by greater exchange rate flexibility.

Policy Challenges

The key policy priorities remain to restore the health of the financial sector and to maintain supportive macroeconomic policies until the recovery is on a firm footing, even though policymakers must also begin preparing for an eventual unwinding of extraordinary levels of public intervention. The premature withdrawal of stimulus seems the greater risk in the near term, but developing the medium-term macroeconomic strategy beyond the crisis is key for maintaining confidence in fiscal solvency and for price and financial stability. The challenge is to map a middle course between unwinding public interventions too early, which would jeopardize the progress made in securing financial stability and recovery, and leaving these measures in place too long, which carries the risk of distorting incentives and damaging public balance sheets.

Timing the Tightening of Accommodative Monetary Conditions

The key issues facing monetary policymakers are when to start tightening and how to unwind large central bank balance sheets. The two objectives do not necessarily present major conflicts, because instruments exist to start tightening monetary conditions even while balance sheets remain much larger than usual. The pace at which the buildup in central bank balance sheets should be unwound depends on progress in normalizing market conditions and the types of interventions in place.

Regarding the timing of monetary policy tightening, advanced and emerging economies face different challenges. In advanced economies, central banks can (with few exceptions) afford to maintain accommodative conditions for an extended period because inflation is likely to remain subdued as long as output gaps remain wide. Moreover, monetary policymakers will need to accommodate the impact of the gradual withdrawal of fiscal support. The situation is more varied across emerging economies; in a number of these economies it will likely be appropriate to start removing monetary accommodation sooner than in advanced economies. In some economies, warding off risks for new asset price bubbles may call for greater exchange rate flexibility, to allow monetary policy tightening to avoid importing an excessively easy policy stance from the advanced economies.

As the October 2009 GFSR emphasizes, continued central bank support will likely be needed through at least next year in many economies, and it could take much longer to unwind the buildup in illiquid assets on some central bank balance sheets. In the meantime, central banks have tools available to absorb reserves as needed to tighten monetary conditions. Looking beyond the short-term challenges, what are some lessons of the crisis for conducting monetary policy? Historical evidence suggests that relatively stable inflation and output growth offer little protection against major shocks to the economy from bursting asset price bubbles: output and inflation are poor predictors of asset price busts. Chapter 3 shows that other variables, notably credit growth and the current account balance, are better predictors and may deserve more attention from monetary policymakers. Thus, if concerns mount about domestic demand and asset prices, monetary policymakers should consider tightening more than required purely for the purpose of keeping inflation under control over the coming year or two. The chapter also argues that policymakers should consider complementing inflation targeting with the introduction of macroprudential tools to help stabilize economies. Macroprudential tools have the advantage of working directly to lean against credit cycles and can therefore be helpful in complementing the role of interest rates in stabilizing economies. Expectations of what can be achieved, however, need to be realistic.

Maintaining Fiscal Support while Safeguarding Fiscal Sustainability

Notwithstanding already large deficits and rising public debt in many countries, fiscal stimulus needs to be sustained until the recovery is on a firm footing and may need to be amplified or extended beyond current plans if downside risks to growth materialize. Governments should thus stand ready to roll out new initiatives as necessary. At the same time, they need to commit to large reductions in deficits once the recovery is on a solid footing and must start addressing long-term fiscal challenges by advancing reforms to put public finances on a more sustainable path. The achievement of such reductions could usefully be supported with more robust fiscal

frameworks, including suitable fiscal rules and strong enforcement mechanisms. Such frameworks and rules can play helpful roles in reining in spending pressures when good times return, thereby providing a degree of reassurance to investors that deficits and debt eventually will be rolled back. This is essential to again create significant room for countercyclical policy and rebuild public support for financial markets, both of which will be needed to respond to future shocks.

Healing Financial Sectors while Reforming Prudential Frameworks

Completing financial sector repair and reforming prudential frameworks are indispensable for a return to sustained growth. Restructuring financial firms' activities is key to a resumption of normal lending. As explained in more depth in the October 2009 GFSR, this will require balance sheet cleansing, recapitalization, and new business plans that are consistent with new funding models and new prudential frameworks. So far, there has been only very limited progress in removing impaired assets from bank balance sheets. The main challenge now is ongoing deterioration of asset quality. In this regard, official stress tests are important instruments through which the condition of banks can be diagnosed in order to design appropriate strategies for the recapitalization and restructuring of viable banks and for the careful resolution of nonviable banks. On this front, progress across countries has been uneven, and it is a source of concern that support for recapitalization faces political obstacles. Exit strategies need to be clearly articulated to help guide markets. Banks face a "wall of maturities" in the next two years, increasing rollover risks. In this setting, programs need to be phased out very gradually, using market-based incentives to encourage reduced reliance on public support.

Regarding fundamental reform, the achievement of a major overhaul must not be jeopardized by growing confidence that the greatest crisis dangers are past, fears that national competitive advantages might be lost, or concerns that first-best solutions are out of reach for technical reasons. As the October 2009 GFSR emphasizes, four challenges deserve particular attention. First, the perimeter of regulation needs to be broadened and made more flexible, covering all systemically important institutions alongside incentives to preclude further buildup of institutions currently considered "too big or too connected to fail." Second, effective market discipline needs to be encouraged through greater transparency and disclosure and reform of governance in financial institutions. Third, macroprudential frameworks must induce banks to build more buffers—by raising capital and making provisions in good times that can be used in bad times. And, fourth, international collaboration and coordination need to be improved to adequately cope with the challenges posed by cross-border institutions.

Structural and Social Policy Challenges

Rising unemployment will present a major challenge in many advanced economies, and poverty will continue to challenge many developing economies. The evidence in Chapter 4 suggests that unemployment rates typically tend to rise significantly and remain higher for many years after financial shocks. Limiting the extent of job destruction will require slower wage growth or even wage cuts for many workers. The impact of the necessary adjustments on poorer segments of the labor force could be cushioned with earned income tax credits or similar programs that limit the social repercussions of wage adjustment. In addition, better job matching and education and training can help limit job and wage losses. Poverty could increase significantly in a number of developing economies, notably in sub-Saharan Africa, where real GDP per capita is contracting in 2009 for the first time in a decade. Continued donor support from advanced economies will be crucial if these economies are to sustain hard-won macroeconomic stability gains.

GLOBAL PROSPECTS AND POLICIES

After a deep global recession, economic growth has turned positive, as wide-ranging public intervention has supported demand and lowered uncertainty and systemic risk in financial markets. Nonetheless, the recovery is expected to be slow, as financial systems remain impaired, support from public policies will gradually have to be withdrawn, and households in economies that suffered asset price busts will continue to rebuild savings. Risks to the outlook remain on the downside. Premature exit from accommodative monetary and fiscal policies is a particular concern because the policy-induced rebound might be mistaken for the beginning of a strong recovery. The key requirement remains to restore financial sector health while maintaining supportive macroeconomic policies until the recovery is on a firm footing. At the same time, policymakers need to begin preparing for an orderly unwinding of extraordinary levels of public intervention. Policies also need to facilitate a rebalancing of global demand, because economies that experienced asset price busts will need to raise saving rates, and there is a need to bolster potential growth in advanced economies, which has suffered as a result of the major financial shocks. Rising unemployment and setbacks to progress in poverty reduction pose social challenges that also must be addressed.

The Global Recession Is Ending

The global economy appears to be expanding again, pulled up by the strong performance of Asian economies and stabilization or modest recovery elsewhere (Figure 1.1). Nonetheless, the pace of recovery is slow, and activity remains far below precrisis levels. Growth is being led by a rebound in manufacturing and a turn in the inventory cycle, and there are some signs of gradually stabilizing retail sales, returning consumer confidence, and firmer housing markets. As prospects have improved, commodity prices have staged a comeback from lows reached earlier this year, and world trade is beginning to pick up.

The triggers for this rebound are strong public policies across advanced and many emerging economies that have supported demand and all but eliminated fears of a global depression. These fears had contributed to the steepest drop in global activity and trade since World War II (Figure 1.2; Box 1.1). Central banks reacted quickly with exceptionally large interest rate cuts as well as unconventional measures to inject liquidity and sustain credit. Governments launched major fiscal stimulus programs, while supporting banks with guarantees and capital injections. Together, these measures reduced uncertainty and increased confidence, fostering an improvement in financial conditions.

The key question is, how far will this initial rebound go? Specifically, is it a harbinger of a strong recovery? Or is a renewed recession in the offing over the next year as expansionary monetary and fiscal policies lose impetus and private demand fails to gain momentum in the face of limited credit? The projections in this *World Economic Outlook* (WEO) describe an intermediate path: there is a recovery, but it will be weak by historical standards.

According to these forecasts, the current rebound will be sluggish, credit constrained, and, for quite some time, jobless. Global growth is projected to reach about 3 percent in 2010, following a contraction in activity of about 1 percent in 2009 (Table 1.1). During 2010–14, global growth is forecast to average just above 4 percent, appreciably less than the 5 percent growth rates in the years just ahead of the crisis. Financial and corporate restructuring will continue to exert considerable downward pressure on activity, and wide output gaps will help keep inflation at low levels. Demand is likely to be dampened by the need in many advanced economies to rebuild savings. Downside risks to growth are receding gradually but remain a concern.

Table 1.1. Overview of the *World Economic Outlook* Projections
(Percent change unless otherwise noted)

	2007	2008	Projections 2009	Projections 2010	Difference from July 2009 WEO projections 2009	Difference from July 2009 WEO projections 2010	Q4 over Q4 Estimates 2008	Q4 over Q4 Projections 2009	Q4 over Q4 Projections 2010
World output[1]	**5.2**	**3.0**	**−1.1**	**3.1**	**0.3**	**0.6**	**−0.1**	**0.8**	**3.2**
Advanced economies	2.7	0.6	−3.4	1.3	0.4	0.7	−2.2	−1.3	1.7
United States	2.1	0.4	−2.7	1.5	−0.1	0.7	−1.9	−1.1	1.9
Euro area	2.7	0.7	−4.2	0.3	0.6	0.6	−1.7	−2.5	0.9
Germany	2.5	1.2	−5.3	0.3	0.9	0.9	−1.8	−2.9	0.8
France	2.3	0.3	−2.4	0.9	0.6	0.5	−1.6	−0.9	1.4
Italy	1.6	−1.0	−5.1	0.2	0.0	0.3	−2.9	−3.2	0.8
Spain	3.6	0.9	−3.8	−0.7	0.2	0.1	−1.2	−3.5	0.5
Japan	2.3	−0.7	−5.4	1.7	0.6	0.0	−4.5	−1.3	1.4
United Kingdom	2.6	0.7	−4.4	0.9	−0.2	0.7	−1.8	−2.5	1.3
Canada	2.5	0.4	−2.5	2.1	−0.2	0.5	−1.0	−1.5	3.0
Other advanced economies	4.7	1.6	−2.1	2.6	1.8	1.6	−2.7	1.8	2.6
Newly industrialized Asian economies	5.7	1.5	−2.4	3.6	2.8	2.2	−4.7	3.9	2.8
Emerging and developing economies[2]	8.3	6.0	1.7	5.1	0.2	0.4	3.3	3.8	5.5
Africa	6.3	5.2	1.7	4.0	−0.1	−0.1	. . .	. . .	. . .
Sub-Sahara	7.0	5.5	1.3	4.1	−0.2	0.0	. . .	. . .	. . .
Central and eastern Europe	5.5	3.0	−5.0	1.8	0.0	0.8	−2.3	−1.4	2.4
Commonwealth of Independent States	8.6	5.5	−6.7	2.1	−0.9	0.1	. . .	. . .	. . .
Russia	8.1	5.6	−7.5	1.5	−1.0	0.0	1.1	−2.7	−0.9
Excluding Russia	9.9	5.4	−4.7	3.6	−0.8	0.4	. . .	. . .	. . .
Developing Asia	10.6	7.6	6.2	7.3	0.7	0.3	5.5	7.7	7.8
China	13.0	9.0	8.5	9.0	1.0	0.5	6.9	10.1	9.2
India	9.4	7.3	5.4	6.4	0.0	−0.1	4.8	5.1	7.0
ASEAN–5[3]	6.3	4.8	0.7	4.0	1.0	0.3	1.9	2.8	3.8
Middle East	6.2	5.4	2.0	4.2	0.0	0.5	. . .	. . .	. . .
Western Hemisphere	5.7	4.2	−2.5	2.9	0.1	0.6	. . .	. . .	. . .
Brazil	5.7	5.1	−0.7	3.5	0.6	1.0	1.2	2.2	3.5
Mexico	3.3	1.3	−7.3	3.3	0.0	0.3	−1.7	−4.1	3.4
Memorandum									
European Union	3.1	1.0	−4.2	0.5	0.5	0.6	−1.6	−2.5	1.1
World growth based on market exchange rates	3.8	1.8	−2.3	2.3	0.3	0.6	. . .	. . .	. . .
World trade volume (goods and services)	**7.3**	**3.0**	**−11.9**	**2.5**	**0.3**	**1.5**	. . .	. . .	. . .
Imports									
Advanced economies	4.7	0.5	−13.7	1.2	−0.1	0.6	. . .	. . .	. . .
Emerging and developing economies	13.8	9.4	−9.5	4.6	0.1	3.8	. . .	. . .	. . .
Exports									
Advanced economies	6.3	1.9	−13.6	2.0	1.4	0.7	. . .	. . .	. . .
Emerging and developing economies	9.8	4.6	−7.2	3.6	−0.7	2.2	. . .	. . .	. . .
Commodity prices (U.S. dollars)									
Oil[4]	10.7	36.4	−36.6	24.3	1.0	1.2	. . .	. . .	. . .
Nonfuel (average based on world commodity export weights)	14.1	7.5	−20.3	2.4	3.5	0.2	. . .	. . .	. . .
Consumer prices									
Advanced economies	2.2	3.4	0.1	1.1	0.0	0.2	2.1	0.6	0.9
Emerging and developing economies[2]	6.4	9.3	5.5	4.9	0.2	0.3	7.7	4.5	4.3
London interbank offered rate (percent)[5]									
On U.S. dollar deposits	5.3	3.0	1.2	1.4	0.0	0.0	. . .	. . .	. . .
On euro deposits	4.3	4.6	1.2	1.6	−0.2	−0.2	. . .	. . .	. . .
On Japanese yen deposits	0.9	1.0	0.7	0.6	−0.2	0.2	. . .	. . .	. . .

Note: Real effective exchange rates are assumed to remain constant at the levels prevailing during July 30–August 27, 2009. Country weights used to construct aggregate growth rates for groups of countries were revised. When economies are not listed alphabetically, they are ordered on the basis of economic size.

[1]The quarterly estimates and projections account for 90 percent of the world purchasing-power-parity weights.

[2]The quarterly estimates and projections account for approximately 77 percent of the emerging and developing economies.

[3]Indonesia, Malaysia, Philippines, Thailand, and Vietnam.

[4]Simple average of prices of U.K. Brent, Dubai, and West Texas Intermediate crude oil. The average price of oil in U.S. dollars a barrel was $97.03 in 2008; the assumed price based on future markets is $61.53 in 2009 and $76.50 in 2010.

[5]Six-month rate for the United States and Japan. Three-month rate for the euro area.

The remainder of this chapter discusses global economic developments and policy challenges in more depth. The next section reviews the forces of contraction and expansion that will determine the shape of the recovery over the short term. This is followed by a discussion of medium-term prospects for potential output growth and a rebalancing of global demand. The subsequent sections discuss the risks to recovery and the macroeconomic, financial, and structural policy priorities for bringing the global economy back onto a healthy growth trajectory. Chapter 2 explores these themes from a regional perspective.

Deleveraging and Slow Job Growth Ahead

Recent data suggest that the world economy has begun to enter recovery. Global activity is estimated to have risen by about 3 percent during the second quarter of 2009, following a 6½ percent contraction in the first quarter, and high-frequency indicators point to stronger growth in the second half of the year. Nonetheless, firms are still going bankrupt at a high rate, employment continues to drop, and private consumption and investment remain anemic as households struggle with income and wealth losses, firms operate with large excess capacity, and lending conditions remain tight. History suggests that these forces tend to be long lasting following financial crises, entailing sluggish recoveries after periods of sharply contracting activity (see Chapter 3 of the October 2008 *World Economic Outlook*). Policies have helped cushion the impact of these forces on growth, but policy stimulus will diminish in the future.

Improving, but Still Difficult, Financial Conditions

The nascent recovery is most evident in financial markets, although conditions are still very difficult for many borrowers. Public intervention, low policy interest rates, and expectations for recovery have spurred strong rallies in many

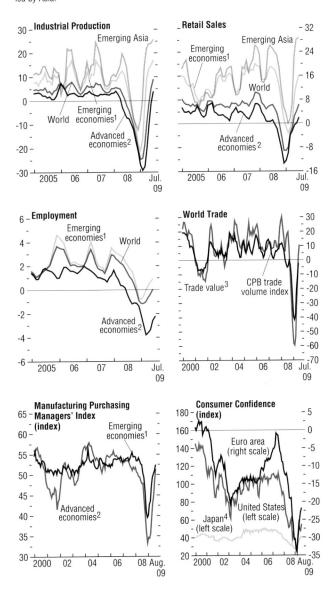

Figure 1.1. Current and Forward-Looking Indicators
(Annualized percent change of three-month moving average over previous three-month moving average unless otherwise noted)

Strong public policies have fostered a rebound of industrial production, world trade, and retail sales, following steep falls at the turn of the year. The rebound in activity is led by Asia.

Sources: CPB Netherlands Bureau for Economic Policy Analysis for CPB trade volume index; for all others, NTC Economics and Haver Analytics.
[1]Argentina, Brazil, Bulgaria, Chile, China, Colombia, Estonia, Hungary, India, Indonesia, Latvia, Lithuania, Malaysia, Mexico, Pakistan, Peru, Philippines, Poland, Romania, Russia, Slovak Republic, South Africa, Thailand, Turkey, Ukraine, and Venezuela.
[2]Australia, Canada, Czech Republic, Denmark, euro area, Hong Kong SAR, Israel, Japan, Korea, New Zealand, Norway, Singapore, Sweden, Switzerland, Taiwan Province of China, United Kingdom, and United States.
[3]In SDR terms.
[4]Japan's consumer confidence data are based on a diffusion index, where values greater than 50 indicate improving confidence.

Figure 1.2. Global Indicators[1]
(Annual percent change unless otherwise noted)

The financial crisis triggered the largest contraction in activity since World War II. The recovery is projected to be modest by past standards.

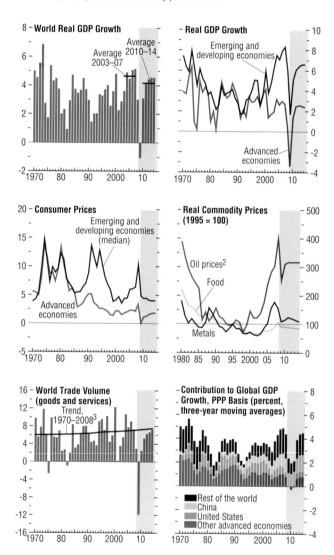

Source: IMF staff estimates.
[1]Shaded areas indicate IMF staff projections. Aggregates are computed on the basis of purchasing-power-parity (PPP) weights unless otherwise noted.
[2]Simple average of spot prices of U.K. Brent, Dubai Fateh, and West Texas Intermediate crude oil.
[3]Average growth rates for individual countries, aggregated using PPP weights; the aggregates shift over time in favor of faster-growing economies, giving the line an upward trend.

markets as well as a rebound in international capital flows (Figure 1.3). Initially, the main driver was public policy, including guarantees for financial institutions, capital injections, provision of ample liquidity, and intervention in credit markets. Now, improving growth prospects are beginning to feed back into financial conditions, with declining risk aversion adding further momentum. However, the environment remains very challenging for lower-tier borrowers, notably small and medium-size enterprises and many households, as emphasized in the October 2009 *Global Financial Stability Report* (GFSR). Securitization markets are still heavily impaired, which severely limits banks' capacity to originate (and distribute) credit. More generally, the risk of a reversal is a significant market concern, and a number of financial stress indicators remain elevated.

Since the first quarter of 2009, equity markets have posted strong gains, corporate risk spreads have declined, and spreads in interbank markets have fallen to levels fairly close to those prevailing before the bankruptcy of Lehman Brothers in September 2008. Investors are allocating an increasing amount of funds away from government bonds in search of higher yields. Confidence in advanced economy banking systems has received a fillip from better-than-expected earnings results and a series of successful bank capital raisings. In addition, stress-testing exercises, completed and published in the United States and ongoing in various other countries, are helping to rebuild trust in banks. Still, questions remain about the sustainability of bank earnings and the implications of elevated credit risks, with loan delinquencies continuing to increase and delays by banks in recognizing loan losses.

International capital flows have recovered, including to emerging markets (Figure 1.4). Since the beginning of the year, sovereign spreads are down and sovereign issues are up for both advanced and emerging economies, consistent with a noticeable pickup in portfolio flows. The recovery in activity has been better than expected, which has buoyed market sentiment, particularly in Asia and Latin America. Since midyear, emerging market corporate and sovereign deals have been oversubscribed and refinancing risks have fallen sharply, although less so in emerging Europe and the Commonwealth of Independent States (CIS). As in mature markets, high-quality corporate borrowers can access funding fairly easily, but the borrowing capacity of those with weaker credit is more constrained. Notwithstanding these favorable market developments, vulnerabilities remain, especially in emerging Europe and other countries heavily dependent on external financing. Cross-border funding for emerging market banks remains vulnerable to the need for mature-market banks to further deleverage. Refinancing and default risks in the corporate sector continue to be relatively high, especially in emerging Europe, but also for smaller, leveraged corporations in Asia and Latin America.

The return of some appetite for risk in international markets has contributed to depreciation of the dollar and yen and appreciation of emerging market currencies. This followed sharp movements in the opposite direction at the height of the crisis (Figure 1.5). The euro recently strengthened against both the dollar and the yen, although it has held more or less steady at the level prevailing before the crisis in nominal effective terms. The renminbi has moved in line with the dollar over the past year.

Even with improving financial market conditions, however, many households and firms in both advanced and emerging economies will continue to face difficult conditions. In particular, bank loans to the private sector are still stagnating or contracting in the United States, the euro area, and the United Kingdom, consistent with surveys among bank loan officers that point to a continuation of very tight credit conditions. Using revised methodologies, the October 2009 GFSR estimates that global bank write-downs could reach $2.8 trillion, of which $1.5 trillion has yet to be recognized. The bulk of these losses are attributable to U.S., U.K., and euro area banks. Furthermore, these banks face a wall of maturing debt, which will reach $1.5

Figure 1.3. Developments in Mature Credit Markets

Public intervention has fostered a significant improvement in financial conditions. Nonetheless, for most households and firms credit will continue to be difficult to obtain, as evidenced by still-tight bank lending conditions and high interest rates on lower-quality credit.

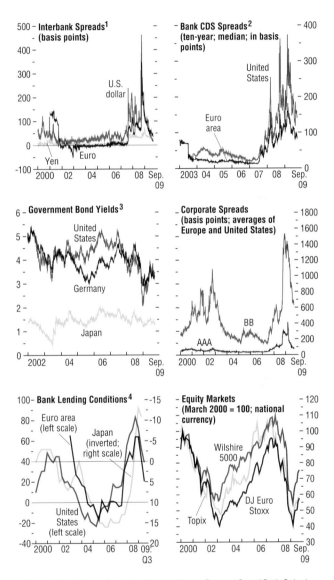

Sources: Bank of Japan; Bloomberg Financial Markets; European Central Bank; Federal Reserve Board of Governors; Merrill Lynch; and IMF staff calculations.
[1]Three-month London interbank offered rate minus three-month government bill rate.
[2]CDS = credit default swap.
[3]Ten-year government bonds.
[4]Percent of respondents describing lending standards as tightening "considerably" or "somewhat" minus those indicating standards as easing "considerably" or "somewhat" over the previous three months. Survey of changes to credit standards for loans or lines of credit to enterprises for the euro area; average of surveys on changes in credit standards for commercial/industrial and commercial real estate lending for the United States; diffusion index of "accommodative" minus "severe," Tankan survey of lending attitude of financial institutions for Japan.

Figure 1.4. Emerging Market Conditions

Capital flows to emerging economies have picked up again, supporting a recovery in equity and bond markets. Lower policy rates have helped ease credit conditions.

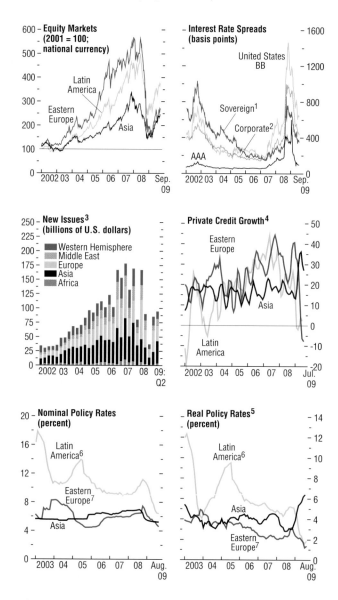

Sources: Bloomberg Financial Markets; Capital Data; IMF, *International Financial Statistics;* and IMF staff calculations.
[1]JPMorgan EMBI Global Index spread.
[2]JPMorgan CEMBI Broad Index spread.
[3]Total of equity, syndicated loans, and international bond issuances.
[4]Annualized percent change of three-month moving average over previous three-month moving average.
[5]Relative to core inflation.
[6]Argentina, Brazil, Chile, Colombia, Mexico, and Peru.
[7]Bulgaria, Estonia, Hungary, Slovak Republic, Latvia, Lithuania, and Poland.

trillion by 2012. At the same time, markets for securitized products remain essentially broken or heavily reliant on public support, which is a particular concern in the United States and other economies where these markets have a major influence on the general availability of credit.

Deleveraging is thus likely to continue for a considerable period in the United States, the euro area, and the United Kingdom. The current outlook for these areas presumes that nonfinancial private sector credit will contract or barely grow during the remainder of 2009 or the first part of 2010, consistent with GFSR estimates. Conditions may ease sooner in the United States, where banks have delevered faster. Because risk premiums remain elevated on high-yield securities and bank lending standards remain tight, financing conditions for many (particularly small and medium-size) enterprises and consumers will remain very difficult.

Projections for emerging economies assume that capital flows, which took a major hit over the past year, will again begin to grow broadly in line with GDP. Credit growth will continue to fall or stay at very low levels, and this will hold back investment, with the notable exception of China. Significant credit contraction is generally unlikely, except in parts of emerging Europe and the CIS, where debt markets are open only to some major corporations and banks and where financial systems are still early in the process of recovering from major credit busts. In general, emerging economies have withstood the financial turmoil much better than expected based on past experience, which reflects improved policy frameworks (Box 1.2).

Sluggish Real Sector Dynamics

The rebound in activity in the real sector is lagging that in the financial sector and will remain subdued over the coming year, particularly in advanced economies. The current recovery in activity is substantially driven by a turn in the inventory cycle, after the sharp destocking that came with the abrupt halt of production at the peak of the crisis. Public policies have successfully improved confidence, demand, and financial conditions, and this has helped industrial production to stabilize and even to increase in a growing number of countries, notably in Asia. As a result, demand for commodities has increased, and with it real sector activity in a number of other emerging economies, boosting international trade. However, in major advanced economies, spare capacity is high and still rising, and household finances are under pressure. Therefore, firms will be cautious about investment, and households will increase their consumption of durables and housing very gradually. Furthermore, many firms and households will continue to struggle to repay debt, which will slow the recovery in housing and financial markets. Subdued demand in advanced economies will hold back the recovery of activity in emerging economies.

Faced with low demand, weak revenue, large excess capacity, and tight credit conditions, non-financial corporations in advanced economies are likely to continue to lay off workers. In the United States, the unemployment rate climbed by over 4 percentage points during the past year to a 26-year high of 9.7 percent in August and is projected to exceed 10 percent by early 2010. Starting from a higher level, the rate in the euro area rose by 2 percentage points to 9½ percent. Countries that experienced particularly large real-estate-related shocks, for example, Ireland and Spain, have seen much larger increases in unemployment because of the sharp contraction in construction jobs. The more moderate increase in the unemployment rate in Europe reflects these economies' greater tendency to adjust payrolls in response to changes in demand by lowering hours worked rather than the number of workers, a practice encouraged in part by labor market policies and institutions (Box 1.3). However, because the euro area is expected to make only a sluggish recovery, more job cuts are likely.

Saving rates are likely to stay high, investment rates low, and labor markets weak. Any substan-

Figure 1.5. External Developments

(Index, 2000 = 100; three-month moving average unless otherwise noted)

Growing risk appetite has accompanied dollar and yen depreciation. Nonetheless, both currencies remain appreciated relative to precrisis levels, whereas those of emerging economies have mostly depreciated, which reflects in part the limited use of currency reserves to buffer external shocks.

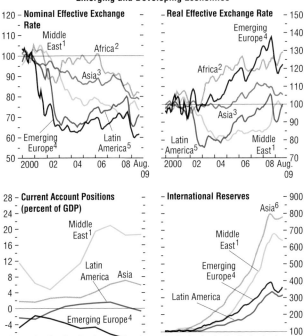

Sources: IMF, *International Financial Statistics;* and IMF staff calculations.
[1]Bahrain, Egypt, I.R. of Iran, Jordan, Kuwait, Lebanon, Libya, Oman, Qatar, Saudi Arabia, Syrian Arab Republic, United Arab Emirates, and Republic of Yemen.
[2]Botswana, Burkina Faso, Cameroon, Chad, Republic of Congo, Côte d'Ivoire, Djibouti, Equatorial Guinea, Ethiopia, Gabon, Ghana, Guinea, Kenya, Madagascar, Mali, Mauritius, Mozambique, Namibia, Niger, Nigeria, Rwanda, Senegal, South Africa, Sudan, Tanzania, Uganda, and Zambia.
[3]Asia excluding China.
[4]Bulgaria, Croatia, Estonia, Hungary, Latvia, Lithuania, Poland, Romania, and Turkey.
[5]Argentina, Brazil, Chile, Colombia, Mexico, Peru, and Venezuela.
[6]Due to data limitations, China's reserves are assumed unchanged since May 2008.

Box. 1.1. Trade Finance and Global Trade: New Evidence from Bank Surveys

The collapse in trade during the crisis was attributed in part to a lack of credit to exporters and importers. Increased uncertainty led exporters and importers to switch from less secure forms of trade finance to more formal arrangements. Exporters increasingly asked their banks for export credit insurance (ECI) or asked importers to provide letters of credit (LCs, a bank's certification that the importer can pay). This increase in the demand for trade credit was assumed to be partly offset by the fact that some merchants switched from bank-financed trade credit to more general loans, as importers were asked to pay for goods before shipment and exporters sought more liquidity to smooth their cash flow. Anecdotes abounded, but there was a lack of information on the extent and types of changes in the demand and supply of trade finance.

To fill this information gap the IMF worked with the Bankers' Association for Finance and Trade to initiate a series of surveys of banks on factors affecting the supply of and demand for trade credit. This box reports the results of a survey comparing conditions in the second quarter of 2009 with those in the fourth quarter of 2008, and conditions in the fourth quarter of 2008 with those in the fourth quarter of 2007. Participants in this survey included a wide range of advanced and emerging market banks. This was the third survey, completed in July and coordinated by FIMetrix.

The survey results suggest that the downturn in trade largely reflected falling demand rather than a lack of trade finance. Trade generally fell

The authors of this box are Irena Asmundson, Armine Khachatryan, and Mika Saito, with assistance from Ioana Niculcea.

by much more than trade finance during 2008 and the first half of 2009, including in the areas hit hardest by the crisis (industrial economies, emerging Europe, Latin America, and—in the first half of 2009—emerging Asia). Correspondingly, six of seven banks pointed to a decrease in trade as the main driver of the decrease in their trade finance activities, and about half also indicated that lower commodity prices contributed to the fall in the value of their trade finance activities. There is, however, some evidence of a separate effect from credit conditions: four of ten banks also cited limited credit at their own banks as a reason for lower trade finance activity, and a similar proportion identified a lack of credit at counterparty banks as a constraint.

Research on the behavior of trade elasticities during downturns also points to demand, rather than trade finance, as a key driver of the downturn. Recent work by Freund (2009) shows that the responsiveness of trade to GDP has increased over time, with elasticities of more than 3.5 during this decade (first figure). The pattern of trade responses across economies also points to increased flexibility: Germany and Japan experienced much larger declines than expected given their diversified export bases and broad access to financial markets. Correspondingly, the rebound may be sharper, and recent data seem to bear this out.

The cost of trade credit also rose during the crisis. Higher funding costs and increased risk continue to put upward pressure on the price of trade credit, for which the increase in demand has been the largest. Even so, the upward price pressures seem to be easing for some instruments, with increasing evidence that the collapse in trade is bottoming out, as demand starts to recover and banks become more positive about

tial pickup in capacity utilization and investment that could lay a foundation for sustained increases in employment appears a long way off. Households struggling with lower pay and job losses and facing weak labor markets will constrain their consumption of durables and

their demand for housing. In addition, saving will increase to help rebuild net household wealth. This is particularly true in the United States and the United Kingdom, where household debt is relatively high, house prices have fallen considerably, and asset price changes tend

Elasticity of World Trade to World Income by Decade

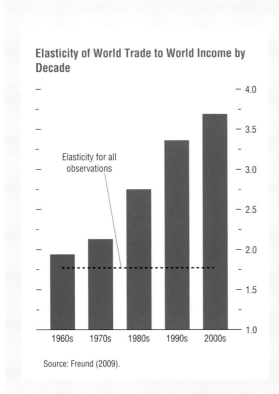

Source: Freund (2009).

Bank Expectations about Trade Finance

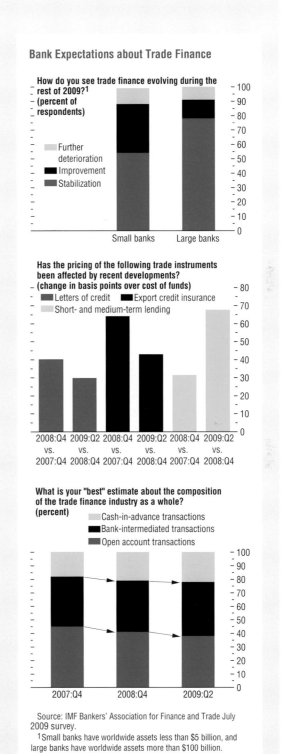

Source: IMF Bankers' Association for Finance and Trade July 2009 survey.
[1] Small banks have worldwide assets less than $5 billion, and large banks have worldwide assets more than $100 billion.

the economic outlook. For example, price increases have started to ease for ECI and LCs (possibly also reflecting competition from official lending bodies whose resources were enhanced).

The shift toward bank-intermediated trade finance appears to be continuing. Surveyed banks estimate that open account transactions (for which exporters provide credit directly to importers) continued to shrink as a share of the total, to less than 40 percent in the second quarter of 2009, from 45 percent at the end of 2007. This has been largely offset by the increasing reliance of traders on bank finance—mainly LCs—as well as by a more modest shift toward cash-in-advance transactions (for which importers pay for goods before shipment). These trends appear to reflect increased risk aversion on the part of both nonfinancial corporations (the decline in the share of open accounts) and banks (increased margins driving some to cash-in-advance transactions), and as such may reflect a more permanent switch in the nature of trade financing (second figure).

Box 1.2. Were Financial Markets in Emerging Economies More Resilient than in Past Crises?

Given the intensity of the global crisis, financial markets in emerging economies have been remarkably resilient. Although many financial institutions in the advanced economies engaged in significant deleveraging, the ruptures in capital markets did not lead to widespread sudden stops of capital flows, and emerging economies with large near-term debt-rollover requirements, such as Turkey, managed to finance such debt relatively well.

The broader economic disruptions in the emerging economies were far from negligible, however. Stock markets fell drastically in the aftermath of the Lehman Brothers bankruptcy, primary funding markets ceased to function for some months, exchange rates came under severe pressure in some regions, and sovereign spreads widened. This box explores how financial markets in emerging economies fared compared with past crises and what might explain any differences (the analysis builds on the approach developed in Chapter 4 of the April 2009 *World Economic Outlook*).

To gauge the resilience of financial markets in emerging economies, we track developments in the Emerging Markets Financial Stress Index (EM-FSI) during the current crisis and during past crises. The EM-FSI measures disruptions in financial intermediation by assessing market signals in various segments of an economy's financial system, including securities markets, the banking system, and foreign exchange markets.[1] By comparing how this index has evolved around the peak of the current crisis with its pattern around past crises, differences in financial market responsiveness can be determined for emerging economies as a whole and by

The main author of this box is Stephan Danninger.

[1]For a description of the EM-FSI and the corresponding index for the advanced economies (AE-FSI), see Balakrishnan and others (2009). The index measures the intensity of stress in the various segments as the deviation from past averages of prices, returns, or volatility indices. The index does not cover corporate bond spreads (CEMBI) due to limited time and country coverage.

region and for different parts of a country's or region's financial system.

Data from the EM-FSI in the top panels of the first figure document that financial stress sharply increased in advanced and emerging economies during the final quarter of 2008 and

Emerging Economies: Resilient Financial Markets

Financial Stress in Advanced and Emerging Economies[1]

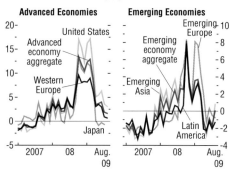

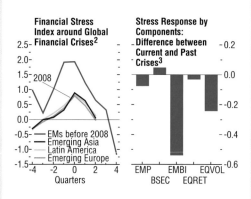

Source: IMF staff calculations.
[1]Purchasing-power-parity-weighted average; the financial stress indices are expressed as a deviation from average since the mid-1990s. See Chapter 4 of the April 2009 *World Economic Outlook*.
[2]Before 2008: 1998 Long-Term Capital Management collapse, 2000 dot-com crash, 2002 default of Enron and WorldCom. Stress response of emerging markets scaled for different size of financial stress in advanced economies in 2008 relative to pre-2008 crises. EMs: emerging markets; Emerging Asia: China, Korea, Malaysia, Philippines, Thailand; Emerging Europe: Hungary, Poland; Latin America: Argentina, Brazil, Colombia, Mexico, Peru.
[3]EMP: exchange market pressure; BSEC: banking sector; EMBI: Emerging Market Bond Index spreads; EQRET: equity market return; EQVOL: equity market volatility.

subsided from historical highs during the first months of 2009. Interestingly, the stress index shows increased resilience across all emerging regions during the current crisis. The bottom panels compare the EM-FSI during the current and past crises in advanced economies—the collapse of Long-Term Capital Management in 1998, the dot-com crash in 2000, and the U.S. corporate crises (WorldCom, Enron, and Arthur Andersen defaults) in 2002—adjusted for the higher level of stress in advanced economies during the current event.[2] Two results stand out: (1) financial stress rose much less compared with past global episodes, and (2) financial market resilience was observed in all emerging regions (lower left-hand panel). These findings were confirmed in a more stringent econometric analysis (see Balakrishnan and others, 2009).

To better understand the forces driving this increased resilience, the differences in response were separated according to the various components of the financial sector: foreign exchange markets, sovereign debt markets, the banking sector, and equity markets (lower right-hand panel). Four of the five components show less responsiveness during the current crisis; only banking sector stress rose, albeit moderately. Because the current crisis is concentrated in the banking sector, the muted increase in stress in this sector is somewhat surprising. The stress response in exchange markets was less strong but broadly the same as in the past. The main contributors to the increased resilience during this crisis were a considerably more moderate widening of sovereign debt spreads and a less sharp increase in equity market volatility. The latter may reflect the fact that earlier crises were centered primarily in the securities markets. The resilience of sovereign debt markets during the current crisis, however, appears to be an important new development.

[2]The regional EM-FSIs for the current crisis were scaled by the intensity of financial stress in advanced economies to obtain comparable responsiveness measures between past and current crises.

What could explain the uniformly more moderate stress response of financial markets in emerging economies? The fact that the more muted financial market response occurred in all emerging regions could indicate that global developments may have played a role, although limited country coverage within some regions hides important variations (for example, the Baltic economies experienced large financial turmoil but are not in the sample). Focusing on the available sample, two factors could have moderated the stress response in sovereign debt markets, exchange markets, and the banking sector: (1) improved macro conditions in emerging economies, such as higher foreign reserves or fiscal balances; and (2) declining foreign currency exposure among borrowers in emerging economies, which was a source of stress during past crises. The analysis first examines whether these variables exhibit a common trend across regions and then assesses the extent to which they can explain differences in resilience across economies.

The two upper panels of the second figure depict trends in fiscal balances and foreign reserves coverage rates across emerging regions. Over the past decade, fiscal vulnerabilities have decreased in most regions and could explain the more limited response of sovereign debt spreads. Similarly, growing reserve buffers may have helped prevent greater exchange market pressure. Further empirical analysis using country-by-country data suggests that rising fiscal balances are associated with a lower financial stress response but there is no strong association with changes in foreign reserves.

The lower left-hand panel depicts trends in local currency lending by foreign banks and domestic subsidiaries in different emerging regions (share of local currency lending in overall foreign lending) to capture the willingness of foreign investors to bear an economy's currency risk. The share of local currency lending has risen in all regions and may reflect the development of more stable financial systems and the implementation of stronger macroeconomic policy frameworks, leading to lower perceived

Box 1.2 *(concluded)*

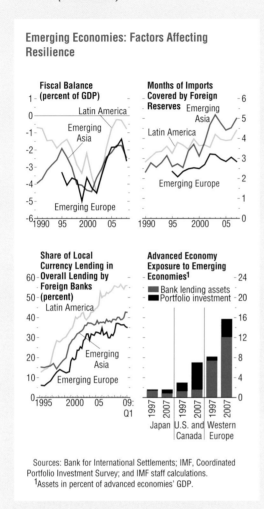

Emerging Economies: Factors Affecting Resilience

Sources: Bank for International Settlements; IMF, Coordinated Portfolio Investment Survey; and IMF staff calculations.
[1]Assets in percent of advanced economies' GDP.

risks from exchange rate fluctuations. There is a negative association between this variable and country-by-country data on the stress response, indicating that economies with higher shares of domestic currency lending have been more resilient (responded less during the current crisis). In a simple regression framework, this variable complements the association between resilience and stronger fiscal balances.[3]

Finally, it may be surprising that financial sectors in emerging Europe were as resilient as those in emerging Asia or Latin America, even though many emerging European economies entered the crisis with weaker macroeconomic fundamentals. One reason is that the available sample omits many of the vulnerable economies in emerging Europe. Another is that investor exposure to emerging Europe was very large in individual economies (Austria, Belgium) and was generally concentrated in the banking sector (lower right-hand panel). As a result, efforts to coordinate the policy response, for instance through multilateral support by the European Union and international financial institutions (European Central Bank, International Monetary Fund, and others), may have led lenders to agree to retract more gently from financial markets in the region to avoid adverse repercussions from an abrupt slowdown.

In sum, the global crisis severely strained the financial systems of emerging economies but by less than would have been indicated by past patterns of financial stress transmission. Stronger fiscal balances and more limited foreign currency exposure among borrowers could have strengthened these economies' resilience, although efforts to coordinate the response of investors, especially in emerging Europe, may also have helped limit the fallout.

---

[3]Given the small number of observations (16), these results are only indicative.

---

to have larger effects on consumption because retirement benefits are more closely related to financial market developments (via defined contribution plans) and borrowing is more dependent on real estate collateral. Furthermore, consumers in many economies that have been hit hard by financial and real-estate-related shocks, such as the United States, are likely to become more prudent, showing a higher propensity to save and a lower appetite for risky assets.

These forces also mean that real-estate-related activity, which along with the related downward pressure on bank balance sheets lies at the origin of the global downturn, may not see a strong rebound for some time. House prices

Box 1.3. Will the Recovery Be Jobless?

The response of unemployment during the current global recession has been very different across economies and regions. In the United States, the unemployment rate has risen by nearly 5 percentage points, to levels not seen since the early 1980s. In contrast, in Germany, despite a major drop in output, the unemployment rate has increased only by ¾ percentage point and remains well below levels seen earlier this decade. This box tries to explain such differences for advanced and emerging economies by comparing current dynamics with those seen around past cycles.

We follow the approach of Chapter 3 of the October 2009 *World Economic Outlook* and compare current labor market dynamics with those around previous recessions.[1] However, we do not look solely at employment dynamics but also at labor productivity and labor participation dynamics.[2] This allows us to get a fuller picture of what is driving output per capita. Specifically, we make use of the fact that the logarithm of output per capita is equal to the sum of the logarithms of labor force participation, the employment rate, and output per employee:

$$\Delta\log\left(\frac{Y}{P}\right) = \Delta\log\left(\frac{Y}{E}\right) + \Delta\log\left(\frac{E}{LF}\right)$$
$$+ \Delta\log\left(\frac{LF}{P}\right),$$

where Y is real GDP, P is population, E is employment, and LF is the labor force.[3]

This allows us to examine how economies adjusted to recent shocks. Has employment adjusted more quickly during this recession? Or is labor hoarding more prevalent than in previous recessions, with productivity initially taking a bigger hit and employment declining only marginally or slowly over time? How uniform are these responses across economies? We apply the decomposition to both advanced and emerging economies, and then use richer data available on labor market institutions and across sectors to take a deeper look at employment dynamics in the advanced economies.

Labor Hoarding or Employment Losses: Which Dominates after a Recession?

As shown in the first figure, during past recessions, the employment rate declines and labor productivity (as measured by output per employee) growth slows, with the latter even turning negative for the average emerging economy, consistent with labor hoarding.[4] During the current crisis, there has been a much bigger impact on output per capita, both in advanced and emerging economies. This is driven mainly by a significantly larger fall in output per employee, which suggests that labor hoarding has been much higher on average during this recession.

However, there is considerable heterogeneity across countries (second figure). For example, among advanced economies, the United States shows a pattern opposite to that of the median country: employment has been cut deeply, helping to maintain labor productivity (whether defined as output per hour or per employee), with little difference in the dynamics of labor force participation. Indeed, during the second quarter of 2009, U.S. nonfarm output per hour grew at its fastest pace in six years (seasonally adjusted annual rate). This is similar to the

---

The main author of this box is Ravi Balakrishnan. Murad Omoev provided research assistance.

[1]This includes recessions going back to the 1970s, and $t = 0$ is the point at which real GDP reaches a peak.

[2]Labor productivity is usually measured here as output per employee because of the lack of comparable data on hours worked for many advanced and emerging economies. However, when comparing German and U.S. labor dynamics, we measure labor productivity as output per hour.

[3]When data on hours worked are available, we can further decompose output per employee:

$$\log\left(\frac{Y}{E}\right) = \log\left(\frac{Y}{H}\right) + \log\left(\frac{H}{E}\right),$$ where H is total hours

worked. This allows us to see which margin is being adjusted: hours worked per employee or employment levels.

[4]Participation trends do not add much insight and so are not discussed in detail.

Box 1.3 *(continued)*

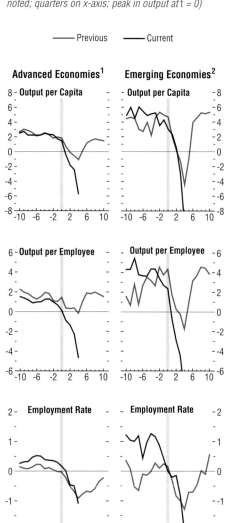

Labor Market Dynamics around Recessions
(Median annual percent change unless otherwise noted; quarters on x-axis; peak in output at t = 0)

——— Previous   ——— Current

Sources: Haver Analytics; IMF staff calculations; and
Organization for Economic Cooperation and Development.
[1]Advanced Economies comprise Australia, Austria, Belgium,
Canada, Czech Rep., Denmark, France, Germany, Greece, Ireland,
Italy, Japan, Korea, Netherlands, New Zealand, Norway, Portugal,
Spain, Sweden, United Kingdom, and United States.
[2]Emerging Economies comprise Argentina, Brazil, Bulgaria,
Chile, Colombia, Estonia, Hungary, Latvia, Lithuania, Malaysia,
Peru, Philippines, Poland, Russia, South Africa, Thailand, and
Turkey.

dynamics of U.S. output per hour following the previous recession, in 2001, which was followed by a so-called jobless recovery, and contrasts with most earlier recessions, when output per hour declined considerably. U.S. employment losses during the current cycle have been significantly larger than for the 2001 recession, or any previous recession. Hours worked per employee have also fallen significantly, but in line with previous cycles.

At the other extreme, Germany, which has also faced an output decline much deeper than during previous recessions, has so far experienced substantially fewer employment losses when compared with previous recessions or with the United States. Output per hour has taken a deep hit, despite hours per employee being cut sharply. This pattern may have been affected by subsidies for part-time work *(Kurzarbeitergeld)*—the availability of which has been lengthened from 6 to 24 months—and by special provisions in collective wage agreements.

Among the emerging economies, during past cycles, southeast Asia tended to demonstrate smaller adjustments in employment and thus had more volatility in output per employee; emerging Europe displayed the opposite pattern. This time around, emerging Europe faces a massive output adjustment, implying declining output per employee, as well as major employment losses. In southeast Asia, employment losses have been minor so far, even relative to previous cycles, whereas in Latin America, there appears to have already been a significant adjustment on the employment margin (third figure).

Can Labor Market Institutions and Regulations Explain the Differences across Advanced Economies?

To explain the heterogeneity, we examine the impact of labor market flexibility, which has many dimensions, such as the types of wage-bargaining arrangements and the level and duration of unemployment benefits. A comprehensive analysis of all facets of labor market flexibility is beyond the scope of this analysis. Instead, we focus on employment protection legislation (EPL), which should be especially important during the current crisis. Research indicates that, although the effect of stricter EPL on the steady-state employment rate is not clear, it could slow the reallocation of labor after major shocks. Of course, EPL may be correlated with other characteristics of labor markets that can affect employment, such as unionization, collective wage bargaining, and various programs to support the unemployed (including subsidies for part-time employment), and EPL could therefore act as a proxy for other labor market characteristics.

Given the lack of data on EPL measures for emerging economies, we focus on advanced economies. We group such economies by their degree of EPL, which we measure by the Organization for Economic Cooperation and Development's index of EPL strictness.[5] Economies are ranked according to their average EPL score during 1985–2007. Canada, the United Kingdom, and the United States are designated as having "low" EPL, and all other advanced economies are designated as having "medium/high" EPL.[6]

The third figure shows the different dynamics of labor productivity (measured by output per employee) and the employment rate across the two groups of advanced economies, during previous recessions and currently. The drop in output per employee is substantial for both groups in the current downturn, but it is particularly sharp among medium/high EPL economies, suggesting a greater degree of labor hoarding given the size of the output drops.

[5]This is produced annually and generally goes back to the mid-1980s. It is a summary indicator, which weighs 14 subcomponents of EPL (on dismissal procedures for regular contracts and the use of temporary contracts).

[6]Of course, many economies have significantly reduced EPL since the mid-1980s (and have made the labor market more flexible in general). However, this doesn't affect the ranking. Moreover, as a robustness check, we examine whether the responses around previous recessions are different before and after the late 1980s, and find that they are quite similar.

Okun's Law and U.S. and German Dynamics
(Median annual percent change unless otherwise noted; quarters on x-axis; peak in output at t = 0)

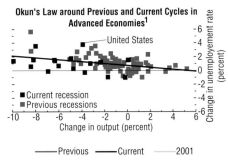

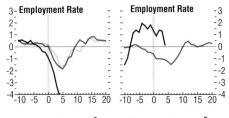

Sources: Haver Analytics; IMF staff calculations; Institute for Employment Research; and Organization for Economic Cooperation and Development (OECD).
[1]Changes in output and the employment rate are defined as year-over-year growth rates at time = 4.
[2]The OECD hours per employee series is used apart from the current period, for which we use Haver Analytics total economy average weekly hours for the United States and Institute for Employment Research total economy quarterly hours per employee for Germany. The series are spliced using year-over-year growth rates of the data used for the current period.

Box 1.3 *(concluded)*

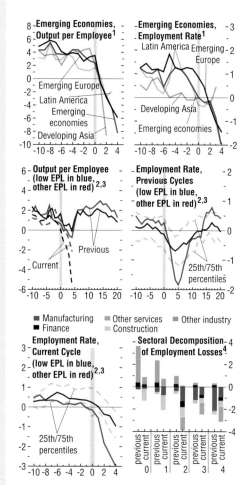

Other Decompositions around Recessions
(Median annual percent change unless otherwise noted; quarters on x-axis; peak in output at t = 0*)*

Sources: Haver Analytics; IMF staff calculations; and Organization for Economic Cooperation and Development.
[1]Emerging economies: all countries in regional groups plus Russia and South Africa; Emerging Europe: Bulgaria, Czech Rep., Estonia, Hungary, Latvia, Lithuania, Poland, Romania, Turkey; Latin America: Argentina, Brazil, Chile, Colombia, Peru; Developing Asia: Malaysia, Philippines, Thailand.
[2]Low employment protection legislation (EPL) countries comprise Canada, United Kingdom, and United States.
[3]Other EPL (medium/high) countries comprise Australia, Austria, Belgium, Czech Rep., Denmark, France, Greece, Ireland, Italy, Japan, Korea, Luxembourg, Netherlands, New Zealand, Norway, Portugal, Spain, and Sweden.
[4]Countries comprise Spain, United Kingdom, and United States. Employment losses are defined as the year-over-year change in employment scaled by the labor force.

The big difference between the two groups is in the employment rate response. During previous cycles and during the current recession, the initial employment losses are much greater among low EPL economies and are even outside the interquartile range for medium/high EPL economies. Regarding job creation once the recovery has taken root, during previous cycles, low EPL economies also tended to register larger employment gains.

What explains this? Clearly, the size of the shock is much larger this time (the biggest global financial crisis since the Great Depression combined with the largest recession since World War II), and this explains the bigger declines in output per capita and output per employee on average. The stronger employment response in low EPL economies, relative to medium/high EPL economies, is consistent with the academic literature, which suggests that employment protection reduces both inflows to and outflows from employment. For medium/high EPL countries, the reduction in employment during this crisis has been similar to that during previous cycles despite substantially bigger output losses, which suggests a higher degree of labor hoarding. Spain, a medium/high EPL economy, is an important exception, most likely because of the dual nature of its labor market. For example, during the current downturn, about half the total employment decline is a result of fixed-term employment losses in the construction sector.[7]

[7]Both historically and during the current recession, Spain has seen bigger employment losses in the downturn phase than low EPL countries. Although employment protection has recently been reduced significantly on regular contracts, at the time fixed-term contracts were introduced (in 1984) it was very high, which led to most new jobs being created on a fixed-term-contract basis. The relatively large stock of fixed-term contracts makes it easier for firms to adjust the level of employment, and also explains why labor productivity (measured as output per hour or employee) doesn't tend to fall in Spain during recessions.

How Are Different Sectors Responding in Advanced Economies?

Because the current recession involves housing busts and systemic banking crises in some of the major advanced economies, we examine whether there is a significantly different sectoral decomposition to employment losses than for previous recessions. We use employment data at the sectoral level, focusing on Spain, the United Kingdom, and the United States, which have all suffered housing busts, and looking at five sectors: manufacturing, construction, other industries, financial and real estate services, and other services (see third figure).

During previous cycles, on average, the service sector provided the bulk of the jobs created during expansions, but most of the job losses during recessions were in the manufacturing sector. Indeed, during downturns, on average, employment increased in services (both financial and other). During this crisis, the manufacturing sector has shed labor as expected, but there have also been big employment losses in construction and financial and other services, consistent with the larger impact of financial crises on financial sector services and of housing busts on construction. The big decline in other services employment may reflect the size of the output drops and spillovers from other sectors.

A Jobless Recovery?

The signs point to substantial labor hoarding in advanced and emerging economies, given that most of the adjustment so far seems to have been in terms of productivity declines rather than employment losses. Of course, this may be part of a rational response by firms, which, because of hiring and firing costs, may be willing to hoard labor if the shock hitting the economy looks transitory. As a recession deepens, however, firms may consider the shock to be more persistent and may start to shed jobs at a faster pace. Given the size and persistence of the recent shocks to the global economy, this harbingers the potential for a jobless recovery,

as excess labor hoarding is gradually unwound, although the analysis suggests that it is critical to distinguish among individual economies.

Advanced economies with low levels of EPL (Canada, United Kingdom, United States) have already experienced major employment losses. If history is any guide, employment in these economies will bounce back strongly, potentially presaging a return to job creation in the not-too-distant future (although after the 2001 recession, employment took a long time to pick up in the United States). The employment losses in the United Kingdom and United States, however, reflect that they have suffered not only recessions but also housing busts and systemic financial crises. As demonstrated in IMF (2009a), such a combination generally leads to large output drops and significantly delays recovery, suggesting a slow and tepid pickup in job creation for these two economies.

Many advanced economies with medium/high levels of EPL have also suffered major recessions but have so far not seen their unemployment rates spike. Some of the adjustment has been through reduced hours, although this may only delay inevitable job losses unless the global recovery is more vigorous than currently expected. For Germany, subsidies for part-time work are making it easier for firms to retain workers by reducing hours worked per employee. These benefits last up to two years, and the result may be reduced job destruction in the downturn, but also significantly less job creation in the recovery period, as hours per employee are simply increased—close to 1.2 million employees, about 3 percent of the labor force, are receiving support under this program.

Emerging economies are expected to recover more strongly than advanced economies, with the notable exception of emerging Europe and the Commonwealth of Independent States, and this should support employment growth. In emerging Europe, the employment adjustment has been severe, and labor market flexibility will be key to the necessary reallocation and future job creation.

are declining at a slower rate or beginning to stabilize in some advanced economies, such as the United States and the United Kingdom, but many markets still face the risk of further price declines (Box 1.4). Even though the heavy drag on growth exerted by falling residential investment is diminishing, a return to more buoyant housing conditions is unlikely as long as households are facing difficult job market prospects and foreclosures continue to mount. Furthermore, the fall in activity has yet to bottom out for commercial real estate, which has lagged the residential sector but is now also going through a severe downturn. Thus, construction activity is likely to stay weak for the foreseeable future, with adverse implications for the financial sector.

Growth dynamics are somewhat stronger in emerging economies. Domestic demand appears relatively robust, particularly in China and India, helped by strong macroeconomic policy support. In addition, many economies are now benefiting from the rebound in commodity prices. Limited information on unemployment in emerging economies points to less difficult although still challenging conditions, with economies in emerging Europe and the CIS suffering large job losses. However, subdued consumption in advanced economies will weigh on many emerging economies' exports, particularly once inventory rebuilding has run its course.

Continued, but Diminishing, Support from Policy

Monetary, fiscal, and financial policies have played a critical role in cutting the adverse feedback loops between the financial and real sectors. However, the policy boost to growth will gradually diminish because room for additional stimulus is limited. Moreover, fundamental financial sector repair is progressing slowly.

Expansionary Monetary Policies

The sharp drop in activity and rise in output gaps have decreased inflation pressures. At the global level, year-over-year inflation moderated to 1.0 percent in July, down from more than 6 percent a year earlier. In the advanced economies, headline inflation has been below zero since May, as oil prices have remained far below levels a year earlier despite their recent pickup. Core inflation has eased to 1.2 percent, down from just over 2 percent a year earlier. Similarly, headline and core inflation in the emerging economies have moderated, falling to 4.2 percent in July and 0.4 percent in June, respectively. However, developments have been uneven, with inflation falling mainly in emerging Asia and less so in emerging Europe.

Policy interest rates have been brought down considerably, close to the zero floor in many advanced economies (Figure 1.6). In response to the growing crisis, central banks proceeded with large cuts in policy rates, which have averaged more than 300 basis points on a global basis since August 2007. In most advanced economies, policy rates were reduced to between 0.25 percent (Canada, Sweden, United States) and 1 percent (euro area). With few exceptions, room for further cuts has thus been exhausted in advanced economies, and markets do not foresee significant rate hikes over the coming year.[1] In an effort to transmit cuts in short-term rates to longer maturities, the U.S. Federal Reserve, the Bank of Canada, and the Swedish Riksbank have explicitly committed to maintaining low policy rates until there are clear signs of recovery. Cuts were generally smaller in emerging economies, reflecting a combination of higher inflation at the onset of the crisis and pressure for exchange rates to depreciate in response to capital outflows. Looking ahead, some central banks in Asia and Latin America may start to tighten again if the strong rebounds there are sustained, although some central banks in emerging Europe are still exploiting

---

[1]Although the European Central Bank (ECB) policy rate remains at 1 percent, after a major one-year repurchase operation, the overnight money market rate in the euro area has dropped to about 0.5 percent and the rate on deposits at the ECB is only 0.25 percent.

room to cut rates in response to more stable external financial conditions.

Central banks in most advanced economies and some emerging economies resorted to a range of unconventional measures to further ease financial conditions during the past year. There have been a variety of different approaches, mainly reflecting different financial system structures.[2] All central banks deployed extensive liquidity support measures for banks, given their importance in every financial system. For example, the ECB introduced much more flexibility into its repurchase facilities, broadening an already wide range of acceptable collateral and introducing six-month and one-year maturities. Many central banks also provided liquidity in U.S. dollars, arranged via swap lines with the Federal Reserve. The Federal Reserve and Bank of England, among others, intervened with outright purchases of government bonds in an effort to lower long-term yields. Given the much greater importance of securities markets for the U.S. economy, the Federal Reserve also intervened heavily in markets for the debt of government-sponsored enterprises,[3] for mortgage-backed securities, and for commercial paper and provided funding and some protection to investors in asset-backed securities.[4]

Together with policy rate cuts and fiscal stimulus, these operations helped to reduce tail risks related to rapidly falling confidence and liquidity constraints. In fact, some interventions are already unwinding naturally in the wake of improvements in financial conditions. Overall, operations targeted at specific dislocated markets appear to have been more effective than purchases of government bonds, although these

[2]For example, in the euro area, bank financing accounted for roughly 70 percent of firms' total external financing during 2004–08. In the United States, market-based sources comprised 80 percent of total external financing (Trichet, 2009). Markets for mortgage-backed securities are also much larger in the United States.

[3]These include the Federal National Mortgage Association (Fannie Mae) and the Federal Home Loan Mortgage Corporation (Freddie Mac).

[4]For further details, see Klyuev, de Imus, and Srinivasan (forthcoming).

Figure 1.6. Measures of Monetary Policy and Liquidity in Selected Advanced Economies
(Interest rates in percent unless otherwise noted)

Central banks have implemented unusually large interest rate cuts to combat the recession. In addition, they have intervened in credit and asset markets to ease financial conditions. With inflation expected to remain constrained, very limited policy tightening is expected over the coming year.

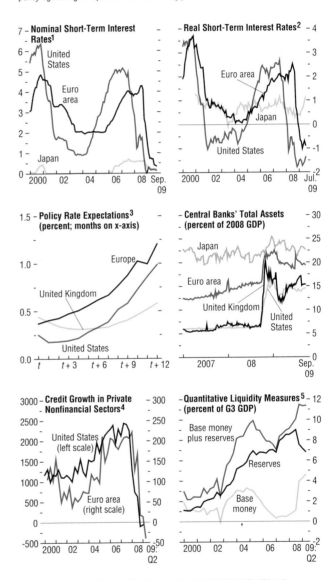

Sources: Bloomberg Financial Markets; Eurostat; Haver Analytics; Merrill Lynch; Organization for Economic Cooperation and Development *Economic Outlook;* and IMF staff calculations.
[1]Three-month treasury bills.
[2]Relative to core inflation.
[3]Expectations are based on the federal funds rate for the United States, the sterling overnight interbank average rate for the United Kingdom, and the euro interbank offered forward rates for Europe; updated September 16, 2009.
[4]Quarter-over-quarter changes; in billions of local currency.
[5]Change over three years for euro area, Japan, and United States (G3); denominated in U.S. dollars.

Box 1.4. Risks from Real Estate Markets

Change in House Prices, 2009:Q1[1]

(Percent, year-over-year, inflation-adjusted)

Sources: Global Property Guide; national sources; Organization for Economic Cooperation and Development; and IMF staff calculations.

[1]Data for Argentina, Belgium, Colombia, Croatia, Czech Republic, Greece, Hungary, India, Korea, Lithuania, Luxembourg, Malaysia, and Slovak Republic are as of 2008:Q4.

The global correction in residential real estate markets has generated large declines in house prices and construction activity across a broad range of economies, although there are some recent signs of stabilization in a few. The median annual decline in real house prices across economies in the year ending in the first quarter of 2009 was 7 percent, with far more dramatic declines in the Baltic economies, Iceland, Singapore, the United Arab Emirates, and the United Kingdom (first figure). Housing activity—measured by the number of transactions or residential investment—has also been falling; housing permits, for instance, showed a median annual decline of about 35 percent in the first quarter of 2009.

With the residential housing bust and the severe global economic downturn, demand for office space and retail/industrial buildings has declined, bringing down the commercial real estate market too. Office vacancy rates increased significantly during 2008 in many cities across the globe. Hardest hit were major cities in some emerging markets, such as Moscow and Shanghai, and international financial centers such as Dublin, New York, London, and Tokyo (second figure).[1] Investment in nonresidential construction has dropped sharply and, in a few cases, has eclipsed the decline in residential construction (third figure).[2] Commercial property sales have come close to a halt (fourth figure), and property prices are falling.

The main authors of this box are Deniz Igan and Prakash Loungani. Heejin Kim and Jair Rodriguez provided research assistance.

[1]Dublin, along with Luxembourg, is one of the main offshore financial centers in Europe.

[2]Nonresidential construction gross fixed capital formation also includes expenditures for public works, but investment in commercial real estate constitutes the bulk of the total. On average, gross fixed capital formation in nonresidential construction constitutes a slightly larger share of GDP (7.4 percent) than residential construction (4.9 percent), but the non-residential sector is considerably larger in the Czech Republic, Korea, Luxembourg, the Slovak Republic, and the United Kingdom.

How much further are house prices likely to fall? And what are the risks to the macroeconomy from the corrections in residential and commercial real estate markets? This box updates the analysis of the housing market in previous issues of the *World Economic Outlook* (WEO) and extends it to commercial real estate.[3]

Corrections in House Prices

On average across advanced economies, upturns in housing markets have lasted about six years, with real house prices going up about 50 percent during that period. Downturns have been characterized by house prices falling by 24 percent over a five-year period (see table). The latest upturn was twice as long as the previous average and more than twice the magnitude (in terms of price). Hence, although house prices have already fallen 20 percent during the ongoing downturn—close to the historical average—there could still be a significant correction to come.

Of course, the extent of the total price correction will vary across economies, and recent price declines have gone further in some than in others. Given the difficulties in assessing house price overvaluation, the fifth figure presents four approaches to computing the likely price correction still to come. The top panel shows the gap between the house price decline in an economy during the current housing downturn and the average declines in that economy during past episodes. If past is prologue, these estimates suggest that the Netherlands and Finland are likely to see further house price declines, whereas the corrections in Australia and the United States are close to complete.

However, this approach does not account for differences across cycles in the driving forces behind house price movements. The estimates in the second panel are based on an econometric model that seeks to explain the increase in house prices that has taken place over the past decade in terms of relevant explanatory

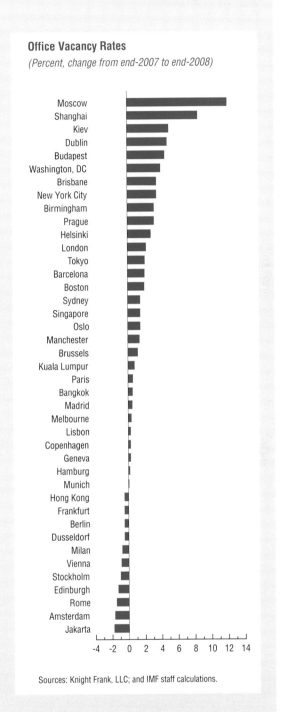

Office Vacancy Rates

(Percent, change from end-2007 to end-2008)

Sources: Knight Frank, LLC; and IMF staff calculations.

[3]See Box 3.1 in the April 2008 WEO, Box 1.2 in the October 2008 WEO, and Chapter 1 (pp. 18–19) in the April 2009 WEO.

variables. To this end, real house price growth is modeled as a function of the following variables: growth in per capita disposable income, working-age population, and credit and equity

Box 1.4 *(continued)*

**Investment in Residential and
Nonresidential Construction**
*(Percent, quarter-over-quarter growth rate as of
2009:Q1)*

█ Gross fixed capital formation in residential construction
■ Gross fixed capital formation in nonresidential
construction

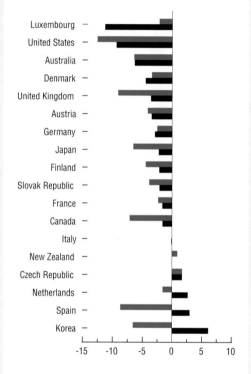

Sources: Organization for Economic Cooperation and
Development; and IMF staff calculations.

Comparison of Current Housing Cycle to Past Cycles

	Upturn		Downturn	
	Duration	Amplitude	Duration	Amplitude
Past cycles	23	48	19	−24
Current cycle	46	124	8	−20

Source: Collyns, Igan, and Loungani (2009).
Note: Average values across 18 advanced economies. Duration is in quarters; amplitude is in percent.

effects of these variables are captured through the inclusion of lagged real house price growth and an affordability ratio (the lagged ratio of house prices to disposable income). This model is estimated for each economy using quarterly data for 1970 to 2008. The increase in house prices between end-2008 or the first quarter of 2009 and the 1997–2001 period that is not explained by these fundamental factors— referred to as the house price gap—provides an estimate of the remaining potential for correction in house prices. This analysis suggests that further price adjustments are likely in Ireland, Italy, and the United Kingdom. Compared with earlier WEO estimates, the average estimated misalignment drops from a 10 percent overvaluation to a 6 percent overvaluation. The ranking of economies remains broadly unchanged.[5]

prices; the level of short-term and long-term interest rates; and construction costs.[4] Dynamic

[4]When compared with Box 3.1 in the April 2008 WEO and Box 1.1 in the October 2008 WEO, this house price model reflects two enhancements. First, to avoid sensitivity to base-year assumptions, the house prices in the first quarter of each year from 1997 to 2001 are used as alternative base levels from which the fitted values of the house price increases are accrued; the cumulative gap is then calculated as the average over these base years. Second, the model now includes

construction costs as a proxy for supply conditions. Although the gap estimates could still partly reflect omitted fundamental factors, they provide an indication of how large those omitted factors would have to be for the rise in house prices over the past years to be considered an equilibrium outcome.

[5]The same data series running from 1970 to 2008 is used to produce estimates under the model used in the earlier reports and under the enhanced model. Hence, the difference in misalignment estimates is due to the enhancement of the model, not to the declines recorded since the date of the last report. Estimates for several economies are sensitive to country-specific factors. For instance, in the case of Australia, if the impact of long-term migration on housing demand is taken into account, the results do not produce evidence of a significant overvaluation of house prices. Similarly, for the Netherlands, the estimated house price gap might be smaller if the rise in single-person households is taken into account, together with institutional factors (strict zoning regu-

Long-term relationships between house prices, rents, and incomes can also be used to gauge the extent of likely declines. The lower panels show the gap between the current price-to-income ratios in different economies and their respective historical averages (third panel) and the gap between the house price-to-rent ratios and their historical averages (bottom panel). For most economies, both ratios are still well above historical averages; this is particularly true for Australia and Spain.

To summarize, all four approaches suggest that for most economies, house price corrections still have some way to go. The analysis most consistently points to further large declines for Denmark, Spain, and the United Kingdom, while in Germany, Korea, and the United States corrections are likely to be small.

Of course, there could be more pronounced corrections at the subnational level than is evident from the aggregate data. In Canada, for instance, the potential for further price corrections is estimated to be much higher in the western provinces (Alberta, British Columbia, Saskatchewan) than in the eastern provinces (Ontario, Quebec).[6] In the United States, the northeast corridor, the West Coast, and three of the four "sand states" (Arizona, Florida, Nevada) appear to be susceptible to continuing corrections, based on analysis of price-to-income ratios.[7]

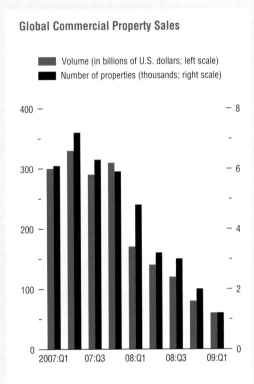

Global Commercial Property Sales

■ Volume (in billions of U.S. dollars; left scale)
■ Number of properties (thousands; right scale)

Sources: Real Capital Analytics; and IMF staff calculations.

lations and generous mortgage interest deductibility). For Italy, low loan-to-value ratios, low household debt levels, and demand from foreigners considerably diminish downside risks to real estate prices. For Japan, given the persistent decline in house prices over the past few decades, gap estimates may be sensitive to specification of trends.

[6]IMF (2009b).

[7]These price-to-income ("affordability ratio") calculations compare the median household income in a state to the income level required to obtain a standard mortgage loan for purchase of a median-priced home in the area. See Collyns, Igan, and Loungani (2009) for details. Further disparities across regions are reflected in delinquency and foreclosure rates, again led by the sand states (Arizona, California, Florida, Nevada).

Corrections in Commercial Real Estate Prices

Commercial real estate markets are facing substantial price corrections. Current rent levels on office, retail, and industrial space are, on average, almost 15 percent above the historical norm (sixth figure). Rents have already started to decline around the world, and this trend is likely to continue given the economic outlook, which will put pressure on commercial property prices. Systematic global price data are not available, but the U.S. market illustrates the scale of the problem. In the United States, commercial real estate prices went through a boom of their own between 2005 and 2007, which has since turned into a bust (seventh figure). As of the second quarter of 2009, U.S. commercial real estate prices had already declined almost 40 percent from their peak in the second quarter of 2007. This compares with a peak-to-trough decline of 27 percent in the market bust of 1987–92. Implications of such a sharp correc-

Box 1.4 *(continued)*

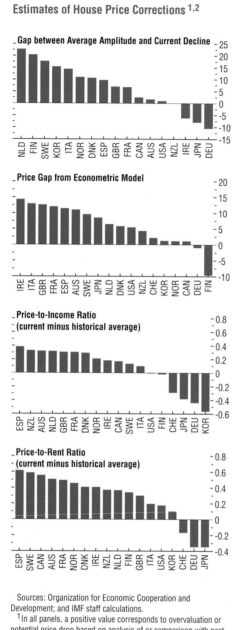

Estimates of House Price Corrections [1,2]

Gap between Average Amplitude and Current Decline

Price Gap from Econometric Model

Price-to-Income Ratio
(current minus historical average)

Price-to-Rent Ratio
(current minus historical average)

Sources: Organization for Economic Cooperation and
Development; and IMF staff calculations.

[1]In all panels, a positive value corresponds to overvaluation or
potential price drop based on analysis of or comparison with past
price movements.

[2]AUS: Australia; CAN: Canada; CHE: Switzerland; DEU: Germany;
DNK: Denmark; ESP: Spain; FIN: Finland; FRA: France; GBR: United
Kingdom; IRE: Ireland; ITA: Italy; JPN: Japan; KOR: Korea; NLD:
Netherlands; NOR: Norway; NZL: New Zealand; SWE: Sweden;
USA: United States.

tion are likely to be considerable: defaults on
commercial real estate loans currently stand at
7.9 percent but, given the size of the bust and
the fact that they reached 12 percent in the
early 1990s, they could more than double.[8]

Impact on the Real Economy

At a conceptual level, the impact of housing
corrections on the real economy depend on the
extent of house price misalignment, as estimated above; the impact of a given house price
correction on macroeconomic variables—which
could vary across economies due to differences
in the characteristics of mortgage markets or
because or differences in policy responses to
housing shocks; and transmission and amplification mechanisms, such as the impact of defaults
on bank balance sheets or the indirect effects
on commercial real estate, which may not be
fully captured in a standard macroeconomic
model of the impacts of housing price shocks.

To provide a baseline assessment of the
impact of house price declines on the economy,
we estimate a vector autoregression (VAR)
model for each of 20 advanced economies for
which we have long series of quarterly data.[9]
Each model includes the following variables:
real GDP, real private consumption, real
residential investment, consumer price index
inflation, short-term interest rate, and real
house prices.[10] The sample period is the first
quarter of 1986 to the fourth quarter of 2008.

---

[8]The delinquency rate reported is for all commercial banks. Default rates tend to lag the price cycle.
Delinquencies peaked in the first quarter of 1991,
more than three years after prices did. Although an
in-depth analysis of the determinants of default rates
is beyond the scope of this box, these estimates are
consistent with forecasts in IMF (2009a). For more
information on modeling defaults, see Igan and Pinheiro (2009) and Box 1.6 in IMF (2008).

[9]Australia, Austria, Canada, Denmark, Finland,
France, Germany, Greece, Ireland, Italy, Japan, Korea,
Netherlands, Norway, New Zealand, Sweden, Switzer-
land, Spain, United Kingdom, United States.

[10]Recent examples of this methodology include
Jarocinski and Smets (2007) and Cardarelli and others
(2009).

We use the model to trace the response of GDP, residential investment, and consumption to a shock to housing prices. The results indicate that, on average, a 10 percent decline in house prices leads to declines after one year of about 2 percent in real GDP, 2½ percent in consumption, and 15 percent in residential investment. In many economies, private consumption growth became closely linked to house price appreciation during the past decade, and house price declines are now driving down consumption growth. Some economies show high responsiveness of the macroeconomy to house prices, including Finland, Greece, and New Zealand. The heterogeneity in the response across economies could be due to numerous factors, but previous work reported in various issues of the WEO suggests that a critical factor is likely to be the ease with which households are able to access mortgage credit.

The VAR model provides baseline estimates of the macro impact of house price declines but may not fully reflect transmission and amplification mechanisms that may be in play. Such mechanisms may be especially important in economies where residential construction has been an important contributor to GDP growth in recent years or where household balance sheets became largely dependent on residential assets. For instance, in Spain, the construction sector grew to account for more than 10 percent of value added in 2007, compared with 6 percent in 1997; in the latest data for 2009, this share has started to shrink, with important implications for income growth and employment. A similar pattern is visible in Estonia and Ireland and, to a lesser extent, in Norway and the United Kingdom.

The indirect effects from weaknesses in commercial real estate are also important at present. Because commercial real estate investors are typically more leveraged than residential homeowners, the impact of price declines on delinquencies and thus on financial institutions' balance sheets is likely to be bigger than the impact of house price declines. In the United States, there are concerns about rising

Rents for Commercial Space[1]
(Current minus historical average, expressed in percent of current level)

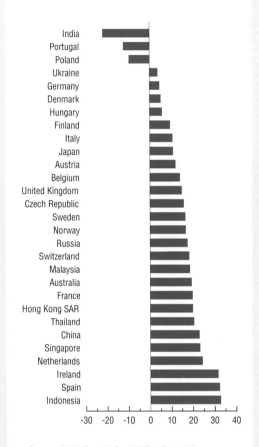

Sources: Knight Frank, LLC; and IMF staff calculations.
[1]Rents in domestic currency. Average for office, retail, and industrial space for each country. Data for different countries start on the following: Australia 2000, Austria 2001, Belgium 1990, China 1991, Czech Republic 2002, Denmark 1996, Finland 2005, France 1990, Germany 1990, Hong Kong SAR 1992, Hungary 2002, India 1999, Indonesia 1997, Ireland 1992, Italy 1990, Japan 1998, Malaysia 1991, Netherlands 1990, Norway 2005, Poland 1993, Portugal 1991, Russia 2003, Singapore 1982, Spain 1990, Sweden 1992, Switzerland 2001, Thailand 1997, Ukraine 2006, United Kingdom 1980. Data are in nominal terms.

delinquency rates for construction loans and commercial-mortgage-backed securities.[11] With

[11]Spreads for investment-grade commercial mortgage-backed securities (CMBSs) soared in summer 2008, along with spreads for other asset-backed securi-

Box 1.4 *(concluded)*

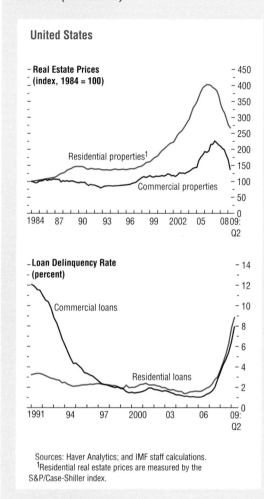

United States

Real Estate Prices
(index, 1984 = 100)

Residential properties[1]

Commercial properties

1984 87 90 93 96 99 2002 05 08 09:
Q2

Loan Delinquency Rate
(percent)

Commercial loans

Residential loans

1991 94 97 2000 03 06 09:
Q2

Sources: Haver Analytics; and IMF staff calculations.
[1]Residential real estate prices are measured by the
S&P/Case-Shiller index.

refinancing needs of commercial real estate
investors expected to peak during 2011–13,
defaults before maturity and property liqui-
dations could start another wave of financial
distress.[12] Other economies also face substan-

ties, and remain elevated. In August 2009, the U.S.
Federal Reserve and the U.S. Treasury Department
announced the extension of the Term Asset-Backed
Securities Loan Facility to mid-2010 for CMBSs to
support the ailing commercial real estate market.
Exposure of nonbank financial institutions to CMBSs
is cause for concern under current market conditions.
    [12]For example, in the United States, Wells Fargo,
Bank of America, and JPMorgan Chase are among
the top commercial real estate lenders. Smaller, more

tial risks from corrections in this sector. These
include the United Arab Emirates, where the
share of construction in non-oil GDP is high,
banks have high direct and indirect exposure
to the sector, and there is high reliance on
external borrowing.

Conclusions

    House prices continue to decline across a
broad range of economies, although signs of
stabilization have emerged recently where the
correction has been ongoing for a number of
years, such as the United States. But an analysis of past house price cycles suggests that for
most economies, there could still be significant
corrections to come given the stronger-than-
average upturn in house prices that preceded
the present downturn. Moreover, the global
recession has put pressure on commercial
property markets, where increasing vacancy
rates and decreasing rents drove down nonresidential construction investment. Leveraged
commercial real estate investors are likely to
face difficulties in refinancing the loans that
are coming due, and soaring delinquencies
therefore have the potential to create a second
wave of financial distress in exposed financial institutions. The ongoing effects on the
real economy of house price corrections and
increasing stress in commercial property markets are being amplified in economies where
construction has been an important contributor to growth in recent years, where consumption was driven by house price appreciations,
and where commercial real estate markets have
been placed in a precarious position by the
weakening of the real economy.

geographically concentrated lenders have already
reported losses associated with such loans. Overall,
commercial banks hold $1.6 trillion in commercial
mortgage loans amounting to 45 percent of the total
outstanding. CMBS issuers (26 percent), life insurance
companies (9 percent), and savings institutions (6 percent) are the other major holders of commercial real
estate debt.

operations may be hard to unwind as long as markets remain illiquid and fundamental market failures remain unaddressed.[5]

Supportive Fiscal Policies

In both advanced and emerging economies, fiscal policy has provided major stimulus in response to the deep downturn, which was particulary important because the transmission of monetary policy has been impaired in many economies (Figure 1.7). Overall fiscal deficits are projected to increase by about 6 percentage points of GDP weighted by purchasing power parity in 2009–10 compared with 2007 pre-crisis levels. The fiscal expansion is greater in advanced economies, reflecting the larger size of their governments and the greater role of automatic stabilizers such as income taxes and transfers (welfare payments, unemployment benefits). For the Group of 20 (G20) economies, crisis-related discretionary measures are estimated at about 2 percent of GDP for 2009 and 1.5 percent of GDP for 2010, both relative to 2007 baselines, with the largest policy packages in Asia, the Middle East, and the United States. The categories of stimulus that were implemented most rapidly—tax breaks and transfer payments—are those that typically have lower effects on activity. Stimulus measures that have higher multipliers will likely be implemented at an accelerated pace during the second half of 2009, reflecting the lags inherent in new and expanded government spending programs, particularly in infrastructure.

With some signs that conditions are stabilizing, most countries are taking a "wait-and-see" approach, focusing on implementing previously announced measures and on assessing their impact before providing additional stimulus. Estimates for 2010 reflect the phased implementation of stimulus spending initiated during 2009 and a carryover of tax provisions as well as the continued operation of automatic stabilizers.

[5]For analysis of early evidence, see McAndrews, Sarkar, and Wang (2008); Čihák and others (2009); Meier (2009); and Taylor and Williams (2009).

Figure 1.7. General Government Fiscal Balances and Public Debt
(Percent of GDP)

Fiscal policy is providing significant stimulus to the global economy. Public debt, however, is rising fast, particularly in advanced economies. Large corrections in fiscal balances will be necessary to reverse this trend once the recovery is on a firm footing.

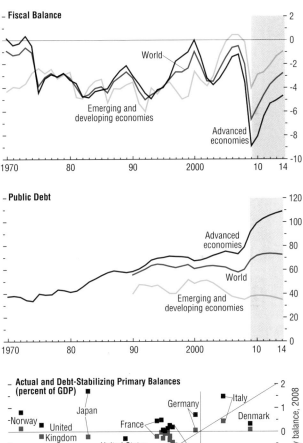

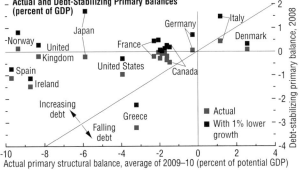

Sources: World Economic Outlook database; and IMF staff estimates.

Figure 1.8. Public Support to Ease Financial Stress

Extraordinary public intervention has helped reduce financial market turmoil. As a result, balance sheets of central banks have expanded considerably, and governments have incurred significant actual and contingent expenditures.

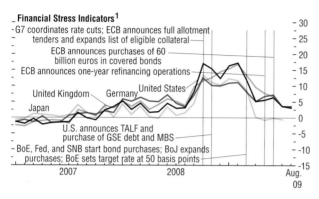

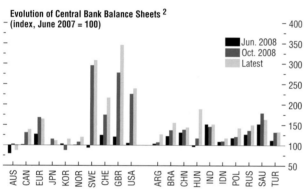

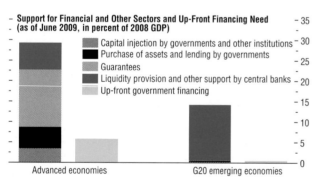

Sources: Horton, Kumar, and Mauro (2009), Table 4; and IMF staff calculations.
[1]Financial stress indicators consist of seven financial market variables, including the beta of banking stocks, the TED spread, the slope of the yield curve, corporate bond spreads, stock market returns, stock market volatility, and exchange rate volatility. BoE: Bank of England; BoJ: Bank of Japan; ECB: European Central Bank; Fed: Federal Reserve; GSE: government-sponsored enterprises; MBS: mortgage-backed securities; SNB: Swiss National Bank; TALF: Term Asset-Backed Securities Loan Facility.
[2]AUS: Australia; CAN: Canada; EUR: Euro area; JPN: Japan; KOR: Korea; NOR: Norway; SWE: Sweden; CHE: Switzerland; GBR: United Kingdom; USA: United States; ARG: Argentina; BRA: Brazil; CHN: China; HUN: Hungary; IND: India; IDN: Indonesia; POL: Poland; RUS: Russia; SAU: Saudi Arabia; TUR: Turkey.

Budget deficits are thus projected to be broadly the same in 2010 as in 2009, implying continued support for activity. For the G20 economies, fiscal policy is estimated to boost GDP by at least 1 percentage point in 2009 and by less in 2010.[6] The continued stimulus to growth in 2010 reflects implementation lags and the growing share of capital (infrastructure) spending, which has larger multipliers than taxes or transfers. In subsequent years, fiscal deficits will start to contract, in the absence of further measures, as stimulus measures phase out and the recovery improves cyclical components of the budget.

Financial Sector Support

In addition to central bank efforts, governments also intervened heavily in financial systems to relieve concerns about a potential systemic collapse and to reestablish trust. Measures included deposit and debt guarantees, recapitalization of financial institutions, and programs to ring-fence or remove bad assets from these entities' balance sheets (Figure 1.8). Differing country circumstances spurred a wide variety of approaches. Most governments provided guarantees, because these entail low up-front fiscal costs and are relatively easy to implement. Programs to recapitalize financial institutions and remove their toxic assets quickly ran into major political obstacles, as skeptical electorates resisted what they considered overly generous bailouts for the very firms seemingly responsible for the crisis or questioned the growing role of government in credit intermediation. Recapitalization also raised a number of specific difficulties, notably how to gauge capital shortfalls with uncertain valuations for bad assets and resistance from existing shareholders who did not want their stakes and influence diluted.

Accordingly, only a limited amount of government funding has been allocated up front

[6]The size of fiscal multipliers is uncertain. Based on plausible ranges, stimulus packages could boost GDP by 1 to 5 percentage points in 2009 and by 0 to 1 percentage point in 2010, both with respect to the previous year. These estimates consider cross-country spillover effects. For details, see Horton, Kumar, and Mauro (2009).

for financial support operations. The advanced G20 economies are estimated to have put aside somewhat less than 6 percent of GDP; for the emerging G20 economies, whose financial systems are affected much less directly by the crisis, that number is below 1 percent of GDP.[7] The amount of financial sector support actually disbursed generally has been even less, reflecting a variety of factors. Some are innocuous, such as the precautionary nature of initial announcements and indications of increasing stability and improved bank liquidity. Others are more worrisome, such as lags in implementation of programs for recapitalization and asset purchases caused by financial institutions' preference to wait out the crisis and deleverage rather than take write-downs and accept government support to increase lending.

Various governments have taken an active role in assessing their banking systems by performing stress tests, which, when accompanied by credible measures to address any shortfalls in capital, have been a useful tool in accelerating balance sheet repair and restoring confidence in banks. But much more work remains to be done on this front in many countries. Accordingly, capital remains far short of the levels required to forestall further bank deleveraging, representing an important drag on the forces of recovery.

A Subdued Recovery and Vulnerability to Mild Deflation

Summing up the short-term prospects, the policy forces that are driving the current rebound will gradually lose strength, and the real and financial forces remain weak but are gradually building. Specifically, fiscal stimulus will diminish and inventory rebuilding will gradually lose its influence, while consumption and investment will slowly build. Thus, after contracting by about 1 percent in 2009, global activity is forecast to expand by about 3 percent in 2010. These projections reflect modest upward

[7]See Horton, Kumar, and Mauro (2009).

revisions to those in the July 2009 *WEO Update* (Table 1.1; Figure 1.9).

Advanced economies are projected to expand sluggishly through much of 2010, with output growth rising toward medium-term potential only later in the year. Thus, average annual growth in 2010 will be only modestly positive, at about 1¼ percent, following a contraction of 3½ percent during 2009. The recovery of activity is more clearly evident on a fourth-quarter-over-fourth-quarter basis: from 2009:Q4 to 2010:Q4, output is expected to rise by about 1¾ percent, up from an expansion of about ½ percent (annualized) during the second half of 2009 and a 2 percent contraction in the first half. The recovery is being felt first by advanced economies in Asia. In the United States, consumption should receive some support from gradually diminishing employment losses, as well as firmer asset prices. In Europe, improvements are being driven by policy support and recovering confidence and trade—output in France and Germany already expanded moderately in the second quarter of 2009. However, a prolonged period of significant job losses is expected to weigh on activity in Europe well into 2010.

In emerging economies, real GDP growth is forecast to reach 5 percent in 2010, up from 1¾ percent in 2009. The rebound is driven by China, India, and a number of other emerging Asian economies. Economies in Africa and the Middle East are also expected to post solid growth of close to 4 percent, helped by recovering commodity prices, whereas Latin America will benefit from higher commodity prices and rising global trade. In emerging Europe and the CIS, the recovery may lag because of tighter external financial constraints that are bringing down very large current account deficits (see Chapter 2).

The gradual pace of recovery points to a prolonged period of subdued inflation and vulnerability to mild deflation (see Figure 1.10). Although the risks of sustained deflation have diminished over the past quarter, deflation pressures—as gauged by a broad indicator that comprises various price indicators, estimates

Figure 1.9. Global Outlook
(Real GDP; percent change from a year earlier)

A recovery is expected to take hold in 2009–10. However, economic growth will be uneven: modest in advanced economies, emerging Europe, the Commonwealth of Independent States (CIS), and Latin America; strong in China and India.

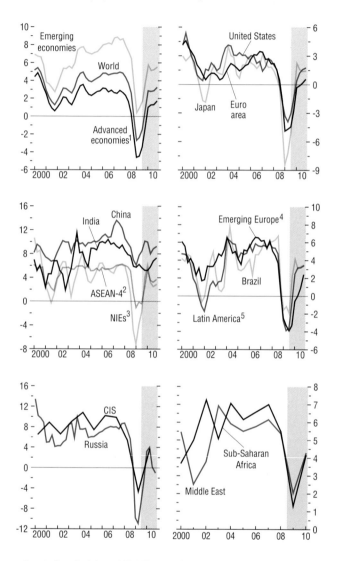

Sources: Haver Analytics; and World Economic Outlook database.
[1]Australia, Canada, Czech Republic, Denmark, euro area, Hong Kong SAR, Israel, Japan, Korea, New Zealand, Norway, Singapore, Sweden, Switzerland, Taiwan Province of China, United Kingdom, and United States.
[2]Indonesia, Malaysia, Philippines, and Thailand.
[3]Newly industrialized Asian economies (NIEs) comprise Hong Kong SAR, Korea, Singapore, and Taiwan Province of China.
[4]Estonia, Hungary, Latvia, Lithuania, and Poland.
[5]Argentina, Brazil, Chile, Colombia, Mexico, Peru, and Venezuela.

of capacity utilization, and asset prices for most G20 economies—are expected to remain relatively high over the coming year.[8] For the United States and the euro area, for example, IMF staff estimates suggest that potential output growth has fallen, is currently close to zero, and will pick up only slowly to about 2 percent and 1¼ percent, respectively, over the medium run (Figure 1.11).[9] Nonetheless, large output gaps are opening, typically measuring about 3–5 percent of potential GDP. Accordingly, inflation in advanced economies is projected to be close to zero in 2009 and to accelerate very modestly to about 1 percent in 2010, largely reflecting rising commodity prices. Prices for many manufactured goods will probably continue to decline for some time. Fortunately, inflation expectations have generally remained well anchored, providing some protection against sustained large price declines. In emerging economies, inflation is forecast to hover around 5 percent in 2009–10, down from more than 9 percent in 2008. Only China, a few of the ASEAN-5,[10] and most emerging European economies are projected to see inflation fall appreciably below 5 percent. Low potential growth and inflation will slow the process of deleveraging, adding to contractionary forces.

[8]For details on the construction of this indicator, see Decressin and Laxton (2009). Notice that Figure 1.10 also features an expanded deflation indicator, which includes house prices.
[9]The (multivariate filter) estimates are obtained by examining various macroeconomic variables and the relationships among them. If falling output translates into falling core inflation, the slowdown is cyclical; to the extent it does not, it is structural, reflecting lower potential growth. Data on output, however, are available only quarterly. More insight can be gleaned about the short term by scrutinizing capacity utilization and unemployment, and their past relationships to output. In general, however, real-time estimates of potential output are subject to wide margins of error, particularly during booms and recessions. See Bernes and others (2009).
[10]Indonesia, Malaysia, Philippines, Singapore, Thailand.

Beyond 2010: How Will the Global Economy Rebalance?

Achieving sustained healthy growth over the medium term will depend critically on addressing the supply disruptions generated by the crisis and rebalancing the global pattern of demand. On the supply side, financial firms will need to be restructured and markets repaired to deliver adequate credit for sustained increases in investment and productivity, and labor will need to be redeployed across sectors. On the demand side, rebalancing hinges on switching from public to private demand and from domestically to externally driven growth in the many economies that experienced asset price busts. By implication, economies that previously relied on export-led growth will need to switch from externally to domestically driven growth.

Lower Potential Output

Historical evidence presented in Chapter 4 indicates that there were typically large, permanent hits to output in the aftermath of past financial crises, although there has been a wide range of outcomes and major losses have been avoided in some cases. In the past, output losses following crises manifested themselves in falling capital, higher unemployment, and lower total factor productivity. Capital accumulation typically plunged as a result of the interaction among surging funding costs, slumping demand, falling collateral values, and growing excess capacity. The dynamics of these interactions tended to be long lasting, pushing unemployment to high levels. Over time, unemployment evolved from cyclical into structural, as the jobless lost skills or were eased out of the labor force with generous early retirement or other long-term benefits. The latter played an important role in boosting structural unemployment in Europe following the big recessions of the 1970s and 1980s.[11] Total factor productivity suffers for several reasons, including short-term

[11]See, for example, Bruno and Sachs (1985).

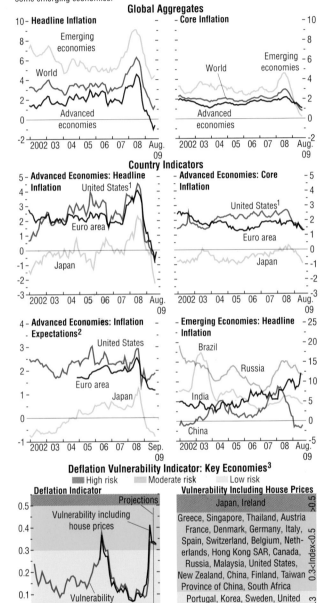

Figure 1.10. Global Inflation

(Twelve-month change in the consumer price index unless otherwise noted)

The global recession has caused a large drop in inflation and rising concern about mild deflation. However, the decline in inflation pressures has been limited among some emerging economies.

Sources: Bloomberg Financial Markets; Haver Analytics; and IMF staff calculations.
[1]Personal consumption expenditure deflator.
[2]One-year-ahead consensus forecasts. The December values are the average of the surrounding November and January values.
[3]For details on the construction of this indicator, see Decressin and Laxton (2009). The figure also features an expanded indicator, which includes house prices. Vulnerability as of 2009:Q3. For the equity, real exchange rate, and nominal house price components, values for August 2009 were used.
[4]Major advanced and emerging economies.

Figure 1.11. Potential Growth and Unemployment Rates

Potential growth is taking a hit from the crisis, particularly in advanced economies and emerging economies suffering balance of payments crises. Unemployment will be above precrisis levels for some time in advanced economies but not in most emerging and developing economies.

Potential Growth (percent)

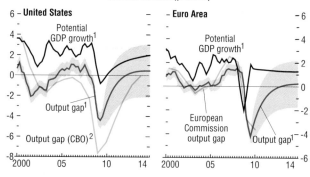

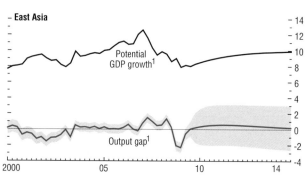

Unemployment Rates (percent)

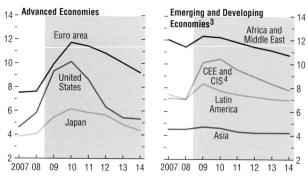

Sources: U.S. Congressional Budget Office; and IMF staff calculations.
[1]Derived using a multivariate filtering approach. For details, see Bernes and others (2009).
[2]CBO: U.S. Congressional Budget Office.
[3]Aggregates are computed on the basis of purchasing-power-parity weights.
[4]CEE: Central and eastern Europe; CIS: Commonwealth of Independent States.

labor hoarding, obsolescence of physical and human capital, and lower research and development expenditures.

The current medium-term output projections are indeed on a much lower path than before the crisis (Figure 1.12), consistent with a permanent loss of potential output. Investment has already fallen sharply, especially in the economies hit by financial and real estate crises. Together with rising scrap rates, as corporations go bankrupt or restructure, this is reducing effective capital stocks. In addition, unemployment rates are expected to remain at high levels over the medium run in a number of advanced economies. In the euro area, for example, rates are projected to rise to close to 12 percent in 2010 and to retreat only gradually to 9½ percent by 2014. By contrast, in the United States, with its more flexible labor market, unemployment is projected to decline from a peak of about 10 percent in 2010 to 5 percent by 2014.

Demand-Side Rebalancing

To complement efforts to repair the supply side of economies, there must also be adjustments in the pattern of global demand in order to sustain a strong recovery. Specifically, many economies that have followed export-led growth strategies and have run current account surpluses will need to rely more on domestic demand—notably emerging economies in Asia and elsewhere and Germany and Japan. This will help offset subdued domestic demand in economies that have typically run current account deficits and have experienced asset price (stock or housing) busts, including the United States, the United Kingdom, parts of the euro area, and many emerging European economies. In these economies, private consumption and investment are unlikely to pick up the slack that will be left by diminishing fiscal stimulus, given that household incomes and corporate profits will be subdued and balance sheet repair will be under way for some time, implying higher saving rates. Hence, these economies' imports will be sluggish and their current account deficits will narrow. In addition, there will need to be sectoral shifts of resources on the supply side to accommodate shifts in demand.

This process of rebalancing global demand will be drawn out. To illustrate the challenge, consumption in China—the main current account surplus economy—amounts to only about one-quarter of total consumption in the United States and the European economies with large current account deficits. Furthermore, the scope for advanced economies such as Germany and Japan to contribute to rebalancing is limited, given their need to build savings to prepare for population aging. Thus, rebalancing must involve a broad range of emerging economies if solid global growth is to be sustained over the medium term. It will also require major changes in consumption patterns, supported by an economic environment that fosters lower precautionary saving and higher investment, including in emerging economies that have traditionally exported large amounts of capital. This is a long-term policy challenge that involves complex issues related to lowering corporate saving, expanding and improving financial intermediation, eliminating distortions that foster production of tradable goods, and strengthening social safety nets. Rapid progress cannot be expected in the near term.

Hence, these projections paint a sobering picture of the path for demand-side rebalancing.[12] In 2009, global current account imbalances decline sharply (Figure 1.13). Current account deficits fall in the United States and various advanced economies (Greece, Ireland, Portugal, Spain, United Kingdom) and in emerging Europe—together, these economies accounted for the bulk of the world's current account deficits before the crisis. Meanwhile, surpluses diminish for oil exporters, as the value of oil

---

[12]Like most forecasts that use both private and official data sources, WEO projections assume unchanged real effective exchange rates. Not surprisingly, WEO projections typically underestimate the amount of rebalancing between surplus and deficit countries that actually takes place.

Figure 1.12. GDP Growth

Historical evidence suggests that declining output after crises is driven to a roughly equal extent by lower employment, lower effective capital stocks, and lower productivity. *World Economic Outlook* (WEO) forecasts for output have been marked down appreciably relative to precrisis levels, in line with historical evidence. With lower investment and consumption, current accounts of advanced economies are expected to improve.

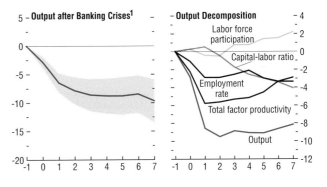

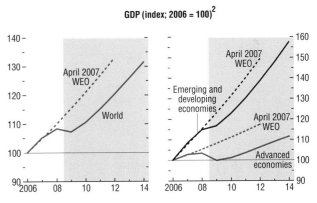

Source: World Economic Outlook database projections.
[1]In percent of precrisis trend; mean difference from year $t-1$; first year of crisis at $t=0$. The figure reports the estimated mean path (line) and the 90 percent confidence interval for the estimated mean (shaded area).
[2]GDP path predicted in the April 2007 WEO (dashed line) versus current GDP path (solid line).

Figure 1.13. Global Imbalances

Output of countries with current account deficits is projected to drop appreciably relative to precrisis trends, driven mainly by lower investment. Consumption is expected to fall as well, however, leading to improvements in their current accounts.

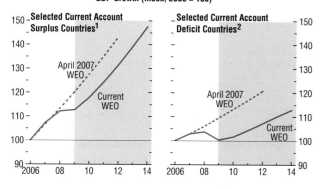

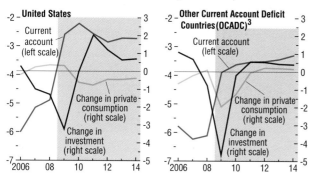

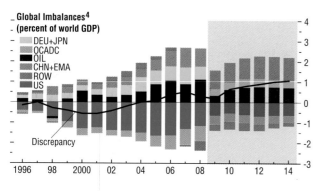

Source: IMF staff estimates.
[1]China, Germany, Hong Kong SAR, Indonesia, Japan, Korea, Malaysia, Philippines, Singapore, Taiwan Province of China, Thailand, and oil exporters (including Islamic Republic of Iran, Nigeria, Norway, Russia, Saudi Arabia, and Venezuela).
[2]Bulgaria, Croatia, Czech Republic, Estonia, Greece, Hungary, Ireland, Latvia, Lithuania, Poland, Portugal, Romania, Slovak Republic, Slovenia, Spain, Turkey, United Kingdom, and United States.
[3]Countries listed in Note 2, excluding United States.
[4]US: United States; DEU+JPN: Germany and Japan; CHN+EMA: China, Hong Kong SAR, Indonesia, Korea, Malaysia, Philippines, Singapore, Taiwan Province of China, and Thailand; OIL: Oil exporters; ROW: Rest of the world.

revenues drops sharply, and for Germany and Japan. Looking further ahead, however, imbalances widen again. The recovery of oil prices is expected to boost the savings and current account surpluses of the oil exporters while lowering those of importers. The turnaround in the global manufacturing cycle is expected to raise surpluses for Germany and to a lesser extent for Japan (because of the recent appreciation of the yen). Nonetheless, these two economies and the oil exporters are expected to contribute less to global imbalances over the medium term than they have recently. At the same time, little current account adjustment is forecast for the emerging economies of Asia, notably China, over the medium term. As a result, global imbalances widen again over the medium term; also, the global current account discrepancy—the sum of all economies' current accounts—is forecast to widen somewhat compared with the recent past (Box 1.5). However, the widening of this discrepancy is limited and, for this and other reasons, its implications for the growth forecast are probably limited.

Risks to a Sustained Recovery

Downside risks to growth are receding gradually but remain a concern. The main short-term risk is that the recovery stalls and deflationary forces become entrenched. This could be triggered by a number of adverse developments. Premature exit from accommodative monetary and fiscal policies, possibly driven by rising concerns about government intervention and unconventional action by central banks, seems to be a significant risk because the policy-induced rebound could be mistaken for the beginning of a strong recovery. Also, there could be resistance to extending policy support long enough to allow private demand to make a sustained recovery. Progress in repairing financial balance sheets could be undercut by rising unemployment, greater-than-expected increases in delinquencies on residential mortgages and commercial real estate, and more corporate bankruptcies. With banks only weakly capital-

Box 1.5. From Deficit to Surplus: Recent Shifts in Global Current Accounts

The global current account discrepancy is a well-known anomaly in economic statistics (IMF, 1987; Annex 3 in the October 1996 *World Economic Outlook* (WEO); and Box 2.1 in the September 2002 WEO). In theory, global exports—the sum of all economies' exports—should equal global imports, but in practice they do not.[1] In fact, the discrepancy has been large on occasion, reaching as much as ½ percent of global GDP in absolute value (figure, upper panel). The origins and behavior of this discrepancy have long been of interest to policymakers and academics who analyze current account developments and prospects. The issue has taken on added importance in light of the necessary rebalancing of global demand in the wake of the current crisis. Specifically, two interrelated sets of questions have arisen.

What factors explain the turnaround in the global discrepancy in recent years to a "surplus" after many decades of "deficit"?

What are the prospects for the global discrepancy? Is the continued increase in the discrepancy implied by the WEO projections consistent with past trends?[2]

The analysis in this box suggests that movements in the discrepancy, including its recent

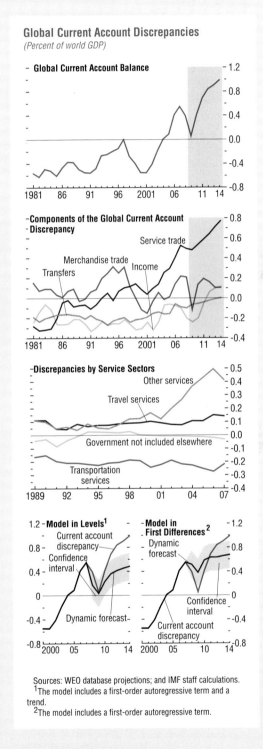

Global Current Account Discrepancies
(Percent of world GDP)

Sources: WEO database projections; and IMF staff calculations.
[1]The model includes a first-order autoregressive term and a trend.
[2]The model includes a first-order autoregressive term.

The main authors of this box are Thomas Helbling and Marco E. Terrones.

[1]The transactions subsumed in the external current account of an economy are typically referred to as international trade transactions. These are referred to as "current transactions" in balance of payments statistics (as opposed to transactions in the capital and financial accounts). Specifically, current transactions include the following major categories: exports and imports of goods and services, receipts of income from assets bought from nonresidents, return payments on liabilities to nonresidents (including returns on human capital), and receipts and payments of current transfers.

[2]The WEO country forecasts are based on common assumptions and consider variables such as growth in trading partner economies, but they do not explicitly incorporate "adding up" constraints for international transactions at the global level. The discrepancy implied by the aggregation of the country trade forecasts has thus long been used as a measure of their global consistency.

Box 1.5 *(continued)*

turnaround from deficit to surplus, reflect changes in global economic conditions and a trend increase in measurement biases toward exports, which is mostly relevant for services. The deceleration in global growth during 2008–09 already resulted in some narrowing of the global current account discrepancy in 2008, and some further narrowing seems likely in 2009. Against this cyclical decline works a growing trend for a global services surplus. However, results from simple econometric models for the global discrepancy suggest that the continued large increases in the global discrepancy during 2013–14 implied by the WEO forecasts might be stronger than consistent with historical trends.

What Factors Are behind the Recent Turnaround in the Global Discrepancy?

As the figure shows, the discrepancy has generally been rising since 2001, became positive in 2005, and peaked in 2007. Based on preliminary data, the discrepancy narrowed from ½ percent of global GDP in 2007 to about ⅓ of global GDP in 2008. Quarterly data for a subset of economies suggest that the discrepancy narrowed sharply in the second half of 2008, when global trade collapsed, but that most of this decline was reversed in the first quarter of 2009.[3]

A breakdown of global trade into major categories, as shown in the second and third panels of the figure, suggests that the switch from a global current account deficit to a surplus reflects primarily increasing positive discrepancies ("surpluses") in the trade of goods and of so-called other services.[4]

The rising surplus in the global goods trade during 2001–07 likely reflects transportation-related lags in the recording of imports compared with exports at a time of rapidly expanding global trade.[5] With some exports recorded one period earlier in the source economy than the corresponding imports in the destination economy, a pickup in global trade growth can lead to an increase in the global trade surplus. With the fragmentation of production processes, trade has expanded at a much faster pace than value added (or GDP) in recent years. The observed decrease in the global trade discrepancy in 2008 could then be explained by the sharp drop in global trade, which was recorded in exports before imports.

The composition of the discrepancy in the trade of services has shifted in recent years.[6] In the 1980s and 1990s, a global deficit in transportation services was the main source of the negative discrepancy in this sector. Since 2001, however, a growing surplus in the trade of other services has more than compensated for the still-negative discrepancy in transportation services, implying a positive discrepancy in services trade overall.

---

[3]The subset of economies accounts for about 93 percent of global GDP.

[4]As discussed in IMF (1987) and Annex 3 in the October 1996 WEO, the negative discrepancy ("deficit") in the 1980s and 1990s was largely a result of deficits in transportation services and investment income. These deficits were attributed to the underrecording and/or failure to report credits by shipping nations (transportation services) and the underreporting by investment credit recipients (tax evasion, etc.).

[5]Other factors could also have played a role. For example, it is often argued that there is a greater incentive to underreport imports, because imports are taxed more heavily than exports. Hence, when global trade picks up, the recorded increase in imports could be systematically biased downward. Nevertheless, with trade in manufacturing components increasingly duty free, this factor may well have played a less prominent role in recent years compared with two decades ago.

[6]Measured international trade in services has been increasing rapidly in recent years. Although this expansion undoubtedly reflects rapid increases in underlying transactions, given the growing tradability of services, it also reflects important progress in measuring this type of international trade. An increasing number of economies have started to record and report trade in services over the past 50 years (Lipsey, 2009). Moreover, the number of economies reporting different kinds of trade in services has increased significantly over the past 30 years. For instance, the number of economies reporting exports and imports of financial services increased from 10 to more than 100 between 1985 and 2005.

The rising discrepancy in other services likely reflects measurement problems associated with the rapid increase in international trade in nontraditional services, such as offshoring of business, financial, and communication services. The measurement problems include the fact that exporters are easier to identify than importers because they specialize partly in providing these services (whereas the need for imports is often more sporadic) and they tend to have larger overall transaction volumes than importers. For example, law firms involved in resolving cross-border legal issues typically are long-established specialist firms, whereas many clients do not have such legal needs on a regular basis. Exporters are thus more likely to be identified and exceed the threshold for participation in the surveys that underpin measurement of a large part of international trade in services.[7] As a result, exports are more likely to be recorded than imports, which can introduce a bias toward a positive discrepancy. And this discrepancy has risen relative to global GDP as such services have greatly increased in importance.

Other reasons for positive discrepancies in the trade of "other services" include policy-related incentive biases—policymakers are often interested primarily in services exports (as a means to stimulate growth), and measurement efforts therefore focus on exports rather than imports. There is also a lack of appropriate data collection systems in services trade in emerging and developing economies, which typically are net importers of services.

It remains difficult to forecast the likely evolution of the discrepancy in the global trade of other services. Rapid trend growth in the trade of other services is likely to continue, but statistical agencies are in the process of improving the related measurements. The extent to which this will affect the magnitude and direction of the discrepancy remains highly uncertain at this point.

What Are the Prospects for the Global Discrepancy?

The current WEO forecasts imply that, after a further decline in 2009, the global discrepancy will again increase relative to global GDP during 2010–14 and will grow well beyond its peak in 2007. Such a pattern seems qualitatively plausible, given the recent trends discussed above, but it would also be desirable to quantitatively assess the consistency with past trends. In other words, the question is whether the fluctuations in the discrepancy implied by the forecasts are within historical margins of error.

Marquez and Workman (2001) examine this question with an econometric model of the global current account discrepancy, which they use to check whether the implied discrepancy falls within the 95 percent confidence interval of the model forecast. This approach was predicated on their finding that during 1972–98, the discrepancy fluctuated systematically with changes in global economic conditions and past values of the discrepancy itself. Building on this work, the IMF staff reexamined these features of the discrepancy, taking into account more recent data and, on this basis, estimated a somewhat modified econometric model.

Simple statistical analysis of the overall global current account discrepancy and its major components suggests the following (first table):[8]

The means of the global discrepancy and its major components are significantly different from zero. This implies that, despite the recent switch from deficit to surplus, the discrepancy has not been on average zero.

Another key property of the global discrepancy and its major components is that they are highly persistent time-series processes. In other

---

[7]Unlike in the trade of goods, there are no customs records available for many types of international trade in services. Indeed, in the areas where the recording of services trade has long been established—transportation and travel—there are at least related customs records available.

[8]The analysis runs from 1981 to 2007. Reliable data start for the early 1980s, and 2007 is the last year for actual data from the IMF's *Balance of Payments Statistics Yearbook*.

Box 1.5 *(concluded)*

Statistical Properties of the Global Current Account Balance
(1981–2007; in percent of global GDP)

	Levels			First Differences		
	Mean	Standard deviation	Persistence	Mean	Standard deviation	Persistence
Merchandise trade	0.085** [0.036]	0.118	0.764*** [0.099]	0.003 [0.018]	0.083	0.236* [0.134]
Services trade	0.014 [0.069]	0.208	1.057*** [0.085]	0.029** [0.013]	0.062	0.289* [0.167]
Income	−0.219*** [0.024]	0.085	0.641*** [0.113]	−0.001 [0.010]	0.071	−0.038 [0.168]
Transfers	−0.186*** [0.013]	0.045	0.786*** [0.084]	0.003 [0.005]	0.033	−0.103 [0.130]
Current Account	−0.305*** [0.093]	0.300	1.080*** [0.124]	0.035 [0.034]	0.139	0.375*** [0.114]

Sources: IMF, World Economic Outlook database; and IMF staff calculations.
Note: Robust standard errors are reported in brackets; *, **, and *** denote significance at the 10 percent, 5 percent, and 1 percent levels, respectively.

words, past levels of the discrepancies matter for their current levels, because the first-order autoregressive coefficients are generally significantly different from zero. The relatively large, positive values of these coefficients imply that the discrepancies at any point in time are typically quite similar to the levels in the previous period.

For services trade and the overall current account balance, the autoregressive coefficients are slightly greater than 1 in value, suggesting that these discrepancies have grown over time.

Simple econometric analysis also confirms the key finding of Marquez and Workman (2001) that the global discrepancies generally fluctuate with global economic conditions but also shows that the discrepancies can grow over time (second table). Two models are fitted to the data for the global discrepancy for the current account as well as its components: one model features a time trend as well as global output growth, oil prices, and the six-month U.S. dollar London interbank offered rate. The other model omits the time trend, working with the first differences of the discrepancy variables rather than the levels. The findings suggest first that the discrepancies tend to be procyclical. In other words, they increase when global growth

picks up and decrease when global growth slows. Second, the discrepancies tend to grow over time.

Hence, in assessing projections for the global discrepancy, the predicted changes in global economic conditions and its trend behavior should be taken into account. Doing this with the two models generates a forecast for the levels of the global current account discrepancy for 2008–14.[9] Comparing the model forecasts for the discrepancy during 2008–14 with the changes implied by the international trade forecasts in the current WEO projections shows that the latter are generally within the 95 percent confidence interval around the model forecasts through 2010 and 2012, respectively (lower

[9]Information criteria and in-sample forecast error comparisons suggest that a first-difference specification is preferable to a specification in levels. The estimation problems associated with highly persistent time-series processes would also argue in favor of such a specification. That said, on theoretical grounds, the global current account discrepancy should be a stationary process when it is scaled with global GDP (as in the analysis presented here). Comparing the model forecasts and the implied forecasts presented below shows that the implications of both specifications are the same. The forecasts for first difference of the global discrepancy were subsequently transformed into levels to allow for a comparison.

Global Current Account Balance and Key Macro Variables[1]

(1981–2007; in percent of global GDP)

	Levels[2]			First Differences Changes in		
	Output growth	Oil prices	Interest rate	Output growth	Oil prices	Interest rate
Merchandise trade	0.023*** [0.006]	0.000 [0.000]	0.003 [0.008]	0.020 [0.015]	0.000 [0.000]	0.000 [0.007]
Services trade	0.022* [0.012]	0.000 [0.000]	−0.009 [0.011]	0.016* [0.010]	0.000 [0.000]	−0.009 [0.006]
Income	0.030** [0.015]	0.000 [0.001]	0.012* [0.007]	0.016 [0.013]	0.000 [0.000]	−0.010 [0.009]
Transfers	0.008 [0.007]	0.000 [0.000]	0.002 [0.004]	0.013*** [0.005]	0.000 [0.000]	−0.001 [0.004]
Current account	0.057** [0.024]	−0.001 [0.001]	0.000 [0.014]	0.052*** [0.019]	0.000 [0.000]	−0.027*** [0.009]

Sources: IMF, World Economic Outlook database; and IMF staff calculations.

[1]These are ARMAX models. The lags for the autoregresive and moving average components have been selected using Akaike and Bayesian criteria, taking into account the usual parsimony considerations.

[2]Regressions include a trend.

panels in the figure). The implied increases in the global discrepancy in 2011–14 and 2013–14, however, are outside the 95 percent confidence interval for the model forecasts. The deviation of the global discrepancy from the upper ends of the confidence intervals on average amounts to 0.1 to 0.2 percent of world GDP. This finding suggests that the growth projections underlying the trade forecasts for individual economies may not be fully consistent with global trade equilibrium, pointing to collective excessive optimism

about growth of export shares. In the context of a need to rebalance global demand, this finding could be an indication that the forecast increases in national savings relative to investment in the economies that recorded current account deficits in recent years are not matched by commensurate declines in national savings in surplus countries at the assumed constant real exchange rates. However, these inconsistencies and their potential implications for the growth forecast are not likely to be large.

ized, this could lead to even tighter financial conditions. (These and other financial sector risks are discussed in the October 2009 GFSR.) More generally, many shocks that otherwise could be absorbed—for example, a virulent return of H1N1 flu or geopolitical tensions that remove excess capacity in the oil sector—may have a significant destabilizing impact, given the vulnerable state of the global economy and financial system.

However, there are some upside considerations, as evidenced by the recent, faster-than-expected improvement in financial conditions. In particular, the success of various policy

measures in allaying fears about a 1930s-style crash in activity and fostering a strong rebound in financial market sentiment could cause consumption and investment to surge in a number of advanced and emerging economies, just as the increase in uncertainty triggered their collapse in late 2008 and early 2009. In other words, just as the crisis in confidence was underestimated during the downward spiral, so too the restoration of confidence may be underestimated during the rebound.

This assessment of the short-term risks to activity is broadly consistent with that of the markets, as embodied in selected data on options

Figure 1.14. Risks to the Global Outlook

Risks to economic growth have diminished somewhat but remain to the downside. Consensus Economics survey information on term spreads and inflation rates and options market information on stock and oil prices suggest that the main downside risk relates to high oil prices.

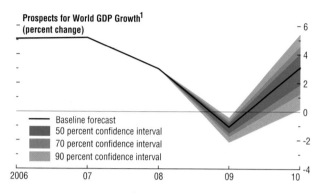

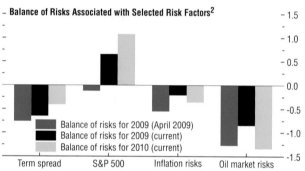

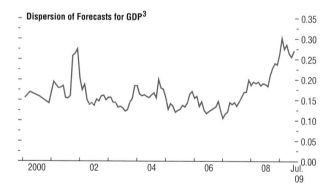

Sources: Bloomberg Financial Markets; Chicago Board Options Exchange; Consensus Economics; and IMF staff estimates.

[1]The fan chart shows the uncertainty around the *World Economic Outlook* (WEO) central forecast with 50, 70, and 90 percent probability intervals. As shown, the 70 percent confidence interval includes the 50 percent interval, and the 90 percent confidence interval includes the 50 and 70 percent intervals. See Appendix 1.2 in the April 2009 WEO for details.

[2]Bars depict the coefficient of skewness expressed in units of the underlying variables. The values for inflation risks and oil market risks are entered with the opposite sign since they represent downside risks to growth.

[3]The series measures the dispersion of GDP forecasts for the G7 economies, Brazil, China, India, and Mexico.

prices and Consensus Economics expectations (Figure 1.14). These data can be used to construct a fan chart, which confirms that risks have narrowed since the April 2009 WEO but suggests that they remain on the downside.[13] The distribution of forecasts for the evolution of term spreads—typically, a high term spread anticipates recovery—points to downside risks to growth, although less so than in the recent past. Options data about the Standard & Poor's 500, by contrast, suggest that stock prices are more likely to surprise on the upside than the downside, consistent with upside risks to growth.

Market data also give indications about other specific short-term risks to the recovery. Much of the recent rebound in oil prices was related to cutbacks in production by the members of the Organization of Petroleum Exporting Countries, which were designed to stabilize prices in response to slumping demand (Appendix 1.1). One key concern in the markets is that higher oil prices could hinder economic recovery. In fact, oil prices have almost doubled from their trough earlier this year, and options prices point to further upside risks. Against this, considerable spare capacity and high inventory levels should reduce the risk of a sustained price surge, barring a major geopolitical event. Thus the projections assume that prices do not rise much further, in line with forward market prices. This does not rule out temporary price spikes, possibly fueled by speculative pressures, although financial factors cannot drive permanent shifts in real prices.

Another market concern is inflation risk, namely, that central banks may need to tighten monetary policy by more than expected to quell inflation pressures. The inflation risk comes from two sources. First, potential output may have slowed more than appreciated, just as during the late 1970s, following a prolonged slowdown in activity that policymakers mistook as cyclical rather than structural. Underlying inflation pressure would then be higher than

---

[13]For a detailed description of the methodology underlying this fan chart, see Elekdag and Kannan (2009).

apparent in current inflation data and could be exacerbated if the recovery surprises on the upside. Second, the large buildup of excess central bank reserves generated by unconventional monetary policy actions could feed a surge in credit growth when the recovery gains strength. As discussed below, central banks therefore must follow market developments closely and use a broad range of tools to tighten monetary conditions in the face of building pressures, although such a situation does not seem imminent.

For a number of emerging economies, by contrast, inflation risks seem more pressing. Inflation pressures have not eased as much as in the advanced economies, except in some emerging Asian and European economies. At the same time, output gaps are smaller and the rebound has been stronger in a number of these economies. Also, higher commodity prices tend to spill over faster into generalized wage pressures. Adding to these concerns, some economies are already seeing large asset price increases in response to low interest rates and easy credit, and such pressures could be exacerbated by strong capital inflows attracted by their dynamic performance.

Extending the horizon to the medium term, there are two important risks to sustained recovery, which mainly affect the advanced economies. On the financial front, continued public skepticism toward what is perceived as bailouts for those responsible for the crisis could undercut public support for financial restructuring, thereby prolonging the crisis. The result would be an even more sluggish recovery or, possibly, a long-lasting credit crunch and the equivalent of a "lost decade" for growth.

On the macroeconomic policy front, the greatest risk revolves around deteriorating fiscal positions, including as a result of measures to support the financial sector. The large increase in public debt and contingent liabilities incurred to provide stimulus to the economy and stabilize financial systems has already raised concerns in financial markets, as suggested by higher credit default swap (CDS)

spreads on sovereign debt and larger sovereign spreads for some advanced economies.[14] If the recovery were to stall and be followed by a prolonged period of stagnation or very low growth, deficits and debt could balloon to difficult-to-sustain levels. There is a low probability that such a development could seriously unsettle global bond markets. Presumably, concerns would surface first in vulnerable advanced and emerging economies, notably those with large financial sectors relative to the size of their economies or with low revenue bases and high (notably short-term) public debt. This could then trigger another retrenchment in capital flows, which could drag down a number of other advanced and emerging economies. There could then be another crisis of confidence, currencies could adjust abruptly, and demand could slump, possibly raising fears about fiscal sustainability in even the larger advanced economies. Investors could react to these fears by taking flight into government or corporate bonds issued in economies with low public debt, including potentially some emerging economies, or by purchasing large amounts of precious metals. In either case, the world economy would go through profound turmoil and a long period of low activity.

Two further risks bear watching. First, whereas oil prices present some short-term risks, they present greater medium- to long-term risks to global growth. In particular, as current excess capacity is absorbed, prices could rise abruptly to very high levels just as they did during the previous upswing. This risk is amplified by cutbacks in investment in new capacity during the present downturn and continued uncertainties about oil investment regimes in some countries that have deferred investment in new fields. Second, although generally solid international collaboration has largely contained pressure for trade and financial protectionism until now, this pressure could strengthen as unemployment

---

[14]For various reasons, including low trading volumes, CDS spreads are imperfect stress indicators for government finance.

and social problems mount. Barriers to trade and financial flows might then be erected in some economies, triggering retaliatory moves by others. Financial markets could react quickly and vigorously, anticipating future losses in profits and productivity, leading to another downward spiral in activity. At the time of writing, however, a surge in protectionism appears to be a low-probability scenario.

From a policy perspective, the key questions are how some of the risks discussed here could interact with the challenges posed by rebalancing and what policymakers can do to prevent significant damage to global growth. The issues are illustrated with two scenarios (Figure 1.15).[15]

In the upside scenario, the major economies make rapid progress in fixing their financial systems, with a resulting increase in productivity. Emerging Asia is assumed to forcefully pursue policies to raise consumption (strengthening social safety nets and implementing financial reforms), while following flexible exchange rate policies that provide room for sustained appreciation of both real and nominal exchange rates. Governments also contribute to demand through government investment spending concentrated on "green" initiatives and infrastructure spending, the latter especially in emerging Asia and other economies where there is the greatest need for additional infrastructure.[16] All these measures encourage a decrease in precautionary saving, especially in emerging Asia, Japan, and the other major economies, and to a lesser extent in the euro area. The exception is the United States, where private saving increases further, because of the ongoing need for consumer deleveraging. Under this scenario, world GDP growth is about 1.3 percentage points higher starting in 2010, contributing to improvements in fiscal positions worldwide. There is some movement toward global current account rebalancing as net debtors' current account

deficits improve and net creditors' surpluses decline, with magnitudes equal to about 0.7 percent of GDP in the United States and emerging Asia and somewhat less elsewhere.

The downside scenario assumes that the process of restoring the health of the financial systems in the major advanced economies is even slower than in the WEO baseline forecast, with a resulting loss of productivity. Economic policy missteps could exacerbate this deterioration, including through protectionist measures that distort incentives and reduce output. In this scenario, emerging Asia makes very limited progress in rebalancing demand toward domestic sources, with private saving failing to decrease by as much as projected in the WEO baseline. In some regions, especially Japan but also the United States, sluggish growth is exacerbated by the fact that monetary policy remains constrained by the zero bound on nominal interest rates, implying rising pressure on real interest rates due to price disinflation. Under this scenario, world GDP growth is about 2.2 percentage points lower starting in 2010. The objective of global current account rebalancing becomes more elusive, as current accounts move toward larger surpluses in emerging Asia and deteriorate in the United States and the euro area.

Policy Challenges: Reconciling Short- and Medium-Term Objectives

The key policy priorities remain to restore the health of the financial sector and to maintain supportive macroeconomic policies until the recovery is on a firm footing, even though policymakers must also begin preparing for an eventual unwinding of extraordinary levels of public intervention. The premature withdrawal of stimulus seems the greater risk in the near term, but developing the medium-term macroeconomic strategy beyond the crisis is key to maintaining confidence in fiscal solvency and for price and financial stability. The challenge is to map a middle course between unwinding public interventions too early, which would jeop-

[15]For further details, see Alichi and others (2009).

[16]Spending on "green" initiatives could be encouraged by a broad multilateral agreement on a new framework to deal with climate change.

Figure 1.15. Global Scenarios

(All variables in levels, unless otherwise stated; years on x-axis)

From a policy perspective, key questions are: How might various risks interact with the challenges posed by rebalancing? And what can policymakers do to prevent significant damage to global growth? In the *upside scenario,* the major economies make rapid progress in fixing their financial systems, and emerging Asia is assumed to forcefully pursue policies to raise consumption, while following flexible exchange rate policies that provide room for sustained appreciation of both real and nominal exchange rates. Under this scenario, world GDP growth is about 1.3 percentage points higher starting in 2010. The *downside scenario* assumes that the process of restoring financial system health in the major advanced economies will be even slower than in the *World Economic Outlook* (WEO) baseline and various economic policy missteps exacerbate output losses. Under this scenario, world GDP growth is about 2.2 percentage points lower starting in 2010. The goal of global current account rebalancing is even farther from resolution, as emerging Asia's current account moves into larger surplus and the United States and the euro area experience current account deterioration.

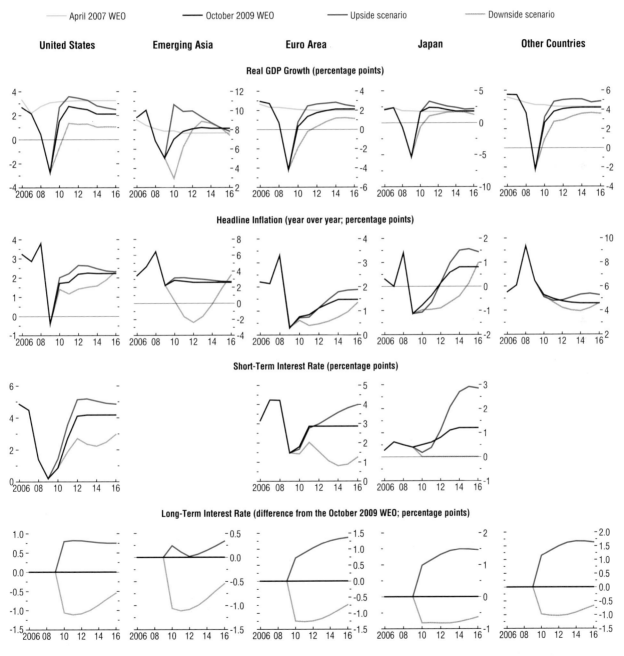

Source: Global Integrated Monetary and Fiscal Model simulations.

ardize the progress made in securing financial stability and recovery, and leaving these measures in place too long, which carries the risk of distorting incentives and damaging public balance sheets. The timing and sequence of action will vary across countries, depending on the momentum of their recoveries, policy room, and progress toward financial sector repair, but coordination will be necessary to avoid adverse cross-border spillovers.

History suggests that both premature and/or delayed exits can be costly. For example, fiscal retrenchment and the U.S. Federal Reserve's doubling of reserve requirements during 1936–37 are blamed for helping to undercut a nascent recovery.[17] Similarly, premature tax hikes in 1997, along with an unfavorable external environment, were among the factors that seem to have contributed to pushing Japan into recession. By contrast, some argue that the withdrawal of monetary accommodation after the bursting of the dot-com bubble was too slow, leaving easy conditions to fuel excessive risk taking and the subsequent house price boom (see Taylor, 2009).

Coordination within and across countries is important, because spillovers from unwinding some measures could compromise the success of unwinding others. For example, the premature withdrawal of liquidity support measures or retail deposit guarantees could delay the unwinding of government guarantees for bank bond issues, which rank among the most distortive types of public intervention.

Timing the Tightening of Accommodative Monetary Conditions

The key issues facing monetary policymakers are when to tighten and how to unwind large balance sheets. The two objectives do not necessarily present major conflicts, because instruments exist to start tightening monetary

[17]The extent to which they contributed is still subject to debate. See Romer and Romer (1989) and Feinman (1993).

conditions even while balance sheets remain much larger than usual.

The pace at which the buildup in central bank balance sheets should be unwound depends on progress in normalizing market conditions and the types of interventions in place. As the October 2009 GFSR emphasizes, continued central bank support will likely be needed through at least 2010 in many economies, and it could take much longer to unwind the buildup in illiquid assets on some central bank balance sheets. Supported by appropriate pricing, short-term liquidity operations will unwind naturally as market conditions improve, and this is already occurring. Assets purchased outright can be resold into markets, starting with government securities and moving toward other securities as their markets normalize. However, getting the timing right is important, because resale of nongovernment securities too soon could undermine the gradual process of stabilizing distressed markets. Specifically, mortgage-backed securities probably need to be held for a while, possibly to maturity if their sale is complicated by the need to continue supporting vulnerable housing markets. In the meantime, central banks can absorb reserves as needed to tighten monetary conditions by engaging in reverse repurchase operations, offering interest-bearing term deposits to banks, or issuing their own paper. Less attractive options include raising reserve requirements or having treasuries sell government paper and deposit the proceeds in central banks. In any case, it would be useful for national treasuries and central banks to develop arrangements to protect central bank balance sheets from the risks associated with holding securities for extended periods, as has been done in some countries, such as the United Kingdom. Such arrangements help mitigate concerns that central banks might delay tightening out of concern for the impact of higher interest rates on the value of the assets on their balance sheets.

Regarding the timing of monetary policy tightening, advanced and emerging economies face different challenges. In advanced economies, central banks can (with few exceptions) afford to maintain accommodative conditions for an extended period. As discussed above, underlying inflation remains very low, with spare capacity high and restructuring and rising unemployment putting downward pressure on labor costs. Fiscal stimulus to growth is diminishing, and therefore tightening prematurely could undercut the recovery. Although a prolonged period of very low interest rates could fuel excessive risk taking, the likelihood of this is limited over the near term, because financial markets and households will take a long time to repair their balance sheets and extend credit. Nonetheless, once the recovery has firmed to such an extent that output gaps narrow and inflation becomes more of a concern, conditions will need to be tightened. Indeed, as credit begins to grow, accommodative policies may need to be removed more quickly than after the bursting of the dot-com bubble in order to limit the scope for renewed excess (consistent with the findings in Chapter 3), especially in the absence of important progress toward strengthening prudential frameworks.

The situation is more varied across emerging economies, but for a number of them, it will likely be appropriate to start removing monetary accommodation sooner than in advanced economies. Inflation pressure has eased in much of Asia and in some emerging European economies, and a number of emerging economies, notably in Asia, are already enjoying relatively vigorous rebounds in activity. Accordingly, unemployment is not forecast to be much higher in 2010 than before the crisis, implying only limited downward pressure on prices going forward. Furthermore, some of these economies are again seeing large asset price increases in response to low interest rates, raising the danger of new asset price bubbles. As Chapter 3 underscores, under such conditions, monetary policymakers may want to tighten more than suggested by output and inflation developments. In some economies, this may

require allowing more exchange rate flexibility to avoid importing an excessively easy policy stance from the advanced economies.

Looking beyond the immediate challenges, what are some lessons of the crisis for conducting monetary policy? Chapter 3 argues that monetary policymakers should put more emphasis on containing macrofinancial risks, helped by the introduction of macroprudential tools. Historical evidence suggests that relatively stable inflation and output growth offer little protection against major shocks to the economy from asset price busts: output and inflation are poor predictors of asset price busts. Chapter 3 shows that other variables, notably credit growth and the current account balance, are better predictors and may deserve more attention from monetary policymakers. Thus, if concerns mount about domestic demand and asset prices, monetary policymakers should consider tightening more than required purely for the purpose of keeping inflation under control over the coming year or two. Macroprudential tools have the advantage of working directly to lean against credit cycles and can therefore be helpful in complementing the role of interest rates in stabilizing economies. Expectations of what can be achieved, however, need to be realistic.

A further question facing central banks is whether to maintain various changes in monetary policy operations introduced in response to the crisis, including those relating to their role as lenders of last resort. The crisis has made apparent the benefits of a large number of central bank counterparties and a broad range of acceptable collateral. However, access to emergency lending must come in exchange for tighter supervision and regulation, and in some cases this requires that supervisors share more information with central banks. Similarly, central banks can continue to accept a broader range of collateral but should adjust pricing and access conditions to ensure that such operations are used only to address temporary liquidity needs and do not become a normal part of financial intermediation.

Maintaining Fiscal Support while Securing Fiscal Sustainability

Notwithstanding already large deficits and high debt in many economies, fiscal stimulus needs to be sustained until the recovery is on a firm footing and may need to be amplified or extended beyond current plans if downside risks to growth materialize. Governments should thus stand ready to roll out new initiatives as necessary. At the same time, they need to commit to large reductions in deficits over the medium term and must start addressing mounting long-term fiscal challenges by advancing reforms to put public finances on a more sustainable path.

A major concern is that the financial shock has saddled advanced economies with a large amount of public debt just as fiscal pressures from population aging are becoming more pressing. Public debt in the advanced economies is projected to exceed 110 percent of GDP by 2014, up from about 80 percent of GDP before the crisis, even building in significant fiscal adjustment (much of which remains to be incorporated into specific measures). This reflects persistent primary deficits, mounting interest bills, and modest economic growth. Population aging will add to deficit pressures and debt trajectories, particularly after 2015. Aging-related spending could rise by about 5 percent of GDP in the European Union by 2060 and by about 4–6 percent of GDP in the United States.[18] Large increases are also expected for Japan. In emerging economies, by contrast, debt levels are expected to decline after the initial postcrisis peak, and few of these economies face a comparable expansion in aging-related spending.

The large increase in government debt is likely to put upward pressure on long-term interest rates as the recovery is sustained, crowding out private investment and some emerging economy sovereign issues.[19] This will have dampening effects on growth, but there may also be other potentially negative effects. Are there debt levels that are simply too high, that will cause investor flight even from traditionally safe assets, for example, U.S. government bonds? Within reasonable debt ranges, there is no straightforward answer to this question. It depends on an economy's growth prospects, on investor preferences and interest rates, and the room available to cut spending or raise taxes to repay the debt in the future, which also brings up political considerations. Some countries, such as Italy and Japan, have sustained very high debt levels for a while already. Fortunately, neither of them featured among the advanced economies whose financial systems were badly hit by the crisis, thus they have avoided major contingent liabilities. Nonetheless, Italy suffered a major increase in risk premiums on its debt for a period during this crisis and had to forego major fiscal stimulus, whereas Japan has been protected by its unique circumstances.[20] Looking forward, pressures on spending and debt in advanced economies will mount, and markets have a tendency to suddenly catch up with slowly increasing vulnerabilities. In the meantime, the price of much higher debt in advanced economies is diminished room for countercyclical

---

[18]See European Commission (2009a, 2009b), IMF (2006), and U.S. Congressional Budget Office (2005).

[19]The October 2009 GFSR presents evidence for a panel of up to 31 advanced and emerging economies over the period 1980–2007, suggesting that an increase in the fiscal deficit raises long-term government interest rates from a minimum of 10 to a maximum of 60 basis points for each percentage point of GDP increase in the fiscal deficit. The impact of debt accumulation on bond yields is smaller but still significant. A 1 percent of GDP increase in debt raises government bond yields by 5 to 10 basis points, with the effects varying depending on country-specific characteristics. However, GFSR projections through the end of 2010 suggest that in the United States and euro area net issuance of total credit (sovereign and private) will be well below the levels seen during the boom years of 2002 to 2007.

[20]Japanese savers have a very strong preference for holding domestic government debt. Also, a significant portion of the domestic debt is held by public institutions.

policy and financial support in the face of any new crises.

However, sustained fiscal support in the near term need not undercut progress toward long-run fiscal sustainability. Reforms to social spending programs—particularly if focused on measures that increase labor force participation (for example, by linking retirement ages to life expectancies) or raise the efficiency of welfare programs—could contribute significantly to lowering spending over the long term, thereby facilitating more fiscal support for the recovery. For example, lowering the growth rate of health care costs by 1 percent a year could lower government spending by about 1½ percent of GDP in the Group of Seven (G7) countries in 15 years. Raising the retirement age by one year could yield fiscal savings of up to ½ percent of GDP after 15 years. Accordingly, with progress on both fronts, up-front government financing costs connected with financial sector support operations would be recouped fairly quickly.

In practice, such reforms certainly face formidable political obstacles, and the room available for stimulus is limited. Thus, it will be crucial to ensure that stimulus spending is allocated in a way that maximizes support for recovery and accelerates a return to solid medium-term growth. This means that any new initiatives should give priority to funding financial sector repair, addressing the heavy social costs of labor market disruptions, and helping to forestall large increases in structural unemployment.

Moreover, rising concerns about fiscal sustainability imply that countries that have accumulated large amounts of debt during this crisis need to adopt ambitious medium-term adjustment targets and support their achievement with fiscal frameworks, including suitable fiscal rules and strong enforcement mechanisms. Such frameworks and rules can play a useful role in reining in spending pressures when good times return, thereby providing a degree of reassurance to investors that deficits and debt eventually will be rolled back. Many countries

have already moved in this direction.[21] Encouragingly, more steps in this direction are being taken or are under consideration (for example, in Germany and the United States), but achieving the right mix of flexibility and discipline will not be straightforward.

Healing Financial Sectors while Reforming Prudential Frameworks

Completing financial sector repair and reforming prudential frameworks are indispensable for a return to sustained growth over the medium term. In many countries, policy actions have been insufficient to return banking systems to a position from which they can sustain the recovery with solid credit growth, and remedying this shortfall must be given priority. In addition, attention must be paid to managing the exit from public support for financial operations and to reforming prudential frameworks to ensure stronger risk management.

Restructuring financial firms' activities is key for normal lending to resume. This will require balance sheet cleansing, recapitalization, and new business plans that are consistent with new funding models and new prudential frameworks. So far, there has been only very limited progress in removing impaired assets from bank balance sheets.[22] The main challenge now is ongoing deterioration of asset quality, and so public policies and financial institutions have to become more forward looking and preemptive. Official stress tests are important instruments through which the condition of banks can be diagnosed and comprehensive recapitalization programs put in place. On this front, progress across countries has been uneven, and it is a source of

---

[21]See Ter-Minassian and Kumar (2008).

[22]Institutional arrangements for dealing with impaired assets are in place in the United States, for example, but have hardly been utilized thus far. The European Union has adopted harmonized guidelines to deal with impaired assets, leaving it up to individual countries to decide whether to do this through a bad bank, guarantee, or hybrid approach.

concern that support for recapitalization faces important political obstacles.

Exit strategies need to be clearly articulated to help guide bank restructuring. Banks face a "wall of maturities" in the next two years, increasing the rollover risks. In this setting, there are risks associated with abrupt changes in the level of support provided to these institutions, and strict deadlines for ending such programs should be avoided—some countries that had announced deadlines for removing wholesale guarantees have had to extend them. Instead, subsidies can be gradually reduced and access terms tightened for any facilities that may need to be extended. Healthy firms should be encouraged to repay capital injections and issue nonguaranteed debt to signal their viability, whereas chronically undercapitalized firms should be resolved rather than kept on life support. Reprivatization can wait until reform is sufficiently advanced, but management of publicly owned financial institutions should focus on limiting distortions to competition or stability.

Regarding fundamental reform, the October 2009 GFSR explains the many challenges facing policymakers. Even though initiatives are getting under way to address these, the achievement of a major overhaul must not be jeopardized by growing confidence that the greatest crisis dangers are past, fears that national competitive advantages might be lost, or concerns that first-best solutions are out of reach for technical reasons. Three challenges deserve particular attention:

- The perimeter of regulation needs to be broadened and made more flexible, covering all systemically important institutions. In this regard, the challenge of dealing with the problem posed by institutions that are too big or too connected to fail will need to be addressed. Proposals have been made to strengthen resolution frameworks, including by requiring such institutions to develop resolution plans and to hold more capital to compensate for their larger contributions to systemic risk, as well as giving authorities the power to impose losses on senior creditors. Other proposals are to separate commercial

from investment banking and to remove proprietary trading activity from commercial and investment banks. The costs and benefits of such proposals require further analysis, weighing potential losses from lower returns to scale and scope against potential benefits from reduced exposures to systemic risks.

- Prudential frameworks must play a greater stabilizing role over the economic cycle. Once the crisis started, mark-to-market rules and constant regulatory capital ratios forced financial institutions to take dramatic measures to reduce their balance sheets, exacerbating fire sales and deleveraging. The opposite forces were driving a credit accelerator during boom times. It is difficult to gauge the extent to which these forces are hardwired into prudential frameworks or imposed by markets. One element of procyclicality could be addressed through establishing minimum capital requirements according to stress-test scenarios and an overall leverage ratio. These could be complemented by raising supervisory risk weights for rapidly growing loan or asset classes. Other proposals include requiring countercyclical capital charges or allowing regulators to alter capital requirements (or other regulatory requirements) over the cycle just as central banks alter interest rates.[23]

- The final challenge is to improve international coordination and avoid financial protectionism. This will require greater supervisory and regulatory convergence, with a view to limiting incentives for cross-border regulatory arbitrage, and robust arrangements (including appropriate bank-specific insolvency frameworks at national levels) to resolve cross-border institutions and counter incentives for beggar-thy-neighbor approaches to addressing crises. Progress is being made on convergence under the auspices of the Financial Stability Board; progress on resolution faces major political hurdles, even within

---

[23]These proposals present major challenges for policymakers, not least of which is determining when buffers need to be built up and when they can be released.

the European Union, which has been debating this issue for some time.

Structural and Social Policy Challenges

Rising unemployment will present a major challenge in many advanced economies. Chapter 4 suggests that unemployment rates tend to rise significantly and for many years after financial shocks, and this time will be no exception. Limiting the extent of job destruction will require slower wage growth or even wage cuts for many workers. The impact of the necessary adjustments on poorer segments of labor forces could be cushioned with earned income tax credits or similar programs that limit the social repercussions of wage adjustment. Subsidizing part-time work to facilitate a broad distribution of reductions in labor input and allow a more gradual reduction in wages may also be appropriate, provided there are reassurances that such programs are cut back as good times return. Those who still lose their jobs should be supported with unemployment benefit programs that are generous (to support demand and prevent hardship) but not too long in duration, appropriately means-tested social support mechanisms, and increased resources for job matching as well as better education and training. In addition, many of the structural reforms that past issues of the WEO have emphasized to improve the flexibility of labor markets remain relevant, possibly even more so to raise medium-term prospects after a damaging crisis.[24]

In some countries, product or services market reforms could help create new employment opportunities and enhance productivity growth.[25] In emerging economies with large external surpluses and tradables sectors, reforms could usefully focus on the service sectors, which tend to be less competitive and more protected, and to generate relatively slower productivity growth.[26] Completion of the Doha Round of global trade negotiations could provide a timely boost to global confidence and trade, although it remains equally critical to avoid any backsliding on trade liberalization and competition policies.

Structural reforms, together with greater exchange rate flexibility, can also make an important contribution to facilitating global demand rebalancing. In this regard, the upside scenario for rebalancing underscores the importance of measures to repair financial systems; improve corporate governance and financial intermediation; support public investment, including in green technologies; and reform social safety nets (including both health care and pension systems) with a view to fostering lower precautionary saving in some countries with large current account surpluses. Even with a strong commitment to reform along these and other lines by all countries, however, rebalancing is likely to be a drawn-out process. In the meantime, the reforms would help strengthen the resilience of a global economy that remains unusually vulnerable to renewed shocks.

Finally, there is a risk that poverty could increase significantly in a number of developing economies, notably in sub-Saharan Africa, where real GDP per capita is contracting in 2009 for the first time in a decade. Past reforms and changes in trade and financial patterns should help soften the blow from lower growth in advanced economies in comparison with past crises. Nonetheless, continued donor support from advanced economies will be crucial

---

[24]Recovery from the major shocks of the 1970s and early 1980s was made more difficult by sometimes well-meaning but often ill-considered initiatives that hindered labor market adjustment, such as the introduction of early retirement programs or the abuse of support for the disabled or the poor through the provision of virtually open-ended support for able but jobless workers. See, for example, Layard, Nickell, and Jackman (1991), and Blanchard and Wolfers (2000).

[25]In fact, evidence on successful labor market reforms in response to crises in Europe suggests that it was often supported with product market reforms, because they boosted job creation and wages. See, for example, Estevão (2005) and Annett (2006).

[26]See *World Economic Outlook*, September 2006, Chapter 3.

Figure 1.16. Commodity and Petroleum Prices

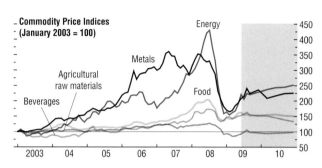

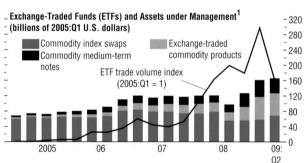

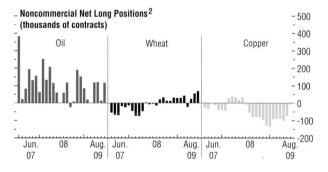

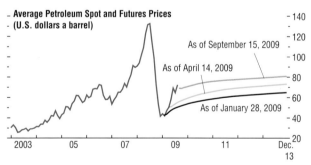

Sources: Barclays Capital; Bloomberg Financial Markets; and IMF staff estimates.
[1]Deflated by IMF Commodity Index.
[2]At the Chicago Board of Trade, New York Mercantile Exchange, and New York Commodity Exchange, respectively.

if these economies are to sustain hard-won macroeconomic stability gains. At the same time, policies need to continue to be geared toward mitigating the impact of the global recession on economic activity and poverty, while strengthening the foundations for sustained growth.

Appendix 1.1. Commodity Market Developments and Prospects

The authors of this appendix are Kevin Cheng, Nese Erbil, Thomas Helbling, Shaun Roache, and Marina Rousset.

After collapsing during the second half of 2008, commodity prices broadly stabilized in early 2009 and subsequently staged a strong rally in the second quarter, despite generally high inventories that resulted from the weak demand through the recession (Figure 1.16; Table 1.2). A rally this strong at such an early stage in the recovery of global industrial production contrasts with past experience.[27] In previous global downturns, prices typically continued to fall into the early phases of recovery (Figure 1.17) or rose at rates far below the increases recorded in recent months. The exception is oil prices, which recorded substantial increases early in previous recoveries as well. However, commodity

[27]Based on data through June 2009, global industrial activity is now estimated to have reached a trough in February 2009.

Table 1.2. Commodity Price Developments, 2008–09

	Percent Change		
	Peak to trough	Trough to June	2009:Q2/ 2009:Q1
IMF Commodity Price Index	−55.6	31.1	15.7
Fuel	−64.1	42.7	20.1
Petroleum	−68.7	66.4	33.8
Nonfuel	−35.5	17.5	9.5
Base metals	−49.6	24.5	15.1
Agricultural raw materials	−33.0	13.6	0.7
Food	−33.4	19.6	10.2

Source: IMF, Primary Commodity Price database.

prices also fell faster and by larger magnitudes during the second half of 2008 than during previous downturns.

The early commodity price rebound has led to renewed discussion of whether prices are increasingly driven by commodity financial investment. The revival in investor risk appetite and improved sentiment since March 2009, together with a renewed tendency toward dollar depreciation, have led to increased financial investment in commodity assets. However, as noted in previous issues of the *World Economic Outlook*, these inflows still tend to follow changes in fundamentals. In the current circumstances, they reflect two interrelated factors. First, there was the growing consensus that the worst of the global recession and the collapse in commodity demand were over and that a recovery would begin in 2009. Second, there was increasing confidence that, with unprecedented financial sector support and macroeconomic policy stimulus, the probability of another systemic financial sector event had decreased.

The perception of an improving near-term outlook has affected physical commodity markets primarily by increasing the incentive to hold inventories. At the same time, improving financial conditions have provided for increased credit availability for inventory financing at more normal costs. The rising inflows into commodity funds, which contributed to the normalization of liquidity conditions in commodity futures markets, likely facilitated the hedging of inventory positions. Against this backdrop, additional expectations-based demand for inventories, and some stabilization in stock buildups as end-user demand bottomed out, allowed for easier absorption of the continued excess supply (current supply minus current end-user consumption). Downward pressure on spot prices eased in turn. Longer-dated futures prices have been less affected by the change in expectations about near-term market conditions, and the upward slope of commodity futures curves has flattened as spot prices have recovered.

The magnitude of recent price increases varied considerably across commodities, irrespec-

Figure 1.17. Commodity Prices in Global Recessions and Recoveries[1]
(Percent change; indices, 2005 = 100)

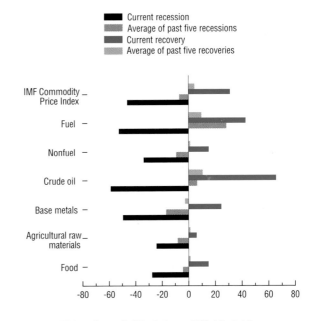

Sources: IMF Primary Commodity Price System; and IMF staff calculations.
[1]Global recessions and recoveries are identified on the basis of monthly peaks and troughs in the log level of a monthly index of global industrial production.

Table 1.3. Commodity Consumption and Market Share

(Percent)

	Global	Emerging Markets
Crude oil		
Cumulative consumption growth		
1985–2008	36.6	58.5
2002–08	10.8	24.8
Market share		
1993	. . .	43.1
2002	. . .	45.8
2008	. . .	51.8
Aluminum		
Cumulative consumption growth		
1985–2008	92.5	140.6
2002–08	48.4	88.8
Market share		
1993	. . .	32.4
2002	. . .	42.8
2008	. . .	59.2
Copper		
Cumulative consumption growth		
1985–2008	61.9	127.0
2002–08	21.4	53.0
Market share		
1993	. . .	35.2
2002	. . .	49.3
2008	. . .	61.7
Wheat		
Cumulative consumption growth		
1985–2008	27.6	20.3
2002–08	7.8	7.7
Market share		
1993	. . .	76.9
2002	. . .	70.5
2008	. . .	70.7
Memorandum		
Real GDP		
Cumulative growth		
1985–2008	84.1	110.6
2002–08	29.2	46.3

Sources: International Energy Agency; U.S. Department of Agriculture; and World Bureau of Metal Statistics.

tive of the relative strength of financial inflows. Underscoring the influence of fundamentals, the variation in price changes reflects differences in the cyclical sensitivity of commodities, but also reflects commodity-specific factors,

as discussed below. In particular, prices in oil markets were supported not only by recovery expectations, but also by Organization of Petroleum Exporting Countries (OPEC) supply cuts, while metal prices have been buoyed by restocking in China.

Commodity demand prospects now depend increasingly on growth in emerging and developing economies, given the steady rise in their market shares (Table 1.3). Moreover, commodity demand in these economies is more income-elastic than in advanced economies. With a buoyant recovery already under way in emerging Asia and the recovery in emerging and developing economies generally advancing ahead of that in advanced economies, commodity demand is strengthening ahead of activity in advanced economies. Commodity prices, especially in cyclically sensitive sectors, have thus responded strongly to news about an earlier-than-expected recovery under way in emerging Asia in the second quarter of 2009.

The extent of further upward price pressure will depend on the timing and strength of the global recovery. With inventories remaining above average except for food commodities and with substantial spare capacity in many commodity sectors, such pressure is likely to remain moderate for some time, unless stronger-than-expected global growth leads to a rapid drawdown of these buffers. There are also near-term risks that the largely expectation-driven price rebound could be partially reversed if the global recovery is more sluggish than currently expected in commodity markets. Probability distributions derived from the option prices of key commodities suggest that the market has become more confident that the recent rebound of commodity prices during the second quarter of 2009 will be sustained and that further price increases are likely (see Box 1.6 for further details). In particular, option pricing for a broad-based commodity index, crude oil, and copper suggests that investors anticipate higher prices during the second half of 2009 compared with the first two quarters. That said, the probability of another commodity price spike is seen

Box 1.6. What Do Options Markets Tell Us about Commodity Price Prospects?

Over the past decade, both exchange-based and over-the-counter commodity derivative markets have grown rapidly. The growth pattern of these markets appears to vary widely across commodities and across derivative types. For example, derivative (options and futures combined) contracts for crude oil trading on the New York Mercantile Exchange grew fivefold during 1998–2008, with options outgrowing futures by five times. For other key commodities, the growth magnitude is smaller, and the divergence in growth rates between options and futures is less prominent (first figure). The number of commodity derivative contracts outstanding, however, plummeted during the second half of 2008—particularly for crude oil—although there have been signs of a rebound for some commodities more recently.

What Is the Logic behind the Use of Option Prices for Economic Analysis?

The rapid growth of commodity futures and options transactions has increased the depth, liquidity, and efficiency of these derivative markets, thereby improving their information content. Indeed, it is well documented that derivatives—particularly options—contain useful information about market expectations that can enrich the analysis of economic and financial prospects.[1] The logic is that option premiums conveying the right to buy or sell an underlying asset at a certain strike price should reflect markets' views of the probability distribution of future prices, which determines the expected option payoff. For example, a bullish and forward-looking investor would be willing to pay a higher premium to exercise a call option at a strike price beyond the current spot price; similarly, a bearish and forward-looking investor would be willing to pay a higher premium to exercise a put option at a strike price below the current spot price.

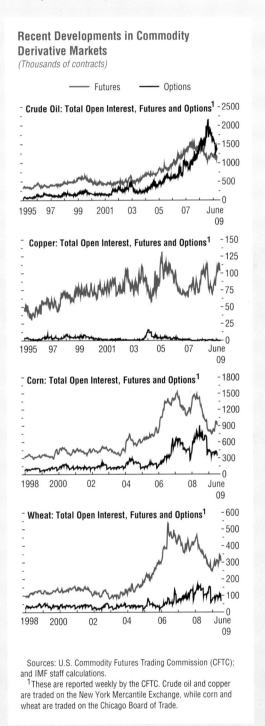

Recent Developments in Commodity Derivative Markets
(Thousands of contracts)

Sources: U.S. Commodity Futures Trading Commission (CFTC); and IMF staff calculations.
[1]These are reported weekly by the CFTC. Crude oil and copper are traded on the New York Mercantile Exchange, while corn and wheat are traded on the Chicago Board of Trade.

The main author of this box is Kevin C. Cheng, with research assistance provided by Marina Rousset.
[1]See, for example, BIS (1999).

Box 1.6 *(concluded)*

Such information extracted from options markets can help in gauging risks in the future, which can help in devising alternative scenarios or stress tests. Furthermore, unlike uncertainty measures from most econometric models that are backward looking, measures from this approach are forward looking, and thus implicitly encompass all risk factors currently considered in the market.

In this respect, the *World Economic Outlook* has presented a so-called risk-neutral probability distribution for Brent crude oil for the past few years. Recently, the IMF staff has developed a new framework that provides for more stable results and can be applied to other futures options as well.[2] The advantage of the new framework is that, unlike the old framework, which required data input of a granular set of artificial price quotes estimated by the Intercontinental Exchange, the new framework relies solely on actual market data. Furthermore, the new model allows a high degree of flexibility to capture a wide range of statistical properties.

This framework has been used to generate probability distributions for the Continuous Commodity Index—a broad-based commodity index consisting of 17 component commodities—as well as a number of key commodities including crude oil, gold, copper, and corn (second figure). The results suggest that compared with distributions estimated in early April, the probability distributions (as of early August and mid-September) of the eight-month-forward contracts for crude oil and copper have shifted to the right—suggesting a higher expected price—while their dispersion has declined—suggesting a decline in perceived volatility (third figure). This decline in dispersion also echoed a decline in the Crude Oil Volatility Index by the Chicago Board Options Exchange in the second

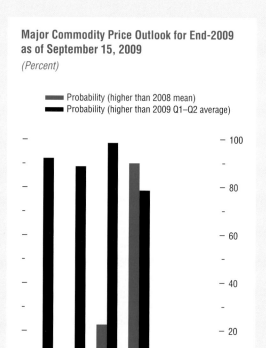

Major Commodity Price Outlook for End-2009 as of September 15, 2009
(Percent)

Source: IMF staff estimates.
[1] West Texas Intermediate crude oil.
[2] CCI = Continuous Commodity Index: 1995 Revision of the Commodity Research Bureau Index; average of 17 commodity futures prices.

quarter of 2009.[3] For corn, the distribution has shifted slightly to the left, but also with a slightly lower dispersion, likely reflecting improved weather conditions in corn-growing regions.

Caveats

The information derived from option prices must be interpreted with some caution. Specifically, the estimated probabilities, as in any other approach, assume that markets are risk neutral. This method tends to exaggerate the likelihood of an undesirable outcome if investors are risk averse. Intuitively, a risk-averse

[2]This framework—which builds on the double-lognormal approach by Bahra (1997)—uses a mixture of multiple lognormal distributions. For a detailed discussion on the technical foundation of the framework and its advantages over other existing methodologies, see Cheng (forthcoming).

[3]In addition, the distributions have also become somewhat less skewed with a less-thick tail, although the differences are marginal.

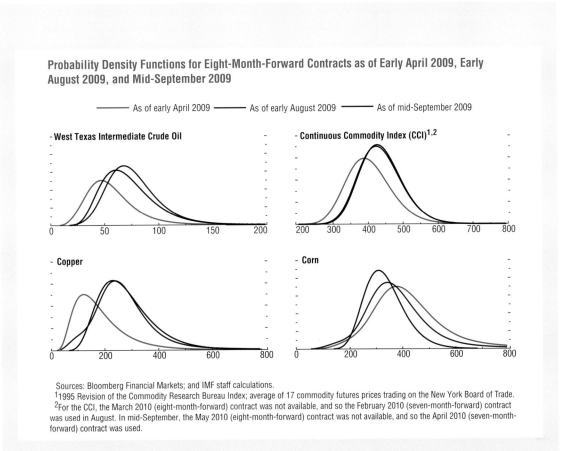

Probability Density Functions for Eight-Month-Forward Contracts as of Early April 2009, Early August 2009, and Mid-September 2009

As of early April 2009 ———— As of early August 2009 ———— As of mid-September 2009

West Texas Intermediate Crude Oil

Continuous Commodity Index (CCI)[1,2]

Copper

Corn

Sources: Bloomberg Financial Markets; and IMF staff calculations.
[1]1995 Revision of the Commodity Research Bureau Index; average of 17 commodity futures prices trading on the New York Board of Trade.
[2]For the CCI, the March 2010 (eight-month-forward) contract was not available, and so the February 2010 (seven-month-forward) contract was used in August. In mid-September, the May 2010 (eight-month-forward) contract was not available, and so the April 2010 (seven-month-forward) contract was used.

investor is willing to pay a higher premium to insure against an unlikely but disastrous outcome than a risk-neutral investor. If the probability of such a disastrous outcome is estimated under the assumption that the inves-

tor is risk neutral while using the *actual observed* premium paid by this risk-averse investor, the estimated probability would be higher than the *objective* probability.

as remote over the near term, with prices not expected to reach their average 2008 levels by the end of the year.

Finally, commodity prices will also partly depend on U.S. dollar developments. Empirically, there has been a generally robust negative association between commodity prices and fluctuations in the effective U.S. dollar exchange rate, both in nominal and real terms.[28] Although the direction of causality may go both ways and

[28]See Box 1.5 in the April 2008 *World Economic Outlook* and the references therein.

may vary over time, depending on the underlying disturbances, the negative correlation is consistent with incentives to hold commodity inventories to hedge against dollar fluctuations in the short term, with the dollar's effect on relative purchasing power becoming more important over the longer term.

Commodity prices are projected to remain high by historical standards through the medium term. The crisis has reduced prices somewhat below their 2008 peaks, but demand is expected to continue rising from current levels at a solid pace as industrialization continues in emerging and developing economies. Accommodating this demand will eventually require a substantial further capacity expansion in many commodity sectors, with some need to tap higher-cost sources. The extent of medium-term price pressure will vary across commodities, depending on the speed of and impediments to capacity buildup, as discussed below.

Oil Markets

Oil prices have responded strongly to perceptions that the worst of the global recession is over and to signs of a demand rebound in China. After reaching a low of $36 a barrel on February 27, 2009, oil prices started to rebound in March and climbed to $70 by midyear.[29] At the same time, oil price volatility declined to levels that were still somewhat elevated compared with pre-2008 values but well below those following the bankruptcy of Lehman Brothers in September 2008.

The strong price response to signs of an expected pickup in activity follows patterns observed during some earlier global slowdowns, notably 2000–01. However, in the current downturn, global oil consumption contracted much more deeply than in any recession since the early 1980s, by well in excess of 2 million barrels a day (mbd) from the fourth quarter of 2008 to the second quarter of 2009 (Table 1.4). The large demand declines are largely attributable to advanced economies, particularly the United States and Japan, although oil-consumption growth in emerging and other developing economies also decelerated and, in some cases, entered negative territory in the first quarter of 2009.

Faced with such demand weakness, OPEC implemented a series of production cuts to support prices. By August 2009, the reduc-

tion in OPEC production from the September 2008 base level was estimated at 2.8 mbd, some 70 percent of the target. This compliance record is broadly in line with the past record, although the downward adjustment in both OPEC production quotas and actual production was faster. Non-OPEC production has broadly stagnated through the contraction. Although excess supply has narrowed in recent months with OPEC production cuts, it remained positive through the first half of 2009, and Organization for Economic Cooperation and Development (OECD) inventories continued to increase, primarily in the United States.

Price developments will partly depend on how strongly supply responds to recovering demand. With non-OPEC supply unlikely to pick up substantially—given high decline rates in some large, mature fields, notably in the North Sea and Mexico, and given sluggish capacity buildup because of barriers to investment in many countries—this response will depend largely on OPEC production. The experience of recent episodes of deliberate production cuts suggests that OPEC members will respond gradually and with some lag to increasing demand and rising price pressure. Indeed, recent statements by key OPEC officials suggest that OPEC production increases will be predicated on a substantial drawdown of OECD inventories to more normal stock-use levels and on an oil price within the target range of $70–$80 a barrel.

Risks of a sustained price surge from current market levels during the recovery should be contained by large excess capacity and high inventories, barring any significant change to the medium-term oil market outlook. Some tightening of demand-supply balances in the second half of 2009 and in 2010 has already been priced in. Measured spare capacity is not necessarily a good indicator of actual oil market tightness in a period of price-oriented production policy decisions. Nevertheless, current spare capacity—which, as of August 2009, is estimated at some 6½ mbd, with about 3½ mbd accounted for by Saudi Arabia—is twice the average level over the past decade and will be boosted by already

---

[29]Unless otherwise stated, oil prices refer to the IMF's Average Petroleum Spot Price (APSP), which is a simple average of the prices for West Texas Intermediate, dated Brent, and Dubai Fateh grades.

Table 1.4. Global Oil Demand and Production by Region[1]
(Millions of barrels a day)

	2008	2009 Proj.	2010 Proj.	2008 H2	2009 H1	Year-over-Year Percent Change							
						2003–05 Avg.	2006	2007	2008	2009 Proj.	2010 Proj.	2008 H2	2009 H1
Demand													
OECD[2]	47.6	45.4	45.4	47.0	45.5	1.3	−0.6	−0.7	−3.2	−4.7	0.1	−4.8	−5.5
North America	24.2	23.1	23.3	23.8	23.2	2.0	−0.8	0.4	−5.1	−4.4	0.8	−6.7	−5.5
of which:													
United States	19.8	18.9	19.1	19.4	19.0	1.7	−0.5	−0.1	−5.9	−4.5	0.9	−3.9	−1.8
Europe	15.3	14.7	14.7	15.5	14.6	0.7	0.1	−2.1	0.0	−4.1	−0.2	−0.6	−4.2
Pacific	8.1	7.5	7.4	7.8	7.7	0.4	−1.6	−1.0	−3.6	−6.8	−1.7	−7.0	−7.9
Non-OECD	38.7	39.1	40.3	38.7	38.8	4.4	4.0	4.4	3.7	0.9	3.2	2.7	0.2
of which:													
China	7.9	8.3	8.6	7.9	8.1	10.1	8.3	4.4	4.3	4.6	4.0	3.6	2.5
Other Asia	9.7	9.7	10.0	9.4	9.9	3.2	2.7	5.7	1.3	0.6	2.2	−1.0	0.2
Former Soviet Union	4.2	4.0	4.1	4.2	3.9	1.2	2.9	2.7	1.5	−4.8	3.0	−0.5	−6.6
Middle East	7.1	7.2	7.5	7.3	7.0	4.8	4.4	3.2	8.5	1.5	3.8	10.0	1.2
Africa	3.2	3.2	3.3	3.2	3.2	4.0	0.5	4.0	3.8	0.5	3.5	3.3	0.9
Latin America	5.9	6.0	6.1	6.0	5.9	2.4	3.4	5.5	3.9	0.7	2.9	2.8	0.6
World	86.3	84.4	85.7	85.7	84.3	2.5	1.2	1.5	−0.2	−2.2	1.5	−1.5	−3.0
Production													
OPEC (current composition)[3]	35.9	...	...	35.8	33.5	6.6	0.8	-0.9	3.0	...	...	1.4	−7.1
of which:													
Saudi Arabia	10.4	...	...	10.4	9.4	7.5	−1.5	−4.4	4.2	...	...	3.0	−9.7
Nigeria	2.2	...	...	2.2	2.1	7.1	−5.2	−4.8	−7.9	...	...	−7.9	−2.3
Venezuela	2.6	...	...	2.6	2.3	1.6	−5.8	−7.8	−1.2	...	...	−2.0	−10.5
Iraq	2.4	...	...	2.4	2.4	2.5	4.9	9.9	14.0	...	...	5.5	−0.8
Non-OPEC	50.6	51.0	51.5	50.4	51.0	1.0	1.2	0.8	-0.4	0.7	0.9	-0.5	0.3
of which:													
North America	13.9	14.0	14.0	13.7	14.0	−0.8	0.8	0.1	−2.5	0.6	0.4	−3.2	−0.5
North Sea	4.3	4.1	3.7	4.3	4.3	−5.7	−7.6	−5.0	−5.1	−6.6	−9.5	−4.5	−2.6
Russia	10.0	10.1	10.2	10.0	10.0	7.7	2.2	2.4	−0.8	1.3	0.4	−0.7	0.7
Other Former Soviet Union[4]	2.8	3.0	3.3	2.7	2.9	7.7	3.9	12.1	2.6	9.5	8.3	−1.4	2.3
Other Non-OPEC	19.6	19.8	20.3	19.7	19.7	1.0	18.6	0.6	2.1	1.0	2.5	2.7	1.0
World	86.5	...	...	86.1	84.5	3.2	1.0	0.1	1.0	...	...	0.3	−2.8
Net demand[5]	−0.2	...	...	−0.5	−0.2	−0.6	−0.4	1.0	−0.3	...	...	−0.5	−0.2

Sources: IMF staff calculations; International Energy Agency; and *Oil Market Report,* August 2009.
[1]Totals refer to a total of crude oil, condensates, natural gas liquids, and oil from nonconventional sources.
[2]OECD = Organization for Economic Cooperation and Development.
[3]OPEC = Organization of Petroleum Exporting Countries. Includes Angola (which joined OPEC in January 2007) and Ecuador (which rejoined in November 2007, after suspending its membership from December 1992 to October 2007).
[4]Other Former Soviet Union includes Azerbaijan, Belarus, Georgia, Kazakhstan, Kyrgyz Republic, Tajikistan, Turkmenistan, Ukraine, and Uzbekistan.
[5]Difference between demand and production.

announced capacity expansion in Saudi Arabia of some 1–1.5 mbd by end-2009 (Figure 1.18). High levels of spare capacity weigh on members who have recently increased their capacity at high cost and will provide for growing incentives to increase production when prices are rising.

Looking to the medium term, the oil price outlook and risks of a renewed price spike will depend on prospects for maintaining sustainable demand-supply balances. Oil demand is expected to return to a path of robust growth in emerging economies but should remain

Figure 1.18. World Energy Market Developments

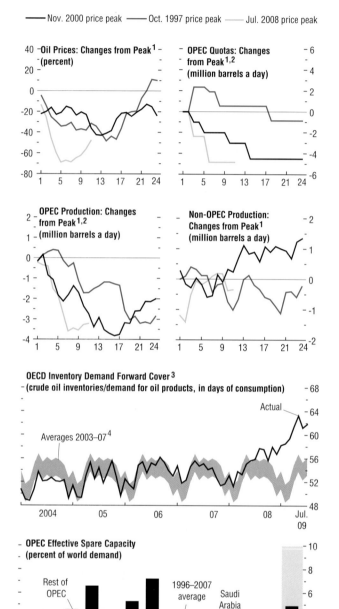

——— Nov. 2000 price peak   ——— Oct. 1997 price peak   ——— Jul. 2008 price peak

Oil Prices: Changes from Peak[1]
(percent)

OPEC Quotas: Changes
from Peak[1,2]
(million barrels a day)

OPEC Production: Changes
from Peak[1,2]
(million barrels a day)

Non-OPEC Production:
Changes from Peak[1]
(million barrels a day)

OECD Inventory Demand Forward Cover[3]
(crude oil inventories/demand for oil products, in days of consumption)

Actual

Averages 2003–07[4]

2004   05   06   07   08   Jul.
09

OPEC Effective Spare Capacity
(percent of world demand)

Rest of
OPEC

1996–2007
average

Saudi
Arabia

1996 97 98 99 2000 01 02 03 04 05 06 07 08 09

Sources: IMF Primary Commodity Price System; International Energy Agency; U.S. Energy Information Administration; and IMF staff calculations.
[1] Months from the price peak on the x-axis.
[2] Organization of Petroleum Exporting Countries (OPEC) composition as of the month of the price peak.
[3] OECD = Organization for Economic Cooperation and Development.
[4] Band is based on averages for each calendar month during 2003–07 and a 40 percent confidence interval based on deviations during this period.

subdued in advanced economies. On the supply side, the concern is that capacity expansion will remain sluggish, as in 2005–08. The financial crisis and the oil price decline of last year have already delayed some projects and led to the suspension of others. Nonetheless, the recession-related setback to capacity expansion is likely to be temporary. Oil prices have already recouped some of the losses of 2008 and are now well above the average price over the past decade. The costs of oil investment have also declined in recent quarters, which should support exploration and development.

The main supply-side concerns, however, continue to be oil investment regimes and geological and technical constraints. First, the deterioration in incentives provided by investment regimes in some producer countries remains a concern.[30] Second, new oil fields are smaller in size and present greater technological and geological challenges, and the decline rates of many existing fields have risen by more than expected. As a result, more investment is needed just to maintain current capacity.

Metals

In line with broad commodity market developments, most metal prices rebounded in the second quarter of 2009. By end-July, the IMF metal daily index had risen by nearly 60 percent from its trough earlier in the year—led by copper, lead, and nickel (Figure 1.19, upper right-hand panel). Besides the improvement in near-term global economic and financial prospects—which elicited strong price responses from the cyclically sensitive base metals—the price rebound also reflected metal-specific factors.

Supply Retrenchment

As metal prices approached or fell below marginal costs, key metal producers began cutting production runs to save costs. Indeed, unlike in the 2001 global downturn, when metal production moved sideways despite a strong decline in

[30]See Box 1.5 in the April 2008 *World Economic Outlook*.

demand, supply cuts were prompt and much more prominent (Figure 1.19). Global production of a few key metals—such as aluminum, tin, and zinc—declined by about or more than 10 percent (seasonally adjusted annual rate) during April 2008–February 2009, when global industrial production was contracting.

Restocking in China

As part of China's fiscal stimulus package, the country's Strategic Reserve Bureau started to boost its inventories to support domestic smelters and refiners. Private metal demand in China also started to increase because of a rebound in industrial production. Along with a rising price differential at the Shanghai Futures Exchange relative to the London Metal Exchange, this boosted net imports to China (Figure 1.19, middle and lower panels).

The impetus from restocking in China will be temporary, and metal price prospects depend on the speed at which activity in China strengthens and on the pace of recovery in the rest of the world. As in the case of oil, a good part of the recovery in metal demand has already been priced in, and further strong price increases in the near term seem unlikely at this point because of substantial excess capacity.

Food

On signs of improving global economic and financial conditions in March, food prices enjoyed a broad-based, albeit modest, recovery. More recently, however, commodity-specific factors—including stabilizing weather conditions and expanded acreage in some major crop producers—have led to wide divergence in price changes across the major global crops. The overall food price index increased by 15 percent through the first seven months of 2009, but corn prices declined by 5 percent and soybean prices rose 20 percent. Corn has been affected by declining demand for industrial usage, including ethanol, while projected harvests for 2009–10 are higher.

Looking ahead, as reflected in futures prices, food prices are expected to rise only gradu-

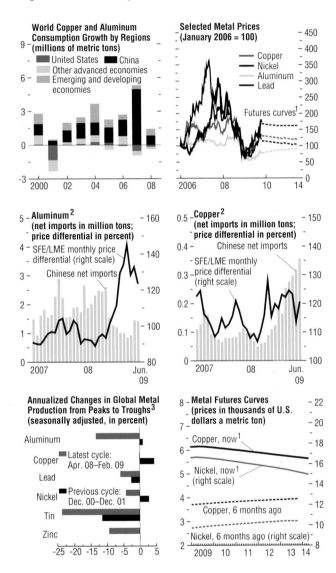

Figure 1.19. Developments in Metal Markets

Sources: Bloomberg Financial Markets; World Bureau of Metal Statistics; and IMF staff calculations.
[1]Prices as of September 15, 2009.
[2]LME: London Metal Exchange; SFE: Shanghai Futures Exchange.
[3]The troughs and peaks are based on purchasing-power-parity-weighted global industrial production.

Figure 1.20. Recent Developments in Markets for Major Food Crops[1]

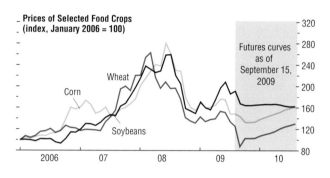

Prices of Selected Food Crops
(index, January 2006 = 100)

Futures curves as of September 15, 2009

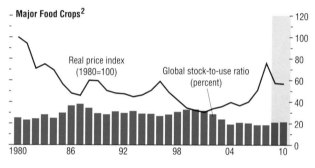

Major Food Crops[2]

Real price index (1980=100)

Global stock-to-use ratio (percent)

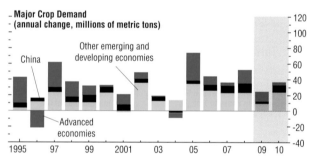

Major Crop Demand
(annual change, millions of metric tons)

Other emerging and developing economies

China

Advanced economies

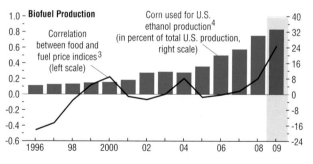

Biofuel Production

Correlation between food and fuel price indices[3] (left scale)

Corn used for U.S. ethanol production[4] (in percent of total U.S. production, right scale)

Sources: Bloomberg Financial Markets; U.S. Department of Agriculture; and IMF staff estimates.
[1] Major food crops are wheat, corn, rice, and soybeans.
[2] Projections for 2009 and 2010 are from the U.S. Department of Agriculture.
[3] Rolling window of 36 months of monthly price changes.
[4] Refers to marketing years (e.g., 2009 refers to September 2009 through August 2010).

ally throughout the global economic recovery. Demand is relatively insensitive to the business cycle compared with other commodities, and future harvests are expected to be fairly abundant, although there is the prospect that the El Niño weather pattern may affect production of some crops, particularly soybeans, through 2010 (Figure 1.20, first panel).

However, there are upside risks to prices. Agricultural supply-demand balances remain relatively tight, with the global stock-to-use ratio for the major crops of corn, rice, soybeans, and wheat expected to remain below their average levels over recent decades (Figure 1.20, second panel). Low inventory ratios are a result, in part, of food demand in emerging economies, which rose quickly during 2001–07 (Figure 1.20, third panel). The renewed pickup in growth in these economies over the coming years will keep market balances tight, and risks are that the increases in food price volatility observed over the past decade or so will be sustained (see Box 1.7).

Another risk concerns the higher cost of energy, particularly as oil prices remain well above their decade averages. Higher energy prices drive up the cost of farming through fuel inputs and fertilizer prices. An indirect effect of higher oil prices is the increased incentive to divert food crops toward biofuel production. Acreage dedicated to biofuel production has increased significantly in recent years—helped by high oil prices and, particularly in advanced economies, by policy incentives. In the United States, the fall in the oil price has led to a sharp decline in ethanol-refining margins and to industry consolidation. However, the U.S. Department of Agriculture projects that the proportion of U.S. corn production used for ethanol will still rise in 2009–10, albeit at a slower pace than had been projected in 2008 (Figure 1.20, fourth panel). These emerging biofuel linkages have led to an increase in the correlation between food and energy prices, and although these prices were possibly inflated by the effects of the extreme volatility of 2008, they will likely remain higher than in the past.

Box 1.7. What Explains the Rise in Food Price Volatility?

The sharp rise and fall of food prices during 2005–08 was associated with a significant increase in price volatility. For the IMF food price index, realized volatility—measured by the annualized standard deviation of monthly price changes—increased from about 8 percent for the decade through 2007 to more than 22 percent since 2008 (first figure, first panel). Although still lower than for other commodities, the volatility of prices for most major crops reached record or multidecade highs during this latest period.

This box presents evidence that long-term real price volatility—variability that is expected to prevail on average over very long time horizons—has risen for most major crops in recent years.[1] Market-determined food prices will always be subject to short-term variability because factors such as weather and crop pests affect harvests, and there is little that policies can do to reduce these effects. Over longer time horizons, stretching beyond the next harvest, other factors could have more persistent effects on longer-term volatility. This box identifies four such factors, including the volatility of U.S. inflation, the volatility of the U.S. dollar exchange rate, the volatility of global economic activity, and changes in futures market trading volumes. Volatility spillovers from energy prices may have only just begun to exert a significant influence.

The macroeconomic effects of elevated food price volatility can be broad and far-reaching, particularly when increases persist for long periods. The direct effects are felt through the balance of payments of importers and exporters, inflation, and poverty levels (food can account for a large share of consumption expenditure in low-income countries). Volatility can also complicate the response of policymakers, including through the effects on budgets and the planning decisions of food producers, processors, and consumers.

Estimating Long-Term Food Price Volatility

Almost all methods to estimate price volatility assume that the long-term level of variation (also known as unconditional volatility) is constant, a restrictive assumption considering the shifts in commodity price volatility observed over long horizons. An alternative approach outlined by Engel and Rangel (2008) is to allow for gradual changes in long-term volatility over time.[2] Applying this method to six major crops—corn, palm oil, rice, soybeans, sugar, and wheat—suggests that although long-term real price volatility moves much more gradually than total volatility (which includes seasonal factors), it has been increasing in recent years (second panel, which shows wheat as an example). The increase for rice has been modest, but for the other five commodities, estimated long-term volatility in annualized terms had increased by between 7 and 13 percentage points as of June 2009 compared with the levels of the mid-1990s and now ranges from 23 to 26 percent for corn, soybeans, and wheat, the most traded commodities (third panel). For most crops, these increases reflects a steady rise in real price variability that predates the most recent boom and bust.

Factors Affecting Unconditional Volatility

Previous research suggests a range of factors that may influence long-term food price volatility. A number of models posit a strong role for the level of inventories, with periods of low stocks characterized by higher volatility as market participants react quickly to the prospects of physical shortages. Macroeconomic factors such as the level and volatility of U.S. inflation, U.S. real interest rates, and the U.S. dollar exchange rate are also potential influences. Commodities are often regarded as stores of wealth, and the incentive to hold them—as financial assets or inventory—increases with inflation and lower

---

The author of this box is Shaun Roache.

[1] Food commodity prices are denominated in U.S. dollars and have been deflated by the U.S. consumer price index for this analysis.

[2] This model uses a nonparametric approach—an exponential quadratic spline—to generate a smooth curve describing long-term volatility based exclusively on data evidence.

Box 1.7 *(concluded)*

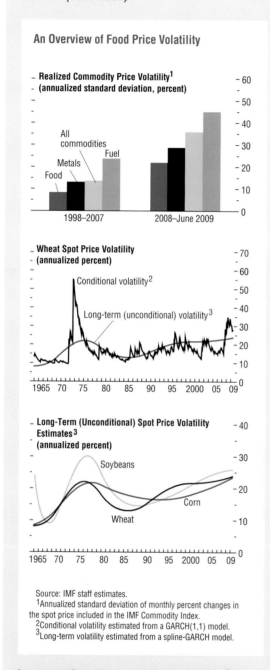

An Overview of Food Price Volatility

Source: IMF staff estimates.
[1]Annualized standard deviation of monthly percent changes in the spot price included in the IMF Commodity Index.
[2]Conditional volatility estimated from a GARCH(1,1) model.
[3]Long-term volatility estimated from a spline-GARCH model.

purchasing power and the effect on margins for producers with non-U.S.-dollar costs. Changes in global economic activity affect commodity demand, and demand volatility is likely to spill over to food price volatility. Crude oil price volatility may play a role, because of the impact on input costs and, more recently, the demand for food crops as biofuels. Global stock market volatility could be influential as a result of its role as a barometer of investor risk aversion and uncertainty. Futures market activity, such as changes in open interest and trading volumes (measured in percentage terms to remove trends) may also affect variability, particularly if new market participants follow price momentum strategies and amplify price movements.[4] The study also includes a measure of the effect of El Niño weather patterns, because some studies have shown that these have a significant influence on commodity prices (Brunner, 2002).[5] One important factor missing from this analysis is the impact of farm policy, which has been shown to be important for some crops during certain periods but which is difficult to measure.

To assess the importance of these factors, long-term real food price volatility was estimated as a function of these factors using harvest year data from 1968 through 2008. The results identified four factors as exerting a significant influence on long-term volatility.[6] U.S. infla-

[4]All variables were tested for endogeneity. Only open interest exhibited endogeneity for most commodities. All regressions were rerun using lags as instruments for open interest, and the results were not qualitatively different.
[5]To take account of the impact of periodic shifts in global weather patterns caused by shifts in Pacific Ocean atmospheric pressure and the resultant El Niño effect, the Southern Oscillation Index and El Niño region 3.4 sea surface temperature anomalies measured by the U.S. National Oceanic and Atmospheric Administration are included as explanatory variables.
[6]Two sets of regressions were estimated: for all commodities on a single factor, and for all commodities on all the factors. This second regression imposed restrictions such that the coefficients on all the factors were the same across commodities, with the excep-

inventory financing costs (interest rates).[3] The exchange rate can affect prices through a number of channels, including international

[3]There is a focus on U.S. inflation as most commodities are priced in U.S. dollars.

tion volatility has a strong effect, which may reflect commodities' role as a store of wealth. For example, one standard deviation increase in annualized inflation volatility (about 70 basis points) increases long-term real food price volatility by between 3 and 7 percentage points, depending on the commodity. Increased variability in global economic activity, as measured by an index of real shipping costs constructed by Kilian (2009), leads to higher food price volatility, which underscores the long-lasting impact of changing demand.[7] U.S. dollar volatility is significant, but only after controlling for

the influence of the real interest rate, because the two variables were highly collinear.[8] Of the financial market measures, only the change in trading volume is significant, with higher futures market activity raising real price volatility. However, the effect is small; for example, the average 68 percent increase in volume over 2008 would lead to an increase in long-term volatility of less than 1½ percentage points.

In summary, the evidence suggests that changes in some macroeconomic and financial variables can have a lasting impact on food price volatility. Other factors included in the study, including El Niño weather patterns and inventories, appear to have only short-term effects. For the two potential sources of volatility that have come to the fore recently—financial speculation and oil prices—there is less evidence of significant effects. However, in the case of energy prices, the linkage process may be at an early stage, and the role of biofuels may strengthen this volatility transmission mechanism in the future.

---

tion of inflation measures, whereas coefficients on the volatility of oil prices, equity prices, and open interest were zero, which was accepted by log-likelihood ratio tests. Rice was excluded from the analysis because it exhibited significantly different behavior from all other commodities. The level of U.S. inflation was highly significant only for sugar.

[7]As noted by Kilian (2009), this provides a direct measure of global economic activity that does not require exchange rate weighting and aggregates activity in all countries, incorporating changes in the composition of real output, or changes in the propensity to import industrial commodities for a given unit of real output. Levels of activity also had an influence, but the sign changed based on the estimation, which makes these results less robust.

[8]The exchange rate variable was a residual from an ordinary least squares regression of monthly log changes on real interest rates.

References

Alichi, Ali, Charles Freedman, M. Johnson, Ondra Kamenik, Turgut Kisinbay, Douglas Laxton, Kevin Clinton, and Huigang Chen, 2009, "Inflation Targeting under Imperfect Policy Credibility," IMF Working Paper 09/94 (Washington: International Monetary Fund).

Annett, Anthony, 2006, "Enforcement and the Stability and Growth Pact: How Fiscal Policy Did and Did Not Change under Europe's Fiscal Framework," IMF Working Paper 06/116 (Washington: International Monetary Fund).

Bahra, Bhupinder, 1997, "Implied Risk-Neutral Probability Density Functions from Option Prices: Theory and Application," Bank of England Working Paper No. 66 (London).

Balakrishnan, Ravi, Stephan Danninger, Selim Elekdag, and Irina Tytell, 2009, "The Transmission of Financial Stress from Advanced to Emerging Economies," IMF Working Paper 09/133 (Washington: International Monetary Fund).

Bank for International Settlements (BIS), 1999, "Estimating and Interpreting Probability Density Functions," Proceedings of a Workshop held on June, 14, 1999 (Basel, Switzerland). http://www.bis.org/publ/bisp06.htm.

Benes, J., K. Clinton, R. Garcia-Saltos, M. Johnson, D. Laxton, and T. Matheson, forthcoming, "The Global Financial Crisis and Its Implications for Potential Output," IMF Working Paper (Washington: International Monetary Fund).

Blanchard, Olivier, and Justin Wolfers, 2000, "The Role of Shocks and Institutions in the Rise of European Unemployment: The Aggregate Evidence," *Economic Journal,* Vol. 110, pp. 1–33.

Brunner, Allan D., 2002. "El Niño and World Primary Commodity Prices: Warm Water or Hot Air?" *Review of Economics and Statistics,* Vol. 84, No. 1, pp. 176–83.

Bruno, Michael, and Jeffrey D. Sachs, 1985, *Economics of Worldwide Stagflation* (Cambridge, Massachusetts: Harvard Univerity Press).

Cardarelli, Roberto, Selim Elekdag, and Subir Lall, 2009, "Financial Stress, Downturns, and Recoveries," IMF Working Paper 09/100 (Washington: International Monetary Fund).

Cheng, Kevin, forthcoming, "The Information Content Embedded in Future Options of Commodities and Other Assets—A New Framework to Estimate the Probability Density Functions," IMF Working Paper (Washington, International Monetary Fund).

Čihák, Martin, Wim Fonteyne, Thomas Harjes, Emil Stavrev, and Erlend Nier, 2009, *Euro Area Policies: Selected Issues,* IMF Country Report No. 09/224 (Washington: International Monetary Fund).

Collyns, Charles, Deniz Igan, and Prakash Loungani, 2009, "House Prices: Global Correction, Local Consequences" (unpublished; Washington: International Monetary Fund).

Decressin, Jörg, and Douglas Laxton, 2009, "Gauging Risks for Deflation," IMF Staff Position Note 09/01 (Washington: International Monetary Fund).

Elekdag, Selim, and Prakash Kannan, 2009, "Incorporating Market Information into the Construction of the Fan Chart," IMF Working Paper 09/178 (Washington: International Monetary Fund).

Engle, Robert F., and Jose Gonzalo Rangel, 2008, "The Spline-GARCH Model for Low-Frequency Volatility and Its Global Macroeconomic Causes," *Review of Financial Studies,* Vol. 21, No. 3, pp. 1187–22.

Estevão, Marcello M., 2005, "Product Market Regulation and the Benefits of Wage Moderation," IMF Working Paper 05/191 (Washington: International Monetary Fund).

European Commission, 2009, "Ageing Report: Economic and Budgetary Projections for the EU-27 Member States (2008–2060), *European Economy,* Vol. 2.

Feinman, Joshua N., 1993, "Reserve Requirements: History, Current Practice, and Potential Reform," *Federal Reserve Bulletin,* Vol. 79, pp. 569–89.

Freund, Caroline, 2009, "The Trade Response to Global Downturns: Historical Evidence," World Bank Policy Research Working Paper No. 5015 (Washington: World Bank).

Horton, Mark, Manmohan Kumar, and Paolo Mauro, 2009, "The State of Public Finances: A Cross-Country Fiscal Monitor," IMF Staff Position Note 09/21 (Washington: International Monetary Fund).

Igan, Deniz, and Marcelo Pinheiro, 2009, "Exposure to Real Estate Losses: Evidence from the U.S. Banks," IMF Working Paper 09/79 (Washington: International Monetary Fund).

International Monetary Fund (IMF), 1987, *Report on the World Current Account Discrepancy* (Washington).

———, 2006, "Euro Area Policies," IMF Country Report No. 06/287 (Washington).

———, 2008, *Global Financial Stability Report: Financial Stress and Deleveraging Macro-Financial Implications and Policy* (Washington, October).

———, 2009a, *Global Financial Stability Report: Responding to the Financial Crisis and Measuring Systemic Risks* (Washington, April).

———, 2009b, "Is the Canadian Housing Market Overvalued? A Tale of Two Regions," in *Canada: Selected Issues,* IMF Country Report No. 09/163 (Washington).

Jarocinski, Marek, and Frank R. Smets, 2008, "House Prices and the Stance of Monetary Policy," Federal Reserve Bank of St. Louis *Review,* Vol. 90, No. 4, pp. 339–66.

Kilian, Lutz, 2009, "Not All Oil Price Shocks Are Alike: Disentangling Demand and Supply Shocks in the Crude Oil Market," *American Economic Review,* Vol. 99, No. 3, pp. 1053–69.

Klyuev, Vladimir, Phil de Imus, and Krishna Srinivasan, forthcoming, "Unconventional Choices for Unconventional Times: Credit and Quantitative Easing in Advanced Economies," IMF Working Paper (Washington: International Monetary Fund).

Layard, Richard, Stephen Nickell, and Richard Jackman, 1991, *Unemployment* (Oxford: Oxford University Press).

Lipsey, Robert, 2009, "Measuring International Trade in Services," in *International Trade in Services and Intangibles in the Era of Globalization,* ed. by Marshall Reinsdorf and Matthew Slaughter (Chicago: University of Chicago Press).

Marquez, Jaime, and Lisa Workman, 2001, "Modeling the IMF's Statistical Discrepancy in the Global Current Account," *IMF Staff Papers,* Vol. 48, No. 43 (Washington: International Monetary Fund).

McAndrews, James, Asani Sarkar, and Zhenyu Wang, 2008. "The Effect of the Term Auction Facility on the London Inter-Bank Offered Rate," Staff Reports No. 335 (New York: Federal Reserve Bank).

Meier, André, 2009, "Panacea, Curse, or Nonevent: Unconventional Monetary Policy in the United Kingdom," IMF Working Paper 09/163(Washington: International Monetary Fund).

Oksanen, Heikki, 2009, "Setting Targets for Government Budgets in the Pursuit of Intergenerational Equity," *Economic Papers 2009*, No. 358 (Brussels: European Commission).

Romer, Christina, and David Romer, 1989, "Does Monetary Policy Matter? A New Test in the Spirit of Friedman and Schwartz," in *NBER Macroeconomics Annual*, Vol. 4, ed. by Olivier Jean Blanchard and Stanley Fischer (Cambridge, Massachusetts: National Bureau of Economic Research).

Taylor, John, 2009, "The Financial Crisis and the Policy Responses: An Empirical Analysis of What Went Wrong," NBER Working Paper No. 14631

(Cambridge, Massachusetts: National Bureau of Economic Research).

Taylor, John B., and John C. Williams, 2009, "A Black Swan in the Money Market," *American Economic Journal: Macroeconomics,* Vol. 1, No. 1, pp. 58–83.

Ter-Minassian, Teresa, and Manmohan Kumar, 2008, "Promoting Fiscal Discipline" (Washington: International Monetary Fund).

Trichet, Jean-Claude, 2009, "The ECB's Enhanced Credit Support," speech at the University of Munich, July 13 (Frankfurt: European Central Bank). www.ecb.int/press/key/date/2009/html/sp090713.en.html.

U.S. Congressional Budget Office, 2005, "Menu of Social Security Options" (Washington). www.cbo.gov/doc.cfm?index=6377.

COUNTRY AND REGIONAL PERSPECTIVES

The global economy seems to be on the verge of recovery. The advanced economies, hit particularly hard by financial crises and the collapse in world trade, are showing signs of stabilization, driven mainly by an unprecedented public policy response. The shape of the recoveries will vary, however, with economies that suffered financial crises likely to experience weaker recoveries than those that were affected mainly by the collapse in global demand. The rebound in emerging and other developing economies is being led by a resurgence in Asia, most notably in China and India, fuelled by policy stimulus and a turn in the global manufacturing cycle. Other emerging economies are benefiting from commodity price increases, as well as from policy frameworks that are stronger than during previous crises. However, recovery in the Commonwealth of Independent States (CIS) and emerging Europe is likely to be difficult, especially for economies most affected by sharply falling capital flows and domestic financial sector turmoil.

The U.S. Economy Is Stabilizing as the Crisis Subsides

The U.S. economy is showing increasing signs of stabilization. Output declined substantially during the first half of 2009, and the unemployment rate rose to a level not seen since the early 1980s. Nevertheless, unprecedented monetary, financial, and fiscal policy interventions are helping stabilize consumer spending and housing and financial markets, which points to renewed moderate growth in the second half of 2009 (Figure 2.1).

Financial conditions have improved by considerably more than anticipated in the April 2009 *World Economic Outlook* (WEO) forecast. Interbank spreads have returned close to precrisis levels, and equity markets have rallied, although they remain way below previous peaks. High-grade corporate issues have rebounded, and corporate bond and mortgage spreads have

tightened considerably, the latter in part reflecting massive purchases of mortgage-backed securities by the U.S. Federal Reserve. On the negative side, although the Term Asset Loan Facility has helped restart some securitization in markets for consumer and small business credit, overall securitization activity remains low. Credit also remains difficult to obtain for many households and businesses, with bank loan standards continuing to tighten, albeit at a slower pace.

For banks, the results of the Supervisory Capital Assessment Program (SCAP) reported in May have bolstered investor confidence, with many banks subsequently raising common equity on public markets and issuing nonguaranteed debt. Results for the second quarter of 2009 outperformed expectations, although in part because of a temporary surge in underwriting revenues, even while provisions for losses on most asset classes continued to rise in view of the likely continued deterioration of loan performance.

Output data confirm that the economy is stabilizing, with the preliminary estimate for 2009 second-quarter real GDP showing a decline of only 1 percent (seasonally adjusted annual rate), a significant improvement from the 6.4 percent fall during the first quarter. Nonetheless, the saving rate continues to climb and business investment to sink. Given the collapse of demand in the rest of the world, exports have made a negative contribution in recent quarters, which has been more than offset by the reduction in imports. Positive contributions were made by state and federal spending in the second quarter, reflecting the impact of fiscal stimulus.

The U.S. economy is projected to contract by 2¾ percent in 2009, mainly because of the sharp contraction during the first half of the year (Table 2.1). Growth is expected to turn positive in the second half of 2009, reflecting the continuing fiscal boost and turns in both

Figure 2.1. United States: Signs of Stabilization

Although significant wealth has been destroyed and unemployment has surged, there are signs that the housing market is stabilizing and credit conditions are normalizing.

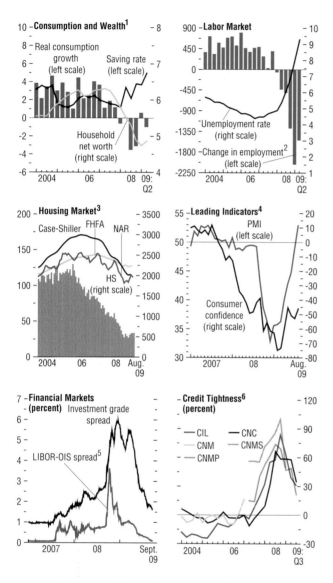

Sources: Bloomberg Financial Markets; Haver Analytics; and IMF staff calculations.
[1] Real consumption annualized quarterly growth and saving rate are in percent; household net worth is ratio to disposable income.
[2] Quarterly change in total nonfarm payrolls, thousands.
[3] Index: January 2002 = 100; Case-Shiller Composite 20; FHFA: Federal Housing Finance Agency; HS: housing starts in thousands; NAR: National Association of Realtors.
[4] PMI: manufacturing purchasing managers composite index. Positive values represent consumer confidence index optimism.
[5] LIBOR-OIS spread is the difference between the three-month London interbank offered rate (LIBOR) and the three-month overnight index swap (OIS) rate.
[6] All series come from the Senior Loan Officer Survey. CIL: banks tightening commercial and industrial loans to large firms; CNC: banks tightening standards for consumer credit cards; CNM: banks tightening standards for mortgages to individuals; CNMS: banks tightening standards for subprime mortgages to individuals; CNMP: banks tightening standards for prime mortgages to individuals.

the inventory and the housing cycles. However, although financial conditions have improved significantly in recent months, markets remain stressed, and this will weigh on investment and consumption. Combined with the impact of rising unemployment, the temporary nature of the fiscal stimulus, and subdued growth in trading partner economies, growth will remain sluggish, reaching 1½ percent for 2010 as a whole. Unemployment is expected to peak at above 10 percent in the second half of 2010, while rising economic slack should keep core inflation below 1 percent through most of next year.

Given the magnitude of shocks and the cloudy outlook for the rest of the world, there remains substantial uncertainty around the near-term outlook. On the upside, the strong policy response and a rapid recovery in emerging markets could lead to a virtuous circle of rising confidence, improving financial conditions, and strong aggregate demand growth. But receding downside risks remain a concern. In particular, continued household deleveraging and rising unemployment may weigh more on consumption than forecast, and accelerating corporate and commercial property defaults could slow the improvement in financial conditions.

Turning to the medium-term outlook, potential growth is likely to fall below 2 percent for a considerable time. Analysis of previous financial crises (see Chapter 4) suggests that many are followed by large, permanent output losses relative to precrisis trends, because impaired financial systems take time to heal and to again intermediate effectively, slowing investment and innovation. High cyclical unemployment could also raise structural unemployment, although the flexible nature of U.S. labor and product markets may make the needed reallocation of employment and capital across sectors more rapid and less painful than in some other regions with greater rigidity. On the demand side, although the personal saving rate has already climbed to about 5 percent, it may have to rise further given the need to rebuild household balance sheets.

Table 2.1. Advanced Economies: Real GDP, Consumer Prices, and Unemployment
(Annual percent change and percent of labor force)

	Real GDP				Consumer Prices				Unemployment			
	2007	2008	2009	2010	2007	2008	2009	2010	2007	2008	2009	2010
Advanced economies	**2.7**	**0.6**	**−3.4**	**1.3**	**2.2**	**3.4**	**0.1**	**1.1**	**5.4**	**5.8**	**8.2**	**9.3**
United States	2.1	0.4	−2.7	1.5	2.9	3.8	−0.4	1.7	4.6	5.8	9.3	10.1
Euro area[1]	2.7	0.7	−4.2	0.3	2.1	3.3	0.3	0.8	7.5	7.6	9.9	11.7
Germany	2.5	1.2	−5.3	0.3	2.3	2.8	0.1	0.2	8.4	7.4	8.0	10.7
France	2.3	0.3	−2.4	0.9	1.6	3.2	0.3	1.1	8.3	7.9	9.5	10.3
Italy	1.6	−1.0	−5.1	0.2	2.0	3.5	0.7	0.9	6.1	6.8	9.1	10.5
Spain	3.6	0.9	−3.8	−0.7	2.8	4.1	−0.3	0.9	8.3	11.3	18.2	20.2
Netherlands	3.6	2.0	−4.2	0.7	1.6	2.2	0.9	1.0	3.2	2.8	3.8	6.6
Belgium	2.6	1.0	−3.2	0.0	1.8	4.5	0.2	1.0	7.5	7.0	8.7	9.9
Greece	4.0	2.9	−0.8	−0.1	3.0	4.2	1.1	1.7	8.3	7.6	9.5	10.5
Austria	3.5	2.0	−3.8	0.3	2.2	3.2	0.5	1.0	4.4	3.9	5.3	6.4
Portugal	1.9	0.0	−3.0	0.4	2.4	2.7	−0.6	1.0	8.0	7.6	9.5	11.0
Finland	4.2	1.0	−6.4	0.9	1.6	3.9	1.0	1.1	6.8	6.4	8.7	9.8
Ireland	6.0	−3.0	−7.5	−2.5	2.9	3.1	−1.6	−0.3	4.5	6.1	12.0	15.5
Slovak Republic	10.4	6.4	−4.7	3.7	2.7	4.6	1.5	2.3	11.0	9.6	10.8	10.3
Slovenia	6.8	3.5	−4.7	0.6	3.6	5.7	0.5	1.5	4.9	4.4	6.2	6.1
Luxembourg	5.2	0.7	−4.8	−0.2	2.3	3.4	0.2	1.8	4.4	4.4	6.8	6.0
Cyprus	4.4	3.6	−0.5	0.8	2.2	4.4	0.4	1.2	3.9	3.7	5.6	5.9
Malta	3.7	2.1	−2.1	0.5	0.7	4.7	2.1	1.9	6.4	5.8	7.3	7.6
Japan	2.3	−0.7	−5.4	1.7	0.0	1.4	−1.1	−0.8	3.8	4.0	5.4	6.1
United Kingdom[1]	2.6	0.7	−4.4	0.9	2.3	3.6	1.9	1.5	5.4	5.5	7.6	9.3
Canada	2.5	0.4	−2.5	2.1	2.1	2.4	0.1	1.3	6.0	6.2	8.3	8.6
Korea	5.1	2.2	−1.0	3.6	2.5	4.7	2.6	2.5	3.3	3.2	3.8	3.6
Australia	4.0	2.4	0.7	2.0	2.3	4.4	1.6	1.5	4.4	4.2	6.0	7.0
Taiwan Province of China	5.7	0.1	−4.1	3.7	1.8	3.5	−0.5	1.5	3.9	4.1	6.1	5.9
Sweden	2.6	−0.2	−4.8	1.2	1.7	3.3	2.2	2.4	6.1	6.2	8.5	8.2
Switzerland	3.6	1.8	−2.0	0.5	0.7	2.4	−0.4	0.5	2.5	2.7	3.5	4.5
Hong Kong SAR	6.4	2.4	−3.6	3.5	2.0	4.3	−1.0	0.5	4.0	3.5	6.0	6.5
Czech Republic	6.1	2.7	−4.3	1.3	2.9	6.3	1.0	1.1	5.3	4.4	7.9	9.8
Norway	3.1	2.1	−1.9	1.3	0.7	3.8	2.3	1.8	2.5	2.6	3.3	3.8
Singapore	7.8	1.1	−3.3	4.1	2.1	6.5	−0.2	1.6	2.1	2.2	3.6	3.7
Denmark	1.6	−1.2	−2.4	0.9	1.7	3.4	1.7	2.0	2.7	1.7	3.5	4.2
Israel	5.2	4.0	−0.1	2.4	0.5	4.6	3.6	2.0	7.3	6.2	8.2	8.6
New Zealand	3.2	0.2	−2.2	2.2	2.4	4.0	1.5	1.0	3.7	4.2	5.9	7.9
Iceland	5.6	1.3	−8.5	−2.0	5.0	12.4	11.7	4.4	1.0	1.6	8.6	10.5
Memorandum												
Major advanced economies	2.2	0.3	−3.6	1.3	2.1	3.2	−0.1	1.1	5.5	5.9	8.2	9.4
Newly industrialized Asian economies	5.7	1.5	−2.4	3.6	2.2	4.5	1.0	1.9	3.4	3.4	4.5	4.4

[1]Based on Eurostat's harmonized index of consumer prices.

The strength and sustainability of the recovery will depend on meeting three key policy challenges:

- continued stabilization of the economy and financial system;
- an appropriately timed and orderly unwinding of public support for the financial system and development of a strategy to shrink the Federal Reserve's balance sheet; and
- addressing long-term imbalances in public, household, and financial balance sheets.

Monetary and fiscal support should be kept in place until the recovery is well established. If downside tail risks materialize and the recovery falters, there will likely be a need for further measures to support demand on the fiscal side given that the federal funds rate is close to the zero bound, although the Federal Reserve could set up additional targeted credit facilities and purchase more assets. Moreover, efforts must continue toward returning financial institutions to full health through recapitalization and the repair of balance sheets—this is the indispensable condition for sustained growth. The results of the SCAP undoubtedly boosted investor confidence in major financial institutions. This could be undermined, however, if the recovery falters, leading to depressed earnings, an increase in nonperforming assets, and further capital losses.

Helping financial institutions clear their balance sheets of troubled assets will also contribute to their renewed ability to resume lending. The Public-Private Investment Program (PPIP) was set up to achieve this, by leveraging both public and private capital within public-private partnerships to purchase distressed assets, allowing banks and other financial institutions to free up capital and stimulate new credit. The PPIP comprises two related parts. The Legacy Loan Program seeks to draw private capital into loan markets by providing debt guarantees from the Federal Deposit Insurance Corporation and equity co-investment from the U.S. Treasury; the Federal Deposit Insurance Corporation is currently proceeding with a pilot. The Legacy Securities Program seeks to target legacy securities by providing debt financing from the Federal Reserve and by matching private capital raised for purchasing such securities. Fund managers have been appointed, although no assets have yet been purchased. It remains to be seen how successful these programs ultimately will be, particularly if banks prefer to hold assets to maturity rather than selling them and recognizing losses up front.

Once a recovery gains traction and wide output gaps start to close, the process of unwinding the monetary stimulus will need to start. Although this point remains well in the future, early communication of a clear exit strategy is key to maintaining market confidence. A premature withdrawal of support before the financial system has healed would impede the recovery. Calibrating the timing will be especially challenging given the uncertainty regarding how much the financial crisis has reduced potential output. Moreover, the massive increase in bank reserves (one consequence of the ballooning Federal Reserve balance sheet) must not be allowed to transform into excessive credit growth and lead to inflation.

Even though many of the short-term liquidity facilities are already unwinding as market conditions improve, the large quantity of longer-term assets on the Federal Reserve's balance sheet will be harder to reduce, and this exposes the Federal Reserve to significant interest rate risk. This is especially true for assets that, unlike government securities and agency mortgage-backed securities, lack a liquid market. Timing the sale of such longer-term assets will be delicate, especially given the potential market impact, but the Federal Reserve can use other tools—reverse repos and interest paid on deposits—to start tightening conditions as needed, even while its balance sheet remains large.

Regarding financial sector regulation, the crisis has revealed major weaknesses, particularly a failure to recognize the buildup of systemic risk. The Obama Administration's proposals for regulatory reform are sensible, including an enhanced focus on systemic risk through creation of a Financial Services Oversight Council and new mechanisms for prompt, corrective action for all large, interconnected institutions (including conservatorship and receivership powers). The key will be to implement the measures as a comprehensive package, rather than in piecemeal fashion, and to tackle the problem of having firms that are "too big or connected to fail." One solution to the latter is penalizing size and complexity via higher capital requirements. This would also help to partly address increasing concentration in the U.S. financial system, which if not resolved could markedly reduce competition and innovation.

The fiscal legacy of the crisis is a high and rising debt trajectory that could become unsustainable without significant medium-term measures. Deficits are forecast to be 10 percent of GDP for 2009/10 and 2010/11. Although deficits will fall below the 10 percent level thereafter, the level of gross general government debt will continue to rise rapidly, reaching nearly 110 percent of GDP by 2014, a worrisome deterioration given looming health care and pension pressures related to population aging. The current budget proposal increases transparency about such pressures by including medium-term forecasts, but these are based on growth assumptions that seem optimistic. More adjustment will likely be needed to ensure long-term fiscal sustainability, particularly on the revenue side, given that non-defense discretionary spending is near historical lows. The shape of health care reform will also be critical. Whereas richer nations such as the United States can be expected to spend relatively more on health care, there are significant inefficiencies in the U.S. health care system, as evidenced by the fact that similar health care outcomes are achieved at different costs across the U.S. states. With this is mind, coverage should only be expanded in a budget-neutral manner, and measures are needed to bring down the rate of cost growth to help maintain debt sustainability.

Asia: From Rebound to Recovery?

Although Asia's export-oriented economies were battered by the abrupt global downturn, the economic outlook for the region improved markedly during the first half of 2009. Recent developments point to a strengthening of domestic demand and exports, but questions remain about whether the rebound can become a self-sustaining recovery—ahead of a stronger growth pickup in the rest of the world.

The recent, swift turnaround of economic fortunes is remarkable. At the onset of the crisis, Asian exporters were hit hard by the collapse of external demand. The deterioration of activity was especially rapid for the more export-oriented economies (Figure 2.2). In Japan, GDP shrunk by well above 10 percent on an annualized basis in the two quarters following the Lehman Brothers bankruptcy in September 2008. Slumping demand for durable goods, especially cars, and a decline in investment

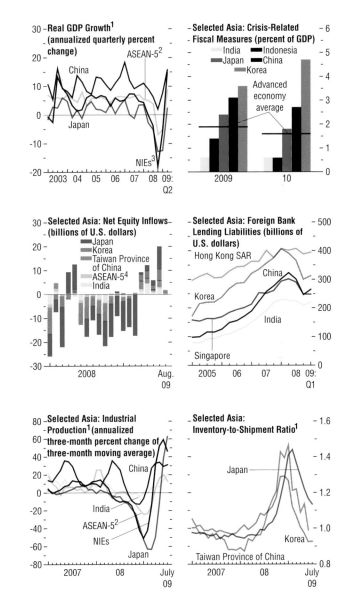

Figure 2.2. Advanced and Emerging Asia: Can the Recovery Be Sustained?

Signs of a strengthening recovery are increasingly helped by large fiscal stimulus packages. Financial markets have rebounded, and capital has begun to flow back into equity markets, while the pullback of foreign banks has ceased. Meanwhile, industrial production began to grow again in the first half of the year helped by an unwinding of inventory adjustments.

Sources: Bank for International Settlements; Horton and others (2009); and IMF staff calculations.
[1]Seasonally adjusted.
[2]Excluding Vietnam.
[3]Newly industrialized Asian economies (NIEs) comprise Hong Kong SAR, Korea, Singapore, and Taiwan Province of China.
[4]Excluding Malaysia.

activity in the emerging economies in the region hurt manufacturing exports. Domestic demand faltered amid rapidly falling confidence, rising uncertainty, weakening labor markets, tightening financial conditions, and rising spare capacity. In other parts of Asia, the manufacturing-oriented economies (Korea, Singapore, Taiwan Province of China) also slumped and, by the end of 2008, had recorded peak declines in industrial production of about 25 percent compared with levels one year earlier. Only China, Indonesia, and India escaped a severe recession, the result of a large policy stimulus and, in the case of India, less dependence on exports.

The downward slide moderated during the first half of 2009. Recent indicators point to a strengthening recovery led by a rapid rebound in China, where growth accelerated to an annual rate of 7.1 percent in the first half of the year, driven entirely by domestic demand. In Japan, the turnaround was more gradual. Industrial production began to grow again in March, and retail sales followed in April, leading to a return to growth in the second quarter (2.3 percent). Other emerging and developing Asian economies showed similar signs of stabilization, with rising industrial production in Hong Kong SAR, India, Korea, Philippines, Taiwan Province of China, and Thailand, which lifted growth during the second quarter into positive territory in several of these economies. The rebound was led by the electronics sector, which had experienced a sharp drop in production right at the onset of the crisis. The overall health of banking sectors in the region also limited the impact of the financial crisis.

The intensifying rebound in Asia can be linked to three factors: (1) expansionary fiscal and monetary policy, which has been very aggressive in some countries; (2) a rebound in financial markets and capital inflows, which eased financing constraints for smaller export enterprises and improved consumer and business confidence; and (3) the growth impulse for industry following large inventory adjustments.

Extensive fiscal and monetary support helped ease tensions in financial markets and helped soften the decline in domestic demand, even bolstering demand in China and India. Central banks provided ample liquidity (Japan) and lowered policy rates (India, Indonesia, Korea, Malaysia, Philippines, Taiwan Province of China, Thailand). In China, a relaxation of credit ceilings and low interest rates buoyed credit growth (private credit grew by 24 percent during the first six months of 2009). Given its comparably robust fiscal position at the onset of the crisis, discretionary support in Asia has been stronger than in other regions. Fiscal packages in China and Japan will reach close to 5 percent of GDP for 2009–10. Most programs are aimed at bolstering consumption, especially for durables (Japan, Korea) and at upgrading infrastructure and retooling factories (China).

The rebound in equity markets and the resumption of capital inflows in the context of a generalized decline in risk aversion is providing a further impetus for the Asian economies. Stock markets rose during the first eight months of the year by 28 percent in Japan, 65 percent in the ASEAN-4 economies,[1] and 52 percent in the newly industrialized Asian economies (NIEs).[2] This upward shift was accompanied by renewed capital inflows. Sovereigns tapped international capital markets, and net equity inflows turned positive in the second quarter. In addition, creditor banks in advanced economies stopped reducing their exposure in emerging Asia. In tandem, most currencies strengthened, although they remained below precrisis levels. These developments were accompanied by a decline in the spread for Asian corporate debt of more than 250 basis points since January 2009, which helped ease financing constraints on corporations and households. Nonetheless, credit growth has stabilized in several Asian economies, including India and the NIEs, as private domes-

---

[1]The largest four economies in the Association of Southeast Asian Nations: Indonesia, Malaysia, Philippines, Thailand.

[2]Hong Kong SAR, Korea, Singapore, Taiwan Province of China. Based on the corresponding Morgan Stanley Capital International indices.

tic demand picked up and banks benefit from ample liquidity and sound capital positions.

A third factor contributing to the rebound in activity has been inventory rebuilding. In much of Asia, firms responded to the sharp decline in demand in the fourth quarter of 2008 by reducing production and inventories. By mid-2009, this destocking process was far advanced in Japan, Korea, and Taiwan Province of China, implying that the current rebound in external demand, together with progress in inventory adjustment, will provide impulses for increased production in the export sector.

Despite these positive signs, a sustained turn-around is not assured. Weakening labor markets will likely put a drag on consumption, and significant excess capacity in industry will dampen investment demand. Furthermore, the main driver of past recoveries—a durable rebound in external demand from outside the region—may be lacking this time around. Overall, exports from Asia are still far below 2008 peaks (about 30 percent lower), including in key sectors such as electronics. That said, the sharp increase in domestic demand has boosted Chinese imports from the region, especially from Indonesia and Korea, and this has helped arrest the sharp con-traction in the region's export sector.

In the baseline projections, growth momen-tum will build during the second half of 2009, forming the basis for a generally moderate recovery in 2010, as external demand from advanced economies strengthens (Table 2.2). China and India will lead the expansion this year and will grow at rates of 8.5 and 5.4 per-cent, respectively, boosted by large policy stimu-lus that is increasing demand from domestic sources. In Japan, after a sharp first-quarter fall, activity is expected to contract by 5.4 percent in 2009 as a whole, although a sizable fiscal stimu-lus and a modest increase in exports will sup-port growth in the second half of 2009 and will lead to a recovery of 1.7 percent in 2010. Given the significant slack in the economy, inflation will remain negative until 2012. The outlook for growth and inflation is similar in the export-oriented NIEs. Output will contract during 2009

by 2.4 percent but will accelerate in the second half of the year, paving the way for a moderate expansion in 2010 (3.6 percent). For the ASEAN economies, the outlook is more mixed. In the more export-oriented economies (Malaysia, Thailand), activity will increase gradually during the second half of 2009, with stronger growth in 2010.

The risks to the growth outlook are gradu-ally becoming more balanced. The pickup in activity is so far being supported by many factors that could turn out to be temporary: rebounding capital markets, inventory adjust-ment, and expansionary fiscal and monetary policy. These forces may not be able to bring about a self-sustaining recovery if activity does not strengthen in other regions. On the upside, however, the policy stimulus in China could sup-port recoveries in other parts of Asia.

With the recovery gaining strength, the policy challenge is to determine when and how to withdraw policy support while ensur-ing a successful transition to more balanced medium-term growth. Asia's dependence on export demand has contributed to rising global imbalances and has made the region vulnerable to global demand developments (Table 2.3). A return to past growth and demand patterns is unlikely—given drawn-out adjustments in the United States and Europe—and many Asian economies therefore need to shift their compo-sition of growth to be more focused on domestic demand.

From this perspective, some caution is war-ranted about the sustainability of the rapid level of credit growth in a few countries, especially China. Maintaining credit growth at this level carries the risk of creating incentives for over-investment, unsustainable asset price inflation, and a worsening of credit quality in the bank-ing system. Recent monetary expansion should therefore be unwound as soon as there are clear signs that economic recovery is established. To promote growth that is based more on strength-ened domestic demand and less on investment and exports, fiscal support should encourage private consumption as in Japan, Korea, and

Table 2.2. Selected Asian Economies: Real GDP, Consumer Prices, and Current Account Balance
(Annual percent change unless noted otherwise)

	Real GDP				Consumer Prices[1]				Current Account Balance[2]			
	2007	2008	2009	2010	2007	2008	2009	2010	2007	2008	2009	2010
Emerging Asia	**9.8**	**6.7**	**5.0**	**6.8**	**4.9**	**7.0**	**2.7**	**3.2**	**6.7**	**5.6**	**5.2**	**5.3**
Newly industrialized Asian economies	**5.7**	**1.5**	**−2.4**	**3.6**	**2.2**	**4.5**	**1.0**	**1.9**	**5.7**	**4.4**	**6.4**	**5.9**
Korea	5.1	2.2	−1.0	3.6	2.5	4.7	2.6	2.5	0.6	−0.7	3.4	2.2
Taiwan Province of China	5.7	0.1	−4.1	3.7	1.8	3.5	−0.5	1.5	8.6	6.4	7.9	8.0
Hong Kong SAR	6.4	2.4	−3.6	3.5	2.0	4.3	−1.0	0.5	12.3	14.2	10.7	10.8
Singapore	7.8	1.1	−3.3	4.1	2.1	6.5	−0.2	1.6	23.5	14.8	12.6	12.5
Developing Asia[3]	**10.6**	**7.6**	**6.2**	**7.3**	**5.4**	**7.5**	**3.0**	**3.4**	**7.0**	**5.9**	**5.0**	**5.2**
China	13.0	9.0	8.5	9.0	4.8	5.9	−0.1	0.6	11.0	9.8	7.8	8.6
India	9.4	7.3	5.4	6.4	6.4	8.3	8.7	8.4	−1.0	−2.2	−2.2	−2.5
ASEAN−5	**6.3**	**4.8**	**0.7**	**4.0**	**4.3**	**9.2**	**2.6**	**4.6**	**4.9**	**2.6**	**3.3**	**2.0**
Indonesia	6.3	6.1	4.0	4.8	6.0	9.8	5.0	6.2	2.4	0.1	0.9	0.5
Thailand	4.9	2.6	−3.5	3.7	2.2	5.5	−1.2	2.1	5.7	−0.1	4.9	2.7
Philippines	7.1	3.8	1.0	3.2	2.8	9.3	2.8	4.0	4.9	2.5	3.2	1.2
Malaysia	6.2	4.6	−3.6	2.5	2.0	5.4	−0.1	1.2	15.4	17.9	13.4	11.0
Vietnam	8.5	6.2	4.6	5.3	8.3	23.1	7.0	11.0	−9.8	−11.9	−9.7	−9.4
Other developing Asia[4]	**6.5**	**3.9**	**3.3**	**4.1**	**10.1**	**12.8**	**11.6**	**8.3**	**0.0**	**−2.3**	**−1.0**	**−1.4**
Pakistan	5.6	2.0	2.0	3.0	7.8	12.0	20.8	10.0	−4.8	−8.3	−5.1	−4.8
Bangladesh	6.3	6.0	5.4	5.4	9.1	7.7	5.3	5.6	1.1	1.9	2.1	1.0

[1]Movements in consumer prices are shown as annual averages. December–December changes can be found in Table A7 in the Statistical Appendix.

[2]Percent of GDP.

[3]The country composition of this regional group can be found in Table F in the Statistical Appendix.

[4]Includes Islamic Rep. of Afghanistan, Bhutan, Brunei Darussalam, Cambodia, Fiji, Kiribati, Lao PDR, Maldives, Myanmar, Nepal, Papua New Guinea, Samoa, Solomon Islands, Sri Lanka, Timor-Leste, Tonga, and Vanuatu.

Taiwan Province of China, for example. In some economies, concerns about fiscal sustainability must be addressed, including through development of credible medium-term consolidation plans (India, Japan, Malaysia). Particular attention also must be given to devising exit strategies from credit-guarantee programs for corporations, which were adopted in many parts of Asia during the crisis. Experiences in Japan and Korea during the past decade show that such programs can encourage excessive risk taking and that scaling them back can be challenging.

Shifting toward a more balanced growth path will require a combination of demand- and supply-side measures.

By developing or improving social safety nets and health care systems, many emerging and developing economies can help reduce precautionary saving by households. This would free up resources for consumption and create a larger market for domestic suppliers.

Development of the financial sector should help ensure efficient allocation of credit. As financial markets become deeper and more robust, they can offer stable saving and investment vehicles, which would reduce reliance on foreign financing and make household savings a more important funding base for the financial sector. Easier access to market-based domestic financing for smaller enterprises may also help lower high corporate saving rates, help develop domestic services sectors, and support consumption. Of course, the development of the financial sector should take place in the context of proper supervisory and regulatory frameworks.

More flexible exchange rate regimes would help rebalance growth. Appreciating exchange rates in economies where there is productivity growth would imply an increase in real house-

Table 2.3. Advanced Economies: Current Account Positions

(Percent of GDP)

	2007	2008	2009	2010
Advanced economies	**−0.9**	**−1.3**	**−0.7**	**−0.4**
United States	−5.2	−4.9	−2.6	−2.2
Euro area[1]	0.3	−0.7	−0.7	−0.3
Germany	7.5	6.4	2.9	3.6
France	−1.0	−2.3	−1.2	−1.4
Italy	−2.4	−3.4	−2.5	−2.3
Spain	−10.0	−9.6	−6.0	−4.7
Netherlands	7.6	7.5	7.0	6.8
Belgium	1.7	−2.5	−1.0	−0.9
Greece	−14.2	−14.4	−10.0	−9.0
Austria	3.1	3.5	2.1	2.0
Portugal	−9.4	−12.1	−9.9	−9.7
Finland	4.1	2.4	0.5	2.0
Ireland	−5.3	−5.2	−1.7	0.6
Slovak Republic	−5.3	−6.5	−8.0	−7.8
Slovenia	−4.2	−5.5	−3.0	−4.7
Luxembourg	9.8	9.1	7.6	7.0
Cyprus	−11.7	−18.3	−10.0	−9.8
Malta	−7.0	−5.6	−6.1	−6.1
Japan	4.8	3.2	1.9	2.0
United Kingdom	−2.7	−1.7	−2.0	−1.9
Canada	1.0	0.5	−2.6	−1.8
Korea	0.6	−0.7	3.4	2.2
Australia	−6.3	−4.6	−3.2	−5.6
Taiwan Province of China	8.6	6.4	7.9	8.0
Sweden	8.6	7.8	6.4	5.4
Switzerland	9.9	2.4	6.1	7.1
Hong Kong SAR	12.3	14.2	10.7	10.8
Czech Republic	−3.1	−3.1	−2.1	−2.2
Norway	15.9	19.5	13.9	15.6
Singapore	23.5	14.8	12.6	12.5
Denmark	0.7	1.0	1.1	1.5
Israel	2.8	1.0	3.2	2.4
New Zealand	−8.2	−8.9	−7.1	−6.7
Iceland	−19.9	−40.6	−5.3	0.7
Memorandum				
Major advanced economies	−1.3	−1.5	−1.1	−0.8
Euro area[2]	0.1	−0.5	−1.0	−1.0
Newly industrialized Asian economies	5.7	4.4	6.4	5.9

[1]Calculated as the sum of the balances of individual euro area countries.

[2]Corrected for reporting discrepancies in intra-area transactions.

hold incomes as import prices decline, thereby strengthening domestic demand, and would also send a signal to businesses to shift supply toward the domestic sector. More flexible exchange rates would also allow Asian economies to develop monetary policy into an independent tool for macroeconomic management, which would help buffer the economic impact of external and domestic shocks.

Europe: A Sluggish Recovery Lies Ahead

Recent data from Europe suggest that the pace of decline is moderating. In the second quarter of 2009, euro area GDP contracted less than previously expected, with France and Germany posting positive growth and the United Kingdom registering a more moderate decline. Although contraction continues in much of emerging Europe, Poland recorded positive growth in both the first and second quarters. Even so, the rebound in Europe is likely to be slow. Financial market conditions in the region have improved, but the largely bank-based financial system will take time to fully resume its intermediating role. Tight credit conditions will limit private investment, and rising unemployment will weigh on consumption, even as public support will need to be gradually withdrawn. Emerging Europe will need to adapt to much tighter external financing constraints.

The output decline across the region was driven by a combination of falling domestic demand—especially investment—and shrinking trade within the tightly integrated region, with individual economies suffering to varying extents depending largely on their precrisis imbalances (Figure 2.3). Abrupt reversals of asset price booms, especially in real estate, caused sharp falls in activity in Ireland, Spain, the United Kingdom, and a number of other economies, including some in emerging Europe. Iceland was hit especially hard and is receiving IMF support following the collapse of its financial sector. Economies with moderate current account deficits or surpluses have generally seen smaller downturns. However, given its export-oriented economy, Germany was severely affected by the fall in external demand, although activity is now benefiting more than elsewhere in the region from the recovery in global trade. In comparison, the downturn in France was somewhat less pronounced, in part because of lower trade openness and a larger public sector.

Figure 2.3. Europe: A Slow Rebound

The recession is giving way to recovery. The depth of the downturn was linked, in part, to the extent of domestic and external imbalances in individual economies. The collapse in intraregional trade and cross-border financing weighed heavily on the closely integrated regional economy.

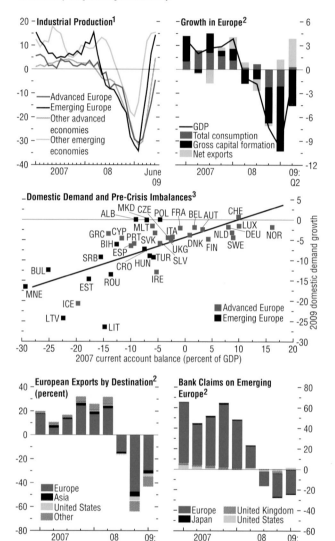

Sources: Bank for International Settlements; Haver Analytics; IMF, *Direction of Trade Statistics*; and IMF staff estimates.

[1]Annualized percent change of three-month moving average over previous three-month moving average. Advanced Europe: Austria (AUT), Czech Republic (CZE), Denmark (DNK), Finland (FIN), France (FRA), Germany (DEU), Greece (GRC), Ireland (IRE), Italy (ITA), Netherlands (NLD), Norway (NOR), Portugal (PRT), Slovak Republic (SVK), Slovenia (SLV), Spain (ESP), Sweden (SWE), and United Kingdom (UKG); Emerging Europe: Bulgaria (BUL), Estonia (EST), Hungary (HUN), Latvia (LTV), Lithuania (LIT), Poland (POL), Romania (ROU), and Turkey (TUR); Other advanced economies: Canada, Israel, Japan, Korea, Singapore, Taiwan Province of China, and the United States; Other emerging economies: Argentina, Brazil, Chile, China, Colombia, India, Indonesia, Malaysia, Mexico, Peru, Philippines, Russia, South Africa, Thailand, and Ukraine.

[2]Annualized quarterly contributions to growth. Croatia, Denmark, Ireland, Luxembourg and Turkey are not included in 2009:Q2.

[3]ALB: Albania; BEL: Belgium; BIH: Bosnia and Herzegovina; CHE: Switzerland; CRO: Croatia; CYP: Cyprus; ICE: Iceland; LUX: Luxembourg; MKD: Macedonia, FYR; MLT: Malta; MNE: Montenegro; SRB: Serbia.

Emerging Europe has been hit particularly hard by the drop in capital inflows. This led to major contractions in the Baltic economies, Bulgaria, and Romania, although exchange rates acted as a shock absorber in economies with flexible regimes. Bosnia, Hungary, Latvia, Romania, and Serbia are currently receiving IMF balance of payments support, whereas Poland has access to the IMF Flexible Credit Line in order to safeguard market confidence. In recent months, the pace of contraction has slowed dramatically in much of the region, with risk appetite returning, exports accelerating, and the inventory drawdown moderating, although private credit remains sluggish and unemployment is on the rise (Figure 2.4).

The strength of the initial macroeconomic policy response has been largely determined by policy room, which varied considerably across the region. With inflation rates low and credit markets severely disrupted, central banks in the advanced economies reduced interest rates aggressively and introduced some unconventional measures, including direct acquisition of assets by the Bank of England and purchases of covered bonds by the European Central Bank. Many advanced economies committed considerable budgetary resources to support the financial sector, mainly through guarantees. Capital injections and asset purchases have generally been more limited so far, with the exception of Austria, Belgium, Ireland, the Netherlands, Norway, and the United Kingdom. A number of countries, including Germany, Spain, and the United Kingdom, introduced large discretionary stimulus packages to support the economy more broadly, in addition to the considerable support provided by automatic stabilizers. At the same time, countries with more limited policy room at the onset of the recession, such as Greece, Italy, and most of the emerging economies, were not in a position to introduce major stimulus. Moreover, most countries of emerging Europe have also been constrained by the outflow of foreign capital (or the risk thereof), with some forced to tighten their monetary stance and consolidate fiscal accounts, particularly those economies with fixed exchange rates. More recently, subsiding risk aversion has allowed some emerging economies to cut interest rates.

The pace of decline in activity appears to be moderating, but the recovery will likely be modest during the coming quarters. The turnaround during the second half of 2009 is expected to be driven mainly by rising exports and a turn in the inventory cycle, with continued support from policy stimulus. The euro area is projected to emerge from the recession in the second half of 2009, with recovery strengthening over the course of 2010, while inflation should remain low (see Table 2.1). The turnaround is most apparent on a fourth-quarter-over-fourth-quarter basis, from a decline of 2.5 percent in 2009 to an increase of 0.9 percent in 2010. The modest pace of recovery is consistent with continued housing market pressures in some economies, enduring strains in the largely bank-based financial sector, and a drag from the labor markets. Even though initial job cuts were moderate, unemployment is projected to approach 10 percent during 2009 and to reach almost 12 percent by 2011, with job creation likely subdued as widespread reductions in hours worked are reversed. In the United Kingdom, real GDP growth is expected to turn positive in the second half of 2009, as the real estate and financial markets stabilize and the weakened sterling supports net exports. In emerging Europe, following a contraction in real GDP of 5¼ percent in 2009, a return to positive growth is expected in 2010 (Table 2.4). The recovery is expected to be slower than in other emerging regions because many economies will continue to face serious adjustment problems, given that cross-border capital flows will likely remain lower for some time. And the recovery will be uneven: some emerging European economies—notably the Baltics—will continue to contract in 2010, but sizable output gains are expected elsewhere, notably in Poland and Turkey.

Downside risks to the outlook for Europe are receding, and some upside risk has surfaced in several economies. The recovery may be more sluggish than expected if conditions in the

Figure 2.4. Europe: Challenges Ahead

The recovery will likely be slow, with tight credit conditions limiting private investment and rising unemployment weighing on consumption. Coordinated policy action remains key to regaining growth momentum in the region, while exit needs to be careful and well timed.

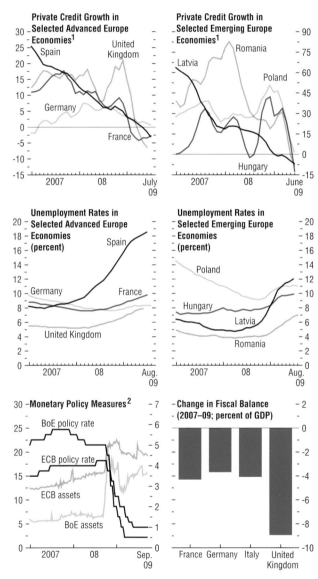

Sources: Haver Analytics; IMF, *International Financial Statistics;* and IMF staff estimates.
[1]Annualized percent change of three-month moving average over previous three-month moving average.
[2]ECB: European Central Bank; BoE: Bank of England. Assets are in percent of 2008 GDP and are on the left scale. Policy rate is in percent and is on the right scale.

Table 2.4. Selected Emerging European Economies: Real GDP, Consumer Prices, and Current Account Balance
(Annual percent change unless noted otherwise)

	Real GDP				Consumer Prices[1]				Current Account Balance[2]			
	2007	2008	2009	2010	2007	2008	2009	2010	2007	2008	2009	2010
Emerging Europe	**5.5**	**2.9**	**−5.2**	**1.8**	**6.2**	**8.0**	**4.7**	**4.2**	**−7.6**	**−7.6**	**−2.7**	**−3.6**
Turkey	4.7	0.9	−6.5	3.7	8.8	10.4	6.2	6.8	−5.8	−5.7	−1.9	−3.7
Excluding Turkey	6.0	4.1	−4.3	0.5	4.5	6.5	3.8	2.5	−8.9	−8.9	−3.2	−3.5
Baltics	**8.9**	**−0.7**	**−17.4**	**−3.7**	**7.3**	**12.2**	**2.6**	**−2.5**	**−17.7**	**−11.4**	**2.3**	**2.6**
Estonia	7.2	−3.6	−14.0	−2.6	6.6	10.4	0.0	−0.2	−17.8	−9.3	1.9	2.0
Latvia	10.0	−4.6	−18.0	−4.0	10.1	15.3	3.1	−3.5	−21.6	−12.6	4.5	6.4
Lithuania	8.9	3.0	−18.5	−4.0	5.8	11.1	3.5	−2.9	−14.6	−11.6	1.0	0.5
Central Europe	**5.5**	**3.9**	**−0.7**	**1.5**	**3.7**	**4.6**	**3.6**	**2.9**	**−5.2**	**−6.1**	**−2.4**	**−3.1**
Hungary	1.2	0.6	−6.7	−0.9	7.9	6.1	4.5	4.1	−6.5	−8.4	−2.9	−3.3
Poland	6.8	4.9	1.0	2.2	2.5	4.2	3.4	2.6	−4.7	−5.5	−2.2	−3.1
Southern and southeastern Europe	**6.1**	**6.1**	**−7.5**	**−0.1**	**5.1**	**8.4**	**4.5**	**3.0**	**−13.9**	**−13.8**	**−6.6**	**−6.0**
Bulgaria	6.2	6.0	−6.5	−2.5	7.6	12.0	2.7	1.6	−25.2	−25.5	−11.4	−8.3
Croatia	5.5	2.4	−5.2	0.4	2.9	6.1	2.8	2.8	−7.6	−9.4	−6.1	−5.4
Romania	6.2	7.1	−8.5	0.5	4.8	7.8	5.5	3.6	−13.5	−12.4	−5.5	−5.6
Memorandum												
Slovak Republic	10.4	6.4	−4.7	3.7	2.7	4.6	1.5	2.3	−5.3	−6.5	−8.0	−7.8
Czech Republic	6.1	2.7	−4.3	1.3	2.9	6.3	1.0	1.1	−3.1	−3.1	−2.1	−2.2

[1]Movements in consumer prices are shown as annual averages. December–December changes can be found in Table A7 in the Statistical Appendix.
[2]Percent of GDP.

financial and corporate sectors get worse and if unemployment rises faster than currently anticipated. Financial institutions are vulnerable to a further deterioration in asset quality, because losses in the corporate sector may rise while capitalization remains fairly low. Emerging Europe is especially vulnerable to further contractions in cross-border funding, and large cross-border exposures by Austria, Belgium, and a number of other advanced economies remain a risk to banks in these countries. The recourse to shortened work hours in an effort to preserve jobs may have slowed the fall in employment so far, but as labor market pressures continue in the months ahead and as employment-support programs reach their limits, job shedding could intensify more than currently projected. The downside risks could become more pronounced if policy support in the advanced economies is withdrawn too early, if political pressures delay financial sector repairs, or if policy coordination falters. The upside risks lie mainly in a faster-than-anticipated recovery of global trade and confidence.

Over the medium term, GDP growth is likely to return to precrisis rates only gradually, as supply remains sluggish and balance sheet adjustment continues to weigh on demand. Unemployment is forecast to remain high for some time, and it is likely that some of the increase will become structural, as displaced labor finds reentry difficult, especially in the euro area and some emerging economies. As credit conditions remain tight and public support is gradually withdrawn, investment will likely remain low, and some of the existing capital stock will need to be scrapped as corporations in a number of countries restructure. Indeed, past experience indicates that employment, capital accumulation, and productivity remain sluggish for a long time following financial crises (see Chapter 4). At the same time, private demand is likely to remain particularly subdued in the many European countries that have undergone an abrupt unwinding of precrisis asset price and credit booms. Linked to this, current account deficits are expected to narrow in a number of countries, in particular, Greece,

Ireland, Spain, and much of emerging Europe. Current account surpluses are forecast to diminish in Germany and a few other countries in 2009 but to widen again later on.

Forceful and innovative policy measures have significantly reduced the negative risks in economies that faced severe pressure, but more needs to be done to ensure a sustained recovery throughout the region. Challenges remain for policy coordination, especially in developing approaches to financial sector stress and providing assistance for hard-hit economies. There have been steps in the right direction, including the recently announced overhaul of the European Union's financial stability architecture, coordinated stress tests of the largest EU banks, and stress tests of banks in central, eastern, and southern Europe conducted with the help of the IMF. However, these steps need to be followed by bank recapitalization to restore confidence in the financial system and rebuild lending capacity. Moreover, considerable uncertainty remains regarding the value of distressed assets and asset quality in general, which continues to raise questions about banks' capital bases and their capacity to extend financial intermediation. Furthermore, a comprehensive and transparent framework for bank resolution, especially for cross-border banks, remains a priority. Steps have also been taken to meet the challenges in the hard-hit emerging economies, including through the Bank Coordination Initiative to support cross-border banking flows, but a common strategy and supporting framework for assisting hard-hit countries and for dealing with accumulating debt is still lacking.

Turning to macroeconomic policies, the policy stance in the advanced economies should continue to support demand until the recovery gains a much stronger foothold. As a result of the severe downturn in activity and the sharp declines in commodity prices from their precrisis peaks, headline inflation is low throughout the region. Against this background, there is ample room to maintain very low interest rates and use unconventional instruments to counter adverse feedback loops between the real and financial sectors. However, as the recovery takes hold, a careful exit needs to be engineered, consistent with continued support for the economy yet forestalling a rise in inflation as output gaps diminish, especially given that potential output has likely fallen. Discretionary fiscal stimulus should not be withdrawn too early, but the fiscal costs of the crisis are high. Public finances in the advanced economies are expected to deteriorate sharply, with the average general government deficit in excess of 5 percent of GDP in 2009 and 2010 and with debt levels rising fast. Debt sustainability is a major concern, as excessive debt buildup may crowd out private capital accumulation and further depress potential growth, amid growing demographic pressures. Thus, fiscal stimulus should be allowed to unwind and consolidation plans should be implemented once the recovery takes hold, supported by effective national fiscal frameworks and by the EU's Stability and Growth Pact.

Given the prospect of slow growth over the medium term, more needs to be done to ensure that unemployed workers can be reabsorbed into the labor force. Labor market policies continue to focus on protecting insiders, while continuing to leave out other groups (for example, migrant workers) that are likely most at risk of hysteresis. At the same time, as economies recover, provisions for higher and longer unemployment and social benefits and subsidies for reduced work time will need to be reversed to prevent lasting damage to employment incentives. Service and product market reforms are needed to raise productivity growth and facilitate a reallocation of resources between the tradable and nontradable sectors. In this regard, the crisis could present an opportunity to push forward with ambitious reforms that would help energize growth in Europe for years to come.

Commonwealth of Independent States: A Difficult Recovery for Some and Damage Containment for Others

The economic fallout of the global crisis on the CIS has been intense and is weighing heavily

Figure 2.5. Commonwealth of Independent States (CIS): An Arduous Road to Recovery

A severe recession in Russia has led to significant spillovers within the region as remittances and demand for exports have fallen sharply. Energy exporters, with the exception of Kazakhstan, experienced a moderate slowdown and declining commodity prices have led to deteriorating fiscal and external balances.

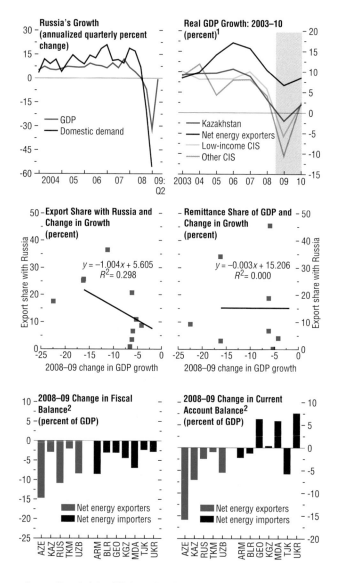

Sources: Haver Analytics; IMF, *International Financial Statistics;* and IMF staff estimates.
[1]Net energy exporters include Azerbaijan, Turkmenistan, and Uzbekistan. Low-income CIS include Armenia, Georgia, Kyrgyz Republic, Moldova, and Tajikistan. Other CIS include Belarus and Ukraine.
[2]ARM: Armenia; AZE: Azerbaijan; BLR: Belarus; GEO: Georgia; KAZ: Kazakhstan; KGZ: Kyrgyz Republic; MDA: Moldova; RUS: Russia; TJK: Tajikistan; TKM: Turkmenistan; UKR: Ukraine; UZB: Uzbekistan.

on the region's economic outlook. A sharp contraction in Russia, on top of the effects of the global recession and financial crisis, has led to painful adjustments in lower-income net energy importers in the region. With many of these economies still dependent on Russia for remittances and export earnings, the crisis depressed domestic demand, upended credit booms, and in some cases shut down access to foreign capital markets. Most of the energy-exporting countries are weathering the financial turmoil and the drop in energy prices comparatively well, because they could draw on large policy buffers and are less dependent on developments in Russia.

Russia is reeling from the unraveling of an oil-boom-related surge in capital inflows, which culminated in the devaluation of the ruble in January 2009 (Figure 2.5). The earlier focus on exchange rate stability had encouraged substantial foreign-currency borrowing by banks and corporations and contributed to unsustainably high rates of credit growth. The drop in commodity prices and a sudden reversal of capital flows led to a fall in fixed investment and shattered the nexus of high growth in investment, productivity, and real wages. As a result, GDP plummeted by almost 10 percent in the first half of 2009 relative to the same period a year earlier. Recent data indicate however that the contraction has begun to moderate: the rate of growth of industrial production recovered to −1.0 percent in the second quarter of 2009 from a trough of −40 percent earlier this year,[3] and the pressure on the capital account and the exchange rate have eased.

Lower-income CIS economies have seen a large fall in activity accompanied by currency devaluations (Armenia, Kyrgyz Republic, Tajikistan). Many economies had previously enjoyed rapid growth based on foreign-financed credit booms and buoyant domestic demand supported by remittance income. As these funding sources dried up, activity came to a halt, espe-

[3]Annualized percentage change of three-month moving average over previous three-month average.

Table 2.5. Commonwealth of Independent States: Real GDP, Consumer Prices, and Current Account Balance

(Annual percent change unless noted otherwise)

	Real GDP				Consumer Prices[1]				Current Account Balance[2]			
	2007	2008	2009	2010	2007	2008	2009	2010	2007	2008	2009	2010
Commonwealth of Independent States[3]	**8.6**	**5.5**	**−6.7**	**2.1**	**9.7**	**15.6**	**11.8**	**9.4**	**4.2**	**4.9**	**2.9**	**4.4**
Russia	8.1	5.6	−7.5	1.5	9.0	14.1	12.3	9.9	5.9	6.1	3.6	4.5
Ukraine	7.9	2.1	−14.0	2.7	12.8	25.2	16.3	10.3	−3.7	−7.2	0.4	0.2
Kazakhstan	8.9	3.2	−2.0	2.0	10.8	17.2	7.5	6.6	−7.8	5.1	−2.0	3.9
Belarus	8.6	10.0	−1.2	1.8	8.4	14.8	13.0	8.3	−6.8	−8.4	−9.6	−7.1
Turkmenistan	11.6	10.5	4.0	15.3	6.3	14.5	0.4	3.5	15.5	18.7	17.8	29.1
Azerbaijan	23.4	11.6	7.5	7.4	16.6	20.8	2.2	5.3	28.8	35.5	19.6	23.1
Low-income CIS countries[3]	**14.2**	**8.8**	**3.0**	**5.4**	**12.6**	**15.9**	**5.8**	**6.6**	**8.2**	**12.0**	**5.5**	**7.9**
Armenia	13.7	6.8	−15.6	1.2	4.4	9.0	3.0	3.2	−6.4	−11.5	−13.7	−13.7
Georgia	12.3	2.1	−4.0	2.0	9.2	10.0	1.2	3.0	−19.7	−22.7	−16.3	−17.6
Kyrgyz Republic	8.5	7.6	1.5	3.0	10.2	24.5	8.0	6.7	−0.2	−8.2	−7.8	−12.4
Moldova	3.0	7.2	−9.0	0.0	12.4	12.7	1.4	7.7	−17.0	−17.7	−11.8	−11.9
Tajikistan	7.8	7.9	2.0	3.0	13.2	20.4	8.0	10.9	−8.6	−7.9	−13.7	−13.3
Uzbekistan	9.5	9.0	7.0	7.0	12.3	12.7	12.5	9.5	7.3	12.8	7.2	6.7
Memorandum												
Net energy exporters[4]	8.6	5.8	−6.1	2.1	9.4	14.5	11.5	9.4	5.6	7.0	3.9	5.5
Net energy importers[5]	8.4	4.4	−9.6	2.4	11.3	21.4	13.5	9.1	−5.2	−8.7	−4.5	−4.2

[1]Movements in consumer prices are shown as annual averages. December–December changes can be found in Table A7 in the Statistical Appendix.

[2]Percent of GDP.

[3]Georgia and Mongolia, which are not members of the Commonwealth of Independent States, are included in this group for reasons of geography and similarities in economic structure.

[4]Includes Azerbaijan, Kazakhstan, Russia, Turkmenistan, and Uzbekistan.

[5]Includes Armenia, Belarus, Georgia, Kyrgyz Republic, Moldova, Mongolia, Tajikistan, and Ukraine.

cially in construction sectors. The crisis is taking a particularly sharp toll in Ukraine, which is a major steel exporter and borrower in international markets and now receives IMF support. Energy exporters in the CIS fared comparatively better, with the recovery of energy prices, and growth slowed only moderately during the first half of 2009. An exception is Kazakhstan, for which the global crisis provided a further blow to a financial sector already weakened by a sudden reversal of capital inflows in early 2008 and then a real estate market meltdown thereafter.

The path toward recovery will be difficult for most CIS economies (Table 2.5). Russia is projected to experience a deep recession in 2009, with GDP contracting by 7.5 percent, followed by a tentative recovery in 2010, helped by expansionary fiscal policy, improving commodity prices, and recovery in Europe and the United States. Without this regional growth locomotive, the lower-income, non-oil-exporting CIS

economies (Armenia, Kyrgyz Republic, Moldova, Tajikistan) are expected to experience steep growth declines in 2009 followed in 2010 by a modest recovery—growth of less than 3 percent. The recession is expected to be very deep for Ukraine, which continues to struggle for external financing—GDP is forecast to be −14 percent in 2009.

For energy-exporting economies, the growth outlook is more benign. Azerbaijan and Uzbekistan are projected to experience only a moderate slowdown in 2009, followed by unchanged growth in 2010, as energy prices recover and fiscal expansions support domestic demand. An exception is Kazakhstan, which is projected to contract by 2 percent this year as its economy works through adjustment in the financial sector. A projected modest recovery in 2010 is mainly the result of a $10 billion anticrisis plan aimed at recapitalizing banks and supporting economic recovery.

The risks to the outlook for the region are tilted downward, with greater risks for economies that are in deeper recessions and face difficult financing conditions. For these economies, room for supportive fiscal policy is limited in light of sustainability concerns, and measures to ease credit may have only a limited effect. A protracted global downturn would also delay the recovery in Russia, with negative repercussions for economies closely tied to its fortune. For energy exporters, the risks to the outlook are linked to energy price developments, which are in turn tied to the fate of the global recovery during 2010. On the upside, positive impulses could come from China, which has growing trade ties with the region, especially for energy exporters, such as Kazakhstan.

A main policy challenge, given the scale of the slowdown, is to provide effective fiscal support. In Russia, planned fiscal measures should be well targeted and temporary to mitigate the risk of deficits becoming entrenched. The hard-hit energy importers should aim to support domestic demand by providing transfers to groups most severely affected (such as those who have lost remittances), but the extent of such support is constrained by the availability of funds and sustainability concerns. Some of these economies may need to draw on multilateral assistance or enhanced donor support. Energy exporters, on the other hand, should use available funds to smooth domestic demand (for example, by advancing infrastructure investment).

The main challenge for monetary policy is to strike the right balance between domestic and external stability. After the currency devaluations earlier in 2009, monetary policy has been directed toward safeguarding stability through higher interest rates. Where these policies have succeeded and external conditions have become more favorable, as in Russia, monetary policy could become more accommodative to respond to rising output gaps. In the lower-income economies of the region, exchange rate flexibility should be maintained to ensure that depreciations protect the competitiveness of ailing export sectors.

The overarching challenge for financial sector policies is to lay the foundation for a resumption of credit growth on a much sounder basis than in the recent past. This will require that many economies draw up a comprehensive approach that includes intensified monitoring by regulators and action to keep rising shares of nonperforming loans from causing systemic problems. Policymakers should also be prepared to act quickly if strains in the financial sector reemerge, by supplying liquidity, providing capital to ailing but sound financial institutions, and facilitating restructuring in the financial sector or elsewhere in the economy.

Other Advanced Economies: On the Path to Recovery

After experiencing severe recessions or slowdowns, Australia, Canada, and New Zealand are transitioning to recovery. Real GDP growth in the first quarter of 2009 was negative for Canada and New Zealand and slightly positive for Australia. However, the recent evolution of industrial production, retail sales, and confidence indicators suggests that Australia is on its way to recovery and that the Canadian and New Zealand economies are stabilizing (Figure 2.6). Activity is expected to grow in the second half of 2009 for all three economies. The recent rebound in commodity prices and reduced reliance on manufactured products have helped exports, particularly for Australia. Because of weak performance during the first half of 2009, the baseline projections show a contraction in real GDP in 2009 followed by modest growth in 2010 (see Table 2.1). On a fourth-quarter-over-fourth-quarter basis, real GDP growth in these economies is projected at about 3 percent in 2010. New Zealand and, to a lesser degree, Australia, with their sizable short-term external debts, are more vulnerable than a number of other advanced economies to a weakening in investor confidence.

Australia, Canada, and New Zealand took advantage of the prolonged period of prosperity in the run-up to the current global recession to put in place sound macroeconomic and regulatory frameworks. As a result, they have had ample room to implement expansionary policies to limit the damage from the global recession and to support recovery as needed. Since September 1, 2008, these central banks have significantly reduced interest rates (between 275 and 550 basis points). Floating exchange rates have acted as a shock absorber and have helped to mitigate the impact of external shocks. Large fiscal stimulus packages for 2009 and 2010 are being implemented to help support domestic demand—in the range of 2 percent of GDP a year for Canada and Australia. In the event that the recovery falters, these economies will have further room for stimulus, both monetary and fiscal (Australia and Canada). Nonetheless, they face important challenges. There is a need to develop and implement strategies to unwind the expansionary policies and to further strengthen financial supervision and regulation. Specifically, the liquidity guidelines to encourage banks in New Zealand and Australia to reduce their reliance on short-term wholesale funding need to be implemented, whereas Canada needs to carry out the announced move to centralized supervision of securities.

Latin America and the Caribbean: Policy Frameworks Have Promoted Resilience

The Latin America and Caribbean region is showing signs of stabilization and recovery. These economies are helped by improving conditions in global financial and commodity markets and stronger policy frameworks that promoted resilience and allowed timely policy responses to support economic activity.

Activity contracted in the fourth quarter of 2008 and the first quarter of 2009, as consumption, investment, and exports fell sharply as a result of tighter external financing conditions, a deterioration in the region's external demand, and lower worker remittances. The deterioration in activity varied across the region and greatly depended on the nature and intensity of the external shocks and on country-specific char-

Figure 2.6. Australia, Canada, and New Zealand: Turning the Page[1]

There are signs that economic activity in these economies is rebounding. Australia's export performance has been remarkable. Export composition (lower manufacturing exports) and markets (more reliant on China) seem to be the key to this performance.

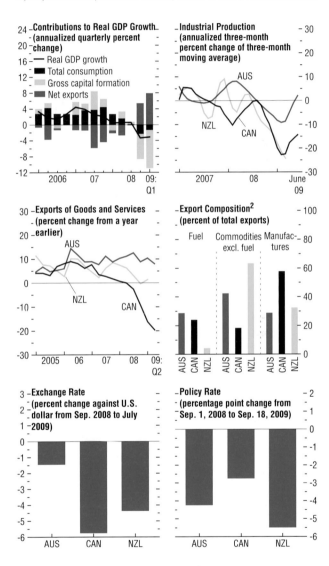

Sources: Haver Analytics; United Nations Comtrade database; and IMF staff calculations.
[1]AUS: Australia; CAN: Canada; NZL: New Zealand.
[2]Average of 2005 and 2008.

Figure 2.7. Latin America: Recovery Is within Reach[1]

Recovery in Latin America is not homogenous across countries, with Brazil leading the recovery in the region. Mexico, the hardest-hit economy in the Western Hemisphere, is expected to start recovering later this year. This heterogeneity can be explained by differences in the composition and destination of exports and by other factors, such as the degree of integration into the world economy and the policy response to the crisis.

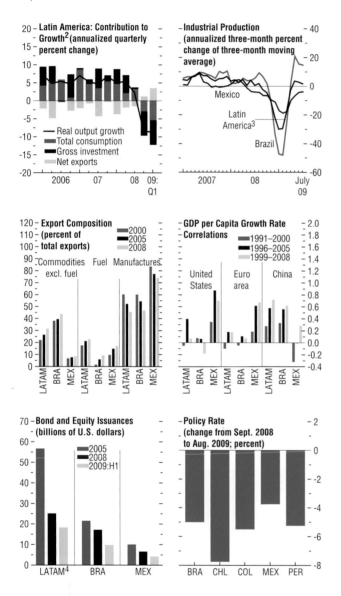

Sources: Dealogic; Haver Analytics; United Nations Comtrade database; and IMF staff calculations.
[1]LATAM: Latin America; BRA: Brazil; CHL: Chile; COL: Colombia; MEX: Mexico; PER: Peru. Latin America consists of the countries above and Argentina, Ecuador, Uruguay, and Venezuela.
[2]LATAM excluding Uruguay.
[3]LATAM excluding Ecuador and Uruguay.
[4]LATAM excluding Ecuador, Uruguay, and Venezuela.

acteristics. For example, the decline in worker remittances and tourism earnings severely affected several economies in Central America and the Caribbean. Net commodity exporters, including the region's largest economies (Argentina, Brazil, Chile, Colombia, Mexico, Peru, Venezuela) suffered terms-of-trade losses. Especially significant export revenue losses were experienced by the energy-intensive economies of Bolivia, Ecuador, and Trinidad and Tobago. For many economies in the region, the intensity of these shocks has been mitigated by an enhanced ability to implement countercyclical monetary and fiscal policies, more resilient financial sectors, and a willingness to use the exchange rate as shock absorber.

There are indications that recovery got under way during the second quarter of 2009, and it should gather moderate speed in the second half of the year, led by Brazil (Figure 2.7). Capital flows have restarted to the region, and sovereign spreads have narrowed. Industrial production has picked up in many economies, notably Brazil, and the contraction in Mexico is moderating. The recent rebound of commodity prices is also improving the overall outlook for the region, given the prominence of commodity exports. Consumer and business confidence have improved, and retail sales have firmed up.

Despite these positive signs, real GDP in the region is still projected to contract by 2.5 percent in 2009 (Table 2.6), reflecting weak activity in the first half of the year, before growing by 2.9 percent in 2010. The pace of recovery, however, is not uniform across economies. Brazil will lead the way, in part because of its large domestic market and its diversified export products and markets, especially its increasing links to Asia. The Peruvian economy, after several years of rapid growth, virtually stagnated in the first half of 2009 but will resume strong growth in the second half of the year. In contrast, Mexico—the hardest-hit economy in the Western Hemisphere[4]—will recover more slowly

---

[4]The swine flu has compounded the adverse impact of the global recession on Argentina and Mexico. The real

Table 2.6. Selected Western Hemisphere Economies: Real GDP, Consumer Prices, and Current Account Balance

(Annual percent change unless noted otherwise)

	Real GDP				Consumer Prices[1]				Current Account Balance[2]			
	2007	2008	2009	2010	2007	2008	2009	2010	2007	2008	2009	2010
Western Hemisphere	**5.7**	**4.2**	**−2.5**	**2.9**	**5.4**	**7.9**	**6.1**	**5.2**	**0.4**	**−0.7**	**−0.8**	**−0.9**
South America and Mexico[3]	**5.7**	**4.2**	**−2.7**	**3.0**	**5.3**	**7.7**	**6.3**	**5.3**	**0.7**	**−0.3**	**−0.6**	**−0.6**
Argentina[4]	8.7	6.8	−2.5	1.5	8.8	8.6	5.6	5.0	1.6	1.4	4.4	4.9
Brazil	5.7	5.1	−0.7	3.5	3.6	5.7	4.8	4.1	0.1	−1.8	−1.3	−1.9
Chile	4.7	3.2	−1.7	4.0	4.4	8.7	2.0	2.3	4.4	−2.0	0.7	−0.4
Colombia	7.5	2.5	−0.3	2.5	5.5	7.0	4.6	3.7	−2.8	−2.8	−2.9	−3.1
Ecuador	2.5	6.5	−1.0	1.5	2.3	8.4	5.0	3.0	3.5	2.3	−3.1	−3.0
Mexico	3.3	1.3	−7.3	3.3	4.0	5.1	5.4	3.5	−0.8	−1.4	−1.2	−1.3
Peru	8.9	9.8	1.5	5.8	1.8	5.8	3.2	2.0	1.1	−3.3	−2.1	−2.3
Uruguay	7.6	8.9	0.6	3.5	8.1	7.9	7.5	7.4	−0.3	−4.6	−1.6	−2.0
Venezuela	8.4	4.8	−2.0	−0.4	18.7	30.4	29.5	30.0	8.8	12.3	1.8	5.4
Central America[5]	**6.9**	**4.2**	**−0.7**	**1.8**	**6.8**	**11.2**	**3.8**	**3.8**	**−7.0**	**−9.3**	**−5.0**	**−6.6**
Caribbean[5]	**5.6**	**3.0**	**−0.5**	**1.6**	**6.7**	**11.9**	**3.5**	**5.2**	**−2.0**	**−3.7**	**−4.1**	**−2.3**

[1]Movements in consumer prices are shown as annual averages. December–December changes can be found in Table A7 in the Statistical Appendix.

[2]Percent of GDP.

[3]Includes Bolivia and Paraguay.

[4]Private analysts estimate that consumer price index inflation has been considerably higher. The authorities have created a board of academic advisors to assess these issues. Private analysts are also of the view that real GDP growth has been significantly lower than the official reports since the last quarter of 2008.

[5]The country composition of these regional groups can be found in Table F in the Statistical Appendix.

because its economy has suffered a sharper drop in trade flows, because of its high trade integration, dependence on the United States, and reliance on manufacturing exports.

Inflation pressures in the region have eased, reflecting the continued weakness in economic activity and large output gaps. In particular, inflation is projected to fall from about 8 percent in 2008 to 6.1 percent in 2009 and 5.2 percent in 2010. Despite the potential pass-through effects of currency depreciation, inflation-targeting regimes have helped anchor price expectations, and inflation in these economies is projected to be in the 2–5 percent range. Venezuela will continue to post the highest inflation rate in the Western Hemisphere because of strong public spending and easy monetary policy, and there continue to be data issues related to the inflation rates recorded in Argentina.[5]

The current account deficit for the region is projected to widen slightly but remain modest in 2009, driven by the collapse of current account surpluses in Venezuela and other energy exporters. Nevertheless, the current account deficits of several economies of the region, including most in Central America, are projected to narrow in 2009, as the large import contraction outweighs the decline in exports.

Downside risks to this outlook are receding but remain a concern. A weaker-than-expected global recovery could lead to a simultaneous drop in exports and remittances, dampening the prospects for recovery in some economies. A tightening of global financial conditions could increase external financing costs and reduce capital inflows, affecting some of the more vulnerable corporations and governments in the region.

The policy response to the external shocks has been rapid and, in some cases, aggressive.[6]

GDP growth losses associated with this illness in Mexico are estimated at between ½ and 1 percent in 2009.

[5]The authorities have created a board of academic advisors to assess these issues.

[6]Some countries in the region are currently receiving IMF support. Costa Rica, El Salvador, and Guatemala

The inflation-targeting economies (Brazil, Colombia, Chile, Mexico, Peru, Uruguay) had more policy room than other economies, reflecting their strengthened policy frameworks and macroeconomic fundamentals at the onset of the global recession. In particular, these economies have cut their policy rates by between 375 and 775 basis points since September 2008, while allowing their currencies to float. Other central banks in the region (including in the Dominican Republic and Venezuela) have also eased monetary conditions. A number have complemented such policies with steps to provide liquidity, including through lower bank reserve requirements (Argentina, Brazil, Colombia, Peru) and an expanded set of instruments that can be used at the discount window. These central banks should keep interest rates low until a recovery is solidly under way and upward inflation pressures become relevant. In the event that growth is weaker than expected, some economies may have room to reduce interest rates still further.

Fiscal policy in many economies in the region has, for the first time in decades, been countercyclical. This is a reflection of improved macroeconomic frameworks, lower debt levels, and larger reserve buffers. Several countries in the region announced fiscal stimulus packages ranging from ½ percent of GDP in Brazil to about 3 percent of GDP in Chile. The timely implementation of these packages has been helpful in supporting the recovery, whereas increased coverage of social programs has mitigated the social costs of the downturn. Falling oil revenues and the drop in economic activity have led to a sharp deterioration in the fiscal balances of some economies (Venezuela), reducing significantly the room for additional fiscal stimulus. In addition, room for countercyclical fiscal policy is limited in many countries in the Caribbean, as a result of a sharp decline in budgetary revenues, high debt, and limited access to external financing.

The domestic financial systems in Latin America have endured the global financial crisis rather well. In particular, the banking systems have generally remained sound, reflecting in part the important regulatory and supervisory changes introduced before the global crisis. As credit growth to the private sector slowed, public banks were encouraged to increase their lending operations to private corporations (most notably in Brazil). This development should be closely monitored to avoid a buildup of contingent fiscal liabilities.

The region faces important medium-term challenges. Continued progress is essential in strengthening fiscal and financial management frameworks, including adopting a long-term approach to fiscal policy. Tax and pension reforms are also needed in some countries, particularly where government revenues rely heavily on energy revenues. In order to increase resilience to future external shocks, oil and commodity exporters should consider developing or enhancing frameworks for countercyclical policies tied to oil and commodity prices, learning from the successful experience of Chile. These countries also need to ensure that investment regimes provide adequate incentives for investment in new facilities to forestall dwindling production capacity.

Middle East: Strengthening Growth Prospects

The outlook for the Middle East has improved recently, with the global economy stabilizing and oil prices rebounding. These economies have been hit hard by the global recession and, as a result, growth has decelerated sharply. In particular, the collapse in oil prices and sharp contraction in worker remittances and foreign direct investment have weighed on the economies in the region. The recent improvement in global financial conditions and rise in commodity prices, however, are helping restore the pace of economic activity. Nonetheless, the aftermath of the regional asset price collapse continues to weigh down the outlook.

---

have balance of payments support, whereas Colombia and Mexico have access to the new Flexible Credit Line.

Real GDP growth for the region is projected at 2 percent in 2009 and almost 4¼ percent in 2010 (Figure 2.8; Table 2.7). Real GDP growth of oil importers is projected at about 4½ percent in 2009, more than three times the growth rate of the oil exporters. The sharp slowdown in activity of oil exporters reflects cutbacks in oil production, a result of efforts by the Organization of Petroleum Exporting Countries to stabilize oil prices, although most oil exporters have maintained strong public spending growth to help their non-oil sector. Part of this spending has spilled over to the non-oil producers in the region, providing important support to these economies. Within these regional aggregates, there are important cross-country differences. For instance, among oil exporters, the United Arab Emirates (UAE) non-oil sector has been most affected by its linkages to global trade and financial markets and by the fall in real estate prices. In contrast, Lebanon continues to demonstrate strong resilience to the global crisis because improved security conditions have buoyed economic activity, particularly in tourism and financial services.

Inflation in the Middle East has subsided as economies have slowed. For the region as a whole, inflation is projected to decline from 15 percent in 2008 to 8.3 percent in 2009. At the country level, Jordan and Lebanon are projected to experience the sharpest drop in inflation (from double digits in 2008 to low single digits in 2009), as a result of the decline in the prices of imported food and fuel experienced by these import-dependent economies. Inflation in Egypt and the Islamic Republic of Iran is projected to remain in double digits, however. The current account surplus of the region is projected to narrow by 15¾ percent of GDP in 2009, primarily from a sharp reduction in oil exports (Kuwait, Qatar, Saudi Arabia).

The key risk to the outlook is the possibility that the global recovery may not be sustained and that oil prices may fall sharply, which could have important implications for oil exporters and their regional trading partners. In an attempt to bolster fiscal positions, oil exporters may need to cut

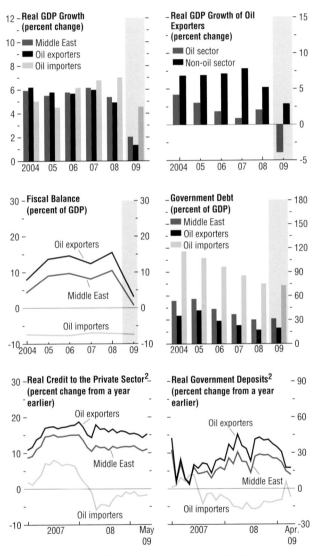

Figure 2.8. Middle East: Resuming Growth[1]

The growth prospects in the Middle East region have strengthened following an improvement in global financial conditions and a rebound in oil prices. Policies should remain supportive of economic growth after the drying up of bank credit and the collapse of asset prices, which weigh on the strength of the recovery.

Sources: Haver Analytics; IMF, *International Financial Statistics;* World Economic Outlook database; and IMF staff calculations.
[1]Oil exporters include Bahrain, Islamic Republic of Iran, Iraq, Kuwait, Libya, Oman, Qatar, Saudi Arabia, United Arab Emirates, and Republic of Yemen. Oil importers include Egypt, Jordan, Lebanon, and Syrian Arab Republic.
[2]Deflated by consumer price index.

Table 2.7. Selected Middle Eastern Economies: Real GDP, Consumer Prices, and Current Account Balance
(Annual percent change unless noted otherwise)

	Real GDP				Consumer Prices[1]				Current Account Balance[2]			
	2007	2008	2009	2010	2007	2008	2009	2010	2007	2008	2009	2010
Middle East	**6.2**	**5.4**	**2.0**	**4.2**	**11.2**	**15.0**	**8.3**	**6.6**	**18.1**	**18.3**	**2.6**	**7.9**
Oil exporters[3]	**6.0**	**4.9**	**1.3**	**4.2**	**11.8**	**15.8**	**7.0**	**6.3**	**21.5**	**21.8**	**4.0**	**10.4**
Iran, Islamic Rep. of	7.8	2.5	1.5	2.2	18.4	25.4	12.0	10.0	11.9	6.7	3.0	3.6
Saudi Arabia	3.3	4.4	−0.9	4.0	4.1	9.9	4.5	4.0	24.3	28.6	4.1	11.4
United Arab Emirates	6.3	7.4	−0.2	2.4	11.1	12.3	2.5	3.3	16.1	15.7	−1.6	5.2
Kuwait	2.5	6.3	−1.5	3.3	5.5	10.5	4.6	4.4	44.7	44.7	29.4	35.3
Mashreq	**6.8**	**7.0**	**4.5**	**4.4**	**9.1**	**12.3**	**13.0**	**7.5**	**−1.6**	**−2.7**	**−4.1**	**−4.4**
Egypt	7.1	7.2	4.7	4.5	11.0	11.7	16.2	8.5	1.9	0.5	−2.4	−2.8
Syrian Arab Republic	4.2	5.2	3.0	4.2	4.7	15.2	7.5	6.0	−3.3	−4.0	−3.2	−4.3
Jordan	8.9	7.9	3.0	4.0	5.4	14.9	0.2	4.0	−17.2	−11.3	−10.0	−8.8
Lebanon	7.5	8.5	7.0	4.0	4.1	10.8	2.5	3.5	−6.8	−11.6	−11.3	−10.5
Memorandum												
Israel	5.2	4.0	−0.1	2.4	0.5	4.6	3.6	2.0	2.8	1.0	3.2	2.4

[1]Movements in consumer prices are shown as annual averages. December–December changes can be found in Table A7 in the Statistical Appendix.
[2]Percent of GDP.
[3]The country composition of the group can be found in Table E of the Statistical Appendix.

public spending. This expenditure compression could have important regional spillover effects on the oil-importing countries by significantly reducing worker remittances. Another risk is that the banking systems of several oil-exporting countries could come under severe stress if global financial conditions tighten again.

Public policies should be geared to supporting domestic demand while recoveries remain fragile, provided countries have enough policy room. Monetary policy should balance the need to continue supporting domestic demand while avoiding the risk of allowing inflation pressures to build (Egypt). Some economies have been reducing interest rates (Kuwait, Saudi Arabia, UAE) as inflation has fallen. Although there is now limited room for further interest rate cuts, some central banks could modestly reduce interest rates if their economies slow.

Fiscal policies have been supportive of domestic demand in many Middle Eastern economies. In particular, oil exporters have maintained high levels of public spending despite a sharp drop in revenues. Countries with fiscal room should continue with these policies (which serve a similar function as automatic stabilizers) to help

the recovery gain momentum. Saudi Arabia, which had sizable government surpluses during the oil boom, is implementing the largest fiscal stimulus program (as a percent of GDP) among the Group of 20 countries. However, countries with weaker fiscal positions will need to cut back unproductive spending to avoid an unsustainable debt path. As part of such efforts, subsidy policies should be reined in.

An important task for some countries in the region is to return financial sectors to health and lay the foundation for greater stability. Bank supervisors should closely monitor the health of these institutions, particularly in the Gulf Cooperation Council, including through regular stress testing, and should assess potential recapitalization needs. Progress is needed in introducing mechanisms for cross-border supervision as well. Bank credit to the private sector in the region dried up following the financial sector problems in Bahrain and Dubai, the region's main financial centers, and this is sapping the strength of the recovery.[7] To support their banking systems,

[7]Dubai has been particularly affected by the correction in asset prices that started in the second quarter of 2008

some central banks injected liquidity, whereas some provided guarantees for private sector deposits and increased their own deposits at commercial banks. Finally, sovereign wealth funds should be managed under more transparent frameworks, particularly given their growing participation in domestic economies.

Africa: Regaining Momentum

Growth in Africa has slowed significantly as a result of the collapse of global trade and disruptions in global financial markets, but growth is expected to regain momentum as the global recovery gets under way. The effect of the global recession was initially felt most strongly in those economies more highly integrated into global financial markets, including South Africa. Subsequently, the impact of the fall in financial flows propagated to oil exporters (including Algeria, Angola, Libya, Nigeria), manufacturing exporters (Morocco, Tunisia), and commodity exporters (Botswana) as global trade collapsed. The recent improvement in financial conditions and commodity prices, however, will help these economies recover from the damage.

Real GDP growth in Africa is projected to decline from an average of 6 percent in 2004–08 to 1¾ percent in 2009, before accelerating to 4 percent in 2010 (Table 2.8). This growth performance, while disappointing in light of the experience of the mid-2000s, is still encouraging given the severity of the external shocks. An important factor behind this outcome has been that many governments in the region have been able to use fiscal balances as shock absorbers, sustaining domestic demand and helping contain employment losses. Net exports are expected to subtract from growth, mainly reflecting the region's sharp drop in exports (Figure 2.9). Relative to their 2004–08 performance, oil exporters (Angola, Equatorial Guinea, Nigeria) are expected to experience the sharpest growth slowdowns in 2009, as oil

and intensified with the escalation of the global financial crisis in September 2008.

Figure 2.9. Africa: Resilient Economies

Africa has been resilient during the global recession. There are indications that economic conditions are improving, driven by domestic demand and higher commodity prices. Policies have played an important role in supporting domestic demand.

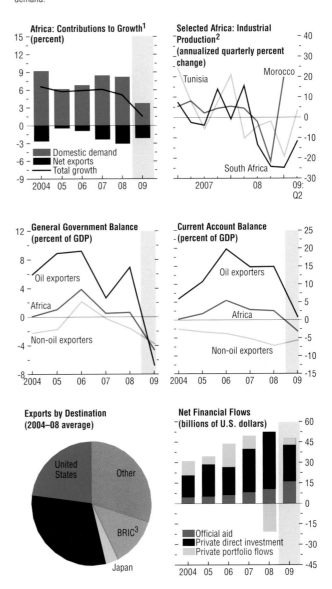

Sources: Haver Analytics; IMF, *Direction of Trade Statistics*; and IMF staff estimates.
[1]Excluding Dem. Rep. of Congo, São Tomé and Príncipe, and Sudan.
[2]Data for Morocco and Tunisia were seasonally adjusted using TRAMO-SEATs methodology developed by the Bank of Spain. Data for South Africa were seasonally adjusted by the source.
[3]Brazil, Russia, India, and China.

Table 2.8. Selected African Economies: Real GDP, Consumer Prices, and Current Account Balance
(Annual percent change unless noted otherwise)

	Real GDP				Consumer Prices[1]				Current Account Balance[2]			
	2007	2008	2009	2010	2007	2008	2009	2010	2007	2008	2009	2010
Africa	**6.3**	**5.2**	**1.7**	**4.0**	**6.0**	**10.3**	**9.0**	**6.5**	**2.9**	**2.5**	**−3.1**	**−1.7**
Maghreb	**3.5**	**4.1**	**3.2**	**3.6**	**3.0**	**4.4**	**3.9**	**3.2**	**12.0**	**10.6**	**−1.1**	**1.8**
Algeria	3.0	3.0	2.1	3.7	3.6	4.5	4.6	3.4	22.6	23.2	2.7	7.3
Morocco	2.7	5.6	5.0	3.2	2.0	3.9	2.8	2.8	−0.1	−5.4	−5.5	−4.7
Tunisia	6.3	4.6	3.0	4.0	3.1	5.0	3.5	3.4	−2.5	−4.2	−3.8	−2.9
Sub-Sahara	**7.0**	**5.5**	**1.3**	**4.1**	**6.8**	**11.9**	**10.5**	**7.3**	**0.2**	**0.2**	**−3.7**	**−2.7**
Horn of Africa[3]	**10.4**	**8.7**	**5.4**	**6.0**	**11.2**	**18.7**	**21.0**	**7.4**	**−10.1**	**−8.1**	**−9.0**	**−9.2**
Ethiopia	11.5	11.6	7.5	7.0	15.8	25.3	36.4	5.1	−4.5	−5.6	−5.6	−9.3
Sudan	10.2	6.8	4.0	5.5	8.0	14.3	11.0	9.0	−12.5	−9.0	−11.2	−9.1
Great Lakes[3]	**7.3**	**5.8**	**4.3**	**5.1**	**9.1**	**11.9**	**14.9**	**8.2**	**−4.8**	**−8.1**	**−8.9**	**−9.4**
Congo, Dem. Rep. of	6.3	6.2	2.7	5.4	16.7	18.0	39.2	14.6	−1.5	−15.3	−14.6	−23.7
Kenya	7.1	1.7	2.5	4.0	9.8	13.1	12.0	7.8	−4.1	−6.8	−8.1	−6.3
Tanzania	7.1	7.4	5.0	5.6	7.0	10.3	10.6	4.9	−9.0	−9.7	−9.9	−9.1
Uganda	8.4	9.0	7.0	6.0	6.8	7.3	14.2	10.8	−3.1	−3.2	−5.5	−5.7
Southern Africa[3]	**11.6**	**8.5**	**0.0**	**6.1**	**7.6**	**12.6**	**11.0**	**10.8**	**6.3**	**0.2**	**−6.3**	**−3.8**
Angola	20.3	13.2	0.2	9.3	12.2	12.5	14.0	15.4	15.9	7.5	−3.4	2.2
Zimbabwe[4]	−6.9	−14.1	3.7	6.0	−72.7	156.2	9.0	12.0	−10.7	−29.5	−21.4	−19.9
West and Central Africa[3]	**5.8**	**5.3**	**2.6**	**4.4**	**4.5**	**10.1**	**8.8**	**6.6**	**8.0**	**9.3**	**1.4**	**4.3**
Ghana	5.7	7.3	4.5	5.0	10.7	16.5	18.5	10.2	−12.0	−18.7	−12.7	−15.4
Nigeria	7.0	6.0	2.9	5.0	5.4	11.6	12.0	8.8	18.8	20.4	6.9	13.8
CFA franc zone[3]	**4.6**	**4.1**	**1.8**	**3.6**	**1.5**	**7.0**	**3.7**	**3.0**	**−2.6**	**−1.0**	**−2.9**	**−4.1**
Cameroon	3.3	2.9	1.6	2.7	1.1	5.3	2.9	2.0	−0.8	−1.0	−7.2	−4.6
Côte d'Ivoire	1.6	2.3	3.7	4.0	1.9	6.3	5.9	3.2	−0.7	2.4	24.6	1.1
South Africa	**5.1**	**3.1**	**−2.2**	**1.7**	**7.1**	**11.5**	**7.2**	**6.2**	**−7.3**	**−7.4**	**−5.0**	**−6.5**
Memorandum												
Oil importers	5.3	4.7	1.4	3.3	6.3	10.8	8.9	5.7	−5.2	−7.1	−5.7	−7.3
Oil exporters[5]	7.8	6.1	2.2	5.1	5.5	9.4	9.4	7.8	14.8	14.9	0.9	6.2

[1]Movements in consumer prices are shown as annual averages. December–December changes can be found in Table A7 in the Statistical Appendix.

[2]Percent of GDP.

[3]The country composition of these regional groups can be found in Table F in the Statistical Appendix.

[4]The Zimbabwe dollar ceased circulating in early 2009. Data are based on IMF staff estimates of price and exchange rate developments in U.S. dollars.

[5]The country composition of the group can be found in Table E of the Statistical Appendix.

revenues have fallen hard. GDP growth in oil importers is projected to decelerate as well, from about 5 percent in 2004–08 to 1½ percent in 2009, as their exports contract. Real GDP in South Africa, the largest economy of the region and an oil importer, is projected to contract by 2.2 percent in 2009. Growth is expected to resume during the second half of 2009, supported by expansive fiscal and monetary policies and the projected recovery in global trade. The recent pickup in capital flows to South Africa is also expected to contribute to the recovery, particularly given the recent upgrade in its sovereign credit rating. Two of the economies hardest hit by the global recession are Botswana and Seychelles. Botswana's economy is being

hit by the collapse in international demand for diamonds; in Seychelles, which is undertaking a comprehensive reform program, the economy is being affected by a sharp contraction in tourism receipts. On the other hand, many low-income countries in the region that have more diversified commodity exports seem to be weathering the global recession fairly well and are placed to quickly return to the higher growth paths of the mid-2000s.

Inflation in the African region is projected to fall from about 10¼ percent in 2008 to 9 percent in 2009, before easing to 6½ percent in 2010. Excluding Zimbabwe, a country for which information is unreliable, there are three economies (Democratic Republic of Congo, Ethiopia,

Seychelles) with projected average inflation rates for 2009 in excess of 20 percent. The majority of economies belonging to the CFA franc zone and Maghreb region, in contrast, are expected to have inflation rates below 5 percent. In contrast with the past, many countries in the region have had the fiscal policy room to allow automatic stabilizers to operate. As a result, the fiscal balance of the region is projected to switch from a surplus of over ½ percent of GDP in 2008 to a deficit of 4½ percent of GDP in 2009. The increased policy room was achieved through relatively prudent fiscal policies, together with debt relief in recent years.

The outlook for the region is subject to significant uncertainty. A weaker-than-expected recovery of the global economy would slow the recovery in commodity markets and worsen the prospects for inflows, including remittances and foreign direct investment. Moreover, a tightening of global financial conditions may have repercussions for the emerging markets of the region, although probably less than elsewhere because of the relatively limited reliance on private financing. However, donor countries, themselves mired in severe recessions, may reduce aid flows to the region with serious repercussions for those countries where external aid finances are a large fraction of total revenues. Poverty could also increase significantly in the sub-Saharan region as real GDP per capita contracts in 2009—the first decline in a decade—unemployment rises, and the region suffers from a lack of extensive social safety nets.

Policies should be geared toward mitigating the impact of the global recession on economic activity and poverty, while continuing to strengthen the foundations for sustained growth.

The fiscal policy response should be supportive of economic recovery. In countries with policy room, the priority is to implement already announced stimulus measures. As the recovery becomes firmly grounded, the focus of fiscal policy should move toward growth and fiscal sustainability considerations. Countries with no policy room should focus on reprioritizing

spending or increasing revenues, which would allow increased spending on infrastructure and social safety nets without worsening debt sustainability.

Monetary policy should continue to be supportive of domestic demand, and exchange rates should act as external shock absorbers. In countries with high inflation, central banks should reiterate their commitment to low inflation and, if needed, should tighten monetary policy. In countries with low inflation and flexible exchange rates, monetary policy should continue to sustain domestic demand until growth is back on a healthy path.

Financial institutions in the region have been largely resilient to the downturn. However, bank balance sheets in some economies have been affected by the region's slowdown. Financial supervisors should identify vulnerabilities in the banking sector, including by conducting frequent bank stress tests to identify credit risks and potential solvency and liquidity issues, and should take action as needed.

Looking beyond the short-term challenges, Africa must move ahead with a series of reforms to strengthen the region's resilience to external shocks and growth prospects. The development and implementation of sound and transparent public policies need to be further promoted, including through improved capacity for public financial management and the implementation of medium-term economic frameworks. A priority for the public sector should be creating and using fiscal room for the enhancement of transport infrastructure and health and education services and introducing well-targeted poverty-reduction programs. To facilitate private sector growth, continued progress is needed in reforming the business environment, including reducing start-up costs for new enterprises. In the financial sector, banking supervisory capacity should be strengthened, and the perimeter of financial sector regulation and supervision should be expanded. Some countries also need to take measures to further integrate their economies with the rest of the world.

LESSONS FOR MONETARY POLICY FROM ASSET PRICE FLUCTUATIONS

The current crisis gives occasion to revisit an old question: should monetary policy be used to prevent asset price busts? The question has at least three aspects, each of which is addressed in this chapter. First, we examine the historical evidence in search of consistent macroeconomic patterns that could be used as reliable leading indicators of asset price busts. Second, we examine the role of monetary policy in the buildup to the current crisis. In particular, we assess the validity of accusations that policymakers created the current crisis by reacting insufficiently to growing inflation pressure or that they raised the likelihood of an asset price bust by placing insufficient weight on credit and asset prices when setting interest rates. Third, we consider whether the goal of monetary policy should be expanded beyond just the stability of goods price inflation, how this could be done, and the potential trade-offs involved.

The chapter presents the following findings. Inflation and output do not typically display unusual behavior ahead of asset price busts. By contrast, credit, the share of investment in GDP, current account deficits, and asset prices typically rise, providing useful leading indicators of asset price busts. These patterns can also be observed in the buildup to the current crisis. Also, in the period since 1985, the stance of monetary policy has not generally been a good leading indicator of future house price busts, consistent with the evidence that inflation and output are poor leading indicators. There is some association between loose monetary policy and house price rises in the years leading up to the current crisis in some countries, but loose monetary policy was not the main, systematic

The main authors of this chapter are Antonio Fatás, Prakash Kannan, Pau Rabanal, and Alasdair Scott, with support from Gavin Asdorian, Andy Salazar, and Jessie Yang. Jordi Galí provided consultancy support.

cause of the boom and consequent bust. If monetary policymakers are to blame, it is mainly for acting too narrowly and not reacting strongly enough to indications of growing financial vulnerability.

This chapter makes the case that putting more emphasis on macrofinancial risk could bring stabilization benefits. Simulations suggest that using a macroprudential instrument designed specifically to dampen credit market cycles would help counter accelerator mechanisms that inflate credit growth and asset prices. In addition, a stronger monetary reaction to signs of overheating or of a credit or asset price bubble could also be useful. Such a broader approach to monetary policy might require that concern for macrofinancial stability be explicitly included in central banks' mandates. However, expectations should be realistic. It is difficult to discern whether credit and asset price booms or surging current account deficits are driven by benign or malign developments. Even the best leading indicators of financial vulnerability are noisy, sometimes sending false signals and raising the risk of policy errors.

The first section of this chapter examines asset price busts during the past 40 years, presenting evidence on the typical costs of such episodes, outlining patterns in macroeconomic variables leading up to the busts, and identifying potential leading indicators of future busts. The second section analyzes whether these patterns held for a cross section of advanced economies in the years leading up to the current crisis. The third section looks at the role of monetary policy in these countries, paying particular attention to the associations between monetary conditions, credit expansion, and house price appreciation. Next, the chapter uses a model-based approach to explore the potential role of monetary and macroprudential policy in dampening house price rises and credit expansion.

The final section discusses policy implications. Data sources and transformations are explained in Appendix 3.2.

Asset Price Busts in the Modern Era

This section examines busts in house and stock prices over the past 40 years. The focus is on key macroeconomic variables in the run-up periods in an attempt to identify systematic patterns in their behavior. The issue of whether or not policymakers should respond to these leading indicators is taken up later in the chapter.

The focus on the run-up to house price and stock price busts is a relatively novel contribution to the literature. Borio and Lowe (2002a) and Gerdesmeier, Reimers, and Roffia (2009) present empirical evidence on how booms in credit, asset prices, and investment have predictive power for banking crises and asset price busts, respectively. In this chapter, house prices and stock prices are examined separately, leading to new results. In particular, we find a recurring pattern of deteriorating current account balances in the run-up to house price busts. Furthermore, this chapter identifies patterns in asset price busts after 1985 that are unique compared with busts that occurred before 1985.[1]

Stylized Facts about Asset Price Busts

The first task for this analysis is to define asset price busts. This chapter uses a simple methodology, similar to that used by Bordo and Jeanne (2002).[2] Busts are defined as periods when the

four-quarter trailing moving average of the annual growth rate of the asset price, in real terms, falls below a particular threshold. The threshold is set at –5 percent for house prices and –20 percent for stock prices.[3] A higher threshold (in absolute terms) is used for stock prices due to the fact that stock prices are typically more volatile. This methodology is objective, easily reproducible, and can be applied consistently across countries. In addition, the thresholds also pick up the major well-known asset price busts—Japan in the early 1990s, the dot-com episode in the 2000s—while still leaving asset price busts as relatively infrequent episodes.

Applying this technique to data for real stock and real house prices identifies 47 house price busts and 98 stock price busts from 1970 to 2008 (Table 3.1).[4] House price busts are generally longer lasting and are associated with greater output loss. The average house price bust lasts for two and a half years, whereas stock price busts last for about one and a half years.[5] The cumulative decline in output below trend is

---

equity busts are roughly equal to the average growth rate of the respective asset prices across the whole sample minus one standard deviation of the growth rates. Bordo and Jeanne use a multiple of 1.3 times the standard deviation of growth rates.

[3]To be clear, a bust occurs when the following condition holds:

$$\frac{g_{t-3} + g_{t-2} + g_{t-1} + g_t}{4} < x \, ,$$

where g is the growth rate of the asset price and x is the relevant threshold (–5 for house prices and –20 for stock prices). If the condition holds, then the periods t–3 through t are labeled as a bust.

[4]The data set consists of quarterly observations on asset prices and macroeconomic variables for 21 advanced economies from 1970 to 2008. Subject to data limitations, the sample includes the following countries: Australia, Austria, Belgium, Canada, Denmark, Finland, France, Germany, Greece, Ireland, Italy, Japan, Netherlands, New Zealand, Norway, Portugal, Spain, Sweden, Switzerland, United Kingdom, and United States. Details are in Appendix 3.2.

[5]The duration of a bust is the amount of time the four-quarter moving average of the growth rate of the asset price remains below the relevant threshold. Because periods t–3 to t are labeled as a bust, there is a minimum duration of one year for all busts.

---

[1]A related strand of literature focuses on asset price booms. Adalid and Detken (2007) and Detken and Smets (2004), for example, document stylized facts on real and financial variables around asset price booms and analyze the influence of liquidity shocks and monetary policy during these episodes. A related paper, Mendoza and Terrones (2008), looks at booms in domestic credit and the associated behavior of macroeconomic and microeconomic variables around these episodes.

[2]Bordo and Jeanne (2002) define a bust as a period when the three-year moving average of the growth rate of asset prices is smaller than the average growth rate minus a multiple of the standard deviation of growth rates. The thresholds that are used in this chapter for housing and

Table 3.1. House Price and Stock Price Busts from 1970 to 2008

	Full Sample		Before 1985		1985–2008	
	House prices	Stock prices	House prices	Stock prices	House prices	Stock prices
Total number of busts	**47**	**98**	**22**	**41**	**25**	**57**
Number of busts per country	2.76	4.67	1.29	1.95	1.47	2.71
Cumulative decline in prices (percent)[1]	−17.71	−37.38	−19.43	−35.27	−15.58	−38.90
Duration (quarters)	10.02	6.98	11.22	7.92	9.74	6.29
Cumulative decline in output (percent relative to trend)[2]	−4.27	−1.31	−5.41	−1.33	−3.27	−1.29

Note: Values are mean values.

[1]Cumulative price decline is measured over the entire duration of the bust period.

[2]Cumulative decline in output is measured as the accumulated deviation from a one-sided Hodrick-Prescott filter with a smoothness parameter of 1600 for the first four quarters of a bust.

roughly 4¼ percent for the first year after the onset of a house price bust,[6] compared with a 1¼ percent decline after stock price busts. These findings mirror those of previous issues of the *World Economic Outlook* (WEO) (April 2003 and April 2008), as well as those of Claessens, Kose, and Terrones (2008).

Figure 3.1 shows that asset price busts are relatively evenly distributed before and after 1985—a year that broadly marks the beginning of the "Great Moderation," a period characterized by substantially lower macroeconomic volatility in advanced economies (see McConnell and Pérez-Quirós, 2000, and Galí and Gambetti, 2009). Several episodes are clustered across countries, including busts in 1974–75, 1983, 1992, and 2008. The current episode is the most widespread cluster of busts for both house prices and stock prices.

Patterns in Macroeconomic Variables in Run-Ups to a Bust

Asset price busts, particularly house price busts, are long and costly. Can they be predicted? Theory suggests that it is not possible to predict the timing of asset price movements, particularly large drops, with a high degree of accuracy. If it were, investors would sell, or short, these assets, and there would be no boom-bust cycles. Even so, there may be some regular

patterns in the behavior of macroeconomic variables that can help indicate the likelihood of a bust, even if they provide only limited insight into its timing.

Before exploring whether there are such macroeconomic patterns, we must first correct for slow-moving trends. Although this analysis focuses, to a large extent, on growth rates, there are slow-moving trends in these rates over the four decades covered by the sample. For example, for almost all the countries, inflation rates were markedly lower during the 1990s than during the 1970s, and therefore looking at deviations from an average calculated on the basis of the full sample would be misleading. The same holds true for output growth, reflecting a diminishing impetus from post–World War II catch-up and population aging. To correct for such slow-moving trends, a trailing eight-year moving average is used as a filter to isolate large or abnormal movements in these variables. The choice of filter was based on three factors. First, it is easily reproducible. Second, the trends for the variables under study are fairly slow moving. Third, this measure—unlike centered moving averages or the popular two-sided Hodrick-Prescott (HP) filter—does not include any information unavailable at the time.[7]

[6]Trend output is measured using a one-sided Hodrick-Prescott (HP) filter with a smoothing coefficient of 1600.

[7]As a robustness check, the analysis was also carried out using a rolling HP filter with a slow-moving trend. Qualitatively similar patterns were obtained. The smoothness parameter was set to 400,000 following Borio and Lowe (2004). See Kannan, Rabanal, and Scott (forthcoming a) for results using this detrending procedure.

Figure 3.1. Asset Price Busts

House price busts and stock price busts have occurred at relatively regular frequencies over the past 40 years. There have been several episodes of clustering, including the present one, during which house price and stock price busts occurred simultaneously in a few economies.

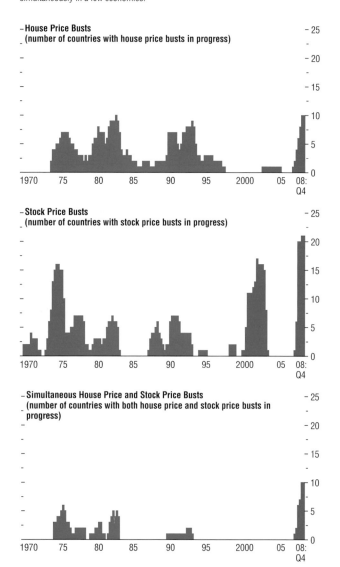

Source: IMF staff calculations.

However, results derived using a one-sided filter should be interpreted carefully. For a variable experiencing a temporary but persistent increase in its growth rate, the deviation from a trailing moving average eventually gets smaller as the trend "catches up" with the higher growth rate. This could, erroneously, be interpreted as a return to normal behavior, even though the variable continues to experience high growth. The choice of an eight-year window for the moving average mitigates this problem somewhat because it lengthens the period over which a boom must persist in order for the trend to catch up.

What patterns do we observe using this detrending procedure? Figure 3.2 shows the behavior of eight key macroeconomic variables around the onset of house price busts before 1985 and during and after 1985. Three factors motivated the decision to split the sample. As mentioned, 1985 marks roughly the beginning of the Great Moderation. Second, the dynamics of asset price busts in the pre-1985 period may have been very different because of the different nature of shocks, such as the two oil crises of the 1970s. Third, during the post-1985 period, financial markets were more liberalized and monetary policy was more consistent—a macroeconomic environment much more similar to today's than to the one before 1985.

Several interesting findings emerge from Figure 3.2. Run-ups to house price busts in 1985 and after feature higher-than-normal growth rates of credit relative to GDP, large deteriorations in current account balances, and higher-than-normal ratios of investment to GDP. Both house and stock prices also grow faster than the eight-year moving average trend, though the difference does not vary significantly from zero within the two years before the busts. Of equal interest, output growth does not display any significant deviation from the measured trend, and inflation is actually *below* its eight-year moving average. Before 1985, there is no pattern of rapid increases in credit relative to GDP or deteriorating current account balances in the run-up to busts, although there are large deviations in inflation coinciding with the two oil crises.

The post-1985 period shows a similar pattern of large increases in credit growth and in the ratio of investment to GDP during the run-up to stock price busts, as shown in Figure 3.3. There are, however, two notable differences between the behavior of macroeconomic variables before stock price busts and before house price busts. First, output growth tends to be significantly higher than trend during the run-up to stock price busts. Second, there is no deterioration in current account balances as there is for house price busts. Even though the median current account balance deteriorates in the year leading up to a stock price bust, the level is not significantly different from zero.

As shown in Table 3.1, asset price busts, particularly house price busts, are costly events. Do macroeconomic variables display different patterns in the run-up to particularly costly house price busts? Figure 3.4 shows the behavior of the same set of variables solely for house price busts from 1985 to 2008. The observations are divided into house price busts that were associated with large falls in output and those that were not.[8] The growth rate of credit relative to output, the share of residential investment in GDP, and the rate of increase of house prices themselves are all higher in costly busts than in episodes that were not as costly. Interestingly, there is no significant difference in inflation and output growth in the run-up to a high-cost bust compared with other busts.

Can These Indicators Predict Asset Price Busts?

There are then some common patterns in the run-up to asset price busts, specifically, a significant expansion in domestic credit and investment shares, often in conjunction with current account deficits, during the two to three years before a bust. But how predictive are

[8]Output losses are computed over the entire duration of a bust. Those that fall in the bottom quartile in terms of total change in output are labeled "high-cost" losses.

Figure 3.2. Selected Macroeconomic Variables before and during House Price Busts

(Median percent deviation from trailing eight-year moving average, unless otherwise noted; asterisk indicates statistically significant difference of post-1985 deviation from zero; t = 1 denotes first quarter of bust)

Since 1985, house price busts have been typically preceded by large deviations in credit relative to GDP, the current account balance, and investment. Output and inflation, on the other hand, do not display such large deviations.

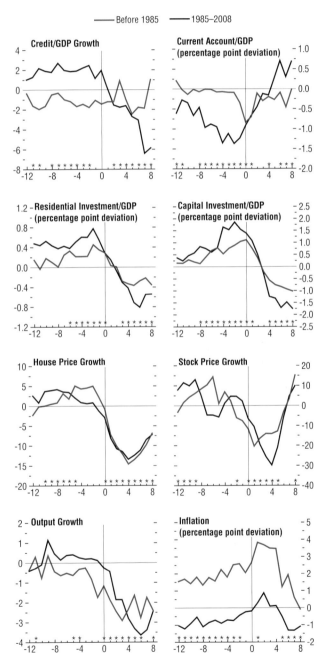

Source: IMF staff calculations.

Figure 3.3. Selected Macroeconomic Variables before and during Stock Price Busts

(Median percent deviation from trailing eight-year moving average, unless otherwise noted; asterisk indicates statistically significant difference of post-1985 deviation from zero; t = 1 denotes first quarter of bust)

The run-up to a stock price bust in the post-1985 period features large increases in credit and capital investment. Unlike house price busts, however, there is no significant deviation in current account balances relative to trend.

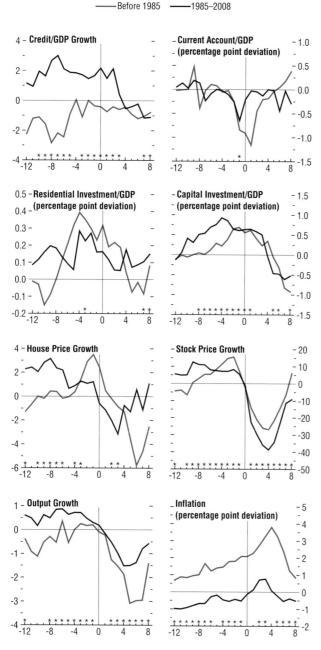

Source: IMF staff calculations.

these variables? From a policymaker's perspective, monitoring, or even reacting to, abnormal growth in these macroeconomic variables can be justified only if they help gauge the risks of asset price busts.

To assess the predictive ability of these variables, we use an approach pioneered by Kaminsky, Lizondo, and Reinhart (1998) and Kaminsky and Reinhart (1999).[9] The approach involves determining whether excessively large movements in particular variables are associated with subsequent busts. Large movements are defined as deviations from an underlying trend, for which the eight-year moving average is used. When the deviation from trend exceeds a particular threshold, we say an "alarm" has been raised. For each quarter, the threshold for each variable for a given country is computed based on observations over the previous 15 years.[10] Whether these alarms are deemed informative depends on their association with subsequent busts.

The choice of a threshold above which an alarm is raised presents an important trade-off between the desire for some warning of an impending bust and the costs associated with a false alarm. A very high threshold, for example, leads to infrequent alarms, because only extreme movements in the variables are captured. These extreme movements may be strong signals of impending asset price busts—and thus reduce the likelihood of a false alarm—but they may miss a large number of busts. With a low threshold, on the other hand, less extreme movements in the variables would more frequently raise alarms. Policymakers would very likely be alerted to impending busts, but would also be subject to a lot of false alarms. Choosing thresholds that minimize the ratio of false to legitimate alarms balances this trade-off.

[9]The analysis of the predictive ability of macroeconomic variables with regard to asset price busts is related to the literature on early warning systems (see Berg and others, 2000, for a survey).
[10]The use of this moving 15-year window dictates that these statistics are calculated and presented only for 1985 and after.

Table 3.2. Classification of Observations Based on Variable Thresholds

	Asset Price Bust 1–3 Years Later	No Asset Price Bust 1–3 Years Later
Alarm raised	A	B
No alarm	C	D

Here, the same percentile threshold is used for a particular variable across all countries, but the actual cutoff value differs from country to country because of the varying distributions of the variables.[11]

Each observation for a given variable can be classified into one of four categories, as shown in Table 3.2. Deviations in the credit-to-GDP ratio illustrate how the observations can be classified. The 90th percentile of the distribution of this variable has the smallest ratio of false alarms to legitimate alarms, which makes this a suitable threshold. An observation on this variable above the 90th percentile is considered to raise an alarm, placing the observation in the first row of the matrix. If an asset price bust occurs within a particular time frame (discussed later) after the alarm, that alarm is considered a legitimate alarm and is placed into cell A. If there is no bust, that alarm is considered to be only noise and is placed into cell B. An analogous classification procedure determines the placement of observations into cells C and D. Ideally, all observations would fall into cells A or D, which correctly predict the occurrence or nonoccurrence of a bust.

Two statistics that can be derived from this approach are of particular interest. The first is a measure of the conditional probability of a bust, which is the probability that a bust will occur within a particular time horizon once an alarm

[11]More specifically, we choose the threshold based on percentiles of the distribution of deviations such that the noise-to-signal ratio—defined as the ratio of the share of false alarms to legitimate alarms—is minimized. To avoid the influence of extreme observations, we limit our grid search to four percentiles: 70th, 75th, 80th, and 90th. For the thresholds used, see Table 3.5 in Appendix 3.1.

Figure 3.4. Selected Macroeconomic Variables before and during High-Cost and Other House Price Busts, 1985–2008

(Median percent deviation from trailing eight-year moving average, unless otherwise noted; asterisk indicates statistically significant difference between medians; t = 1 denotes first quarter of bust)

House price busts that are associated with larger output losses typically feature larger deviations in credit growth, residential investment, and house price growth. No significant differences are found for output growth and inflation.

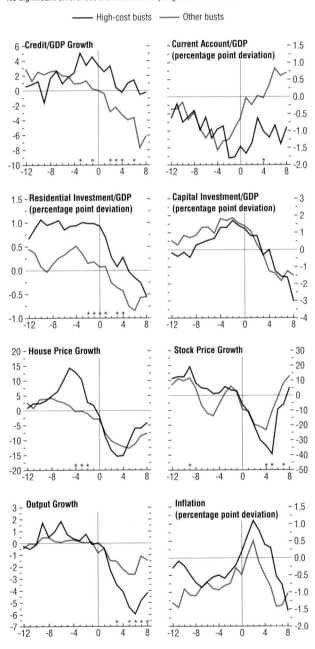

Source: IMF staff calculations.

Figure 3.5. The Probability of an Asset Price Bust

(Percent of times a bust occurs 1–3 years after an alarm is raised relative to the unconditional probability of a bust)

For house price busts since 1985, large deviations in credit, current account, and residential investment to GDP are particularly predictive of the likelihood of an impending bust. In the case of stock price busts, these variables are also more predictive than the unconditional probability, though the difference is smaller.

■ 1985–2008

House Price Busts

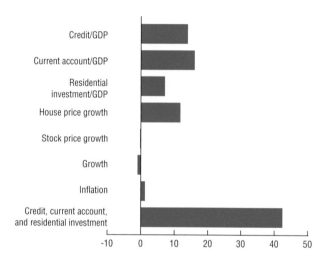

Stock Price Busts

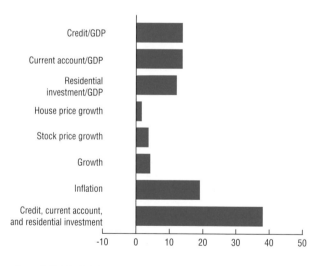

Source: IMF staff calculations.

has been raised based on a particular variable.[12] The second is a measure of the predictive ability (or lack thereof) of the variables, which essentially captures the proportion of periods during which a bust occurred one to three years in the future but for which no alarm was raised.[13] These two statistics capture the trade-off involved in the choice of a suitable threshold. An extremely high threshold that identifies only one observation from the sample will perform well on the conditional probability measure if a bust occurs within a particular time horizon, but will fare poorly on the other measure because no alarm would be raised for most of the busts.

Computing these probabilities also involves selecting the appropriate time horizon. If the horizon is too short, the alarm will have no operational relevance because any action by policymakers would be too late to affect the economy and forestall or mitigate the bust. If the horizon is too long, the alarm becomes uninformative, meaning that it loses its predictive ability. We chose a horizon that considers an alarm legitimate if it successfully predicts a bust within three years, with a minimum lead time of one year.

Figure 3.5 shows the difference between the conditional probability of a bust occurring one to three years after an alarm has been raised and the unconditional probability of a bust over the same horizon. This gauges the predictive ability of the conditional probability measures. In the sample, the unconditional probability of a house price bust occurring one to three years in the future is 14 percent during the post-1985 period. For stock price busts, the corresponding probability is 29 percent.

In the post-1985 period, large deviations in credit relative to GDP, in the current account balance, in the residential investment share of GDP, and in house prices themselves are particularly predictive of an impending house

[12]In terms of the matrix presented in Table 3.2, this statistic can be computed as A divided by (A+B).

[13]In this case, the relevant statistic is C divided by (A+C).

price bust. Large deviations in the credit-to-GDP ratio, for example, are associated with a 28 percent probability of a house price bust one to three years in the future, which is twice the unconditional probability of such a bust. Large deviations in output and inflation—the conventional components of monetary policy rules in the academic literature—have little ability to predict house price busts. For stock price busts, output and inflation perform slightly better as leading indicators, but credit, the current account balance, and residential investment have much more predictive ability, as they do for house price busts. The degree of significance of the marginal predictive ability of these variables is confirmed in a formal econometric (probit) analysis (see Table 3.6 in Appendix 3.1).

These results suggest that large deviations in the ratios of credit, the current account, and residential investment to GDP are significant predictors of asset price busts. What happens when all three variables raise alarms at the same time? The bottom bars in each panel of Figure 3.5 indicate that 56 percent of these occasions were associated with a house price bust one to three years in the future.[14] The ratio is roughly the same in the case of predicting stock price busts.

These results should be interpreted with caution. As mentioned, the most predictive thresholds for these variables may be those that result in identification of just a few observations that yield particularly reliable alarms. When considering the simultaneous raising of alarms by all three variables, this restriction becomes more severe. To complement the analysis, therefore, we look at the proportion of periods during which the indicators fail to raise an alarm one to three years ahead of a bust (Figure 3.6). Large deviations in variables such as credit to GDP, current account to GDP, and residential investment to GDP raise alarms in advance of a bust only one-quarter to one-half of the time during

[14]The percentage is computed as the sum of the percentage indicated in the bar and the unconditional probability of each type of bust.

Figure 3.6. The Failure of the Indicators to Predict an Asset Price Bust
(Percent of quarters the variables failed to raise an alarm 1–3 years before a bust)

Even though large deviations in credit, the current account, and investment to GDP are good predictors of asset price busts, they raised alarms only about one-quarter to one-half of the time prior to a bust in the post-1985 period.

1985–2008

House Price Busts

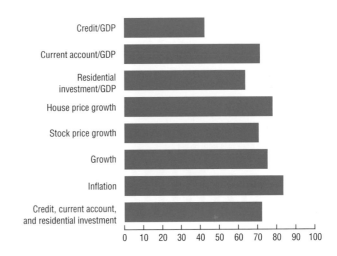

Stock Price Busts

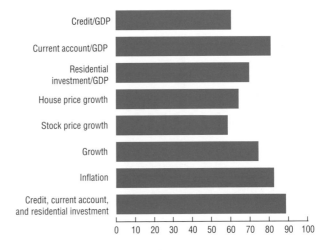

Source: IMF staff calculations.

Figure 3.7. Recent Developments in House and Stock Prices[1]

With the exception of Germany and Japan (which are experiencing secular declines in house prices), most economies have experienced strong rises in asset prices, followed by sharp falls. The extent of house price falls is related to the extent of previous house price rises. The extent of recent stock price falls is similar across countries but does not closely relate to the extent of previous rises.

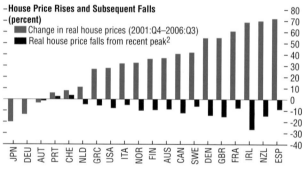

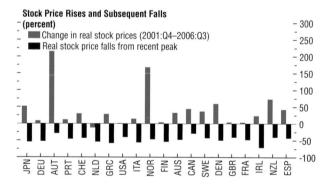

Sources: Bank for International Settlements; Bloomberg Financial Markets; Haver Analytics; IMF, *International Financial Statistics;* Organization for Economic Cooperation and Development; and IMF staff calculations.

[1]AUS: Australia; AUT: Austria; BEL: Belgium; CAN: Canada; CHE: Switzerland; DEN: Denmark; DEU: Germany; ESP: Spain; GBR: United Kingdom; GRC: Greece; FIN: Finland; FRA: France; IRL: Ireland; ITA: Italy; JPN: Japan; NLD: Netherlands; NOR: Norway; NZL: New Zealand; PRT: Portugal; SWE: Sweden; USA: United States.

[2]Not shown for Germany and Japan as real prices declined through the 2001:Q4–2006:Q3 period.

the post-1985 period. The most reliable indicator is credit, which raises an alarm in one-half of all cases.

In summary, large booms in credit and investment, as well as deteriorating current account balances, substantially increase the probability of a bust occurring in the near future. When these indicators raise an alarm, the probability of a bust is more than twice the unconditional probability. Nonetheless, even the best indicator failed to raise an alarm one to three years ahead of roughly one-half of all busts since 1985. Thus, asset price busts are difficult to predict.

Macroeconomic Patterns ahead of the Current Crisis

These findings lead to the following question: Do the patterns associated with previous episodes of asset price busts show up ahead of the current crisis? Undoubtedly, recent years saw several important developments, such as innovations in securitization, that might suggest the current crisis is fundamentally different from previous crises. However, for house prices, this crisis had a very familiar macroeconomic pattern: house price busts were preceded by strong growth in credit, worsening current account balances, and house price booms.

Figure 3.7 shows average annual real house and stock price growth across all economies in the sample from the start of 1995 through 2008. Apart from the current episode, stock prices experienced one other boom-bust cycle during this period. Real house prices registered strong growth rates, on average, until 2007. Subsequently, most economies experienced falls in asset values that are severe by historical standards. Asset price paths differ widely across countries. From the fourth quarter of 2001 through the third quarter of 2006, real house prices rose strongly in Ireland, New Zealand, and Spain, but fell in Austria, Germany, and Japan.[15] Consistent with the results from

[15]These dates were chosen because they cover the period during which most economies (except for Austria,

previous issues of the *World Economic Outlook* (April 2003 and April 2008), larger house price increases have generally, though not uniformly, been followed by larger decreases from recent peaks. Except for Germany and Japan, which have been experiencing long-term declines in real house prices, the correlation between house price rises and subsequent falls is 0.79.[16] In contrast, the recent fall in stock prices was relatively uniform across countries and was largely unrelated to previous stock price rises.

Were the macroeconomic indicators identified in the previous section associated with the recent asset price busts? Figure 3.8 shows the proportion of countries that experienced house price busts for which the credit-to-GDP, residential-investment-to-GDP, and current-account-to-GDP variables were raising alarms, based on the definitions in the previous section. Signs of a residential investment boom, in some cases funded by current account declines, are apparent in at least half the economies one to three years before the onset of house price busts. Credit growth was unusually high in roughly half the economies over almost the entire three-year period. The alarm from the current account is more muted until about one year ahead of the bust, when it was raised for nearly half the countries.

Figure 3.9 shows how recent cross-country variations in house price changes are associated with variations in credit growth, residential investment, and current account relative to GDP. Economies with the largest house price appreciations also had large increases in residential investment as a share of GDP, large current account deficits as a share of GDP, and large expansions of credit relative to the expansion in output. Furthermore, stronger credit growth was also typically matched by more severe deteriorations in household balance sheets: a version of a

Germany, and Japan) experienced steady rises in house prices, ending with the peak in house prices in Ireland.

[16]House price falls are defined as the percentage difference between the recent peak in the economy's house prices and the latest data available (either 2008:Q3 or 2008:Q4, depending on the economy).

Figure 3.8. Warning Signs for Recent House Price Busts
(Percent of countries with recent house price busts that raised alarms)

Residential investment booms were observed for more than half the economies that subsequently experienced a house price bust. Credit booms and large deviations from trend in current account balances were also observed for a significant proportion of these economies.

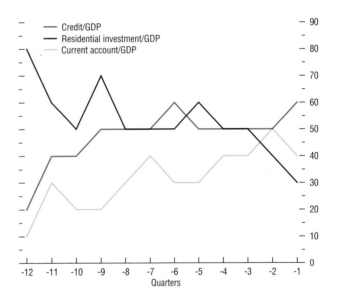

Source: IMF staff calculations.

Figure 3.9. Macroeconomic Patterns Underlying Recent House Price Booms[1]

Larger real house price booms in recent years have been associated with larger increases in residential investment, deteriorations in current account balances, and larger expansions in credit.

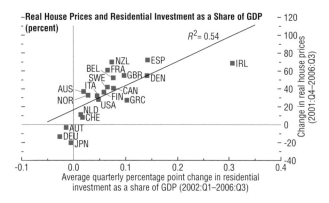

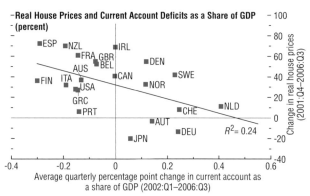

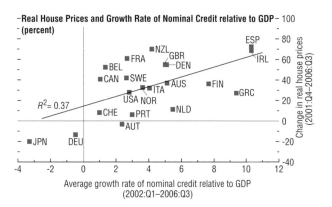

Sources: Bank for International Settlements; Bloomberg Financial Markets; Haver Analytics; IMF, *International Financial Statistics;* Organization for Economic Cooperation and Development; and IMF staff calculations.

[1]See Figure 3.7 for country abbreviations.

household "quick ratio"—the ratio of liabilities to liquid assets (deposits and currency)—was found to be highly associated with house price growth (Figure 3.10).[17] At the macroeconomic level, therefore, the evidence suggests that this was a conventional crisis in that it displayed patterns historically evident in asset price booms and busts. A key question, then, is whether these boom-bust cycles resulted from monetary policy actions.

The Role of Monetary Policy

Two criticisms have been leveled against monetary policymakers:

- The first criticism is that monetary policy was too loose from 2002 to 2006—in particular, that central banks held the policy rate below the level specified by a simple rule for reacting to an output gap and inflation.[18] Had monetary policymakers not deviated from a Taylor rule, goes the argument, the rise in asset prices—and, by implication, the current crisis—would have been avoided. Note that the essence of this argument is that monetary excesses were the main cause of the booms and subsequent busts.

- The second criticism argues that setting monetary policy by looking only at consumer price index (CPI) inflation and the output gap is too narrow an approach: in a simple version, monetary policy should lean against unsustainable asset price rises or developments that raise financial vulnerability, even at the cost of more variability in inflation and output.[19]

[17]These measures were constructed from nonconsolidated household balance sheet data from the Organization for Economic Cooperation and Development (OECD). The ratio of loans to disposable income fitted poorly. The United Kingdom and United States stand out with very high maturity ratios (ratios of long- to short-term liabilities), but these do not have explanatory power for house price changes during this period.

[18]See Taylor (2007 and 2008). Taylor cites Ahrend, Cournède, and Price (2008) as support for the argument that policy failures were widespread and not limited to the U.S. Federal Reserve.

[19]See, among others, Borio and Lowe (2002b and 2004) and White (2006). A more far-reaching ver-

These criticisms are difficult to answer conclusively because they require assessing the counterfactual—what would have happened had different policy choices been made. However, an analysis of monetary conditions and asset prices during the years before the recent asset price busts sheds some light on the validity of the first criticism. (The validity of the second is evaluated in the following section using a model-based approach.)

Overall, since 1985, monetary policy conditions are generally not a good leading indicator of house price busts. Figure 3.11 tracks two standard measures of monetary policy stance in the run-up to house price busts. As in the previous section, patterns around busts before 1985 and during and after 1985 are examined separately. The upper panel shows the behavior of real policy rates,[20] and the lower panel shows the deviation of these rates from a standard Taylor rule, which takes into account business cycle developments.[21] There is some evidence of loose monetary policy in the run-up to house price busts before 1985. One interpretation is that monetary policy during that period did not react sufficiently to inflation, such as that generated by the oil shocks.

In the period since 1985, taken as a whole, real policy rates were typically above trend in the run-up to a house price bust and high when compared with those implied by a Taylor rule. Furthermore, the dynamics of real rates suggest that, if anything, rates actually increased in the years leading up to a bust. However, both real interest rates and residuals from Taylor rules

sion of this criticism is that current implementations of best-practice monetary policy—especially in formal inflation-targeting regimes—can themselves raise overall macroeconomic instability by focusing exclusively on too narrow a definition of stability—namely, goods market inflation. A related criticism—the "paradox of credibility"—is that success at lowering and anchoring inflation expectations may encourage a form of money illusion (see, for example, Borio and Shim, 2007).

[20]As in the previous section, these data are presented as deviations from an eight-year trailing average.

[21]The rule has weights of 1.5 on deviations of inflation from its target level and 0.5 on the output gap. See Taylor (1993).

Figure 3.10. Recent House Price Booms and Household Balance Sheets[1]

Larger credit expansions have been associated with larger deteriorations in balance sheets.

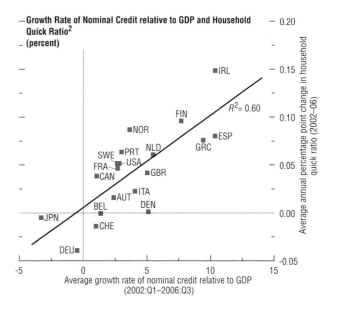

Sources: Bank for International Settlements; Haver Analytics; IMF, *International Financial Statistics;* Organization for Economic Cooperation and Development; and IMF staff calculations.
[1]See Figure 3.7 for country abbreviations.
[2]Ratio of liabilities to liquid assets (deposits and currency).

Figure 3.11. Monetary Policy before House Price Busts

(Percentage points; t *= 1 denotes first quarter of bust)*

In the post-1985 period as a whole, house price busts have typically not been preceded by loose monetary policy. However, monetary policy may have been too loose, on average, in recent years.

——— Busts before 1985 ——— 1985–2008 busts ——— Recent busts[1]

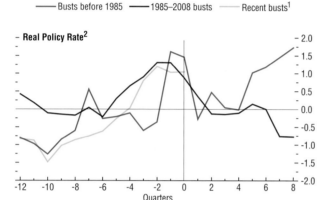

Source: IMF staff calculations.
[1]Recent busts comprise 10 busts beginning after 2007:Q1 in Australia, Canada, Denmark, Finland, Ireland, New Zealand, Norway, Spain, United Kingdom, and United States.
[2]Deviation from eight-year moving average.
[3]Deviation from a policy rule of the form $r = r^* + 0.5\,(\pi - \pi^*) + 0.5\,(y - y^*)$, where the starred variables are computed as the trailing eight-year moving average.

were negative, on average, one to three years before the recent busts, followed by a sharp tightening of monetary conditions during the year preceding the crash. This may be evidence of overly loose monetary policy. However, in most economies, policymakers looking only at CPI inflation would not have seen obvious signs of a problem during this period. Figure 3.12 shows that core inflation in the United States, the euro area, and, on average, the other advanced economies (with the exception of Japan) stayed within 1–3 percent throughout the period during which credit was expanding and asset prices were booming. One interpretation advanced at the time—which is addressed in the next section—is that higher asset prices and demand for credit reflected expected gains in productivity.

If monetary policy were the fundamental cause of house price booms over the past decade, there would be a systematic relationship between monetary policy conditions and house price gains across economies. Certainly, average real policy rates were low and even negative in some economies, and Taylor rule residuals were mostly negative, suggesting that monetary policy was generally accommodative across economies during this period. But there is, at best, a weak association with house price developments within the euro area (Figure 3.13, blue lines).[22] And there is virtually no association between the measures of monetary policy stance and house price increases in the full sample (Figure 3.13, black lines). For example, whereas Ireland and Spain had low real short-term rates and large house price rises, Australia, New Zealand, and the United Kingdom had relatively high real rates and large house price rises. Moreover, the association between measures of the monetary policy stance and real stock price growth is

---

[22]The real policy rate here is constructed by deflating nominal gross policy rates by Consensus Economics expectations of gross CPI inflation one year forward. (Consensus Economics expectations data are not available for all economies in the sample before 1995, which prevented their use in measuring real rates in the previous sections.)

extremely weak, whether assessed during the global house price boom (2001:Q4–2006:Q3; not shown) or during a later period, when stock markets rallied from their troughs (2003:Q1) through the stock market declines of 2007 (Figure 3.14).

The fairly regular behavior of inflation and output and the fact that Taylor rule residuals were not associated with recent asset price rises across economies in the sample suggest that monetary policy was not the main or systematic source of the recent asset price booms.[23] At the same time, evidence outlined in previous sections underscores that the asset price bust that started in 2007 did not come out of the blue, in the sense that key macroeconomic variables showed patterns similar to those ahead of historical asset price booms and busts. Should policymakers have reacted to these signals and alarms, by placing greater emphasis on financial stability and less emphasis on inflation? This question is addressed in the next section.

Should Policymakers React to Asset Market Fluctuations?

This analysis has identified a number of macroeconomic variables that are often associated with asset price busts, although their predictive ability is not as consistent nor as strong as policymakers might hope. Those same variables do reasonably well in explaining the differences across economies in house price rises leading up to the current crisis. This suggests that central bankers should consider reacting more strongly to indicators other than just output and inflation in order to mitigate damaging asset price boom-bust cycles. There are three important

[23]One assumption in this analysis is that monetary policy decisions in one economy were independent of those in other economies, which is a common conclusion given floating exchange rates and a free flow of capital. Some argue that monetary policy decisions in the United States have more influence on monetary conditions in other economies than this assumption allows. This awaits rigorous empirical testing.

Figure 3.12. Inflation and Output for Advanced Economies in Recent Years

(Percent)

Core consumer price index (CPI) inflation and output gaps stayed within narrow ranges for most economies in recent years, during which time credit expanded rapidly and asset prices boomed.

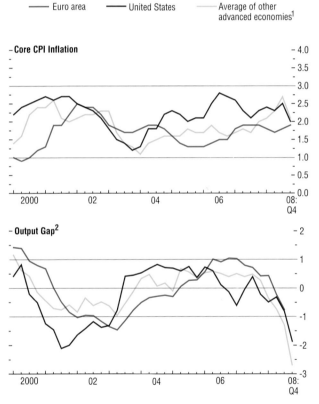

Sources: Haver Analytics; and IMF staff calculations.
[1]Japan omitted.
[2]Estimate of output gap using rolling Hodrick-Prescott filter.

Figure 3.13. House Prices and Monetary Conditions[1]

In economies with common nominal monetary policy rates, looser real monetary conditions in recent years were associated with larger rises in real house prices. Across advanced economies as a whole, there was little significant correlation in recent years between real monetary conditions and real house prices.

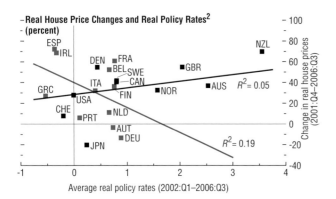

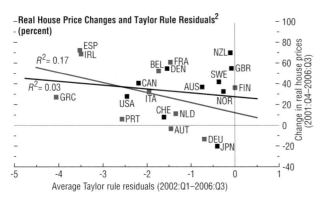

Sources: Bank for International Settlements; Bloomberg Financial Markets; Haver Analytics; national authorities; Organization for Economic Cooperation and Development; Thomson Datastream; and IMF staff calculations.
[1] See Figure 3.7 for country abbreviations.
[2] Euro area economies are designated by blue squares. Other advanced economies are designated by red squares. Blue lines are fitted to a subsample of euro area economies. Black lines are fitted to the whole sample of advanced economies.

questions to be addressed in assessing the appropriate policy responses:

- What are the potential gains from reacting to signs of emerging financial vulnerability, such as excessive credit growth?
- Is monetary policy the appropriate tool for reacting to such indicators, or should other policies be used?
- What are the trade-offs between focusing policy on stabilizing output and CPI inflation and attempting to reduce the risk of asset price booms and busts?

This section addresses these questions with simulations conducted using a model economy with some of the key features relevant for examining the potential role of monetary policy in mitigating the effects of asset price booms. Because housing wealth is generally more important than equities for most households, and because house purchases typically require bank credit, the focus is on house price booms rather than stock price booms.[24]

A Model for Analyzing House Price Booms

The model used here has conventional New Keynesian foundations; in particular, prices generally do not adjust immediately. This means that monetary policy has a potential role in stabilizing the economy because it influences real interest rates. Consumption and residential investment adjust slowly, and it is costly for workers to shift from producing consumption goods to building houses, and vice versa. In addition, there are a number of modifications to the standard model with regard to the characterization of households and financial markets, which create a special role for the housing market.[25] First, households make choices about

---

[24]For a model that considers the monetary policy implications of stock price fluctuations, see Christiano, Motto, and Rostagno (2007). For simplicity, there is no capital used in production, and the economy is closed.

[25]The model draws on elements of models by Aoki, Proudman, and Vlieghe (2004); Cúrdia and Woodford (2009); Iacoviello (2005); and Monacelli (2009). See also the April 2008 WEO. The accelerator mechanism goes

the consumption of nondurable goods and how much to invest in housing. Housing is an asset that provides services and is the main vehicle for accumulating wealth in this economy. Second, there is a distinction between borrowers and lenders, creating conditions for leverage. Third, the lending rate is modeled as a spread over the policy rate that depends on loan-to-value ratios, the markup charged over funding (policy) rates, and, in some cases (discussed later), a macroprudential instrument. Hence, lending rates can change for a number of reasons: for example, a rise in house prices will raise market valuations of borrowers' collateral, lower the average loan-to-value ratio, and therefore lead to a fall in lending rates even if monetary policy has not eased. Credit market conditions can change—because of, say, changes in perceptions of risk or competitiveness in lending—which could lead banks to adjust their markups and therefore alter the lending spread. Both of these mechanisms help accelerate a rise in residential investment, nondurable consumption, and prices. In some simulations, policymakers can affect spreads directly, using a macroprudential tool, in addition to influencing lending rates via policy rates. Finally, debt is important for financing the purchase of houses—the loan-to-value ratio fluctuates around an average over time of 80 percent.

The behavior of the model economy is examined under different policy regimes, following shocks that produce sustained rises in residential investment and house prices.[26] The objective is

---

back to Bernanke, Gertler, and Gilchrist (BGG, 1998); unlike BGG, the accelerator in this model works through housing finance rather than firms' capital. For a detailed description of the model, see Kannan, Rabanal, and Scott (forthcoming b).

[26]We rank policy regimes in terms of the evenly weighted variances of the output gap and CPI inflation. The output gap in this model is the difference between aggregate and potential output (GDP). Potential output is defined as the level of aggregate production in this economy when nominal rigidities and financial frictions are removed—that is, prices are assumed to be flexible in both sectors, all agents have the same discount factor, and there is no spread between borrowing and lending rates. The output gap is an appropriate target, from a welfare

Figure 3.14. Stock Prices and Monetary Conditions[1]

There has been little significant correlation between real monetary conditions in recent years and real stock prices, whether in economies with common nominal monetary policy rates or across advanced economies as a whole.

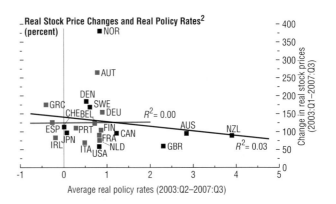

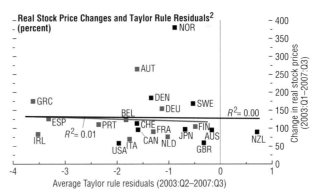

Sources: Bloomberg Financial Markets; IMF, *International Financial Statistics;* and IMF staff calculations.
[1]See Figure 3.7 for country abbreviations.
[2]Euro area economies are designated by blue squares. Other advanced economies are designated by red squares. Blue lines are fitted to a subsample of euro area economies. Black lines are fitted to the whole sample of advanced economies.

to determine which policy regime is better at stabilizing the economy in the face of pressures on the housing market—policies that can help prevent financial vulnerabilities, rather than help pick up the pieces after a bust. The conclusions that can be drawn from this analysis depend crucially on which shocks drive the house price boom. To illustrate the importance of correctly identifying the drivers of the housing boom, we test the policy regimes with two shocks: a financial shock that prompts a relaxation in lending standards, and a positive productivity shock.[27] Although asset booms can arise from expectations of future capital gains, without any change in fundamentals, we do not model bubbles or "irrational exuberance."[28] Similarly, we do not attempt to model events that trigger house price crashes.

Policymakers are assumed to have nominal short-term interest rates and, potentially, the macroprudential instrument at their disposal. The macroprudential instrument affects lending rates—policymakers can directly offset, to some degree, fluctuations in spreads caused by the

changes in collateral values and financial shocks. This is a simple shortcut intended to mimic the effects of, say, regulations that require banks to set aside more capital as asset prices rise, hence raising the margin that banks have to charge over funding costs (the policy rate).

The baseline policy regime is a *standard Taylor rule,* specified with a weight of 1.5 on CPI inflation and 0.5 on the output gap. With that benchmark, we investigate gains to be achieved by incorporating indicators of potential financial vulnerability. Hence, the second regime is implemented as an *augmented Taylor rule,* in which monetary policy rates react to changes in nominal credit, in addition to CPI inflation and the output gap.[29] The third regime introduces a *macroprudential rule* that specifies the reaction of a macroprudential instrument (which alters the spread between the lending and the policy rate) to lagged nominal credit changes (the same variable as in the augmented Taylor rule). Combining the macroprudential instrument with the augmented Taylor rule produces the third policy regime.[30] The final policy regime is a variation on the third, in which the weight on each variable is determined by an optimization procedure that seeks the best response to the particular shock being considered. All variables in these policy rules are lagged.[31]

---

perspective, because GDP is the sum of output of both consumption and the housing sector. Monetary and regulatory policy should aim to reduce the impact of nominal and financial distortions in the economy. CPI inflation is the rate of change of prices for consumption goods and does not include house price inflation; hence, it is not fully appropriate as a welfare metric. We deliberately assess the policies in terms of CPI inflation to facilitate comparison with most of the monetary policy literature and conventional goals of central bankers; in general, assessing policies in terms of house price inflation as well would strengthen the case for broader policies.

[27]The financial shock can be thought of as a reduction in the margin banks charge over funding costs, caused by an increase in competition and a quest for market share or by a reduction in perceived lending risk. The productivity increase is modeled as a shock to labor-augmenting productivity of nondurable consumption goods. Both shocks are temporary but quite persistent—they follow AR(1) processes with persistence parameters set at 0.95. Note that, once the shock hits the economy, we assume both households and policymakers immediately understand what the shock is and how it will be transmitted through the economy.

[28]This is not a comment on the likelihood of bubbles; it is a reflection of the fact that there are currently no tractable models of irrational bubbles that can be incorporated into models of this type.

[29]Nominal credit is defined as real credit multiplied by the GDP deflator, which is a weighted average of CPI and house price indices.

[30]In these three regimes, all monetary policy reactions are smoothed by imposing a weight of 0.7 on the lagged nominal interest rate and 0.3 on the policy variables. (The weight is optimized in the fourth regime.)

[31]These lags are introduced on the grounds that, in real life, policymakers have data for the output gap and inflation only after some delay; data for money aggregates and credit are available more readily. Including contemporaneous credit in the rules would increase the value of credit as an indicator and therefore bias the conclusions in favor of extended frameworks. To avoid this, credit is also introduced with a lag.

The Performance of Policy Rules in Reaction to Financial Shocks

Figure 3.15 shows the response to a financial shock, modeled as a relaxation in lending standards that immediately reduces lending rates by 100 basis points in the baseline Taylor policy regime (black line). Three other paths are shown, corresponding to the other policy regimes. In the Taylor policy regime, monetary policy is guided by the simple Taylor rule with no macroprudential reaction. The financial shock causes an immediate increase in residential investment and house prices. Because banks are assumed to lower lending rates when collateral rises, the shock feeds on itself: housing demand raises house prices, collateral values increase, lending rates are lowered, and households take out more loans. This is the credit accelerator mechanism at work. In addition, lower rates lead to higher demand for nondurable consumption goods, pushing up CPI inflation. Some characteristics of a house price bust are evident in the aftermath of this shock: as financial conditions normalize, residential investment—and with it, house prices—must *undershoot* for a period to bring the housing stock back to equilibrium. This process spills over to the rest of the economy, causing a temporary recession and raising volatility in all markets. The reaction of a central bank following a simple Taylor rule is straightforward: to the extent that the output gap and CPI inflation are positive following the increase in housing demand, policy rates are raised. Eventually, output and inflation stabilize.

The second policy regime is the augmented Taylor rule, under which the central bank reacts directly to credit in addition to the output gap and inflation. For illustration, we assume the central bank puts the same weight (0.5) on changes in nominal credit as on the output gap (Table 3.3, upper panel, second row). This rule produces greater stability across the board as shown in the figure: the volatility of residential investment is lower, there is a considerable reduction in the volatility of GDP and the

Figure 3.15. Effects of a Financial Shock

(Deviation from steady state; quarters on x-axis)

The figure shows impulse response to an unanticipated financial shock in the first quarter. The size of the shock is normalized such that it leads to a 1 percent decline of the lending rate on impact under the Taylor rule regime. Paths denote different policy regimes.

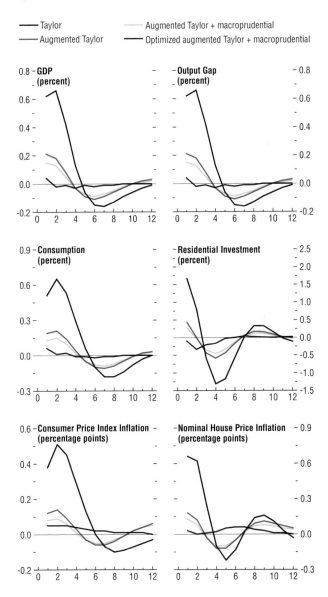

Source: IMF staff calculations.

Table 3.3. Parameters and Performance of Policy Regimes in Reaction to Financial Shocks

	Weights under Each Regime				
	Lagged interest rates in monetary policy rule	Inflation in monetary policy rule	Output gap in monetary policy rule	Nominal credit in monetary policy rule	Nominal credit in macroprudential rule
Taylor	0.7	1.5	0.5	. . .	. . .
Augmented Taylor	0.7	1.5	0.5	0.5	. . .
Augmented Taylor + macroprudential	0.7	1.5	0.5	0.5	0.5
Optimized augmented Taylor + macroprudential	0.0	13.2	3.2	0.0	0.8

	Performance			
	Standard deviation of inflation	Standard deviation of output gap	Loss[1]	Ranking
Taylor	0.512	0.624	0.652	4
Augmented Taylor	0.110	0.076	0.018	3
Augmented Taylor + macroprudential	0.092	0.061	0.012	2
Optimized augmented Taylor + macroprudential	0.018	0.040	0.002	1

Source: IMF staff calculations.

[1]Loss equals the sum of the variances of output gap and consumer price index inflation.

output gap, and house prices and CPI inflation are less volatile (see also the standard deviations in Table 3.3, lower panel, second row, compared with those in the first row).[32]

Macroeconomic stabilization is even better served under the third policy regime, under which the central bank complements the augmented Taylor rule with the use of the macroprudential instrument (Table 3.3, lower panel, third row). For illustration, the growth rate of nominal credit in the macroprudential rule has a weight of 0.5, with the other weights maintained as for the augmented Taylor rule. The

macroprudential rule allows policymakers to directly counter the relaxation of lending standards that induces borrowers to take on more debt as house prices rise.

To summarize, adding another indicator to the monetary policy reaction function can improve macroeconomic stability when the economy is hit by a financial shock. The responses hint that policy reactions guided by the standard Taylor rule are too weak in the face of loosened lending standards and credit accelerator effects, with the consequence that housing investment is insufficiently dampened. But the parameters in the augmented Taylor and macroprudential rules used here are ad hoc. In fact, if the objective is simply to stabilize the output gap and inflation, the optimal weights on the output gap and inflation in the monetary policy rules under this sort of "microfounded" model are generally much higher than the Taylor weights (see Woodford, 2001). This implies that the improvement in stability

[32]The volatility of interest rates is lower as well, even though the policy rule is more aggressive. This is because a model with fully forward-looking private agents, such as this one, has very strong expectational effects—households anticipate a stronger reaction from the central bank and factor it into their decision making. The result is that monetary policy works through the threat of a stronger reaction, rather than by actually delivering that stronger reaction.

from adding nominal credit to the monetary policy rule and employing the macroprudential instrument could simply indicate that, under the baseline Taylor rule, the reaction to the output gap and inflation is insufficient.

To address this issue, we also model a policy regime with the augmented Taylor and macroprudential rules optimized to minimize the variation in the output gap and in inflation. As expected, the optimized rules are the most successful in stabilizing the economy and come close to producing the efficient reaction—no output gap at all.[33] More interesting are the optimized weights (Table 3.3, upper panel, fourth row). Optimal monetary policy is very aggressive—the weights on the output gap and inflation are multiples of those in either the standard Taylor rule or typical estimated monetary reaction functions, and the optimized weight on interest rate smoothing is zero. The weight on nominal credit in setting the policy rate is zero.[34] Crucially, however, the optimal weight on nominal credit in the macroprudential rule is *not* zero; in fact, it is slightly more than the weight used before (0.8). Hence, macroprudential policy is unambiguously useful for dealing with financial shocks, even when the central bank is free to use policy rates very aggressively. Using the macroprudential tool is a more efficient reaction to loosening credit markets than simply raising policy rates, because it tackles the problem at its root.

The Performance of Policy Rules in Reaction to Productivity Shocks

Broader and more aggressive policy regimes can improve stability in the face of financial

shocks, but they raise the possibility of policy mistakes in the face of other types of shocks. This is evident from the second set of simulations, which shows the reactions to an increase in productivity in the nondurable goods sector that, in the case of the Taylor rule, delivers an immediate 1 percent increase in output (Figure 3.16).[35] The results of this shock also resemble a housing boom: residential investment, house prices, and the demand for credit all rise, just as in response to a financial shock. However, the prices of consumption goods fall. Indeed, the fact that CPI inflation was contained in recent years while asset prices surged led many policymakers to conclude that asset price rises were being driven by positive productivity shocks.

The best policy for dealing with a productivity shock is for the central bank to accommodate the improvement in productivity as much as possible. Policies to suppress private sector borrowing would be misguided, as shown in the figure: following the augmented Taylor and macroprudential rules, with the same parameter values as for the financial shock, accentuates the downward pressure on prices (CPI index) and output, because of the reaction to credit growth. The result is that the output gap and inflation are *more* volatile, not less (Table 3.4, lower panel, second and third rows). Among the first three policy regimes—Taylor, augmented Taylor, augmented Taylor with macroprudential instrument—the best is the standard Taylor rule. The optimized regime has higher weights on the output gap and inflation, as before, but the model does not support using the macroprudential tool at all (Table 3.4, upper panel, fourth row). These results suggest that policy reactions to indicators of potential financial vulnerability should be neither automatic nor rigid—policymakers need room for discretion.

[33]The efficient reaction is desirable from a welfare point of view but is not possible within this model because of nominal rigidities and distortions in financial markets.

[34]In the augmented Taylor rule, the weight on credit was positive, and this held even when this rule was combined with a macroprudential instrument. This reflected lower-than-optimal Taylor rule weights on the output gap and inflation (0.5 and 1.5, respectively). A similar result is documented in Iacoviello (2005).

[35]Although the shock is centered on the production of nondurable consumption goods, households spend more on residential investment and nondurables consumption because of expectations for higher income.

Figure 3.16. Effects of a Productivity Shock

(Deviation from steady state; quarters on x-axis)

The figure shows impulse response to an unanticipated productivity shock in the first quarter. The size of the shock is normalized such that it leads to a 1 percent increase in real GDP on impact under the Taylor rule regime. Paths denote different policy regimes.

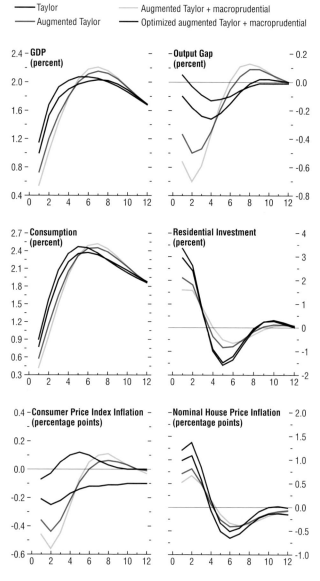

Source: IMF staff calculations.

Policy Rules with Multiple Shocks

In the real world, economies are affected by multiple shocks of various types. Optimal policy rules must strike a balance among the optimal responses to each different type of shock and must reflect the relative importance of the shocks in driving the economy. Consequently, the case for using a macroprudential tool will depend, among other things, on the mixture of shocks facing a particular economy. Figure 3.17 shows how the optimal weight on changes in nominal credit in the macroprudential rule rises as financial shocks become relatively more important than productivity shocks.[36] When there are no financial shocks, there is no need for the macroprudential tool. When there are only financial shocks, the optimal weight on nominal credit in the macroprudential rule in this model is 0.8, as shown above. Ideally, then, policymakers would be able to use discretion to deal appropriately with different types of shocks as they arise, rather than reacting rigidly with fixed rules.

How do these conclusions compare with those from other studies? As far as we know, this is the first time the coordination of monetary and macroprudential rules has been formally evaluated using a macroeconomic model of this type,[37] although there is abundant literature on monetary policy and asset prices. The debate persists over whether central banks should react directly to asset prices.[38] The analysis here sug-

[36]More precisely, the exercise involves specifying a sequence of variance-covariance matrices in which the ratio of the variance of the financial shock increases, while the variance of the productivity shock and the covariance of the two shocks stay fixed at 1 and zero, respectively, then optimizing the weights for all variables in the augmented Taylor and macroprudential rule regime for each of the variance-covariance matrices in the sequence.

[37]Gray and others (forthcoming) find a role for a financial stability indicator in the monetary policy rule. Gruss and Sgherri (2009) study the welfare implications of pro-cyclical loan-to-value ratios in a two-country model. However, because the model does not have a nominal side, the reaction of monetary policy cannot be addressed.

[38]Two well-known examples are Bernanke and Gertler (2001), who conclude that there is no role for asset prices in monetary policy rules, and Cecchetti and others

gests that policymakers should be concerned not so much with asset price rises per se as with other conditions that can be associated with them: lax lending standards, excessive credit expansion, overinvestment, and deteriorating external balances. These conditions give policy-makers a strong reason to react.

Nonetheless, the simulations presented here are highly stylized, and many potentially important factors are omitted. The model captures some relevant features of the world, but it has not been adapted to fit any particular economy. In particular, the characterization of the macro-prudential tools is very simple and glosses over important practical questions about how such tools would be managed and how effective they would be in certain financial systems.[39] Hence, the results are only suggestive, and a great deal more research is required.

Policy Conclusions

Monetary policymakers in advanced economies with flexible exchange rate regimes have been guided in recent years by the principle that stabilizing inflation forms the best policy for promoting economic growth and welfare. At the time this approach was gaining favor, it was suggested that stable inflation would also reduce risk premiums and increase financial stability. A number of central banks now have explicit mandates to target CPI inflation, and they have been strikingly successful in keeping inflation in check. But this approach has not been sufficient to prevent asset price busts; the current crisis is no exception. Asset price busts have typically been preceded by rising investment, expanding credit, and deteriorating current account balances. Again, the current bust is no exception.

Monetary policy does not appear to be the main cause of recent asset price booms. To the extent that monetary policymakers bear responsibility for the crisis, it is for acting too narrowly—

Figure 3.17. Optimal Weight on Nominal Credit in the Macroprudential Rule

As the importance of financial shocks increases, the macroprudential tool becomes more useful.

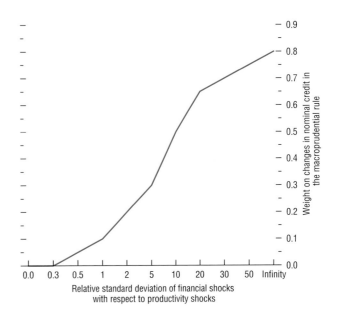

Relative standard deviation of financial shocks with respect to productivity shocks

Source: IMF staff calculations.

(2000), who argue that central banks should react to asset prices.

[39]See BIS (2009) for a useful discussion.

Table 3.4. Parameters and Performance of Policy Regimes in Reaction to Productivity Shocks

	Weights under Each Regime				
	Lagged interest rates in monetary policy rule	Inflation in monetary policy rule	Output gap in monetary policy rule	Nominal credit in monetary policy rule	Nominal credit in macroprudential rule
Taylor	0.7	1.5	0.5	. . .	. . .
Augmented Taylor	0.7	1.5	0.5	0.5	. . .
Augmented Taylor + macroprudential	0.7	1.5	0.5	0.5	0.5
Optimized augmented Taylor + macroprudential	0.0	3.5	12	0.3	0.0

	Performance			
	Standard deviation of inflation	Standard deviation of output gap	Loss[1]	Ranking
Taylor	0.199	0.162	0.066	2
Augmented Taylor	0.184	0.220	0.082	3
Augmented Taylor + macroprudential	0.233	0.276	0.130	4
Optimized augmented Taylor + macroprudential	0.072	0.080	0.011	1

Source: IMF staff calculations.

[1]Loss equals the sum of the variances of output gap and consumer price index inflation.

paying too little attention to emerging signs of financial vulnerability—rather than for failing to control CPI inflation. By accommodating loosening credit conditions and rising debt, monetary policymakers increased the risks of a bust.

The evidence suggests that policymakers should react more strongly to signs of increasing macrofinancial risk. The findings in this chapter do not support the idea that central banks should react automatically to changes in asset prices, still less that they should try to determine some appropriate level for asset prices. But they should examine what is driving asset price movements and be prepared to act in response. This applies particularly to housing, which represents a larger share of wealth than equities for most households and typically involves significant levels of debt. One possibility is that central bank mandates be expanded to include concern for financial vulnerabilities. In addition, macroprudential tools could be used to help tackle problems in financial markets, which may help

limit the need for aggressive monetary policy reactions.

However, expectations must be realistic. Even the best leading indicators of asset price busts are imperfect—in the process of trying to reduce the probability of a dangerous bust, central banks may raise costly false alarms. Also, rigid reactions to indicators and inflexible use of policy tools will likely lead to policy mistakes. Discretion is required. Therefore, implementing a broader framework for monetary policy in order to mitigate macrofinancial risks further increases the importance of correctly identifying the sources of shocks driving changes in credit, investment, balance sheets, and external balances. Central bankers implementing broader policies would need to explain very carefully the basis for their actions, their immediate objectives, and how their actions are consistent with the longer-term objective of price stability. Moreover, monetary and macroprudential policies need to be coordinated, requiring greater information exchange and more consultation among monetary and supervisory authorities. These represent significant practical issues that must be carefully addressed before the framework for monetary policy is broadened or additional instruments are implemented. And neither a broader mandate nor additional instruments replace the need for fiscal and regulatory frameworks that are designed to make economies as robust as possible to asset price busts and provide policymakers the flexibility to respond to such events with stimulus policies.

Appendix 3.1. Econometric Methods

The main author of this appendix is Prakash Kannan.

This appendix addresses two issues. First, in most cases, the indicators of impending asset price busts could be highly correlated, such that the marginal information from some of the variables is insignificant when the information from other variables is accounted for. (Table 3.5 shows the thresholds used for the indicators.) Second, it is not straightforward to compute the statistical significance of these indicators, making it difficult to state the level of confidence associated with particular indicators. To remedy these problems, the analysis is complemented with a probit model. Probit models are non-linear regressions that seek to explain binary variables. In the case of this exercise, the binary variable in question takes on a value of 1 if there is an asset price bust between one and three years in the future and zero otherwise.[40]

The results from the probit analysis are shown in Table 3.6. The coefficients represent the marginal increase in the probability of a bust evaluated at the mean level of the other variables.[41] For the post-1985 sample, a 10

[40]Probit models have been used in the context of predicting currency crises (Frankel and Rose, 1996, and Milesi-Ferretti and Razin, 1998).

[41]Variables are measured as deviations relative to the eight-quarter trailing moving average, as earlier.

Table 3.5. Percentiles Used as Thresholds for Alarms

	House Price Bust	Stock Price Bust
Credit/GDP	90	90
Current account/GDP	90	90
Residential investment/GDP	90	90
House price growth	90	70
Stock price growth	70	70
Growth	75	80
Inflation	90	90

Note: Entries in the table denote the percentile of the distribution of the respective variable where the noise-to-signal ratio (defined as the ratio of false alarms to correct alarms) is minimized. The grid search was limited to the 70th, 75th, 80th, and 90th percentiles.

percentage point increase in the credit-to-GDP ratio relative to an eight-year moving average—the typical increase in the run-up to a house price bust—increases the probability of a house price bust by 4.4 percent, which is roughly one-third higher than the unconditional probability of about 15 percent. Current account balances and residential investment are also significant predictors of house price busts; for example, a 1½ percentage point deterioration of the current account relative to its eight-year moving average, a magnitude typically found in the run-up to a bust, implies a one-third increase in the probability of a house price bust over the unconditional probability. Meanwhile, for house price busts during 1985–2008, output growth and inflation are not significantly associated with the likelihood of a bust.

Deviations in residential investment shares and credit are also found to be significant predictors of a stock price bust. A 10 percentage point increase in the credit-to-GDP ratio is associated with an increase in the probability of a stock price bust of 6.4 percent—roughly 20 percent higher than the unconditional probability of a stock price bust. The coefficient on current account balances with regard to stock price busts, however, appears to be of the wrong sign for the post-1985 portion of the sample.

Table 3.6. Marginal Probabilities Based on Probit Regressions

	Full Sample		Before 1985		1985–2008	
	House price bust (1)	Stock price bust (2)	House price bust (3)	Stock price bust (4)	House price bust (5)	Stock price bust (6)
Credit/GDP	0.241**	0.546***	−0.864*	0.052	0.443***	0.638***
	(2.180)	(4.070)	(−1.740)	(0.130)	(4.280)	(4.210)
Current account balance	−3.910***	0.691	−3.472***	−2.851***	−3.191***	1.768**
	(−7.560)	(1.200)	(−3.640)	(−2.990)	(−5.440)	(2.510)
Residential investment/GDP	1.956	6.392***	4.621	4.801	2.456*	7.327***
	(1.520)	(5.280)	(1.370)	(1.550)	(1.930)	(5.290)
House price growth	0.798***	0.577***	2.147***	1.046***	0.455***	0.318
	(5.240)	(3.110)	(5.140)	(3.170)	(2.910)	(1.340)
Stock price growth	0.249***	0.337***	0.577***	0.323***	0.111***	0.349***
	(6.060)	(5.250)	(4.890)	(2.660)	(2.680)	(4.660)
Output growth	−0.413	1.686**	−0.916	0.280	−0.160	2.428
	(−0.810)	(2.540)	(−0.940)	(0.290)	(−0.300)	(2.620)
Inflation	2.511***	4.373***	3.786***	4.721***	0.681	3.732***
	(7.180)	(7.030)	(5.460)	(5.470)	(1.640)	(4.130)
N	1,699	1,580	435	419	1,264	1,161
Pseudo R^2	0.14	0.10	0.16	0.15	0.15	0.10

Source: IMF staff calculations.

Note: Dependent variable takes a value of 1 if there is a bust between 12 and 4 quarters ahead and zero otherwise. Estimation is carried out using robust standard errors. Z-statistics are reported in parentheses. ***, **, and * refer to significance at the 1, 5, and 10 percent level, respectively. Marginal probabilities computed at the mean values of other variables are reported. Variables are measured as deviations from an eight-year moving average

Appendix 3.2. Data Sources

Variable	Source
Nominal house prices	Bank for International Settlements, Haver Analytics, Organization for Economic Cooperation and Development (OECD)
Real house prices	OECD
Real stock prices	Bloomberg Financial Markets, International Financial Statistics (IFS) database
Real credit	IFS database
Nominal credit	IFS database
Real private consumption	OECD
Real residential investment	OECD
Output	OECD
Current account	OECD
Consumer price index	Haver Analytics (Core Personal Consumption Expenditures), OECD, IFS database
Quick ratio	OECD
Policy rates	Bloomberg Financial Markets, national authorities, Thomson Datastream
Real long-term interest rates	IFS database

References

Adalid, Ramón, and Carsten Detken, 2007, "Liquidity Shocks and Asset Price Boom/Bust Cycles," ECB Working Paper No. 732 (Frankfurt: European Central Bank).

Ahrend, Rudiger, Boris Cournède, and Robert Price, 2008, "Monetary Policy, Market Excesses and Financial Turmoil," OECD Economics Department Working Paper No. 597 (Paris: Organization for Economic Cooperation and Development).

Aoki, Kosuke, James Proudman, and Gertjan Vlieghe, 2004, "House Prices, Consumption, and Monetary Policy: A Financial Accelerator Approach," *Journal of Financial Intermediation,* Vol. 13, No. 4, pp. 414–35.

Bank for International Settlements (BIS), 2009, *Annual Report* (Basel: Bank for International Settlements).

Berg, Andrew, Eduardo Borensztein, Gian Maria Milesi-Ferretti, and Catherine Pattillo, 2000, "Anticipating Balance of Payments Crises: The Role of Early Warning Systems," IMF Occasional Paper No. 186 (Washington: International Monetary Fund).

Bernanke, Ben, and Mark Gertler, 2001, "Should Central Banks Respond to Movements in Asset Prices?" *American Economic Review,* Vol. 91, No. 2, pp. 253–57.

———, and Simon Gilchrist, 1998, "The Financial Accelerator in a Quantitative Business Cycle Framework," NBER Working Paper No. 6455 (Cambridge, Massachusetts: National Bureau of Economic Research).

Bordo, Michael, and Olivier Jeanne, 2002, "Boom-Busts in Asset Prices, Economic Instability, and Monetary Policy," NBER Working Paper No. 8966 (Cambridge, Massachusetts: National Bureau of Economic Research).

Borio, Claudio, and Philip Lowe, 2002a, "Asset Prices, Financial and Monetary Stability: Exploring the Nexus," BIS Working Paper No. 114 (Basel: Bank for International Settlements).

———, 2002b, "Assessing the Risk of Banking Crises," *BIS Quarterly Review* (December), pp. 43–54.

———, 2004, "Securing Sustainable Price Stability: Should Credit Come Back from the Wilderness?" BIS Working Paper No. 157 (Basel: Bank for International Settlements).

Borio, Claudio, and Ilhyock Shim, 2007, "What Can (Macro-)Prudential Policy Do to Support Monetary Policy?" BIS Working Paper No. 242 (Basel: Bank for International Settlements).

Cecchetti, Stephen G., Hans Genberg, John Lipsky, and Sushil Wadhwani, 2000, "Asset Prices and Central Bank Policy," *Geneva Reports on the World Economy* 2 (Geneva: International Centre for Monetary and Banking Studies).

Christiano, Lawrence J., Robert Motto, and Massimo Rostagno, 2007, "Two Reasons Why Money and Credit May Be Useful in Monetary Policy," paper presented at the fourth ECB Central Banking Conference, "The Role of Money: Money and Monetary Policy in the Twenty-First Century," Frankfurt, November 9–10, 2006.

Claessens, Stijn, Ayhan Kose, and Marco Terrones, 2008, "What Happens During Recessions, Crunches, and Busts?" IMF Working Paper 08/274 (Washington: International Monetary Fund).

Cúrdia, Vasco, and Michael Woodford, 2009, "Credit Spreads and Monetary Policy" (unpublished).

Detken, Carsten, and Frank Smets, 2004, "Asset Price Booms and Monetary Policy," ECB Working Paper No. 364 (Frankfurt: European Central Bank).

Frankel, Jeffrey A., and Andrew K. Rose, 1996, "Currency Crashes in Emerging Markets: An Empirical Treatment," *Journal of International Economics,* Vol. 41 (November), pp. 351–66.

Galí, Jordi, and Luca Gambetti, 2009, "On the Sources of the Great Moderation," *American Economic Journal: Macroeconomics,* Vol. 1, No. 1, pp. 26–57.

Gerdesmeier, Dieter, Hans-Eggert Reimers, and Barbara Roffia, 2009, "Asset Price Misalignments and the Role of Money and Credit," ECB Working Paper No. 1068 (Frankfurt: European Central Bank).

Gray, Dale, Carlos García, Leonardo Luna, and Jorge E. Restrepo, forthcoming, "Incorporating Financial Sector Risk into Monetary Policy Models: Application to Chile," IMF Working Paper (Washington: International Monetary Fund).

Gruss, Bertrand, and Silvia Sgherri, 2009, "The Volatility Costs of Procyclical Lending Standards: An Assessment Using a DSGE Model," IMF Working Paper 09/35 (Washington: International Monetary Fund).

Iacoviello, Matteo, 2005, "House Prices, Borrowing Constraints, and Monetary Policy in the Business Cycle," *American Economic Review,* Vol. 95, No. 3, pp. 739–64.

Kaminsky, Graciela, Saul Lizondo, and Carmen Reinhart, 1998, "Leading Indicators of Currency Crisis," *IMF Staff Papers,* Vol. 45 (March), pp. 1–48.

Kaminsky, Graciela L., and Carmen M. Reinhart, 1999, "The Twin Crises: The Causes of Banking and Balance-of-Payments Problems," *American Economic Review,* Vol. 89, No. 3 (June), pp. 473–500.

Kannan, Prakash, Alasdair Scott, and Pau Rabanal, forthcoming a, "Macroeconomic Patterns and Monetary Policy in the Run-Up to Asset Price Busts," IMF Working Paper (Washington: International Monetary Fund).

———, forthcoming b, "Monetary and Macroprudential Policy Rules in a Model with House Price Booms," IMF Working Paper (Washington: International Monetary Fund).

McConnell, Margaret M., and Gabriel Pérez-Quirós, 2000, "Output Fluctuations in the United States: What Has Changed since the Early 1980s?" *American Economic Review,* Vol. 90, No. 5, pp. 1464–76.

Mendoza, Enrique G., and Marco E. Terrones, 2008, "An Anatomy of Credit Booms: Evidence from Macro Aggregates and Micro Data," IMF Working Paper 08/226 (Washington: International Monetary Fund).

Milesi-Ferretti, Gian Maria, and Assaf Razin, 1998, "Current Account Reversals and Currency Crises: Empirical Regularities," NBER Working Paper No.

6620 (Cambridge, Massachusetts: National Bureau of Economic Research).

Monacelli, Tommaso, 2009, "New Keynesian Models, Durable Goods, and Collateral," *Journal of Monetary Economics,* Vol. 56, pp. 242–54.

Taylor, John B., 1993, "Discretion versus Policy Rules in Practice," *Carnegie-Rochester Conference Series on Public Policy,* Vol. 39, No. 1, pp. 195–214.

———, 2007, "Housing and Monetary Policy," paper presented at the Federal Reserve Bank of Kansas City 31st Economic Policy Symposium, "Housing, Housing Finance and Monetary Policy," Jackson Hole, Wyoming, August 31–September 1.

———, 2008, "The Financial Crisis and the Policy Responses: An Empirical Analysis of What Went Wrong," keynote lecture at the Bank of Canada, Ottawa, November.

White, William R., 2006, "Procyclicality in the Financial System: Do We Need a New Macrofinancial Stabilisation Framework?" BIS Working Paper No. 193 (Basel: Bank for International Settlements).

Woodford, Michael, 2001, "The Taylor Rule and Optimal Monetary Policy" (unpublished; Princeton, New Jersey: Princeton University).

WHAT'S THE DAMAGE? MEDIUM-TERM OUTPUT DYNAMICS AFTER FINANCIAL CRISES

The global economy is beginning to recover from the most severe financial crisis since the Great Depression and the deepest recession since World War II. Global economic activity is starting to pick up, but financial systems remain impaired and domestic and external imbalances persist in many economies. The recovery is expected to be slow, and there are concerns about the prospect of long-term damage to the path of global output, as financial institutions and markets worldwide struggle to restore their ability to intermediate and unemployment rises to high levels. In this context, the aftermath of past financial crises may provide useful insights into the medium-term prospects for economies now in the midst of financial crisis and for the global economy.

This chapter builds on Chapter 3 of the April 2009 *World Economic Outlook*, which analyzed the short-term dynamics of output in advanced economies and found that recessions following financial crises are unusually long, particularly with a global downturn. This chapter goes beyond the short term to concentrate on medium-term developments following financial crises in advanced, emerging, and developing economies over the past 40 years.

A first glance at several previous crisis episodes illustrates that although financial crises typically lead to large output losses in the short term, what happens to output over the medium term has varied widely (Figure 4.1). Some economies persistently grow at a slower rate than before, moving further away from their precrisis trend. Some return to growth at a similar rate as before but fail to recover the initial output loss. Some return to their precrisis trend, and

some recover quickly and outperform their previous trend.

This chapter addresses a number of questions:
- What happens to output over the medium term following financial crises? Does the path of output per capita remain below its precrisis trend? Do growth rates recover? How much do outcomes vary across crisis episodes?
- What factors account for shifts in medium-term output dynamics: changes in the factors of production (capital and labor) or changes in the efficiency of their use (total factor productivity)?
- What are the underlying determinants of medium-term output dynamics? For example, do different country characteristics and macroeconomic conditions before the crisis affect medium-term postcrisis outcomes? What can be said about the role of policies after a crisis?

To explore these issues, this chapter examines medium-term output performance following 88 banking crises that occurred over the past four decades across a wide range of economies, as well as the behavior of world output following major financial crises going back to the 19th century. Building on work by Cerra and Saxena (2008), the main contributions of this analysis are the focus on medium-term output and its driving forces (capital, labor, and total factor productivity) for a broad sample of economies that experienced banking crises, and the assessment of the underlying determinants of postcrisis performance.[1]

---

[1] A great deal of work has been done on the output effects of financial crises in the short term (for example, Reinhart and Rogoff, 2009; Haugh, Ollivaud, and Turner, 2009; Bordo, 2006; Hutchison and Noy, 2002; and Gupta, Mishra, and Sahay, 2007, among others). Until recently, the emphasis on the medium term has been much more limited, with the notable exceptions of Boyd, Kwak, and Smith (2005) and Cerra and Saxena (2008). With the current crisis, interest in the topic has surged. For instance, Furceri and Mourougane (2009)

The main authors of this chapter are Ravi Balakrishnan, Petya Koeva Brooks, Daniel Leigh, Irina Tytell, and Abdul Abiad, with support from Stephanie Denis, Murad Omoev, and Min Kyu Song.

Figure 4.1. Medium-Term Output per Capita after Financial Crises: Case Studies
(Log scale)

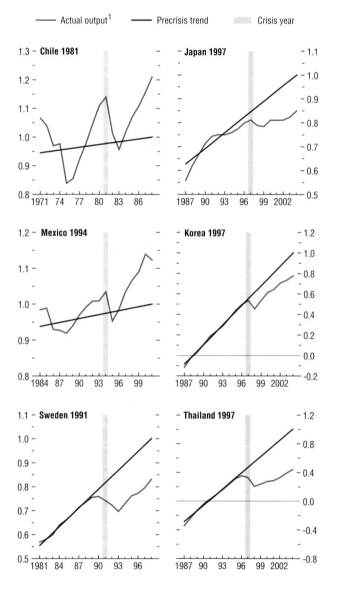

Sources: World Bank, *World Development Indicators;* and IMF staff calculations.
[1]Output = logarithm of per capita real GDP.

Our general approach is to use an event-study methodology that compares the medium-term level of output to the level it would have reached following the precrisis trend, with the medium term defined as seven years after the crisis. Measured this way, the resulting underperformance ("output loss") is then decomposed into its underlying components: capital, labor, and productivity.[2] Output losses are also related to a range of pre- and postcrisis macroeconomic and policy factors, using both statistical methods and a narrative approach, to explore which underlying factors may have contributed to different outcomes across crisis episodes.

The main findings of the chapter are as follows:

- The path of output tends to be depressed substantially and persistently following banking crises, with no rebound on average to the precrisis trend over the medium term. Growth does, however, eventually return to its precrisis rate for most economies.

- The depressed output path tends to result from long-lasting reductions of roughly equal proportion in the employment rate, the capital-to-labor ratio, and total factor productivity. In the short term, the output loss is mainly accounted for by total factor productivity, but, unlike the employment rate and capital-to-labor ratio, the level of total factor productivity recovers somewhat to its precrisis trend over the medium term. In contrast, capital and employment suffer enduring losses relative to trend.

apply the Cerra-Saxena approach, which involves using an autoregressive model of output growth rates augmented by crisis dummies, to growth rates of potential output for Organization for Economic Cooperation and Development (OECD) member countries. Pisani-Ferry and van Pottelsberghe (2009) also discuss the persistent impact on output of banking crises using several case studies. Haugh, Ollivaud, and Turner (2009) analyze the impact of banking crises on potential growth in Finland, Japan, Norway, and Sweden.

[2]Because of data limitations, the decompositions into factor components are based on a smaller sample of 27 observations.

- Initial conditions have a strong influence on the size of the output loss. What happens to short-term output is also a good predictor of the medium-term outcome, as is the joint occurrence of a currency and a banking crisis. This is consistent with the notion that the output drop is especially persistent following large shocks, carrying over into the medium term. A high precrisis investment share of GDP is a reliable predictor of high medium-term output losses, because of its correlation with the dynamics of capital after the crisis. There is also evidence suggesting that limited precrisis policy room tends to be associated with more muted medium-term recoveries. Interestingly, postcrisis output losses are not significantly correlated with the level of income.
- The medium-term output loss is not inevitable. Some economies succeed in avoiding it, ultimately exceeding the precrisis trajectory. Although postcrisis output dynamics are hard to predict, the evidence suggests that economies that apply countercyclical fiscal and monetary stimulus in the short run to cushion the downturn after a crisis tend to have smaller output losses over the medium run. There is also some evidence that structural reform efforts are associated with better medium-term outcomes. In addition, a favorable external environment is generally associated with smaller medium-term output losses.

How do these findings relate to shifts in potential output following financial crises? The term "potential output" typically refers to the level of output consistent with stable inflation and is associated with structural and institutional factors. If an economy experiences a decline in output relative to its previous trend over the medium term, it could reflect a decline in potential output, but it could also partly reflect a persistent fall in aggregate demand. The experience of a number of economies, including Japan, suggests that if output remains below its precrisis trend over the medium term, then a substantial part of the shortfall reflects lower potential. Therefore, to the extent that this chapter identifies output losses seven years after a financial crisis, it is likely that lower potential explains most of those losses. However, attempting to precisely identify shifts in potential output is beyond the scope of this chapter.

The first section of this chapter describes key features of medium-term output dynamics following financial crises based on international experience over the past 40 years. The second section decomposes medium-term output losses into their factor components (capital, labor, and productivity), as well as their demand-side drivers (consumption, investment, exports, and imports). The third section analyzes how medium-term output performance relates to country characteristics and macroeconomic conditions prevailing before the crisis. It also examines the role of domestic policies and the external environment after the onset of the crisis, based on both case studies of successful medium-term recoveries and statistical analysis. The last section puts the recent financial crisis into historical perspective and discusses implications of the analysis for the outlook.

Does Output Recover over the Medium Term?

This section presents key stylized facts on the output losses associated with financial crises. We start with methodological issues and then report some stylized facts on the estimated output losses at both the country and the global levels.

The analysis focuses on banking crises, although currency crises are also considered for purposes of comparison.[3] It uses a comprehensive set of financial crisis events from the early 1970s to 2002. Banking crisis dates are taken from Laeven and Valencia (2008).[4] Currency

[3]Currency crises seem to be a natural choice for comparison, given that they represent a different type of financial crisis.

[4]The Laeven-Valencia data set is constructed by combining quantitative indicators measuring banking sector distress, such as a sharp increase in nonperforming loans and bank runs, with a subjective assessment of the situation.

crisis dates are identified based on the method-ology of Milesi-Ferretti and Razin (1998).[5] Our sample includes 88 banking crises and 222 currency crises, distributed across high-, middle-, and low-income economies (Figure 4.2).[6] We also use a set of major international financial crises dating to the end of the 19th century to analyze the impact at the global level (Box 4.1).

We compute the medium-term output loss for each episode, as illustrated in Figure 4.3.[7] The idea is to measure the output loss associated with a crisis as the difference between the actual level of output and the level that would have been expected based on the prevailing precrisis trend. To focus on the medium term, the postcrisis window is seven years, beyond the effects of short-term fluctuations in the economy. Estimating the precrisis trend is tricky in terms of insulating the analysis from the impact of any immediate precrisis boom or slump, and there is no well-established method of doing this. We estimate a linear trend through the actual output series during a seven-year precrisis period that ends three years before the onset of the crisis.[8] The appeal of this approach is that it is simple, transparent, and easy to implement for a large set of economies. Given its linearity, it also facilitates the decomposition of output losses into the factors of production,

Figure 4.2. Distribution of Crises across Time and Economy Type
(Number of countries)

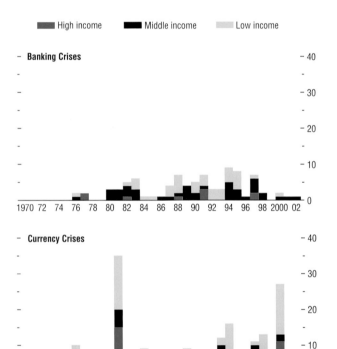

Sources: Laeven and Valencia (2008); and IMF staff calculations.

[5]This definition requires (1) a 15 percent minimum rate of nominal depreciation vis-à-vis the U.S. dollar, (2) a minimum 10 percent increase in the rate of depreciation with respect to the previous year, and (3) a rate of depreciation of below 10 percentage points in the previous year. For the rationale behind this definition, see Milesi-Ferretti and Razin (1998).

[6]The sample excludes transition economies, because the output developments in these economies were strongly related to the shift away from central planning rather than to financial crises. Countries with populations of less than 1 million are also dropped.

[7]See Angkinand (2008) for a literature review of alternative methods for estimating output losses associated with a crisis.

[8]In a number of cases, however, the above procedure yielded negative trend growth rates, implying that output per capita would decline indefinitely even in the absence of a crisis. In these cases, the precrisis window was extended from 10 to 20 years before the crisis and used instead if it produced a more plausible trend growth rate.

namely losses in capital, labor, and total factor productivity. The robustness of the results is checked by considering alternative approaches to estimating the precrisis trend.[9] The actual level of output is measured as the logarithm of real GDP per capita.

The key stylized facts that emerge from the analysis are as follows:

- Typically, output does not recover to its pre-crisis trend. On average, output falls steadily below its precrisis trend until the third year after the crisis and does not rebound thereafter (Figure 4.4).
- The medium-term output losses following banking crises are substantial. Seven years after the crisis, output has declined relative to trend by close to 10 percent on average. As indicated by the shaded area measuring the 90 percent confidence band, the average decline relative to trend is statistically significant (see Figure 4.4).
- Medium-term growth rates tend to eventually return to the precrisis rate. As illustrated in Figure 4.5, the medium-term growth rate is typically statistically indistinguishable from the precrisis trend growth rate.[10]
- The variation in outcomes is substantial. For example, whereas the change in output relative to trend following banking crises has a mean of –10 percent, the middle 50 percent of cases had a range of –26 percent to +6

---

[9]Several robustness checks were performed. First, the calculations were repeated with the precrisis window ending one year rather than three years before the crisis. Second, an alternative approach was applied to computing the trend growth rates, by which a longer precrisis window from $t = -20$ (rather than $t = -10$) to $t = -3$ was applied to the lowest and the highest 10 percent of trend growth rates. Third, the precrisis trend was computed based solely on the longer precrisis window (from $t = -20$ to $t = -3$). Finally, the output losses were recomputed using real-time medium-term growth projections from IMF country desk economists as the trend growth rates. Note, however, that these real-time forecasts were available only after 1989. Overall, the output losses obtained using the different approaches were highly correlated (see Appendix 4.1).

[10]The mean difference with respect to the precrisis trend growth rate is –0.2 percentage point, with a standard error of 0.4 percentage point.

Figure 4.3. Methodology Example (Korea 1997)
(First year of crisis at t *= 0; years on x-axis)*

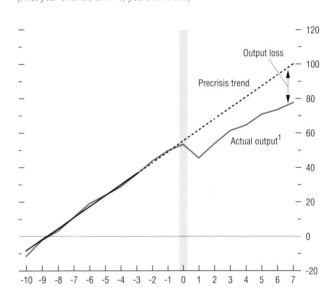

Sources: World Bank, *World Development Indicators;* and IMF staff calculations.
Note: The precrisis trend is estimated up to year $t = -3$, and is extrapolated linearly thereafter. The dotted line indicates the extrapolation of the trend up to the year $t = 7$.
[1]Output = logarithm of real GDP per capita; 100 equals trend in year 7.

Figure 4.4. Output Evolution after Banking and Currency Crises

(Percent of precrisis trend; mean difference from year t = − 1; *first year of crisis at* t = 0; *years on x-axis)*

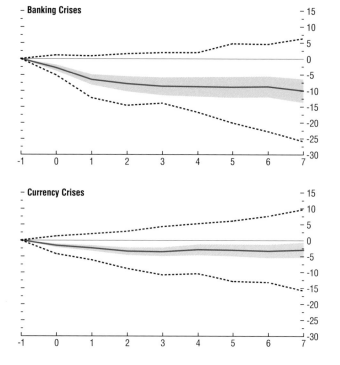

Sources: World Bank, *World Development Indicators;* and IMF staff calculations.
[1] The interquartile range indicates the middle 50 percent of all crises.

percent (see Figure 4.4).[11] On average, there is no rebound to the precrisis trend, but in more than a quarter of cases, output ultimately exceeded this level.

To put the losses associated with banking crises in perspective, Figure 4.4 also reports the evolution of output relative to trend following currency crises. Estimated losses following currency crises are much smaller, about one-third (3 percent) of the average loss associated with banking crises.

At the global level, the picture is broadly similar: major international financial crises during the past 140 years were typically followed by persistent output losses relative to precrisis trend, with gradual recoveries in output growth rates. Medium-term output losses were particularly large for both advanced and nonadvanced economies following the Great Depression (see Box 4.1).

Decompositions: Why Does Aggregate Output Fail to Recover after a Banking Crisis?

This section decomposes medium-term output losses, in terms of factor inputs and demand components, to help explain which factors drive them. Exploring these underlying forces could provide insights into both the likely trend in output after the current banking crises and the types of policies that may help reduce the ultimate losses.

Before presenting the results, we briefly review the main channels through which banking crises may affect output in the medium term.

[11]Part of the variation in outcomes reflects the variation in the estimates of the country-specific precrisis trends and not just the heterogeneity of postcrisis output paths. However, the wide range of outcomes is robust to using alternative measures of the precrisis trends.

What Are Possible Effects on the Key Sources of Output?

A useful way to examine why output per capita often fails to recover to its precrisis trend is to analyze what happens to the key elements of an economy's production process, namely labor inputs (which can be thought of as depending on the employment rate and labor force participation), capital inputs, and total factor productivity. From a theoretical perspective, banking crises may affect these components in several ways.[12]

- *Impact on labor force participation:* In theory, the medium-term effect of a crisis on this component of labor input is uncertain. There are two opposing forces. On the one hand, grim employment prospects may discourage jobseekers and prompt employed workers to leave the labor force, especially if there are incentives to retire early. On the other hand, in times of economic hardship, second-income earners may enter the labor force to help compensate for a loss in family income or wealth.[13]

- *Impact on employment rate:* The medium-term employment rate may be adversely affected if a financial crisis leads to an increase in the underlying ("structural") unemployment rate. Why? The crisis may imply the need for a substantial reallocation of labor across sectors, something that may take time and increase medium-term frictional unemployment. Perhaps more important, the large initial increase in the actual unemployment rate induced by the crisis could persist for a long time if rigid labor market institutions (strict employment protection laws, gener-

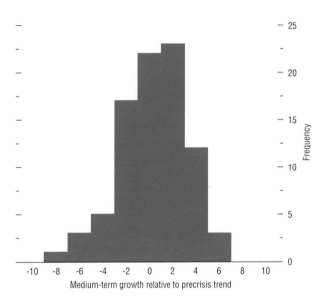

Figure 4.5. Medium-Term Growth after Banking Crises[1]
(Difference from precrisis trend; percentage points)

Sources: World Bank, *World Development Indicators;* and IMF staff calculations.
[1]Medium-term growth is derived as the five-year average growth starting in the fourth year after the crisis.

---

[12]Changes in these components following a banking crisis could reflect a deterioration in the economy's productive potential, as well as a persistent fall in aggregate demand, although the latter is likely to explain only a small part of medium-term losses..

[13]Indeed, there is some evidence suggesting that the additional worker effect may already be playing a role in the current crisis, with the female participation rate rising as the male participation rate has fallen in the United States (see FRBSF, 2009).

Box 4.1. A Historical Perspective on International Financial Crises

International financial crises have been a feature of the global economy for a very long time. This box undertakes a historical comparison of output paths following these crises going back to 1870.[1]

Since 1870, global output has grown at an average rate of about 3 percent a year (first figure). During this period, the trend in the pace of global growth has shifted, most notably in the aftermath of the two world wars and the Great Depression and in the early 1970s. The level and the growth rate of global output were also affected to varying degrees by a number of international financial crises described below.

Following the literature, it is possible to identify at least eight episodes of major international financial crisis since 1870 (see first figure).[2] In 1873, the German and Austrian stock markets collapsed, causing declines in capital inflows, debt servicing problems, and crises throughout Europe and the Americas. In 1890, a boom in lending to the Americas came to an end, leading to debt crises in Latin America, notably Argentina, and to the near failure of the London-based Baring Brothers bank. In 1907, a fall in copper prices caused financial panic in the United States, with spillovers to a number of countries in Europe, Latin America, and Asia.

In 1929, a stock market crash in the United States ushered in the Great Depression. Monetary policy tightening during the preceding year, aimed at stemming speculation, is widely

seen as a key initial cause.[3] Debt deflation, bank runs and failures, and severe recession in the United States intensified through 1933 amid an incoherent policy response. The crisis was transmitted worldwide through wealth losses and declines in trade and capital flows, with monetary policies constrained by the gold standard.

There were another four episodes of major international financial crisis during the postwar period. The Latin American crisis began in 1981–82 and set off a nearly decade-long debt crisis across emerging economies. In 1991–92, real estate and equity price bubbles burst in Scandinavia and Japan, while the exchange rate mechanism (ERM) in Europe came under pressure. In 1997–98, the Asian and Russian crises led to widespread capital outflows from emerging economies. Finally, in 2007–08, bursting real estate bubbles and a collapse of securitization in the United States and other advanced economies marked the beginning of the current financial crisis.

To compare the output effects of these international crises, output losses following each episode are measured in the same way as in the main text. In short, the precrisis trend line is calculated by fitting a linear regression through the output series (in logs) between 10 and 3 years before the onset of the crisis; then the output loss is defined as the difference (in logs) between the actual level of output and its precrisis trend. To focus the discussion, the comparison is limited to five crises associated with major global downturns and for which sufficient data are available: the New York panic of 1907; the Great Depression; the Latin American debt crisis of the early 1980s; the Scandinavian, Japanese, and ERM crises of the early 1990s; and the current crisis.[4] It is clear that the Great

The main author of this box is Irina Tytell. Stephanie Denis provided research assistance.

[1]Global GDP is constructed by aggregating individual country series in 2008 purchasing-power-parity dollars. The data sources are the IMF World Economic Outlook database, the Total Economy Database of the Conference Board (www.conference-board.org/economies/database.cfm), and the Historical Statistics Database of Angus Maddison (www.ggdc.net/madison).Changes in sample composition are smoothed by pasting together the aggregate growth rates before and after each change. The World War II data rely on approximations in a number of cases and should be treated cautiously.

[2]See Bordo (2006), Reinhart and Rogoff (2008a and 2008b), and references therein.

[3]See Box 3.1 in the April 2009 *World Economic Outlook* and the references therein.

[4]There is a potential bias associated with the way these crises are selected, given that they are all associated with downturns. For the current crisis, only the information available to date is used. The Asian and Russian crises were not associated with major down-

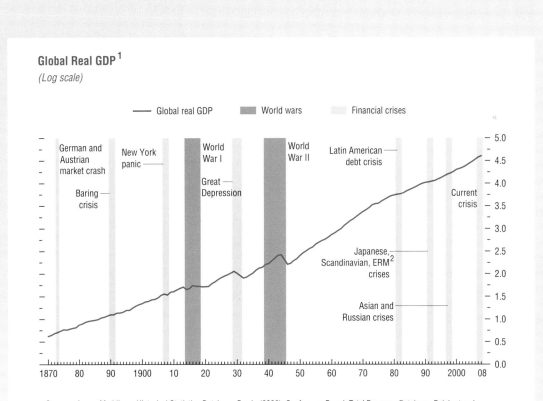

Global Real GDP [1]

(Log scale)

Sources: Angus Maddison, Historical Statistics Database; Bordo (2006); Conference Board, Total Economy Database; Reinhart and Rogoff (2008a and 2008b); and IMF staff calculations.

[1]For advanced economies, data start in 1870, except for Greece and Ireland data, which start in 1921. For emerging and developing economies, data start in 1950, except for Ecuador and Paraguay, which start in 1939; Poland and Romania in 1929; Bulgaria, Hungary, and Turkey in 1924; Costa Rica, Czechoslovakia, El Salvador, Guatemala, Honduras, and Yugoslavia in 1920; Malaysia, Korea, and Taiwan Province of China in 1912; Philippines in 1902; Argentina, Colombia, Mexico, Peru, and Venezuela in 1900; India in 1884; and Brazil, Chile, Indonesia, Sri Lanka, and Uruguay in 1870.

[2]ERM = European exchange rate mechanism.

Depression was associated with by far the largest medium-term output losses: 28 percent in advanced and 21 percent in nonadvanced economies in 1936, seven years after the onset of the crisis (second figure). Both country groups were least affected by the New York panic, with output losses close to zero two years after the crisis and no medium-term consequences.[5] Advanced economies experienced significant losses in

the 1990s (10 percent as of 1998), whereas the effects on emerging and developing economies were relatively short lived. However, emerging and developing economies experienced large losses after the 1980s debt crisis (13 percent as of 1988), whereas advanced economies were not affected much beyond the short term. In the current crisis, advanced economies have taken the greater hit; emerging and developing economies have fared better so far.

In all three crises associated with medium-term losses in the past—the Great Depression, the 1980s in emerging and developing economies, and the 1990s in advanced economies—output grew more slowly relative to the precrisis trend for a number of years. The fastest

---

turns at the global level (see Box 1.1 in the April 2009 *World Economic Outlook*). The data available at the time of the German stock market crash and the Baring crisis are not sufficient for the analysis, in part because of limited coverage of nonadvanced economies.

[5]Rising output losses in 1914 reflect the outbreak of World War I.

Box 4.1 *(concluded)*

turnaround in growth rates occurred after the Great Depression: growth returned to trend by 1934 in advanced economies and by 1936 in nonadvanced economies. However, growth rates remained about 1 percentage point below the precrisis trend seven years after the onset of the two more recent crises: the 1980s crisis in

emerging and developing economies and the 1990s crisis in advanced economies. By implication, in none of these three episodes did output growth accelerate sufficiently in the aftermath of the crisis to return output to its precrisis trend. It remains to be seen whether the current crisis will follow a similar pattern.

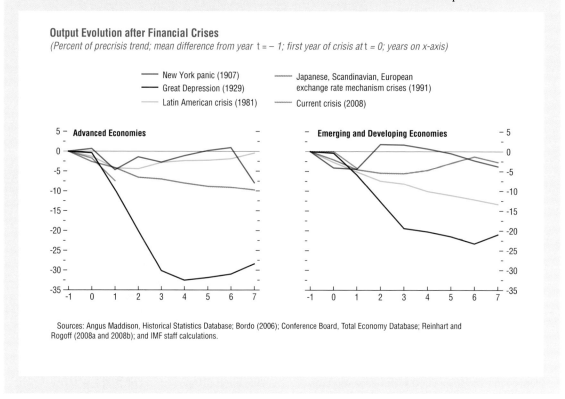

Output Evolution after Financial Crises
(Percent of precrisis trend; mean difference from year t = – 1*; first year of crisis at* t = 0*; years on x-axis)*

Sources: Angus Maddison, Historical Statistics Database; Bordo (2006); Conference Board, Total Economy Database; Reinhart and Rogoff (2008a and 2008b); and IMF staff calculations.

ous unemployment benefits) complicate the task of finding a new job. Long spells without employment may also impair professional and on-the-job skills, making it even more difficult for the long-term unemployed to find jobs.[14]

- *Impact on capital accumulation:* A financial crisis may depress investment and slow capital accumulation over a protracted period. As the supply of credit becomes more limited, firms face

tougher financing conditions in the form of tighter lending standards and higher effective costs of borrowing, and profit rates are likely to suffer (see Bernanke and Gertler, 1989 and 1995; and Bernanke and Blinder, 1988). The ability of firms to borrow and invest may be hampered further if the crisis leads to lower asset prices that weaken corporate balance sheets and erode collateral values (see Kiyotaki and Moore, 1997). Investment may also suffer if the crisis leads to a sustained increase in uncertainty and risk premiums.

[14]These are often called "hysteresis effects." See Blanchard and Wolfers (2000); Bassanini and Duval (2006); and Nickell, Nunziata, and Ochel (2005), among others.

- *Impact on total factor productivity:* The effect on total factor productivity is ambiguous, based on theoretical considerations. On the negative side, as it recovers from the crisis, the financial system may not be able to allocate loanable funds as productively as before the crisis, particularly if high-risk but high-return projects are discouraged by more cautious lending attitudes.[15] In addition, productivity may also suffer due to less innovation, as research and development spending tends to be scaled back in bad times (see Guellec and van Pottelsberghe, 2002). Also, high-productivity firms may go under for lack of financing. On the positive side, however, financial crises may have a cleansing effect on the economy by removing inefficient firms and activities and creating incentives to restructure and improve efficiency.[16]

What Do the Data Show?

Medium-term output losses following banking crises are decomposed into underlying components using the following approach. The starting point is the observation that the logarithm of output per capita is equal to the weighted sum of the logarithms of labor force participation, employment rate, capital-to-labor ratio, and total factor productivity.[17]

Applying the same procedure for estimating precrisis trends and computing output losses to their underlying components allows us to decompose output losses into losses due to changes in the employment rate, labor force participation, capital-to-labor ratio, or total factor productivity.[18] To complement the analysis, an analogous decomposition is done for the demand-side components of output: investment, consumption, exports, and imports.[19]

The results for both types of output loss decompositions are presented in Figures 4.6 and 4.7. For each component of output, the 90 percent confidence bands are reported to indicate the statistical significance of the estimates. Note that due to limited data availability, the size of the sample shrinks from 88 to 27 observations for these decompositions.

What do the results tell us?

- The measured medium-term losses in GDP per capita can be attributed to roughly equal losses in three of the four components of output, namely, the employment rate, capital-to-labor ratio, and total factor productivity (see Figure 4.6).[20]

- After a significant initial decline, total factor productivity gradually moves closer to the precrisis trend toward the end of the seven-year horizon. This is consistent with the notion that labor hoarding decreases over time. Nevertheless, the medium-term loss in total factor productivity still accounts for about one-third of the total output loss. Its magnitude, however, is not statistically significant

[15]In some countries, the efficiency of financial intermediation could be low both before and after a crisis.

[16]See Caballero and Hammour (1994) and Aghion and Saint-Paul (1998). The underlying concept of "creative destruction" was first introduced by Schumpeter (1942).

[17]The decompositions are based on a Cobb-Douglas production function of the form $Y = AE^{\alpha}K^{1-\alpha}$, where A denotes total factor productivity, E denotes employment, and K denotes the capital stock. The employment share α is assumed to be 0.65. Given the assumption of constant returns to scale, the production function can be expressed in per capita terms by dividing by population, P, yielding $\frac{Y}{P} = A\left(\frac{E}{P}\right)^{\alpha}\left(\frac{K}{P}\right)^{1-\alpha}$. Finally, taking logs and noting that $\frac{E}{P} = \left(\frac{E}{LF} \times \frac{LF}{P}\right)$ and $\frac{K}{P} = \left(\frac{K}{E} \times \frac{E}{LF} \times \frac{LF}{P}\right)$ —where LF denotes the labor force—yields the decomposition used in the analysis: $\log\left(\frac{Y}{P}\right) = (1-\alpha)$ $\log\left(\frac{K}{E}\right) + \log\left(\frac{E}{LF}\right) + \log\left(\frac{LF}{P}\right) + \log(A)$, where $\frac{K}{E}$ rep-

resents the capital-to-labor ratio, $\frac{E}{LF}$ is the employment rate, and $\frac{LF}{P}$ is the labor force participation rate.

[18]Specifically, for each output component, the precrisis trend is estimated over the same precrisis period as the output trend. This approach ensures that, based on the assumed Cobb-Douglas production function, the factor input contributions add up exactly to the total output loss.

[19]Because the demand components are additive, the losses of the aggregate demand components do not sum exactly to the total output loss.

[20]The contribution of labor force participation is positive, albeit small and statistically insignificant.

Figure 4.6. Output Decomposition

(Percent of precrisis trend; mean difference from year t = – 1;
first year of crisis at t = 0; *years on x-axis)*

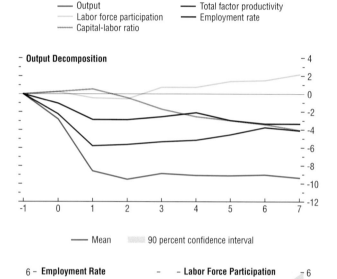

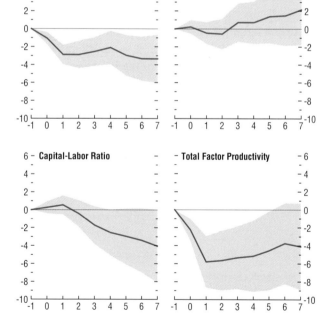

Sources: Bosworth and Collins (2003); World Bank, *World Development Indicators;* and IMF staff calculations.

seven years after the crisis, although it is in the short term.

- The initial loss in the employment rate persists into the medium term, whereas capital losses worsen steadily over time.

The finding of an adverse impact on the capital-to-labor ratio is consistent with demand-side decompositions that show a large and significant decline in investment of about 30 percent relative to its precrisis trend (see Figure 4.7). The consumption loss is also notable and significant, at about 15 percent. These losses are partially offset by an overall improvement in net exports relative to trend.

Overall, the decompositions suggest that higher unemployment rates, slower capital accumulation, and lower productivity growth play an important role in explaining medium-term output losses following banking crises. In other words, output per capita does not recover to its precrisis trend because capital per worker, the unemployment rate, and productivity do not typically return to their precrisis trends within seven years after the crisis. This finding suggests that pre- and postcrisis macroeconomic conditions and policies could play a role in shaping medium-term output dynamics—an issue examined in the next section.

What Factors Are Associated with Medium-Term Output Losses?

To explain the substantial variations in medium-term output losses across banking crises, this section explores how output losses are related to various macroeconomic, structural, and policy conditions, both before and after the crisis.

The analysis uses a broadly similar empirical strategy, which examines the associations of pre- and postcrisis macroeconomic factors with medium-run output losses as follows:

- We first present the results of small-scale ordinary least squares (OLS) regressions that consider several factors at a time. These small-scale regressions typically include one or two variables of interest in addition to key control variables.

- We then explore the robustness of the results using a large-scale OLS regression that includes all of the factors considered simultaneously and using Bayesian model averaging (BMA). Unlike the large-scale OLS regression, BMA allows us to examine whether the associations found for each variable are robust to including additional controls in *all* the possible ways that those additional controls can be added.[21] BMA is particularly useful in our investigation because theory is not sufficiently explicit regarding which variables should be included in the "true" regression. At the same time, however, BMA has substantial data requirements that, here, reduce the number of available observations by half. This is why we use both the small-scale results (based on a broad sample) and the larger-scale models (based on a restricted sample).
- Finally, in the postcrisis analysis, we complement the statistical methods described above with a more narrative approach based on country case studies.

Do Precrisis Conditions Help to Predict Medium-Term Output Losses?

What are the precrisis factors that may explain the magnitude of the eventual output losses? Our analysis examines the importance of a range of macroeconomic, structural, and policy variables:

[21]The procedure summarizes the results obtained across all possible specifications using two key statistics: (1) the average coefficient value obtained for each variable, and (2) the probability that each variable is statistically "effective" and should be used to predict output losses. A conventional approach in the BMA literature is to refer to a variable as "effective" if its estimated inclusion probability is greater than 50 percent. For additional details on BMA, see, for example, Hoeting and others (1999) and Masanjala and Papageorgiou (2008). We are grateful to Chris Papageorgiou for providing us with R programs that implement BMA.

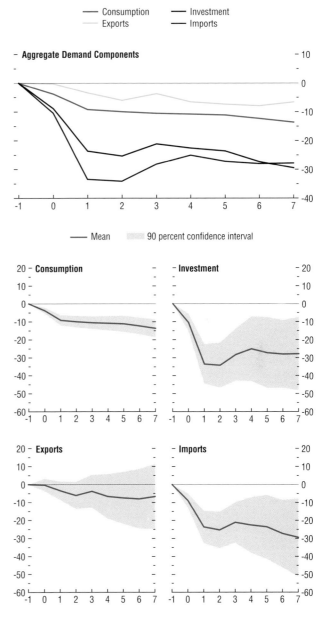

Figure 4.7. Demand-Side Decomposition
(Percent of precrisis trend; mean difference from year t = – 1; *first year of crisis at* t = 0; *years on x-axis)*

Sources: World Bank, *World Development Indicators;* and IMF staff calculations.

Table 4.1. Output Losses versus Initial Conditions

(Dependent variable: output at t=7 in percent of precrisis trend)

		(1)	(2)	(3)	(4)	(5)	(6)	(7)	(8)	(9)	(10)	(11)	(12)	(13)
(1)	Investment/GDP		−0.989***										−1.211***	−1.602
			[−3.120]										[−2.825]	(1.000)
(2)	Investment/GDP gap		0.335										−1.049	−0.388
			[0.889]										[−1.671]	(0.381)
(3)	Current account/GDP			0.765**									0.063	0.000
				[2.016]									[0.167]	(0.000)
(4)	Current account/GDP gap			0.964									0.525	0.189
				[1.593]									[0.571]	(0.196)
(5)	Inflation				0.116								0.005	−0.002
					[1.500]								[0.063]	(0.042)
(6)	Inflation gap				−0.196**								−0.063	−0.032
					[−2.243]								[−0.475]	(0.258)
(7)	Fiscal balance					0.501							−0.541	0.000
						[1.205]							[−1.102]	(0.000)
(8)	Fiscal balance gap					1.256**							0.480	0.013
						[2.042]							[0.796]	(0.022)
(9)	Real exchange rate gap						−0.176						...	...
							[−1.274]						...	...
(10)	Real interest rate gap						−0.127						...	...
							[−0.166]						...	...
(11)	Log (PPP GDP per capita)							0.018					0.028	0.000
								[0.736]					[0.635]	(0.000)
(12)	Credit/GDP								−0.152				−0.032	0.005
									[−1.616]				[−0.299]	(0.073)
(13)	Credit/GDP gap								0.204				0.438	0.027
									[0.503]				[0.993]	(0.109)
(14)	Currency crisis									−0.141*			−0.155	−0.082
										[−1.878]			[−1.483]	(0.558)
(15)	U.S. Treasury bill rate										0.543		1.011	0.026
											[0.528]		[0.999]	(0.038)
(16)	External demand shock										−0.100		−0.113*	−0.012
											[−1.200]		[−1.960]	(0.089)
(17)	Financial openness/GDP											0.059***	0.008	0.002
												[3.031]	[0.499]	(0.094)
(18)	Trade openness/GDP											−0.133	−0.030	0.000
												[−1.549]	[−0.421]	(0.000)
(19)	Precrisis output	1.601***	1.328***	1.598***	1.027***	0.950***	1.425**	1.538***	0.900***	1.685***	1.632***	0.751**	0.901	0.916
		[3.844]	[3.875]	[4.855]	[2.691]	[3.174]	[2.435]	[3.639]	[2.700]	[3.931]	[3.807]	[2.175]	[1.437]	(0.871)
(20)	First-year output change	1.681***	1.583***	1.573***	1.781***	1.841***	1.069	1.752***	1.665***	1.552***	1.699***	1.799***	1.289***	1.175
		[3.051]	[3.551]	[3.608]	[3.406]	[3.547]	[0.992]	[3.039]	[3.280]	[2.694]	[3.046]	[3.271]	[3.379]	(1.000)
(21)	Constant term	−0.056**	0.162**	−0.018	−0.093***	−0.051*	−0.066	−0.077**	−0.021	−0.045**	−0.086	−0.049	0.125	0.337
		[−2.652]	[2.156]	[−0.726]	[−2.759]	[−1.970]	[−1.182]	[−2.036]	[−0.806]	[−2.003]	[−1.271]	[−1.159]	[0.791]	(1.000)
Number of observations		88	85	80	87	81	26	88	77	88	88	52	44	44
R^2		0.334	0.408	0.409	0.334	0.369	0.256	0.338	0.295	0.353	0.339	0.314	0.763	...

Source: IMF staff calculations.

Note: columns 1–12 report estimation results based on ordinary least squares with robust *t*-statistics in square brackets. ***, **, and * indicate significance at the 1, 5, and 10 percent level, respectively. Column 13 reports estimation results based on Bayesian model averaging with the probability of inclusion of each variable in parentheses. The term "gap" denotes the deviation of the variable from the precrisis historical average (years *t* = −10 to *t* = −3, where *t* = 0 denotes the crisis year) during the last three years preceding the crisis. PPP = purchasing power parity.

- *Output:* The precrisis output position (which identifies the starting position of output relative to trend) and the initial change in output during the first year of the crisis (which indicates the severity of the crisis in the short run) are potentially important control variables. The small-scale OLS results indicate that the severity of the crisis, measured by the first-year change in output, has strong predictive power for medium-term output losses (Table 4.1, row 20). Similarly, a depressed level of output relative to trend before the crisis appears to carry over and is associated with a significantly larger medium-term output loss (Table 4.1, row 19).[22] Based on these results, the two initial output variables are included as controls in all remaining regressions.[23]

- *Investment:* The prominent role of investment and capital losses suggests that the level and evolution of precrisis investment would be good predictors of eventual output losses. Indeed, regression results provide strong evidence that economies with high precrisis investment-to-GDP ratios, measured as the average investment-to-GDP ratio during the three years before the crisis, tend to have large output losses (Table 4.1, row 1; Figure 4.8). In contrast, the investment gap, defined as the deviation from its historical average of the investment-to-GDP ratio during the three years before a crisis, is not statistically significant (Table 4.1, row 2).[24] We return to potential interpretations of these results later in this section, but it is worth mentioning that the precrisis investment share is particularly robust as a leading indicator, even after controlling for the level of the current account balance. This suggests that countries that have high investment rates tend to experience larger output declines following banking crises, irrespective of whether the investment is financed by foreign or domestic savings.

[22]In the three years prior to a banking crisis, the level of output is, on average, below its trend, suggesting that banking crises are not typically preceded by a precrisis boom. In the sample of 88 banking crises, the average deviation is about –3 percent.

[23]A possible concern about controlling for short-run crisis severity, proxied by the decline in output in the crisis year, is that crisis severity could be correlated with other explanatory variables, potentially complicating the interpretation of the regression coefficients. For example, a greater precrisis investment-to-GDP ratio could be associated with a sharper short-run decline in output. To address this possible concern, all the regressions are also implemented while omitting the short-run crisis severity control variable (see Tables 4.3 and 4.4 in Appendix 4.1), and the coefficient estimates do not change substantially.

[24]The precrisis historical average level is based on the seven-year period ending three years before the crisis.

Figure 4.8. Output Evolution versus Precrisis Investment

Output in Percent of Precrisis Trend
(Percent of precrisis trend; mean difference from year t = – 1; *first year of crisis at* t = 0; *years on x-axis)*

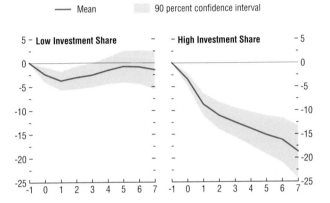

Precrisis Investment Share versus Corporate Leverage

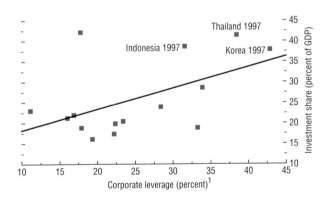

Sources: Ueda (2008); World Bank, *World Development Indicators;* and IMF staff calculations.
[1]Corporate leverage is measured by the debt-to-assets ratio.

Figure 4.9. Output Evolution versus Precrisis Imbalances[1]

(Output in percent of precrisis trend; mean difference from year t = – 1; *first year of crisis at* t = 0; *years on x-axis)*

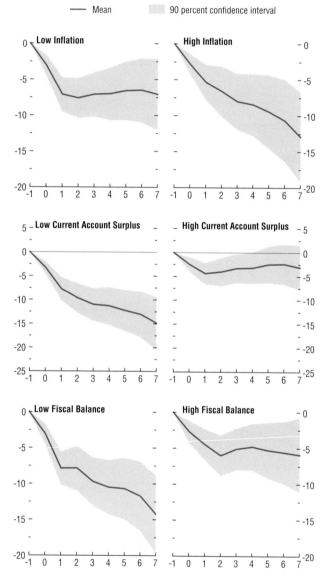

Sources: World Bank, *World Development Indicators;* and IMF staff calculations.
[1]The figure reports the output evolution for banking crises with inflation, current account, and fiscal balance below and above the sample median, respectively. Inflation and fiscal balance are measured in deviation from country-specific historical averages.

- *Policy room:* By limiting the room for policy maneuver, the buildup of macroeconomic imbalances may also imply higher medium-term output losses after a crisis. We consider the precrisis levels and dynamics of several variables—inflation, current account balance, fiscal balance, real exchange rate, and real interest rate—that may capture the notion of macroeconomic imbalances.[25] We find mixed evidence that rising imbalances are associated with larger output losses, and, by implication, that more limited policy room that constrains the ability of countries to run countercyclical macroeconomic policies is associated with larger output losses. In particular, the results based on the small-scale regressions suggest that economies with larger current account deficits, rising inflation, and a deteriorating fiscal balance before a crisis experienced significantly larger output losses (Table 4.1, rows 3, 6, 8; Figure 4.9). But the results from the BMA analysis (Table 4.1, column 13) are less conclusive. Here it is important to bear in mind that having more policy room does not necessarily mean using that policy room—an issue addressed later.[26]

- *Level of income and financial development:* Postcrisis output losses are not significantly correlated with the level of income (Table 4.1, row 11). In fact, the evolution of output after

[25]The dynamics are captured by considering the deviations of these variables from their country-specific historical averages during the precrisis period (the "gaps"). Using country-specific averages allows for the possibility that different countries may have different explicit or implicit inflation targets or fiscal rules. For example, a 3 percent inflation rate may imply less room for monetary easing in an economy with inflation normally at 1 percent than in an economy with an inflation norm of 5 percent. For each variable, the "gap" value is constructed as a deviation of the average precrisis value (from $t = -3$ to $t = -1$) from the country-specific average value (from $t = -10$ to $t = -3$). Using government debt to measure fiscal room was not possible for the sample of economies considered here due to data limitations.

[26]Two other domestic policy variables—the real interest rate and real exchange rate before the crisis, measured relative to their historical averages—do not appear to have predictive power for medium-term output losses (see Figure 4.1, rows 9, 10).

banking crises for upper-income, middle-income, and low-income economies is similar (Figure 4.10). At the same time, there is weak evidence that a higher precrisis level of financial development is associated with larger output losses (Table 4.1, row 12; Figure 4.10).[27]

- *Openness, external conditions, and currency crises:* Currency crises that coincide with banking crises—"twin crises"—are robustly associated with larger output losses (Table 4.1, row 14, Figure 4.11). The results for the openness indicators, on the other hand, are mixed (Table 4.1, rows 17, 18; Figure 4.11). The small-scale regression approach suggests that financial openness is associated with smaller losses and is consistent with recent work that finds that deeper financial integration reduces the risk of a sudden stop in capital flows and enhances the ability to smooth spending.[28] However, the evidence is weaker based on the broader specification. Evidence for trade is even weaker. Turning to external conditions, the U.S. Treasury bill rate before the crisis is not found to be a significant predictor of output losses (Table 4.1, row 15). The evidence that an adverse external demand shock occurring at the time of a banking crisis is correlated with larger output losses is mixed (Table 4.1, row 16).

- *Structural policy environment:* The precrisis levels of various structural policy reform indicators are not significantly correlated with medium-run output losses and are not presented in Table 4.1.[29] Nevertheless, one

[27]The analysis also considers whether an increase in the credit-to-GDP ratio relative to each country's own historical average level (the credit-to-GDP "gap") plays a role and finds it to be statistically insignificant. The question of whether there is a nonlinear link between the level of financial deepening and output losses is left for further research.

[28]See Calvo, Izquierdo, and Mejía (2008) and Abiad, Leigh, and Mody (2009).

[29]The analysis draws on the database of structural reforms prepared by the Research Department of the IMF. It covers 150 industrial and developing economies and eight sectors. In this chapter, we use the domestic financial sector reform index (which includes measures of securities markets and banking sector reforms) and the

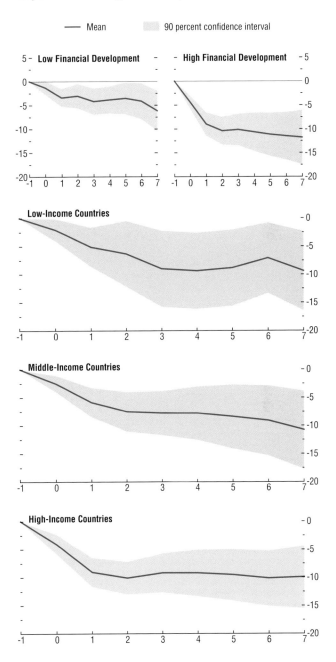

Figure 4.10. Output Evolution versus Financial Development and Income[1]

(Output in percent of precrisis trend; mean difference from year t = − 1; *first year of crisis at* t = 0; *years on x-axis)*

Sources: World Bank, *World Development Indicators;* and IMF staff calculations.
[1]The figure reports the output evolution for banking crises with financial development below and above the sample median and by income level. Financial development is measured by the credit-to-GDP ratio. Income level is measured by real purchasing-power-parity GDP per capita.

finding is worth highlighting: countries with higher precrisis levels of employment protection tend to experience larger postcrisis employment losses. This link is illustrated for OECD economies that have experienced banking crises, using the OECD's comprehensive measure of employment protection, and for the broader banking crisis sample using a cruder measure (Figure 4.12).[30] Because this result is based on a smaller sample, it needs to be interpreted cautiously.

What do the regression results tell us?

The empirical analysis suggests that the first-year loss is important in predicting the eventual output losses following a banking crisis. This is consistent with the notion that output dynamics are especially persistent following large shocks. What could explain this? Some possible candidates include (1) bankruptcies that lead to fire sales of capital assets that have significant sunk costs and take time to rebuild, (2) an impaired financial system that needs time to heal before it can intermediate financial capital effectively, and (3) labor and product market rigidities that impede the necessary reallocation of labor and capital following a crisis. These explanations are consistent with the finding that all factors of production contribute to medium-term output losses.

Figure 4.11. Output, Twin Crises, and Financial Openness[1]

(Output in percent of precrisis trend; mean difference from year t = − 1; *first year of crisis at* t = 0; *years on x-axis)*

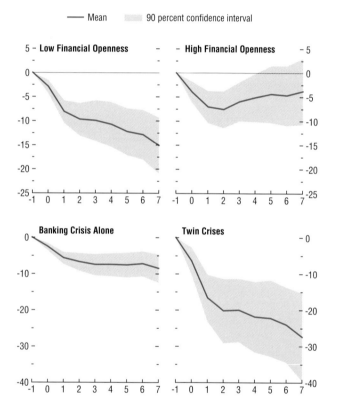

Sources: Lane and Milesi-Ferretti (2006); and IMF staff calculations.
[1]Financial openness is measured using the ratio of external assets and liabilities to GDP. Twin crises are defined as simultaneous banking and currency crises. The figure reports output evolution for banking crises and twin crises and for crises with financial openness below and above the sample median, respectively.

capital account liberalization index (which summarizes a broad set of restrictions), the trade liberalization index (based on average tariffs), and the fiscal sector reform index (based on tax rates and the efficiency of revenue collection and public spending). We also use various measures of labor market flexibility, including for employment protection, unemployment benefit replacement ratios, and tax wedges. See IMF (2008) and Giuliano, Mishra, and Spilimbergo (2009) for more details. The indices for product market reforms were not used in the analysis because of insufficient data coverage.

[30]The OECD employment protection legislation (EPL) strictness index is produced annually and generally goes back to the mid-1980s. It is a summary indicator of EPL strictness, which weights 14 subcomponents (on dismissal procedures for regular contracts and the use of temporary contracts). For the broader sample, two of the subcomponents that are used to construct this index are available (on notice periods required and severance payments involved in employment termination).

Related to the dynamics of capital accumulation, the precrisis investment share is a particularly robust predictor of the postcrisis output loss. This finding, together with the earlier result that investment and the capital-to-labor ratio decline over the medium term following banking crises, is consistent with a number of potential interpretations. In some cases, it may be that the output loss reflects the unwinding of excessive investment built up over a protracted period, such as the real estate bubble in the case of Thailand's 1997 crisis.[31] Corporate sector indebtedness may also play a role. Figure 4.8 shows a link between the precrisis investment-to-GDP ratio and the level of precrisis corporate leverage. During the bubble period, when collateral may be valued excessively, some firms issue debt in order to invest. When the bubble bursts, these same firms have to delever, which may take time, leading to a stagnation of investment over the medium term. For economies affected during the Asian crisis, such as Indonesia, Korea, and Thailand, there is some firm-level evidence supporting this hypothesis (Coulibaly and Millar, 2008). Nevertheless, these interpretations may not fully explain the remarkably strong correlation between the precrisis investment share and medium-term output losses—an issue that merits further investigation.

Regarding employment dynamics, there is some tentative evidence linking eventual employment losses to the level of employment protection. Theoretically, employment protection has an ambiguous effect because it reduces inflows to and outflows from employment. However, while the effect on the steady-state employment rate is unclear, many academic papers argue that stricter employment protection makes the labor market less effective at reallocating labor after a shock.[32] Specifically, in the immediate aftermath of a banking crisis,

Figure 4.12. Employment Losses and Employment Protection Legislation

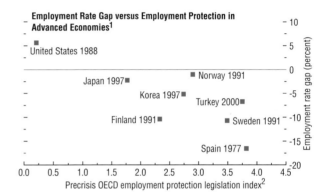

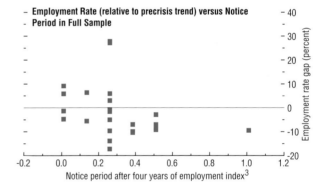

Sources: IMF, Structural Reform Database; and IMF staff calculations.
[1]The employment rate gap measures the employment rate relative to its precrisis trend.
[2]The index is a summary indicator of the OECD employment protection legislation strictness. Because employment protection legislation index data start in the mid-1980s, the 1985 observation is used for Spain 1977.
[3]The index is constructed based on the notice period required to terminate employment.

---

[31]To the extent that some investment during the precrisis period was wasteful, output losses may have taken place even without a crisis, albeit gradually.

[32]See Blanchard and Portugal (2001) and Balakrishnan and Michelacci (2001), for example.

unemployment may rise independently of the level of protection because firms can more easily justify layoffs during crises (or are more willing to pay firing costs) and because the number of bankruptcies rises. After the crisis, however, countries with stricter employment protection may experience lower job creation, explaining the larger overall employment rate losses.

After the Crisis: Which Policies Are Associated with Lower Output Losses?

What role do policies play in mitigating the ultimate output loss after a crisis? It is important to acknowledge that the following discussion seeks to identify patterns rather than establish causality between policies and postcrisis output trends.[33] The discussion focuses on domestic macroeconomic policies and structural reforms and on external conditions and policies abroad. As in the analysis of precrisis factors, we present the regression results, which are supplemented by some relevant charts. As before, all regressions control for key initial output variables.

- *Macroeconomic policy support:* Short-run demand management policies (monetary and fiscal) implemented after the beginning of a crisis may play a role both in reducing the size of the initial output loss and in aiding the recovery. Dependent on data availability, we measure the monetary policy stance as the change in real lending rates. To measure changes in discretionary fiscal policy, we follow the approach of the April 2009 *World Economic Outlook* and use the growth in real government consumption. In both cases, to capture the short-term response of macroeconomic policies, the variables are computed for the

first year of the crisis and the following three years. The variables are designed to measure a notion of stimulus (rather than policy room) and thus differ from those used in the precrisis analysis. We find that a stronger short-term fiscal policy response (a larger increase in government consumption) is significantly associated with smaller medium-term output losses (Table 4.2, row 1; Figure 4.13).[34] The evidence on the monetary policy stance is mixed, possibly reflecting a weaker monetary policy transmission mechanism after banking crises. A decline in real lending rates is associated with smaller output losses, but only in some specifications (Table 4.2, row 2; Figure 4.13). There is also some mixed evidence that real exchange rate depreciations are associated with smaller output losses (Table 4.2, row 3).

- *Structural reforms:* Structural reforms may also play a role in boosting output during the postcrisis period. We consider reform efforts in several areas, such as domestic financial reform, capital account and trade liberalization, and structural fiscal reform. In each case, the reform effort is measured as the *change* in various indices mentioned earlier during the postcrisis period (rather than

---

[33]As discussed in the literature, the two-way relationship between postcrisis policies and outcomes complicates any causal inference. For example, is it that financial reform during or after a banking crisis leads to increased financial intermediation and a lower output loss? Or that a lower output loss leads to higher demand and thus higher financial intermediation and also gives the authorities the policy room to implement important financial sector reforms? These difficult questions cannot be answered within our regression framework.

[34]The results imply that raising government consumption by 1 percent of GDP is associated with a reduction in the medium-term output loss of about 1.5 percentage points. The change in government consumption, rather than the change in tax revenue or the fiscal balance, is used as a measure of fiscal stimulus, because it lessens reverse-causality concerns. Measuring fiscal stimulus based on the change in tax revenue or the change in the fiscal balance would be problematic. A larger deterioration in output implies a greater deterioration in tax revenue and the fiscal balance, complicating the interpretation of the regression coefficients. As expected, repeating the analysis using the change in the fiscal balance yields a regression coefficient that is statistically indistinguishable from zero. Exploring the possibility of "expansionary contractions" associated with cuts in government spending, or of "crowding-out" effects associated with fiscal stimulus in economies with unsustainable government debt levels, was complicated by insufficient data on government debt. Some evidence of such effects is presented in Chapter 3 of the April 2009 *World Economic Outlook*.

the levels, which were used in the precrisis analysis).[35] Overall, there is mixed evidence that structural reform efforts are significantly associated with smaller output losses. Liberalization of the capital account is highly correlated with smaller output losses in small-scale regressions, although its statistical significance declines when considered in larger-scale frameworks (Table 4.2, row 4; Figure 4.14). Domestic financial reforms are also significantly associated with output losses in small-scale regressions, but less so in larger-scale frameworks (Table 4.2, row 5; Figure 4.14). Trade liberalization is not significantly related to output losses (Table 4.2, row 6). Finally, there is some positive evidence of a link between improvements in government efficiency and output losses, although the increased significance of this structural variable in the broader specifications appears to be partly due to the change in the sample composition (as the number of observations drops to 30).

- *External conditions:* Policies and conditions abroad may also be important in reducing output losses by improving the external environment during the postcrisis period. The results indicate that larger domestic output losses are significantly related to the occurrence of adverse external demand shocks, defined as very low partner growth during the postcrisis period (Table 4.2, row 9). In addition, there is weak evidence that larger output losses are significantly associated with higher global short-term interest rates (Table 4.2, row 8).[36]

How should we interpret these empirical findings? Overall, our findings suggest that

---

[35]Regarding labor market liberalization indicators, data availability is limited for the sample of banking crisis countries. Moreover, when data are available, there is often little change after a crisis. For both these reasons, we do not report results for postcrisis labor market indicators.

[36]Unlike in the small-scale regressions, the global interest rate is significantly related to output losses in the large-scale OLS regression and has a relatively high probability of inclusion (0.63) in the BMA framework.

Figure 4.13. Output Losses and Macroeconomic Stimulus[1]

Expansionary macroeconomic policies are associated with smaller output losses.

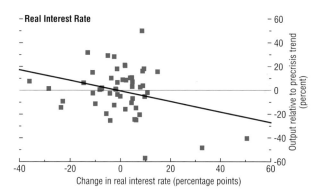

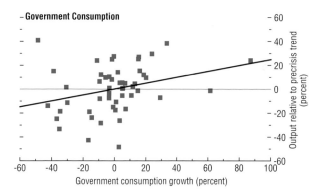

Sources: World Bank, *World Development Indicators;* and IMF staff calculations.
[1]Scatter plots report conditional plots that take into account the effect of several other controlling variables (as reported in column 11 of Table 4.2). The change in the real interest rate and the growth of government consumption is measured over the crisis year and the following three years.

Figure 4.14. Postcrisis Associations of Key Variables with Output Losses

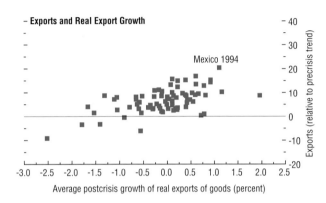

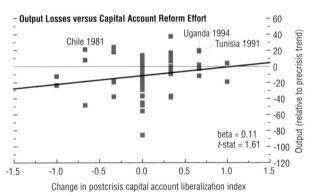

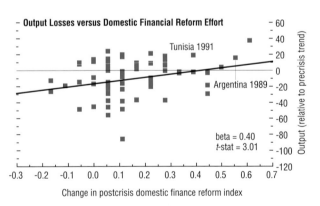

Sources: IMF, Structural Reform database; World Bank, *World Development Indicators;* and IMF staff calculations.

expansionary short-term macroeconomic policies are associated with smaller medium-term output losses. This is consistent with the notion that countercyclical fiscal and monetary policies may help cushion the downturn after the crisis, which would carry over into smaller measured output losses in the medium term. At the same time, these results do not imply that countercyclical macroeconomic stimulus is the right solution for all economies at all times—it is likely to depend on country-specific characteristics, such as the credibility of fiscal and external sustainability and borrowing costs. In fact, fiscal expansions in economies with unsustainable debt levels could be counterproductive—an issue that is not explored here because of data limitations.

The relationship between postcrisis structural policy reform and output losses is somewhat weaker. However, this could be the result of well-known difficulties in measuring the timing, magnitude, and sequencing of structural reforms,[37] as well as the possibility that structural reforms and capacity building may take longer than seven years to bear fruit in terms of output. At the same time, the spillover effects of global conditions may be important, given the association between the external environment and the eventual output losses.

What about the role of structural policies based on country experiences?

To gain further insight into the effects of structural policy reform, we supplement the regression analysis by looking at the experiences of several countries. Specifically, we focus on episodes—such as Chile (1981) and Mexico (1994) in Figure 4.1—that were followed by significant

---

[37]Measurement error in the structural reform indicators will bias the regression coefficients toward zero, making it more difficult to find that the results are statistically significant. Also, the size of the bias depends directly on the magnitude of the measurement error, which is likely to be much larger for unobserved structural reform indicators (such as labor market flexibility or financial sector reform) than for macroeconomic variables (such as government consumption or interest rates).

Table 4.2. Output Losses versus Postcrisis Conditions and Policies

(Dependent variable: output at t=7 in percent of precrisis trend)

	(1)	(2)	(3)	(4)	(5)	(6)	(7)	(8)	(9)	(10)	(11)	(12)	(13)
(1) Real government consumption growth	0.202** [2.520]									0.244* [1.843]		0.405** [2.264]	0.263 (0.648)
(2) Change in real interest rate		−0.085 [−0.404]								−0.493** [−2.280]		−0.580 [−1.577]	−0.530 (0.708)
(3) Real appreciation			0.135* [1.785]							−0.011 [−0.075]		−0.418* [−2.047]	−0.038 (0.166)
(4) Change in capital account liberalization index				0.166*** [4.267]							0.147** [2.290]	0.030 [0.433]	0.007 (0.085)
(5) Change in financial liberalization index					0.108** [2.583]						0.017 [0.302]	0.149* [1.769]	0.002 (0.044)
(6) Change in trade liberalization index						−0.046 [−0.950]					−0.063 [−1.123]	−0.122 [−1.506]	−0.013 (0.149)
(7) Change in government efficiency index							−0.005 [−0.077]				0.0132 [0.213]	0.129* [2.044]	0.078 (0.608)
(8) U.S. Treasury bill rate								−1.404 [−1.012]		0.490 [0.178]		−4.459 [−1.524]	−2.820 (0.400)
(9) External demand shock									−0.960*** [−3.156]	−1.161 [−1.611]		−1.073 [−1.668]	−0.415 (0.411)
(10) Precrisis output	1.213*** [4.666]	1.038*** [2.791]	1.371*** [4.292]	1.079*** [3.537]	0.997*** [4.358]	1.384*** [4.456]	1.162** [2.398]	1.601*** [3.783]	1.753*** [4.427]	1.137*** [3.453]	1.124*** [3.061]	0.907 [1.687]	0.143 (0.184)
(11) First-year output change	2.032*** [3.396]	2.107*** [2.941]	1.750*** [2.884]	2.191*** [3.560]	2.262*** [3.529]	2.145*** [3.526]	1.749** [2.591]	1.714*** [3.158]	1.875*** [3.558]	2.365** [2.667]	2.220*** [3.330]	3.136*** [2.889]	2.693 (1.000)
(12) Constant term	−0.056** [−2.065]	−0.047** [−2.059]	−0.034 [−1.471]	−0.093*** [−4.010]	−0.088*** [−3.510]	−0.020 [−0.869]	−0.054 [−1.485]	0.023 [0.284]	−0.004 [−0.177]	−0.037 [−0.260]	−0.079* [−1.964]	0.064 [0.385]	0.052 (1.000)
Number of observations	77	59	74	65	65	78	53	88	88	50	49	30	30
R^2	0.398	0.283	0.342	0.459	0.397	0.388	0.281	0.344	0.396	0.506	0.450	0.709	...

Source: IMF staff calculations.

Note: Columns 1–12 report estimation results based on ordinary least squares with robust *t*-statistics in square brackets. ***, **, and * indicate significance at the 1, 5, and 10 percent level, respectively. Column 13 reports estimation results based on Bayesian model averaging with the probability of inclusion of each variable in parentheses. Structural reform variables (trade, financial, capital account, and government efficiency) measure change in index from $t = 0$ to $t = 7$, where $t = 0$ denotes the crisis year.

output gains (based on our measure of medium-term output losses) and try to identify associated major policy reforms. The following experiences are interesting.

- *Mexico (1994):* Mexico bounced back rapidly from its banking crisis in 1994 and indeed registered a significant output gain relative to precrisis trend (see Figure 4.1). Compared with most other banking crisis countries, Mexico had much stronger export growth following its crisis (see Figure 4.14). Yet partner growth—particularly in the United States— did not increase notably after 1994, suggesting that the implementation of a major trade reform—the signing of the North American Free Trade Agreement in January 1994— was the key driver of spectacular export growth, along with the impact of a substantial exchange rate depreciation during the first few years following the crisis.[38]

- *Uganda (1994):* Uganda had a significant output gain after its banking crisis in 1994. It also significantly liberalized its capital account, freeing its exchange rate and then completing the liberalization of the exchange and payments systems after the crisis. This is reflected as major capital account reform according to the structural reform index (see Figure 4.14). Uganda also implemented other important reforms, such as divesting or liquidating 115 of 150 public enterprises and liberalizing its trade regime (IMF, 2006).

[38]See for example, Kose, Meredith, and Towe (2004).

- *Argentina (1989):* After its banking and currency crisis of 1989, Argentina undertook major liberalization that led to a spectacular increase in financial intermediation (see Figure 4.14) and investment and imports, which may be observed as a significant output gain relative to the precrisis trend seven years after the crisis. The country implemented major financial reforms in the early 1990s, introducing capital and reserve requirements and increasing banking competition by allowing foreign entry. On the capital account side, restrictions on the entry and exit of portfolio and direct investment were lifted and the convertibility plan was adopted (introduction of the currency board). Trade was also liberalized, as export taxes were eliminated and import restrictions/duties lifted (see Pou, 2000).

- *Chile (1981):* Chile implemented some important structural reforms in the 1980s, including major pension and tax reforms, and registered a significant medium-term output gain. However, in the aftermath of its major financial and balance of payments crises in 1981, Chile also partially reversed major trade and capital account reforms that were implemented in the 1970s. During the late 1970s, combined with a fixed exchange rate and high real indexation, trade and capital account liberalization facilitated rising current account deficits, which were financed by large amounts of foreign lending. The imbalances continued to grow, which, combined with high global interest rates and a collapse of commodity prices, led to faltering confidence, capital flight, and a major recession. The authorities reacted by increasing tariffs and severely restricting capital flows and holdings of foreign assets by residents. The latter can be seen as a major reversal of capital account liberalization relative to how other countries reacted to banking crises (see Figure 4.14). Of course, the trade and capital account restrictions imposed after the crisis were gradually lifted during the 1980s and 1990s (Le Fort, 2005).

Overall, the case studies show that there is certainly no "one size fits all" when it comes to explaining the factors behind strong performances after banking crises. Big neighbors and trade agreements can play a role (Mexico), as can liberalization (Argentina and Uganda). Nevertheless, it is not easy to draw strong general conclusions about the growth impact of postcrisis structural reforms. Moreover, there are countries for which other factors help to explain the significant output gains relative to precrisis trend (for example, Zambia after 1995 and El Salvador after 1989).[39]

What is the bottom line?

The results suggest that proactive domestic macroeconomic policies in the short term may mitigate medium-term output losses. There is also some evidence of the beneficial role of structural policy reform and favorable global conditions. However, there is still much to learn about the processes and interactions that lead to strong growth performance.

Implications for the Outlook after the Current Financial Crisis

This section discusses some tentative implications for output in the wake of the current crisis and how policy can be used to help mitigate medium-term output losses.

For the most part, the implications of our analysis are sobering for the medium-term output prospects in economies with recent banking crises. The historical evidence suggests that output in many of these economies may remain well below precrisis trends in the medium run. The associated losses in capital, employment, and total factor productivity could be long-lasting, leaving an enduring imprint on the productive capacity of these economies. Medium-term

---

[39]After its banking crisis in 1991, Tunisia also had a significant output gain. In the years following the crisis, the country ratified the agreement to establish the African Union, established a free trade zone with the European Union, and implemented major financial and capital account reforms (see Figure 4.14).

output dynamics may also be affected at the global level. The combined output of economies currently in the midst of a banking crisis comprises close to one-half of real GDP for the advanced economies and one-quarter of world GDP. This suggests that real output in advanced economies is unlikely to rebound to its precrisis trend, which was the experience of emerging economies following the 1980s debt crises (see Box 4.1). The global nature of the current crisis also implies that external demand is less likely to play the same role it did in many of the previous banking crises in mitigating output losses.

For policymakers, the prospects of large permanent output losses raise major challenges. The macroeconomic policy response has been forceful so far, in the form of substantial fiscal and monetary stimulus. However, it remains uncertain how much potential output has been reduced by the recent financial crisis, which makes it difficult to measure the amount of slack in the economy, the so-called output gap. This makes calibrating macroeconomic policy especially challenging. Looking ahead, the timing for the withdrawal of the extraordinary amount of monetary and fiscal stimulus that has been implemented in many countries will be important. On the one hand, a premature exit could stifle the recovery. On the other hand, delaying the withdrawal of stimulus could be inflationary.

At the same time, the dramatic increase in fiscal deficits and government debt levels exacerbates sustainability concerns for a number of economies. These pressures will worsen if output losses are permanent and constrain government revenues in the future. A fall in medium-term output would also worsen the expected deterioration in government debt dynamics due to factors related to population aging.

These concerns underscore the importance of implementing reforms to help raise medium-term output and facilitate the shift of resources across sectors. On the employment side, previous crises suggest that medium-term employment losses will be large, a prediction seemingly confirmed by recent unemployment dynamics. As discussed in Chapter 1, this pros-

pect highlights the importance of labor market policies that facilitate the requisite adjustment of workers and jobs across sectors within crisis-hit economies and thereby avert increases in structural unemployment.

Appendix 4.1. Data Sources and Methodologies

The main author of this appendix is Daniel Leigh.

This appendix provides details on the data used in the analysis. It also reports the results of robustness exercises on measuring output losses and on the estimation results reported in Tables 4.1 and 4.2.

Data Sources

The main data sources for this chapter are the IMF's World Economic Outlook (WEO) and International Financial Statistics (IFS) databases and the World Bank's World Development Indicators (WDI) database. Additional data sources are listed in the table.

Data on real GDP and its demand components are from the WDI and are spliced with WEO data for observations after 2007 for which WDI data are unavailable. The current account balance, the GDP deflator, and the fiscal balance are also taken from the WEO database; the exchange rate series are taken from the IFS database. The domestic real interest rate is defined as the difference between the nominal lending rate, taken from the IFS, and GDP deflator inflation.

For the growth accounting exercises, the capital stock data are taken from Bosworth and Collins (2003). For observations not included in the Bosworth and Collins data set, the capital stock is constructed using the perpetual inventory method, with a depreciation rate of 5 percent, and real investment data. The employment and labor force data come from the WEO database.

Financial development is measured using the ratio of bank credit to GDP. Bank credit to the private nonfinancial sector is taken from the IFS database. Breaks in these data are identified

Variable	Source
Real GDP	World Bank World Development Indicators (WDI) database, World Economic Outlook (WEO) database
Population	WDI database, WEO database
Real consumption	WDI database, WEO database
Real government consumption	WDI database, WEO database
Real private investment	WDI database, WEO database
Real exports	WDI database, WEO database
Real imports	WDI database, WEO database
Current account balance	Christiansen and others (forthcoming)
GDP deflator	WEO database
Fiscal balance	WEO database
Real exchange rate	International Financial Statistics (IFS) database
Nominal exchange rate vis-à-vis U.S. dollar	IFS database
Nominal lending rate	IFS database
Capital stock	Bosworth and Collins (2003)
Employment	WEO database
Labor force	WEO database
Bank credit	WDI database, IFS database
Corporate leverage	Brooks and Ueda (2005)
Financial openness	Lane and Milesi-Ferretti (2006)
Partner-country growth	WDI database, WEO database
U.S. Treasury bill rate	Thomson Datastream
Trade liberalization index	IMF
Financial liberalization index	IMF
Capital account liberalization index	IMF
Government efficiency index	IMF
Employment protection legislation index	Organization for Economic Cooperation and Development
Employment notice period index	IMF

using the IFS *Country Notes* publication, and data are growth-spliced at these points.

Financial openness is calculated as the sum of foreign assets and foreign liabilities divided by GDP, using the External Wealth of Nations Mark II Database (see Lane and Milesi-Ferretti, 2006). Trade openness is defined as the sum of exports and imports divided by GDP. Partner-country

growth, used to compute external demand shocks, is taken from the WEO database; the three-month U.S. Treasury bill rate is obtained from Thomson Datastream.

The structural reform indicators measuring trade liberalization, capital account liberalization, financial liberalization, and government efficiency come from the IMF, and are described in greater detail by Giuliano, Mishra, and Spilimbergo (2009) and IMF (2008).

Robustness: Alternative Measures of Output Losses

The baseline measure of the output loss is compared with the following four alternative measures based on different versions of the precrisis trend.

- *Alternative 1: Precrisis window ending one year before crisis.* Here, the precrisis trend is computed as in the baseline, except that the estimation window for the precrisis trend ends one year before the crisis, rather than three years before as it does in the baseline.

- *Alternative 2: Longer estimation window application.* As in the baseline, an initial estimate of the precrisis trend is obtained based on the seven-year sample ending three years before the crisis. In the baseline approach, initial estimates that were negative were replaced with trends based on a longer precrisis window going back 20 years before the crisis. Here, the longer precrisis window is applied to the lowest and the highest 10 percent of the initial estimates of the trend growth rates. As in the baseline approach, if the trend estimate based on the longer sample is unavailable, or even farther from zero than the initial estimate, the initial estimate is kept.

- *Alternative 3: Longer estimation window applied to all crises.* Here, the estimate of the precrisis trend is obtained based solely on the longer precrisis window going back 20 years before the crisis and ending three years before the crisis.

- *Alternative 4: Precrisis trend based on real-time IMF country desk forecasts.* Here, the output losses were recomputed using the real-time medium-term growth projections of IMF country desks prepared for the April 2009 *World Economic Outlook* in the year before the crisis. In particular, the precrisis trend growth rate is defined as the desk forecast for real GDP growth in year $t = 4$ made in year $t = -1$, where $t = 0$ is the year of the crisis. The corresponding per capita growth forecast is obtained by subtracting population growth in year $t = -1$. Note that these real-time forecasts were available only for the post-1989 period.

As Figure 4.15 illustrates, the output losses obtained using the different approaches were highly correlated and all confirm the finding of large and statistically significant output losses after banking crises. The 90 percent confidence bands for each measure overlap with the 90 percent confidence band of the baseline measure. In the case of alternatives 1, 2, and 3, the overlap is substantial, and the mean output losses are statistically indistinguishable from the baseline. In the case of alternative 4, the average output loss is even greater than in the baseline. This is because the IMF country desk forecasts were, on average, more optimistic than the baseline precrisis trend. Therefore, the corresponding underperformance relative to the forecast (output loss) is, on average, significantly greater than in the baseline.

Estimation Results without Controlling for Short-Term Crisis Severity

The short-term crisis severity variable, measured by the change in output relative to trend in the crisis year, was found to be a strong predictor of medium-term output losses (Tables 4.1 and 4.2). However, there is a possible concern that short-term crisis severity may be correlated with other explanatory variables included in the regression, potentially complicating the interpretation of the regression coefficients. To address this concern, the regressions are repeated with the omission of the short-term crisis severity variable, and the results are reported in Tables 4.3 and 4.4. Overall, the coefficients are similar.

Figure 4.15. Output Evolution after Banking Crises: Alternative Measures of Precrisis Trend
(Percent of precrisis trend; mean difference from year t = − 1; *first year of crisis at* t = 0; *years on x-axis)*

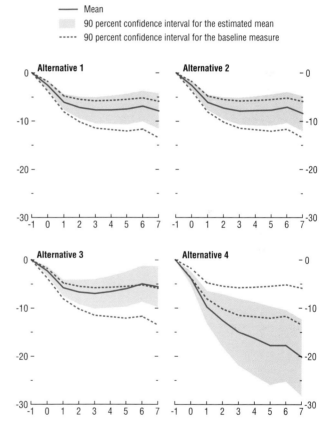

Sources: World Bank, *World Development Indicators;* and IMF staff calculations.

However, given the strong predictive power of the short-term crisis severity variable, the regression fit, measured by the R^2 statistic, declines substantially relative to the baseline specifications, in some cases by more than one-half.

References

Abiad, Abdul, Daniel Leigh, and Ashoka Mody, 2009, "Financial Integration, Capital Mobility, and Income Convergence," *Economic Policy,* Vol. 24, No. 58, pp. 241–305.

Aghion, Philippe, and Gilles Saint-Paul, 1998, "On the Virtue of Bad Times: An Analysis of the Interaction Between Economic Fluctuations and Productivity Growth," *Macroeconomic Dynamics,* Vol. 2, No. 3, pp. 322–44.

Angkinand, Apanard P., 2008, "Output Loss and Recovery from Banking and Currency Crises: Estimation Issues." http://ssrn.com/abstract=1320730.

Table 4.3. Robustness: Output Losses versus Initial Conditions, Crisis Severity Omitted
(Dependent variable: output at t = 7 in percent of precrisis trend)

	(1)	(2)	(3)	(4)	(5)	(6)	(7)	(8)	(9)	(10)	(11)	(12)	(13)
(1) Investment/GDP		−1.242***										−0.930	−1.167
		[−4.195]										[−1.660]	(0.962)
(2) Investment/GDP gap		0.687										−1.233*	−0.698
		[1.597]										[−1.724]	(0.575)
(3) Current account/GDP			0.677*									−0.002	−0.002
			[1.848]									[−0.003]	(0.019)
(4) Current account/GDP gap			1.245*									1.178	0.037
			[1.814]									[0.819]	(0.070)
(5) Inflation				0.145*								0.018	0.000
				[1.781]								[0.221]	(0.054)
(6) Inflation gap				−0.246***								−0.081	−0.023
				[−3.004]								[−0.668]	(0.199)
(7) Fiscal balance					0.428							−0.247	−0.012
					[0.754]							[−0.354]	(0.064)
(8) Fiscal balance gap					0.983							0.006	0.000
					[1.032]							[0.008]	(0.000)
(9) Real exchange rate gap						−0.182							...
						[−1.143]							
(10) Real interest rate gap						−0.184							...
						[−0.232]							
(11) Log (PPP GDP per capita)							−0.005					0.001	0.000
							[−0.225]					[0.0137]	(0.044)
(12) Credit/GDP								−0.191				−0.021	0.001
								[−1.583]				[−0.192]	(0.022)
(13) Credit/GDP gap								0.041				0.398	0.016
								[0.095]				[0.923]	(0.083)
(14) Currency crisis									−0.201***			−0.255**	−0.217
									[−2.729]			[−2.292]	(0.962)
(15) U.S. Treasury bill rate										0.082		0.295	0.005
										[0.063]		[0.215]	(0.023)
(16) External demand shock										−0.093		−0.117	−0.015
										[−0.908]		[−1.601]	(0.108)
(17) Financial openness/GDP											0.026	−0.022	0.000
											[1.675]	[−1.149]	(0.044)
(18) Trade openness/GDP											−0.126	−0.040	−0.001
											[−1.483]	[−0.442]	(0.032)
(19) Precrisis output	1.695***	1.421***	1.833***	1.138**	1.189***	1.386**	1.712***	1.117***	1.804***	1.707***	1.057***	1.283*	1.225
	[4.127]	[3.751]	[5.138]	[2.569]	[3.289]	[2.220]	[4.199]	[2.961]	[4.266]	[4.048]	[3.267]	[1.759]	(0.958)
(20) constant term	−0.099***	0.176**	−0.061**	−0.147***	−0.098***	−0.104*	−0.093**	−0.047	−0.079***	−0.100	−0.070*	0.168	0.219
	[−3.974]	[2.497]	[−2.651]	[−4.170]	[−2.717]	[−1.892]	[−2.221]	[−1.375]	[−2.935]	[−1.179]	[−1.770]	[0.817]	(1.000)
Number of observations	88	85	80	87	81	26	88	77	88	88	52	44	44
R^2	0.214	0.294	0.282	0.185	0.201	0.195	0.214	0.135	0.254	0.218	0.134	0.676	...

Note: columns 1–12 report estimation results based on OLS with robust *t*-statistics in square brackets. ***, **, and * indicate significance at the 1, 5, and 10 percent level, respectively. Column 13 reports estimation results based on Bayesian model averaging with the probability of inclusion of each variable in parentheses. The term "gap" denotes the deviation of the variable from the precrisis historical average (years *t* = −10 to *t* = −3, where *t* = 0 denotes the crisis year). PPP = purchasing power parity.

Table 4.4. Robustness: Output Losses versus Postcrisis Conditions, Crisis Severity Omitted

(Dependent variable: output at t = 7 in percent of precrisis trend)

	(1)	(2)	(3)	(4)	(5)	(6)	(7)	(8)	(9)	(10)	(11)	(12)	(13)
(1) Change in trade liberalization index	−0.045 [−0.806]										−0.052 [−0.714]	−0.0547 [−0.448]	−0.003 (0.059)
(2) Change in financial liberalization index		0.114** [2.243]									−0.004 [−0.0631]	0.0586 [0.509]	0.000 (0.045)
(3) Change in capital account liberalization index			0.179*** [3.684]								0.183** [2.276]	0.0371 [0.343]	0.003 (0.068)
(4) Change in government efficiency index				−0.030 [−0.489]							−0.025 [−0.386]	0.125 [1.352]	0.053 (0.402)
(5) Real government consumption growth					0.270** [2.257]					0.366** [2.270]		0.491 [1.459]	0.368 (0.751)
(6) Change in real interest rate						0.0016 [0.009]				−0.367 [−1.677]		−0.515 [−1.571]	−0.392 (0.595)
(7) Real appreciation							0.148* [1.689]			0.023 [0.157]		−0.196 [−0.944]	−0.001 (0.061)
(8) U.S. Treasury bill rate								−1.142 [−0.783]		0.535 [0.176]		−2.199 [−0.537]	−1.330 (0.100)
(9) External demand shock									−0.735** [−2.133]	−0.930 [−1.138]		−1.002 [−1.035]	−0.234 (0.251)
(10) Precrisis output	1.620*** [4.410]	1.274*** [4.327]	1.357*** [3.534]	1.450*** [3.228]	1.377*** [4.485]	1.165*** [2.873]	1.518*** [3.782]	1.694*** [4.076]	1.817*** [4.668]	1.230*** [3.646]	1.627*** [3.669]	1.133* [1.869]	0.373 (0.0322)
(11) Constant term	−0.074*** [−2.968]	−0.142*** [−4.906]	−0.147*** [−4.657]	−0.088* [−1.990]	−0.105*** [−3.345]	−0.098*** [−3.289]	−0.075*** [−2.670]	−0.036 [−0.414]	−0.064** [−2.426]	−0.089 [−0.602]	−0.125*** [−2.980]	−0.080 [−0.376]	−0.116 (1.000)
Number of observations	78	65	65	53	77	59	74	88	88	50	49	30	30
R^2	0.204	0.167	0.243	0.126	0.246	0.105	0.204	0.219	0.250	0.343	0.203	0.440	...

Note: columns 1–12 report estimation results based on ordinary least squares with robust t-statistics in square brackets. ***, **, and * indicate significance at the 1, 5, and 10 percent level, respectively. Column 13 reports estimation results based on Bayesian model averaging with the probability of inclusion of each variable in parentheses. Structural reform variables (trade, financial, capital account, and government efficiency) measure change in index from $t = 0$ to $t = 7$, where $t = 0$ denotes the crisis year.

Balakrishnan, Ravi, and Claudio Michelacci, 2001, "Unemployment Dynamics Across OECD Countries," *European Economic Review*, Vol. 45, No. 1, pp. 135–65.

Bassanini, Andrea, and Romain Duval, 2006, "The Determinants of Unemployment across OECD Countries: Reassessing the Role of Policies and Institutions," OECD *Economic Studies*, No. 42, pp. 7–86.

Bernanke, Ben S., 1983, "Nonmonetary Effects of the Financial Crisis in the Propagation of the Great Depression," *American Economic Review*, Vol. 73 (June), pp. 257–76.

———, and Alan S. Blinder, 1988, "Credit, Money, and Aggregate Demand," *American Economic Review*, Vol. 78 (May), pp. 435–39.

Bernanke, Ben S., and Mark Gertler, 1989, "Agency Costs, Net Worth, and Business Fluctuations," *American Economic Review*, Vol. 79 (March), pp. 14–31.

———, 1995, "Inside the Black Box: The Credit Channel of Monetary Policy Transmission," *Journal of Economic Perspectives*, Vol. 9 (Autumn), pp. 27–48.

Blanchard, Olivier, and Pedro Portugal, 2001, "What Hides Behind an Unemployment Rate: Comparing Portuguese and U.S. Labor Markets," *American Economic Review*, Vol. 91, No. 1, pp. 187–207.

Blanchard, Olivier, and Justin Wolfers, 2000, "The Role of Shocks and Institutions in the Rise of European Unemployment: The Aggregate Evidence," *The Economic Journal*, Vol. 110 (March), pp. 1–33.

Bordo, Michael, 2006, "Sudden Stops, Financial Crises, and Original Sin in Emerging Countries: Déjà Vu?" NBER Working Paper No. 12393 (Cambridge, Massachusetts: National Bureau of Economic Research).

Bosworth, Barry P., and Susan M. Collins, 2003, "The Empirics of Growth: An Update," *Brookings Papers on Economic Activity 2:2003*, 2, pp. 113–206.

Boyd, John H., Sungkyu Kwak, and Bruce Smith, 2005, "The Real Output Losses Associated with Modern Banking Crises," *Journal of Money, Credit, and Banking*, Vol. 37, No. 6, pp. 977–99.

Brooks, Robin, and Kenichi Ueda, 2005, "User Manual for the Corporate Vulnerability Utility." (unpublished; Washington: International Monetary Fund).

Caballero, Ricardo, and Mohammed Hammour, 1994, "The Cleansing Effect of Recessions," *American Economic Review*, Vol. 84, No. 5, pp. 1350–68.

Calvo, Guillermo A., Alejandro Izquierdo, and Luis-Fernando Mejía, 2008, "Systemic Sudden Stops: The Relevance of Balance-Sheet Effects and Financial Integration," NBER Working Paper No. 14026 (Cambridge, Massachusetts: National Bureau of Economic Research).

Cerra, Valerie, and Sweta Saxena, 2008, "Growth Dynamics: The Myth of Economic Recovery," *American Economic Review*, Vol. 98, No. 1, pp. 439–57.

Christiansen, Lone, Alessandro Prati, Luca Antonio Ricci, and Thierry Tressel, forthcoming, "External Balance in Low-Income Countries," NBER International Seminar on Macroeconomics 2009, ed. by Lucrezia Reichlin and
Kenneth D. West (Chicago: University of Chicago Press, for National Bureau of Economic Research).

Coulibaly, Brahima, and Jonathan Millar, 2008, "The Asian Financial Crisis, Uphill Flow of Capital, and Global Imbalances: Evidence from a Micro Study," FRB International Finance Discussion Paper No. 942 (Washington: Board of Governors of the Federal Reserve System).

Federal Reserve Bank of San Francisco (FRBSF), 2009, "Labor Supply Response to Changes in Wealth and Credit," *FRBSF Economic Letter* No. 2009–05 (January 20).

Furceri, Davide, and Annabelle Mourougane, 2009, "The Effect of Financial Crises on Potential Output: New Empirical Evidence from OECD countries," OECD Economics Department Working Paper No. 699 (Paris: Organization for Economic Cooperation and Development).

Giuliano, Paola, Prachi Mishra, and Antonio Spilimbergo, 2009, "Democracy and Reforms," IZA Discussion Paper No. 4032 (Bonn: Institute for the Study of Labor).

Guellec, Dominique, and Bruno van Pottelsberghe de la Potterie, 2002, "R&D and Productivity Growth: Panel Data Analysis for 16 OECD Countries," *OECD Economic Studies*, Vol. 2001, No. 2, pp. 128–63.

Gupta, Poonam, Deepak Mishra, and Ratna Sahay, 2007, "Behavior of Output during Currency Crises," *Journal of International Economics*, Vol. 72, No. 2, pp. 428–50.

Haugh, David, Patrice Ollivaud, and David Turner, 2009, "The Macroeconomic Consequences of Banking Crises in OECD Countries," OECD Economics Department Working Paper No. 683 (Paris: Organization for Economic Cooperation and Development).

Hoeting, Jennifer A., David Madigan, Adrian E. Raftery, and Chris T. Volinsky, 1999, "Bayesian Model Averaging: A Tutorial," *Statistical Science*, Vol. 14, No. 4, pp. 382–401.

Hutchison, Michael, and Ilan Noy, 2002, "How Bad Are Twins? Output Costs of Currency and Banking Crises," *Journal of Money, Credit, and Banking*, Vol. 37, No. 4, pp. 725–52.

International Monetary Fund (IMF), 2005, "Uruguay: Ex Post Assessment of Longer-Term Program Engagement," IMF Country Report No. 05/202 (Washington: International Monetary Fund).

———, 2006, "Uganda: Ex Post Assessment of Performance under Fund-Supported Programs," IMF Country Report No. 06/24 (Washington).

———, 2008, "Structural Reforms and Economic Performance in Advanced and Developing Countries" (Washington). www.imf.org/external/np/res/docs/2008/0608.htm.

Kiyotaki, Nobuhiro, and John Moore, 1997, "Credit Cycles," *Journal of Political Economy*, Vol. 105 (April), pp. 211–48.

Kose, M. Ayhan, Guy Meredith, and Christopher Towe, 2004, "How Has NAFTA Affected the Mexican Economy? Review and Evidence," IMF Working Paper 04/59 (Washington: International Monetary Fund).

Laeven, Luc, and Fabian Valencia, 2008, "Systemic Banking Crises: A New Database," IMF Working Paper 08/224 (Washington: International Monetary Fund).

Lane, Philip R., and Gian Maria Milesi-Ferretti, 2006, "Systemic Banking Crises: A New Database," IMF Working Paper 08/224 (Washington: International Monetary Fund).

Le Fort, Guillermo, 2005, "Capital Account Liberalization and the Real Exchange Rate in Chile," IMF Working Paper 05/132 (Washington: International Monetary Fund).

Masanjala, Winford H., and Chris Papageorgiou, 2008, "Rough and Lonely Road to Prosperity: A Reexamination of the Sources of Growth in Africa Using Bayesian Model Averaging," *Journal of Applied Econometrics*, Vol. 23, No. 5, pp. 671–82.

Milesi-Ferretti, Gian Maria, and Assaf Razin, 1998, "Current Account Reversals and Currency Crises: Empirical Regularities," NBER Working Paper No. 6620 (Cambridge, Massachusetts: National Bureau of Economic Research).

Nickell, Stephen, Luca Nunziata, and Wolfgang Ochel, 2005, "Unemployment in the OECD since the 1960s: What Do We Know?" *The Economic Journal*, Vol. 115, No. 500, pp. 1–27.

Pisani-Ferry, Jean, and Bruno van Pottelsberghe, 2009, "Handle with Care! Post-Crisis Growth in the EU," Bruegel Policy Brief No. 2009/02 (Brussels: Bruegel).

Pou, Pedro, 2000, "Argentina's Structural Reforms of the 1990s," *Finance and Development*, Vol. 37, No. 1, pp. 13–15.

Reinhart, Carmen, and Kenneth Rogoff, 2008a, "This Time Is Different: A Panoramic View of Eight Centuries of Financial Crises," NBER Working Paper No. 13882 (Cambridge, Massachusetts: National Bureau of Economic Research).

———, 2008b, "Banking Crises: An Equal Oppotunity Menace," NBER Working Paper No. 14587 (Cambridge, Massachusetts: National Bureau of Economic Research).

———, 2009, "The Aftermath of Financial Crises," NBER Working Paper No. 14656 (Cambridge, Massachusetts: National Bureau of Economic Research).

Schumpeter, Joseph, 1942, *Capitalism, Socialism and Democracy* (New York: Harper, 1975; originally published in 1942).

IMF EXECUTIVE BOARD DISCUSSION OF THE OUTLOOK, SEPTEMBER 2009

The following remarks by the Acting Chair were made at the conclusion of the Executive Board's discussion of the World Economic Outlook *on September 16, 2009.*

Executive Directors welcomed signs that the global economy appears to be recovering and that financial conditions have improved markedly. Decisive and wide-ranging public interventions in key advanced economies have allayed concerns about systemic financial collapse and a global depression, while stimulative macroeconomic policies have shored up domestic demand across many other economies. Directors observed that emerging and developing countries, notably strong Asian performance, are leading the global recovery, supported by accommodative policies and recent increases in commodity prices.

Directors nevertheless expected the pace of global recovery to be subdued, with activity remaining far below precrisis levels. Downside risks to growth, though receding, remain a concern. First, a key constraint on activity is credit availability, as bank deleveraging is expected to limit the supply of credit for some time. Second, forces driving the current rebound will fade, as fiscal stimulus diminishes and inventory rebuilding gradually loses impetus. Third, consumption and investment are muted by the need to repair balance sheets, as well as rising unemployment, high excess capacity, and financing constraints. All these provide grounds to be cautious about the course of the global recovery.

Directors stressed that the key policy tasks remain restoring financial sector health, while maintaining supportive macroeconomic policies until the recovery is on a firm footing. Directors agreed that, while it is still too early for an exit from extraordinary public interventions and fiscal and monetary stimulus, policymakers need to begin preparing for the exit. The challenge is to calibrate the timing for the unwinding of public support, suited to individual country circumstances, communicating clear, coordinated exit strategies to the public. A premature withdrawal could jeopardize achievements in securing financial stability and economic recovery, while a delayed exit runs the risk of damaging public balance sheets, amplifying inflation prospects, and distorting incentives. Directors underscored the importance of international coordination and the advisory role of the IMF in the design and timing of exit strategies, recognizing that recovery paths differ from country to country.

Directors considered that the key issues facing monetary policymakers are when and how to unwind accommodative conditions, anticipating the impact of the withdrawal of fiscal support. In advanced economies, most central banks can afford to maintain accommodative conditions for an extended period so long as output gaps remain wide. While the rise in central bank liquidity will largely run off naturally as financial conditions improve, it could take much longer to reverse the buildup in illiquid assets on some central banks' balance sheets. Directors noted that central banks have the tools available to absorb reserves as needed to drain liquidity. They thought that the need to remove monetary accommodation is likely to materialize sooner in emerging economies than in advanced economies, although the situation varies across emerging economies. In some emerging economies, warding off risks of new asset price bubbles may also call for greater exchange rate flexibility.

Beyond the short-term horizon, Directors considered that monetary authorities should regularly monitor asset price movements along with other economic developments and, where and when possible, complement changes in policy rates with macroprudential instruments under appropriate circumstances. That said, they recognized that many unresolved practical issues exist regarding macrofinancial linkages, and hence it is too early to draw firm operational conclusions for monetary policy.

Notwithstanding already large deficits and rising public debt in many countries, Directors generally believed that fiscal stimulus needs to be sustained until the recovery is firmly established. They broadly felt that support may even need to be amplified or extended beyond current plans if downside risks to growth materialize, although a few saw very limited fiscal room in major advanced economies. Directors agreed that more progress in putting public finances back on a sustainable path could be achieved by governments' committing to large reductions in deficits and advancing reforms to entitlement systems. The credibility of such commitments could usefully be supported with more robust fiscal frameworks, including suitable fiscal rules and strong enforcement mechanisms that help constrain spending pressures in the upswing.

Directors stressed that completing financial sector repair and reforming prudential frameworks are urgently needed to return to sustained growth and to fully exit from liquidity and credit provision. Renewed efforts to increase bank capital and to cleanse bank balance sheets would help underpin the recovery. Official stress tests provide key diagnostics in order to design appropriate strategies for recapitalization of viable banks and for careful resolution of nonviable banks. In addition, exit strategies need to be clearly articulated to help guide bank restructuring. Public support programs need to be phased out gradually, using well-designed, market-based incentives. Moreover, clarity on new standards for capital regulation, liquidity risk requirements, provisioning, and accounting,

and, where possible, resolution strategies are necessary in order for banks to decide properly how to deploy their resources and which business lines are likely to be profitable.

Directors noted that the pace of sustained medium-term growth depends critically on addressing the supply disruptions caused by the crisis and rebalancing the global pattern of demand. While past banking crises have tended to result in appreciable permanent output losses, this need not be the case if appropriate policies are deployed. Beyond the restructuring of financial firms and repair of markets, measures to help facilitate the redeployment of capital and labor are necessary. Countries with significant impediments to growth need to accelerate structural reforms to lift productivity and potential output.

To offset likely subdued domestic demand in deficit economies, many current account surplus economies will need to rely more on domestic demand growth, boosting private consumption, increasing the efficiency of capital allocation, and allowing greater exchange rate flexibility where necessary. Deficit countries must also do their part, tackling impediments to public and private saving, boosting potential output through labor and product market reforms, and improving corporate governance. It will be important for all countries to avoid trade and financial protectionism.

Directors cautioned that rising unemployment will present a major challenge in many advanced economies, while the crisis has been a setback to growth, employment, and poverty-alleviation efforts in many low-income economies. They underscored the need to help the unemployed with income support, strong job intermediation services, education and training, and measures to buffer the impact of income losses from lower wages in response to the shocks. Directors called for continued international support for low-income countries in their efforts to alleviate poverty and maintain macroeconomic stability.

STATISTICAL APPENDIX

The Statistical Appendix presents historical data, as well as projections. It comprises five sections: Assumptions, What's New, Data and Conventions, Classification of Countries, and Statistical Tables.

The assumptions underlying the estimates and projections for 2009–10 and the medium-term scenario for 2011–14 are summarized in the first section. The second section presents a brief description of changes to the database and statistical tables. The third section provides a general description of the data and of the conventions used for calculating country group composites. The classification of countries in the various groups presented in the *World Economic Outlook* is summarized in the fourth section.

The last, and main, section comprises the statistical tables. Data in these tables have been compiled on the basis of information available through mid-September 2009. The figures for 2009 and beyond are shown with the same degree of precision as the historical figures solely for convenience; because they are projections, the same degree of accuracy is not to be inferred.

Assumptions

Real effective *exchange rates* for the advanced economies are assumed to remain constant at their average levels during the period July 30–August 27, 2009. For 2009 and 2010, these assumptions imply average U.S. dollar/SDR conversion rates of 1.532 and 1.556, U.S. dollar/euro conversion rates of 1.373 and 1.409, and yen/U.S. dollar conversion rates of 94.9 and 93.2, respectively.

It is assumed that the *price of oil* will average $61.53 a barrel in 2009 and $76.50 a barrel in 2010.

Established *policies* of national authorities are assumed to be maintained. The more specific policy assumptions underlying the projections for selected economies are described in Box A1.

With regard to *interest rates*, it is assumed that the London interbank offered rate (LIBOR) on six-month U.S. dollar deposits will average 1.2 percent in 2009 and 1.4 percent in 2010, that three-month euro deposits will average 1.2 percent in 2009 and 1.6 percent in 2010, and that six-month yen deposits will average 0.7 percent in 2009 and 0.6 percent in 2010.

With respect to *introduction of the euro*, on December 31, 1998, the Council of the European Union decided that, effective January 1, 1999, the irrevocably fixed conversion rates between the euro and currencies of the member states adopting the euro are as follows.

1 euro	= 13.7603	Austrian schillings
	= 40.3399	Belgian francs
	= 0.585274	Cyprus pound[1]
	= 1.95583	Deutsche mark
	= 5.94573	Finnish markkaa
	= 6.55957	French francs
	= 340.750	Greek drachma[2]
	= 0.787564	Irish pound
	= 1,936.27	Italian lire
	= 40.3399	Luxembourg francs
	= 0.42930	Maltese lira[3]
	= 2.20371	Netherlands guilders
	= 200.482	Portuguese escudos
	= 30.1260	Slovak koruna[4]
	= 239.640	Slovenian tolars[5]
	= 166.386	Spanish pesetas

---

[1]Established on January 1, 2008.
[2]Established on January 1, 2001.
[3]Established on January 1, 2008.
[4]Established on January 1, 2009.
[5]Established on January 1, 2007.

Box A1. Economic Policy Assumptions Underlying the Projections for Selected Economies

Fiscal Policy Assumptions

The short-term fiscal policy assumptions used in the *World Economic Outlook* (WEO) are based on officially announced budgets, adjusted for differences between the national authorities and the IMF staff regarding macroeconomic assumptions and projected fiscal outturns. The medium-term fiscal projections incorporate policy measures that are judged likely to be implemented. In cases where the IMF staff has insufficient information to assess the authorities' budget intentions and prospects for policy implementation, an unchanged structural primary balance is assumed, unless otherwise indicated. Specific assumptions used in some of the advanced economies follow (see also Tables B5–B7 in the Statistical Appendix for data on fiscal and structural balances).[1]

Australia. The fiscal projections are based on the May 2009 budget and IMF staff projections.

Austria. Projections for 2009 and 2010 incorporate two separate fiscal stimulus packages, tax reform, and other decisions made in Parliament. These measures are estimated to amount to 1.5 percent of GDP in 2009 and 1.9 percent of GDP in 2010.

[1]The output gap is actual less potential output, as a percent of potential output. Structural balances are expressed as a percent of potential output. The structural budget balance is the budgetary position that would be observed if the level of actual output coincided with potential output. Changes in the structural budget balance consequently include effects of temporary fiscal measures, the impact of fluctuations in interest rates and debt-service costs, and other noncyclical fluctuations in the budget balance. The computations of structural budget balances are based on IMF staff estimates of potential GDP and revenue and expenditure elasticities (see the October 1993 *World Economic Outlook*, Annex I). Net debt is defined as gross debt minus financial assets of the general government, which include assets held by the social security insurance system. Estimates of the output gap and of the structural balance are subject to significant margins of uncertainty.

Belgium. Projections for 2009 are IMF staff estimates based on the 2009 budgets approved by the federal, community, and regional parliaments and adjusted for macroeconomic assumptions. Projections for the outer years are IMF staff estimates, assuming unchanged policies.

Brazil. The 2009 forecasts are based on the budget law and IMF staff assumptions. For the outer years, the IMF staff assumes unchanged policies, with a further increase in public investment in line with the authorities' intentions.

Canada. Projections use the baseline forecasts in the 2009 Budget Statement and June 2009 Economic Action Plan—Second Report, and the September 2009 Update of Economic and Fiscal Projections. The IMF staff makes some adjustments to this forecast for differences in macroeconomic projections. The IMF staff forecast also incorporates the most recent data releases from Statistics Canada, including provincial and territorial budgetary outturns through the end of 2009:Q2.

China. For 2009–10, the government has announced a large fiscal stimulus (although there is a lack of clarity on the precise size, which complicates analysis). The IMF staff is assuming a total fiscal stimulus of 4 percent on budget in 2009 (of which 1.0 percent of GDP is revenue, 0.5 percent of GDP is automatic stabilizers, and 2.5 percent of GDP is spending), as well as 1 percent in support for government-owned enterprises. For 2010, the assumption is that the stimulus is not withdrawn.

Denmark. Projections for 2009 and 2010 are aligned with the latest official budget estimates and the underlying economic projections, adjusted where appropriate for the IMF staff's macroeconomic assumptions. For 2011–14, the projections incorporate key features of the medium-term fiscal plan as embodied in the authorities' 2008 Convergence Program submitted to the European Union (EU) and additional information obtained during the 2008 Article IV discussions with authorities.

France. Projections for 2009 are IMF staff estimates based on the 2009 budget and the two revised budget laws voted by Parliament and adjusted for macroeconomic assumptions. Projections for the outer years are IMF staff estimates based on unchanged policies.

Germany. Projections for 2009 are based on the 2009 budget, fiscal stimulus measures announced since the budget was passed, and a cyclical widening of the deficit. These amount to a fiscal stimulus of 1.5 percent of GDP in 2009 and an additional fiscal stimulus of 0.5 percent of GDP in 2010. Over the medium term, the path of health expenditures accelerates as a result of population aging, and costs increase because significant health care reform measures have not been taken.

Greece. Projections are based on the 2009 budget, the latest Stability Program, and other forecasts and data provided by the authorities.

Hong Kong SAR. Fiscal projections for 2007–10 are consistent with the authorities' medium-term strategy as outlined in the fiscal year 2009/10 budget, with projections for 2011–14 based on the assumptions underlying the IMF staff's medium-term macroeconomic scenario.

India. Estimates for 2007 are based on budgetary execution data. Projections for 2008 and beyond are based on available information on the authorities' fiscal plans, with some adjustments for the IMF staff's assumptions. For 2008/09, the fiscal projections incorporate the estimated provisions under the 2008/09 budget, as well as the cost of fiscal stimulus measures in relation to the crisis (about 0.6 percent of GDP). Beyond 2008/09, the IMF staff projects that the government will not return to its fiscal rules target of 3 percent deficit in 2009/10 or in 2010/11, in order to provide some countercyclical stimulus to sagging economic activity. However, the central government will remain relatively prudent in its fiscal management and will not use all the fiscal room created by falling commodity prices, taking into account the slower growth in revenues and worsening subnational fiscal situation. This fiscal stance would result in a gradual reduction in the over-all fiscal deficit and a sustainable medium-term debt path.

Indonesia. The 2009 fiscal projections are based on IMF staff estimates of the revised 2009 budget realization. Staff projections are adjusted for changes in macroeconomic assumptions as well as the execution of fiscal stimulus measures. For 2010, staff estimates are based on the assumption that the fiscal stimulus will not be withdrawn. Because the authorities were still in the process of finalizing the 2010 budget at the time of the WEO submission, the following elements of the additional fiscal stimulus were identified and reflected in the 2010 projections: (1) Rp 25 trillion in tax cuts, and (2) Rp 12 trillion in new infrastructure spending. The financing of the budget was based on an assumption that additional financing costs would be split between further drawdown of government deposits and additional bond issues.

Ireland. The fiscal projections are based on the April 2009 supplementary budget. The authorities announced their intention to take steps to bring the deficit down to 2.6 percent of GDP by 2013, but have yet to implement measures to bring this about.

Italy. The fiscal projections for 2009–10 incorporate the budget estimates as presented in the government's 2010–13 Economic and Financial Planning Document approved by Parliament in July, including the fiscal stimulus packages, with further adjustments for the IMF staff's macroeconomic projections and assumptions. Thereafter, a broadly constant structural primary balance is assumed.

Japan. The 2009 projections assume that fiscal stimulus will be implemented as announced by the government. The medium-term projections typically assume that expenditure and revenue of the general government (excluding the social security fund) are adjusted in line with current government policies (3 percent cut a year in public investment).

Korea. The fiscal projections assume that fiscal stimulus will be implemented in 2009 and 2010,

Box A1 *(concluded)*

as announced by the government. These discretionary stimulus measures amount to 3.6 percent of GDP in 2009 and 1.2 percent of GDP in 2010. Expenditure numbers for 2009 correspond to the budget numbers (original plus supplementary). Revenue projections reflect the IMF staff's macroeconomic assumptions, adjusted for the estimated costs of tax measures included in the stimulus package. The medium-term projections assume that the government will resume its consolidation plans and balance the budget (excluding social security funds) over the years.

Mexico. Fiscal projections for 2009 are based on budgeted discretionary spending, with revenues and nondiscretionary spending driven by the IMF staff's macroeconomic projections. Projections for 2010 and beyond are based on (1) IMF staff macroeconomic projections, (2) the modified balanced budget rule under the Fiscal Responsibility Legislation, and (3) authorities' projections of the spending pressures in pensions and health care and of the wage bill restraint. A fiscal stimulus package of about 1 percent of GDP was introduced in the context of the 2009 budget (effective early 2009). The main elements were (1) an increase in infrastructure spending (0.4 percent of GDP), (2) an increase in net lending by development banks (0.2 percent of GDP), and (3) an increase in current spending on public security, social transfers, and economic development (0.3 percent of GDP).

Netherlands. Fiscal projections for 2009–10 are based on the Bureau for Economic Policy Analysis budget projections, after adjusting for differences in macroeconomic assumptions. For the remainder of the projection period, the IMF staff projection assumes further consolidation efforts in line with the authorities' objective of reducing the sustainability gap.

New Zealand. The fiscal projections are based on the authorities' May 2009 budget update and IMF staff estimates. The New Zealand fiscal

accounts switched to new generally accepted accounting principles beginning in fiscal year 2006/07, with no comparable historical data.

Portugal. For 2008–10, the fiscal projections take into account the impact of discretionary measures taken so far in response to the downturn. In addition, automatic stabilizers are allowed to play fully. For 2011–14, the deficits are projected to decline gradually, assuming the government will contain further current spending to achieve structural adjustment of at least 0.5 percent of GDP a year in compliance with the EU's Stability and Growth Pact.

Russia. The deficit projection for 2009 is based on the revised 2009 supplementary budget. Consolidated regional budgets are expected to be broadly balanced, reflecting strict deficit and debt limits at the local government level. For 2010, the projection is based on the IMF staff's revenue forecast and the authorities' nominal expenditures presented in the draft 2010–12 medium-term budget. The deficit projection for 2011–12 is based on the IMF staff's revenue projections and the non-oil deficit implied by the draft 2010–12 medium-term budget. Over the longer term, the overall balance is assumed to evolve in line with the authorities' intention to gradually reduce the non-oil deficit to 4.7 percent of GDP—a target that the IMF staff assumes will be attained by 2014.

Saudi Arabia. The authorities systematically underestimate revenues and expenditures in the budget relative to actual outturns. The WEO baseline oil prices are discounted by 5 percent, reflecting the higher sulfur content in Saudi crude. Regarding non-oil revenues, customs receipts are assumed to grow in line with imports, investment income in line with the London interbank offered rate (LIBOR), and fees and charges as a function of non-oil GDP. On the expenditure side, wages are assumed to rise above the natural rate of increase, reflecting a salary increase of 15 percent distributed over 2008–10, and goods and services are projected to grow in line with inflation over the medium term. Interest payments are projected to decline in line with the authorities' policy of repaying public debt. Capital spending in 2009 is projected to be higher than in the budget by about 40 percent and in line with the authorities' announcements to maintain spending at current levels. The pace of spending is projected to slow over the medium term.

Singapore. For fiscal year 2009/10, projections are based on budget numbers. Medium-term projections assume that capital gains on fiscal reserves will be included in investment income.

South Africa. The authorities did not explicitly enact a stimulus package in response to the weakening economy but instead accelerated the existing public investment program to help support economic activity. Thus, the IMF staff estimates of the magnitude of the stimulus rely on the authorities' 2009 budget and are derived from a cyclical adjustment of the public sector borrowing requirement based on tax-specific elasticities.

Spain. The fiscal projections for 2009 take into account the impact of discretionary measures taken so far in response to the economic downturn. In addition, automatic stabilizers are allowed to operate fully. For 2010–14, the deficit is projected to decline gradually as spending declines (the stimulus has sunset clauses) and as the government contains further current spending to bring the deficit down.

Sweden. For 2009, the fiscal projections take into account the impact of the stimulus measures introduced in response to the downturn. No further measures are assumed for the future, consistent with the authorities' projections in the 2009 Spring Bill. The impact of cyclical developments on the fiscal accounts is calculated using the Organization for Economic Cooperation and Development's latest semi-elasticity.

Switzerland. Projections for 2008–14 are based on IMF staff calculations, which incorporate measures to restore balance in the federal accounts and strengthen social security finances.

Turkey. Fiscal projections are based on the IMF staff's assessment of the fiscal policies and measures identified in the authorities' medium-term macroeconomic program.

United Kingdom. The projections incorporate a fiscal stimulus of about 1.5 percent of GDP in 2009 (1.3 percent revenue measures, 0.2 percent expenditure measures).

United States. The fiscal projections are based on the administration's budget for fiscal year 2009 and the U.S. Congressional Budget Office's baseline budget outlook for 2009–19. These projections include the $787 billion stimulus package under the American Recovery and Reinvestment Act of 2009. The projections are adjusted for differences in forecasts of (1) macroeconomic and financial variables, (2) the timing of stimulus disbursements, (3) additional costs to support financial institutions and government-sponsored enterprises, and (4) the effect of financial sector support on government-owned financial assets.

Monetary Policy Assumptions

Monetary policy assumptions are based on the established policy framework in each country. In most cases, this implies a nonaccommodative stance over the business cycle: official interest rates will increase when economic indicators suggest that inflation will rise above its acceptable rate or range, and they will decrease when indicators suggest that prospective inflation will not exceed the acceptable rate or range, that prospective output growth is below its potential rate, and that the margin of slack in the economy is significant. On this basis, the LIBOR on six-month U.S. dollar deposits is assumed to average 1.2 percent in 2009 and 1.4 percent in 2010 (see Table 1.1). The rate on three-month euro deposits is assumed to average 1.2 percent in 2009 and 1.6 percent in 2010. The interest rate on six-month Japanese yen deposits is assumed to average 0.7 percent in 2009 and 0.6 percent in 2010.

See Box 5.4 of the October 1998 *World Economic Outlook* for details on how the conversion rates were established.

What's New

Starting with the October 2009 *World Economic Outlook*, the Islamic Republic of Afghanistan, Bosnia and Herzegovina, Brunei Darussalam, Eritrea, Iraq, Liberia, Montenegro, Serbia, and Timor-Leste are included in the regional and analytical group compositions. Zimbabwe has been returned to the group compositions as a result of recent price stabilization, which facilitates the measurement of macroeconomic variables and allows for cross-country data comparisons. Georgia officially withdrew from the Commonwealth of Independent States on August 18, 2009, but is included in that group for reasons of geography and similarities in economic structure.

Data and Conventions

Data and projections for 182 economies form the statistical basis for the *World Economic Outlook* (the WEO database). The data are maintained jointly by the IMF's Research Department and regional departments, with the latter regularly updating country projections based on consistent global assumptions.

Although national statistical agencies are the ultimate providers of historical data and definitions, international organizations are also involved in statistical issues, with the objective of harmonizing methodologies for the compilation of national statistics, including analytical frameworks, concepts, definitions, classifications, and valuation procedures used in the production of economic statistics. The WEO database reflects information from both national source agencies and international organizations.

The comprehensive revision of the standardized *System of National Accounts 1993*, the IMF's *Balance of Payments Manual, Fifth Edition*, the *Monetary and Financial Statistics Manual*, and the *Government Finance Statistics Manual 2001* represented significant improvements in the standards

of economic statistics and analysis.[1] The IMF was actively involved in all these projects, particularly the *Balance of Payments, Monetary and Financial Statistics*, and *Government Finance Statistics* manuals, which reflect the IMF's special interest in countries' external positions, financial sector stability, and public sector fiscal positions. The process of adapting country data to the new definitions began in earnest when the manuals were released. However, full concordance with the manuals is ultimately dependent on the provision by national statistical compilers of revised country data; hence, the *World Economic Outlook* estimates are still only partially adapted to these manuals.

Several countries have phased out their traditional *fixed-base-year* method of calculating real macroeconomic variable levels and growth by switching to a *chain-weighted* method of computing aggregate growth, in line with recent improvements in standards for reporting economic statistics. Recent dramatic changes in the structure of these economies have caused these countries to revise the way they measure real GDP levels and growth. Switching to the chain-weighted method of computing aggregate growth, which uses current price information, allows countries to measure GDP growth more accurately by eliminating upward biases in new data.[2] Currently, real macroeconomic data for Albania, Australia, Austria, Azerbaijan, Belgium, Bulgaria, Canada, Cyprus, the Czech Republic, Denmark, Estonia, the euro area, Finland, France, Georgia, Germany, Greece, Guatemala, Hong Kong SAR, Iceland, Ireland, Israel, Italy, Japan, Kazakhstan, Korea, Lithuania, Luxembourg, Malta, the Netherlands, New Zea-

---

[1]Commission of the European Communities, International Monetary Fund, Organization for Economic Cooperation and Development, United Nations, and World Bank, *System of National Accounts 1993* (Brussels/Luxembourg, New York, Paris, and Washington, 1993); International Monetary Fund, *Balance of Payments Manual, Fifth Edition* (Washington, 1993); International Monetary Fund, *Monetary and Financial Statistics Manual* (Washington, 2000); and International Monetary Fund, *Government Finance Statistics Manual* (Washington, 2001).

[2]Charles Steindel, 1995, "Chain-Weighting: The New Approach to Measuring GDP," *Current Issues in Economics and Finance* (Federal Reserve Bank of New York), Vol. 1 (December).

land, Norway, Poland, Portugal, Romania, Russia, Singapore, Slovenia, Spain, Sweden, Switzerland, the United Kingdom, and the United States are based on chain-weighted methodology. However, data before 1994 (Azerbaijan, Kazakhstan), 1995 (Belgium, Cyprus, Czech Republic, Estonia, euro area, Ireland, Luxembourg, Poland, Russia, Slovenia, Spain), 1996 (Albania, Georgia), 2000 (Greece, Korea, Malta, Singapore), and 2001 (Bulgaria) are based on unrevised national accounts and are subject to revision in the future.

Composite data for country groups in the *World Economic Outlook* are either sums or weighted averages of data for individual countries. Unless otherwise indicated, multiyear averages of growth rates are expressed as compound annual rates of change.[3] Arithmetically weighted averages are used for all data except inflation and money growth for the emerging and developing economies group, for which geometric averages are used. The following conventions apply.

- Country group composites for exchange rates, interest rates, and growth rates of monetary aggregates are weighted by GDP converted to U.S. dollars at market exchange rates (averaged over the preceding three years) as a share of group GDP.
- Composites for other data relating to the domestic economy, whether growth rates or ratios, are weighted by GDP valued at purchasing power parity (PPP) as a share of total world or group GDP.[4]
- Composites for data relating to the domestic economy for the euro area (16 member countries throughout the entire period unless

otherwise noted) are aggregates of national source data using GDP weights. Annual data are not adjusted for calendar day effects. For data prior to 1999, data aggregations apply 1995 European currency unit exchange rates.

- Composite unemployment rates and employment growth are weighted by labor force as a share of group labor force.
- Composites relating to the external economy are sums of individual country data after conversion to U.S. dollars at the average market exchange rates in the years indicated for balance of payments data and at end-of-year market exchange rates for debt denominated in currencies other than U.S. dollars. Composites of changes in foreign trade volumes and prices, however, are arithmetic averages of percent changes for individual countries weighted by the U.S. dollar value of exports or imports as a share of total world or group exports or imports (in the preceding year).

All data refer to calendar years, except for the following countries, which refer to fiscal years: Islamic Republic of Afghanistan, Islamic Republic of Iran, and Myanmar (April/March); Australia, Egypt, Ethiopia, Mauritius, Nepal, New Zealand, Pakistan, Samoa, and Tonga (July/June); and Haiti (October/September).

Classification of Countries

Summary of the Country Classification

The country classification in the *World Economic Outlook* divides the world into two major groups: advanced economies and emerging and developing economies.[5] This classification is not based on strict criteria, economic or otherwise, and it has evolved over time. The objective is to facilitate analysis by providing a reasonably meaningful method for organizing data. Table A provides an overview of the country classifica-

---

[3]Averages for real GDP and its components, employment, per capita GDP, inflation, factor productivity, trade, and commodity prices are calculated based on the compound annual rate of change, except for the unemployment rate, which is based on the simple arithmetic average.

[4]See Box A2 of the April 2004 *World Economic Outlook* for a summary of the revised PPP-based weights and Annex IV of the May 1993 *World Economic Outlook*. See also Anne-Marie Gulde and Marianne Schulze-Ghattas, "Purchasing Power Parity Based Weights for the *World Economic Outlook*," in *Staff Studies for the World Economic Outlook* (International Monetary Fund, December 1993), pp. 106–23.

[5]As used here, the term "country" does not in all cases refer to a territorial entity that is a state as understood by international law and practice. It also covers some territorial entities that are not states, but for which statistical data are maintained on a separate and independent basis.

Table A. Classification by *World Economic Outlook* Groups and Their Shares in Aggregate GDP, Exports of Goods and Services, and Population, 2008[1]
(Percent of total for group or world)

	Number of Countries	GDP		Exports of Goods and Services		Population	
		Advanced economies	World	Advanced economies	World	Advanced economies	World
Advanced economies	**33**	**100.0**	**55.1**	**100.0**	**65.0**	**100.0**	**15.1**
United States		37.4	20.6	14.2	9.3	30.3	4.6
Euro area	16	28.5	15.7	44.1	28.6	32.4	4.9
Germany		7.6	4.2	13.3	8.7	8.2	1.2
France		5.6	3.1	6.0	3.9	6.2	0.9
Italy		4.8	2.6	5.2	3.4	5.9	0.9
Spain		3.7	2.0	3.3	2.2	4.5	0.7
Japan		11.5	6.3	7.0	4.5	12.7	1.9
United Kingdom		5.8	3.2	6.1	4.0	6.1	0.9
Canada		3.4	1.9	4.1	2.7	3.3	0.5
Other advanced economies	13	13.3	7.3	24.5	15.9	15.3	2.3
Memorandum							
Major advanced economies	7	76.2	42.0	56.0	36.4	72.6	11.0
Newly industrialized Asian economies	4	6.7	3.7	13.1	8.5	8.3	1.3

	Number of Countries	Emerging and developing economies	World	Emerging and developing economies	World	Emerging and developing economies	World
Emerging and developing economies	**149**	**100.0**	**44.9**	**100.0**	**35.0**	**100.0**	**84.9**
Regional groups							
Africa	50	6.9	3.1	7.8	2.7	15.3	13.0
Sub-Sahara	47	5.4	2.4	5.8	2.0	14.0	11.9
Excluding Nigeria and South Africa	45	2.8	1.3	3.1	1.1	10.5	8.9
Central and eastern Europe	14	8.1	3.6	10.6	3.7	3.1	2.6
Commonwealth of Independent States[2]	13	10.2	4.6	11.5	4.0	5.0	4.2
Russia		7.3	3.3	7.6	2.7	2.5	2.1
Developing Asia	26	46.7	21.0	38.6	13.5	61.9	52.6
China		25.3	11.4	22.9	8.0	23.5	19.9
India		10.6	4.8	3.9	1.4	21.0	17.8
Excluding China and India	24	10.8	4.9	11.8	4.1	17.5	14.8
Middle East	14	9.0	4.0	16.9	5.9	4.9	4.1
Western Hemisphere	32	19.2	8.6	14.6	5.1	9.8	8.4
Brazil		6.3	2.8	3.3	1.2	3.4	2.8
Mexico		5.0	2.2	4.5	1.6	1.9	1.6
Analytical groups							
By source of export earnings							
Fuel	27	19.5	8.8	30.9	10.8	11.3	9.6
Nonfuel	122	80.5	36.2	69.1	24.2	88.7	75.3
of which, primary products	20	1.6	0.7	1.9	0.7	4.1	3.5
By external financing source							
Net debtor countries	120	51.1	23.0	41.1	14.4	61.1	51.8
of which, official financing	31	2.5	1.1	1.4	0.5	10.9	9.3
Net debtor countries by debt-servicing experience							
Countries with arrears and/or rescheduling during 2003–07	48	6.7	3.0	4.8	1.7	13.1	11.1
Other net debtor countries	72	44.5	20.0	36.3	12.7	48.0	40.8
Other groups							
Heavily indebted poor countries	35	2.1	0.9	1.5	0.5	9.5	8.0
Middle East and North Africa	20	10.7	4.8	19.2	6.7	7.0	5.9

[1]The GDP shares are based on the purchasing-power-parity valuation of countries' GDP. The number of countries comprising each group reflects those for which data are included in the group aggregates.

[2]Georgia and Mongolia, which are not members of the Commonwealth of Independent States, are included in this group for reasons of geography and similarities in economic structure.

tion, showing the number of countries in each group by region and summarizing some key indicators of their relative size (GDP valued by purchasing power parity, total exports of goods and services, and population).

Some countries remain outside the country classification and therefore are not included in the analysis. Cuba and the Democratic People's Republic of Korea are not IMF members, and their economies therefore are not monitored by the IMF. San Marino is omitted from the group of advanced economies for lack of a fully developed database. Likewise, Aruba, Kosovo, the Marshall Islands, the Federated States of Micronesia, Palau, and Somalia are omitted from the emerging and developing economies group because of data limitations.

General Features and Composition of Groups in the World Economic Outlook Classification

Advanced Economies

The 33 advanced economies are listed in Table B. The seven largest in terms of GDP—the United States, Japan, Germany, France, Italy, the United Kingdom, and Canada—constitute the subgroup of *major advanced economies,* often referred to as the Group of Seven (G7). The 16 members of the *euro area* and the four *newly industrialized Asian economies* are also distinguished as subgroups. Composite data shown in the tables for the euro area cover the current members for all years, even though the membership has increased over time.

Table C lists the member countries of the European Union, not all of which are classified as advanced economies in the *World Economic Outlook.*

Emerging and Developing Economies

The group of emerging and developing economies (149 countries) includes all countries that are not classified as advanced economies.

The *regional breakdowns* of emerging and developing economies—*Africa, central and eastern Europe, Commonwealth of Independent States, developing Asia, Middle East, and Western Hemisphere*—largely conform to the regional breakdowns in the IMF's *International Financial Statistics.* In both classifications, Egypt and Libya are included in the *Middle East* region rather than in Africa. In addition, the *World Economic Outlook* sometimes refers to the regional group of Middle East and North African countries, also referred to as the MENA countries, whose composition straddles the Africa and Middle East regions. This group is defined as the Arab League countries plus the Islamic Republic of Iran (see Table D).

Emerging and developing economies are also classified according to *analytical criteria.* The analytical criteria reflect countries' composition of export earnings and other income from abroad; exchange rate arrangements; a distinction between net creditor and net debtor countries; and, for the net debtor

Table B. Advanced Economies by Subgroup

Major Currency Areas	Euro area		Other Subgroups			
			Newly industrialized Asian economies	Major advanced economies	Other advanced economies	
United States	Austria	Italy	Hong Kong SAR[1]	Canada	Australia	New Zealand
Euro area	Belgium	Luxembourg	Korea	France	Czech Republic	Norway
Japan	Cyprus	Malta	Singapore	Germany	Denmark	Singapore
	Finland	Netherlands	Taiwan Province	Italy	Hong Kong SAR[1]	Sweden
	France	Portugal	of China	Japan	Iceland	Switzerland
	Germany	Slovak Rep.		United Kingdom	Israel	Taiwan Province
	Greece	Slovenia		United States	Korea	of China
	Ireland	Spain				

[1]On July 1, 1997, Hong Kong was returned to the People's Republic of China and became a Special Administrative Region of China.

Table C. European Union

Austria	Finland	Latvia	Romania
Belgium	France	Lithuania	Slovak Republic
Bulgaria	Germany	Luxembourg	Slovenia
Cyprus	Greece	Malta	Spain
Czech Republic	Hungary	Netherlands	Sweden
Denmark	Ireland	Poland	United Kingdom
Estonia	Italy	Portugal	

Table D. Middle East and North African Economies

Algeria	Iraq	Mauritania	Sudan
Bahrain	Jordan	Morocco	Syrian Arab Republic
Djibouti	Kuwait	Oman	Tunisia
Egypt	Lebanon	Qatar	United Arab Emirates
Iran, I.R. of	Libya	Saudi Arabia	Yemen, Rep. of

countries, financial criteria based on external financing sources and experience with external debt servicing. The detailed composition of emerging and developing economies in the regional and analytical groups is shown in Tables E and F.

The analytical criterion, by *source of export earnings,* distinguishes between categories: *fuel* (Standard International Trade Classification—SITC 3) and *nonfuel* and then focuses on *nonfuel primary products* (SITCs 0, 1, 2, 4, and 68).

The financial criteria focus on *net creditor countries, net debtor countries,* and *heavily indebted poor countries* (HIPCs). Net debtor countries are further differentiated on the basis of two additional financial criteria: by *official external*

financing and by *experience with debt servicing.*[6] The HIPC group comprises the countries considered by the IMF and the World Bank for their debt initiative, known as the HIPC Initiative, with the aim of reducing the external debt burdens of all the eligible HIPCs to a "sustainable" level in a reasonably short period of time.[7]

[6]During 2003–07, 48 countries incurred external payments arrears or entered into official or commercial bank debt-rescheduling agreements. This group of countries is referred to as *countries with arrears and/or rescheduling during 2003–07.*

[7]See David Andrews, Anthony R. Boote, Syed S. Rizavi, and Sukwinder Singh, *Debt Relief for Low-Income Countries: The Enhanced HIPC Initiative,* IMF Pamphlet Series, No. 51 (Washington: International Monetary Fund, November 1999).

Table E. Emerging and Developing Economies by Region and Main Source of Export Earnings

	Fuel	Nonfuel Primary Products		Fuel	Nonfuel Primary Products
Africa	Algeria Angola Chad Congo, Rep. of Equatorial Guinea Gabon Nigeria Sudan	Burkina Faso Burundi Congo, Dem. Rep. of Guinea Guinea-Bissau Malawi Mali Mauritania Mozambique Namibia Sierra Leone Zambia Zimbabwe	**Developing Asia**	Brunei Darussalam Timor-Leste	Papua New Guinea Solomon Islands
			Middle East	Bahrain Iran, I.R. of Iraq Kuwait Libya Oman Qatar Saudi Arabia United Arab Emirates Yemen, Rep. of	
Commonwealth of Independent States[1]	Azerbaijan Kazakhstan Russia Turkmenistan	Mongolia Uzbekistan	**Western Hemisphere**	Ecuador Trinidad and Tobago Venezuela	Chile Guyana Suriname

[1]Mongolia, which is not a member of the Commonwealth of Independent States, is included in this group for reasons of geography and similarities in economic structure.

Table F. Emerging and Developing Economies by Region, Net External Position, and Status as Heavily Indebted Poor Countries

	Net External Position		Heavily Indebted Poor Countries		Net External Position		Heavily Indebted Poor Countries
	Net creditor	Net debtor[1]			Net creditor	Net debtor[1]	
Africa				**CFA franc zone**			
Maghreb				Benin		*	*
Algeria	*			Burkina Faso		•	*
Morocco		*		Cameroon		*	*
Tunisia		*		Central African Republic		•	*
Sub-Sahara				Chad		*	*
South Africa		*		Congo, Rep. of		•	*
Horn of Africa				Côte d'Ivoire		*	*
Djibouti		*		Equatorial Guinea		*	
Eritrea		•		Gabon	*		
Ethiopia		•	*	Guinea-Bissau		*	*
Sudan		*		Mali		*	*
Great Lakes				Niger		•	*
Burundi		•	*	Senegal		*	*
Congo, Dem. Rep. of		•	*	Togo		•	*
Kenya		*		**Central and eastern Europe**			
Rwanda		•	*	Albania		*	
Tanzania		•	*	Bosnia and Herzegovina		*	
Uganda		*	*	Bulgaria		*	
Southern Africa				Croatia		*	
Angola	*			Estonia		*	
Botswana	*			Hungary		*	
Comoros		•		Latvia		*	
Lesotho		*		Lithuania		*	
Madagascar		•	*	Macedonia, FYR		*	
Malawi		•	*	Montenegro		•	
Mauritius		*		Poland		*	
Mozambique		•	*	Romania		*	
Namibia	*			Serbia		*	
Seychelles		*		Turkey		*	
Swaziland		*		**Commonwealth of Independent States[2]**			
Zambia		*	*	Armenia		•	
Zimbabwe		•		Azerbaijan	*		
West and Central Africa				Belarus		*	
Cape Verde		*		Georgia		*	
Gambia, The		*	*	Kazakhstan		*	
Ghana		•	*	Kyrgyz Republic		*	
Guinea		•	*	Moldova		*	
Liberia		*	*	Mongolia		•	
Mauritania		*	*	Russia	*		
Nigeria	*			Tajikistan		*	
São Tomé and Príncipe		*	*	Turkmenistan	*		
Sierra Leone		•	*	Ukraine	*		
				Uzbekistan	*		

Table F. *(concluded)*

	Net External Position		Heavily Indebted Poor Countries
	Net creditor	Net debtor[1]	
Developing Asia			
Afghanistan, I.R. of		•	*
Bangladesh		•	
Bhutan		•	
Brunei Darussalam	*		
Cambodia		*	
China	*		
Fiji		*	
India		*	
Indonesia	*		
Kiribati	*		
Lao PDR		*	
Malaysia	*		
Maldives		*	
Myanmar		*	
Nepal		•	
Pakistan		*	
Papua New Guinea	*		
Philippines		*	
Samoa		*	
Solomon Islands		•	
Sri Lanka		*	
Thailand		*	
Timor-Leste	*		
Tonga		•	
Vanuatu		*	
Vietnam		*	
Middle East			
Bahrain	*		
Iran, I.R. of	*		
Iraq	*		
Kuwait	*		
Libya	*		
Oman	*		
Qatar	*		
Saudi Arabia	*		
United Arab Emirates	*		
Yemen, Rep. of		*	
Mashreq			
Egypt		*	
Jordan		*	

	Net External Position		Heavily Indebted Poor Countries
	Net creditor	Net debtor[1]	
Lebanon		*	
Syrian Arab Republic		•	
Western Hemisphere			
Mexico		*	
South America			
Argentina		*	
Bolivia		•	*
Brazil		*	
Chile		*	
Colombia		*	
Ecuador		*	
Paraguay		*	
Peru		*	
Uruguay		*	
Venezuela	*		
Central America			
Costa Rica		*	
El Salvador		*	
Guatemala		*	
Honduras		*	*
Nicaragua		*	*
Panama		*	
Caribbean			
Antigua and Barbuda		*	
Bahamas, The		*	
Barbados		*	
Belize		*	
Dominica		*	
Dominican Republic		*	
Grenada		*	
Guyana		*	*
Haiti		•	*
Jamaica		*	
St. Kitts and Nevis		*	
St. Lucia		*	
St. Vincent and the Grenadines		*	
Suriname		*	
Trinidad and Tobago	*		

[1]Dot instead of star indicates that the net debtor's main external finance source is official financing.

[2]Georgia and Mongolia, which are not members of the Commonwealth of Independent States, are included in this group for reasons of geography and similarities in economic structure.

List of Tables

Table A1. Summary of World Output[1]

(Annual percent change)

	Average 1991–2000	2001	2002	2003	2004	2005	2006	2007	2008	2009	2010	2014
World	**3.1**	**2.3**	**2.9**	**3.6**	**4.9**	**4.5**	**5.1**	**5.2**	**3.0**	**−1.1**	**3.1**	**4.5**
Advanced economies	**2.8**	**1.4**	**1.7**	**1.9**	**3.2**	**2.6**	**3.0**	**2.7**	**0.6**	**−3.4**	**1.3**	**2.4**
United States	3.4	1.1	1.8	2.5	3.6	3.1	2.7	2.1	0.4	−2.7	1.5	2.1
Euro area	...	1.9	0.9	0.8	2.2	1.7	2.9	2.7	0.7	−4.2	0.3	2.1
Japan	1.2	0.2	0.3	1.4	2.7	1.9	2.0	2.3	−0.7	−5.4	1.7	1.8
Other advanced economies[2]	3.5	1.8	3.2	2.5	4.1	3.4	3.9	3.8	1.2	−2.7	2.1	3.4
Emerging and developing economies	**3.6**	**3.8**	**4.8**	**6.2**	**7.5**	**7.1**	**7.9**	**8.3**	**6.0**	**1.7**	**5.1**	**6.6**
Regional groups												
Africa	2.4	4.9	6.5	5.4	6.7	5.7	6.1	6.3	5.2	1.7	4.0	5.3
Central and eastern Europe	2.0	0.2	4.4	4.8	7.3	6.0	6.6	5.5	3.0	−5.0	1.8	4.0
Commonwealth of Independent States[3]	...	6.1	5.2	7.8	8.2	6.7	8.4	8.6	5.5	−6.7	2.1	5.3
Developing Asia	7.4	5.8	6.9	8.2	8.6	9.0	9.8	10.6	7.6	6.2	7.3	8.5
Middle East	4.0	2.5	3.8	6.9	5.9	5.5	5.8	6.2	5.4	2.0	4.2	4.8
Western Hemisphere	3.3	0.7	0.6	2.2	6.0	4.7	5.7	5.7	4.2	−2.5	2.9	4.0
Memorandum												
European Union	2.2	2.1	1.4	1.5	2.7	2.2	3.4	3.1	1.0	−4.2	0.5	2.5
Analytical groups												
By source of export earnings												
Fuel	−0.1	4.3	4.8	7.0	7.9	6.7	7.2	7.4	5.4	−2.1	3.1	4.6
Nonfuel	4.7	3.6	4.8	6.0	7.4	7.2	8.1	8.5	6.1	2.6	5.6	7.0
of which, primary products	3.6	3.7	3.1	4.3	6.1	5.6	5.4	5.6	4.8	1.3	4.6	5.4
By external financing source												
Net debtor countries	3.5	2.1	3.2	4.5	6.4	6.0	6.7	6.6	4.8	−0.1	3.8	5.5
of which, official financing	3.3	4.6	4.1	3.9	6.1	6.6	6.5	6.4	6.4	4.2	5.0	6.0
Net debtor countries by debt-servicing experience												
Countries with arrears and/or rescheduling during 2003–07	3.1	1.8	0.5	6.1	7.6	7.8	7.4	7.3	5.4	0.6	2.9	4.9
Memorandum												
Median growth rate												
Advanced economies	3.1	1.9	1.9	1.9	3.8	3.0	3.8	3.6	1.1	−3.6	0.9	2.8
Emerging and developing economies	3.3	3.5	3.9	4.8	5.4	5.6	6.0	6.3	5.1	1.5	3.3	5.0
Output per capita												
Advanced economies	2.1	0.7	1.1	1.3	2.6	2.0	2.4	2.0	−0.1	−4.0	0.8	1.9
Emerging and developing economies	2.0	2.4	3.4	4.8	6.1	5.8	6.6	7.0	4.7	0.4	3.8	5.3
World growth based on market exchange rates	**2.6**	**1.6**	**2.0**	**2.7**	**4.0**	**3.4**	**3.9**	**3.8**	**1.8**	**−2.3**	**2.3**	**3.7**
Value of world output in billions of U.S. dollars												
At market exchange rates	28,350	31,892	33,187	37,301	41,974	45,385	49,115	55,270	60,917	57,228	60,495	74,660
At purchasing power parities	33,452	43,993	45,963	48,607	52,452	56,453	61,198	66,122	69,490	69,743	72,980	93,043

[1]Real GDP.

[2]In this table, "other advanced economies" means advanced economies excluding the United States, euro area countries, and Japan.

[3]Georgia and Mongolia, which are not members of the Commonwealth of Independent States, are included in this group for reasons of geography and similarities in economic structure.

Table A2. Advanced Economies: Real GDP and Total Domestic Demand[1]

(Annual percent change)

	Average 1991–2000	2001	2002	2003	2004	2005	2006	2007	2008	2009	2010	2014	Fourth Quarter[2] 2008	2009	2010
Real GDP															
Advanced economies	**2.8**	**1.4**	**1.7**	**1.9**	**3.2**	**2.6**	**3.0**	**2.7**	**0.6**	**−3.4**	**1.3**	**2.4**	**−2.2**	**−1.3**	**1.7**
United States	3.4	1.1	1.8	2.5	3.6	3.1	2.7	2.1	0.4	−2.7	1.5	2.1	−1.9	−1.1	1.9
Euro area	...	1.9	0.9	0.8	2.2	1.7	2.9	2.7	0.7	−4.2	0.3	2.1	−1.7	−2.5	0.9
Germany	2.1	1.2	0.0	−0.2	1.2	0.7	3.2	2.5	1.2	−5.3	0.3	1.8	−1.8	−2.9	0.8
France	2.0	1.8	1.1	1.1	2.3	1.9	2.4	2.3	0.3	−2.4	0.9	2.3	−1.6	−0.9	1.4
Italy	1.6	1.8	0.5	0.0	1.5	0.7	2.0	1.6	−1.0	−5.1	0.2	1.9	−2.9	−3.2	0.8
Spain	2.9	3.6	2.7	3.1	3.3	3.6	4.0	3.6	0.9	−3.8	−0.7	2.1	−1.2	−3.5	0.5
Netherlands	3.1	1.9	0.1	0.3	2.2	2.0	3.4	3.6	2.0	−4.2	0.7	2.6	−0.8	−3.2	1.2
Belgium	2.3	0.8	1.5	1.0	2.8	2.2	3.0	2.6	1.0	−3.2	0.0	2.4	−1.0	−2.2	0.5
Greece	2.3	4.2	3.4	5.6	4.9	2.9	4.5	4.0	2.9	−0.8	−0.1	1.9	2.4	−1.8	1.0
Austria	2.5	0.5	1.6	0.8	2.5	2.5	3.5	3.5	2.0	−3.8	0.3	2.4	0.2	−3.3	1.0
Portugal	3.0	2.0	0.8	−0.8	1.5	0.9	1.4	1.9	0.0	−3.0	0.4	1.3	−2.0	−1.4	0.7
Finland	2.0	2.7	1.6	1.8	3.7	2.8	4.9	4.2	1.0	−6.4	0.9	2.8	−3.0	−3.5	1.0
Ireland	7.1	5.7	6.5	4.4	4.6	6.2	5.4	6.0	−3.0	−7.5	−2.5	2.6	−8.0	−4.6	−1.5
Slovak Republic	0.2	3.4	4.8	4.7	5.2	6.5	8.5	10.4	6.4	−4.7	3.7	4.2	2.2	−3.2	0.7
Slovenia	...	2.8	4.0	2.8	4.3	4.3	5.9	6.8	3.5	−4.7	0.6	3.3	−0.9	0.9	1.8
Luxembourg	5.0	2.5	4.1	1.5	4.5	5.2	6.4	5.2	0.7	−4.8	−0.2	2.9	−0.9	−2.6	1.7
Cyprus	4.2	4.0	2.1	1.9	4.2	3.9	4.1	4.4	3.6	−0.5	0.8	3.3	2.7	−1.4	2.1
Malta	4.4	−1.6	2.6	−0.3	0.4	4.1	3.8	3.7	2.1	−2.1	0.5	2.9	0.5	0.0	1.3
Japan	1.2	0.2	0.3	1.4	2.7	1.9	2.0	2.3	−0.7	−5.4	1.7	1.8	−4.5	−1.3	1.4
United Kingdom	2.5	2.5	2.1	2.8	3.0	2.2	2.9	2.6	0.7	−4.4	0.9	2.9	−1.8	−2.5	1.3
Canada	2.9	1.8	2.9	1.9	3.1	3.0	2.9	2.5	0.4	−2.5	2.1	2.1	−1.0	−1.5	3.0
Korea	6.1	4.0	7.2	2.8	4.6	4.0	5.2	5.1	2.2	−1.0	3.6	4.5	−3.4	4.3	3.5
Australia	3.4	2.1	4.2	3.0	3.8	2.8	2.8	4.0	2.4	0.7	2.0	3.0	0.7	1.4	2.8
Taiwan Province of China	6.5	−2.2	4.6	3.5	6.2	4.2	4.8	5.7	0.1	−4.1	3.7	5.0	−8.0	5.5	0.9
Sweden	2.0	1.1	2.4	1.9	4.1	3.3	4.2	2.6	−0.2	−4.8	1.2	3.9	−5.1	−0.7	1.9
Switzerland	1.1	1.2	0.4	−0.2	2.5	2.6	3.6	3.6	1.8	−2.0	0.5	1.5	−0.2	−1.9	1.9
Hong Kong SAR	3.9	0.5	1.8	3.0	8.5	7.1	7.0	6.4	2.4	−3.6	3.5	4.3	−2.7	−0.2	3.5
Czech Republic	0.2	2.5	1.9	3.6	4.5	6.3	6.8	6.1	2.7	−4.3	1.3	4.0	0.5	−2.6	1.7
Norway	3.7	2.0	1.5	1.0	3.9	2.7	2.3	3.1	2.1	−1.9	1.3	2.1	0.5	−2.1	2.6
Singapore	7.6	−2.4	4.1	3.8	9.3	7.3	8.4	7.8	1.1	−3.3	4.1	4.6	−4.0	2.5	4.3
Denmark	2.6	0.7	0.5	0.4	2.3	2.4	3.3	1.6	−1.2	−2.4	0.9	2.3	−3.7	−0.5	2.0
Israel	5.8	0.0	−0.7	1.5	5.0	5.1	5.3	5.2	4.0	−0.1	2.4	4.4	2.1	0.3	2.8
New Zealand	2.9	2.6	4.9	4.1	4.5	2.8	2.0	3.2	0.2	−2.2	2.2	3.3	−2.0	−0.6	2.8
Iceland	2.5	3.9	0.1	2.4	7.7	7.5	4.3	5.6	1.3	−8.5	−2.0	4.0	−1.5	−11.9	−5.0
Memorandum															
Major advanced economies	2.6	1.2	1.3	1.8	2.9	2.3	2.6	2.2	0.3	−3.6	1.3	2.1	−2.3	−1.6	1.6
Newly industrialized Asian economies	6.1	1.2	5.6	3.1	5.9	4.7	5.6	5.7	1.5	−2.4	3.6	4.6	−4.7	3.9	2.8
Real total domestic demand															
Advanced economies	**2.8**	**1.3**	**1.8**	**2.1**	**3.2**	**2.7**	**2.8**	**2.3**	**0.2**	**−3.5**	**1.2**	**2.3**	**−1.9**	**−1.8**	**1.5**
United States	3.7	1.2	2.4	2.8	4.0	3.2	2.6	1.4	−0.7	−3.6	1.7	2.3	−2.5	−1.8	2.0
Euro area	...	1.3	0.4	1.4	1.9	1.9	2.8	2.5	0.7	−3.2	−0.3	1.8	−0.4	−3.0	0.7
Germany	2.0	−0.5	−2.0	0.6	−0.1	0.0	2.2	1.0	1.7	−1.8	−0.9	1.5	2.0	−2.5	0.5
France	1.8	1.7	1.1	1.8	3.0	2.8	2.7	3.2	0.7	−2.1	0.7	1.8	−0.7	−1.4	1.3
Italy	1.4	1.6	1.3	0.8	1.3	0.9	2.0	1.4	−1.3	−4.3	0.2	1.7	−2.4	−2.7	0.9
Spain	2.8	3.8	3.2	3.8	4.8	5.1	5.2	4.2	−0.5	−6.5	−1.9	2.0	−3.6	−6.0	−0.5
Japan	1.0	1.0	−0.4	0.8	1.9	1.7	1.2	1.2	−0.9	−3.4	1.2	1.5	−1.8	−2.0	1.3
United Kingdom	2.6	2.9	3.2	2.9	3.6	2.1	2.4	3.0	0.5	−5.2	0.5	2.8	−2.9	−3.1	1.1
Canada	2.4	1.2	3.2	4.6	4.2	4.9	4.2	4.2	2.4	−2.9	2.4	1.6	−1.0	−1.3	2.8
Other advanced economies	4.0	0.6	4.1	1.8	4.7	3.3	4.0	4.5	1.8	−2.9	3.1	3.7	−3.1	1.7	2.2
Memorandum															
Major advanced economies	2.7	1.2	1.4	2.2	3.0	2.4	2.4	1.7	−0.2	−3.4	1.1	2.0	−1.8	−2.0	1.6
Newly industrialized Asian economies	5.7	0.1	4.9	0.6	4.9	2.9	4.2	4.5	1.6	−3.8	4.1	4.4	−5.0	3.6	1.6

[1]When countries are not listed alphabetically, they are ordered on the basis of economic size.
[2]From the fourth quarter of the preceding year.

Table A3. Advanced Economies: Components of Real GDP

(Annual percent change)

	Ten-Year Averages		2001	2002	2003	2004	2005	2006	2007	2008	2009	2010
	1991–2000	2001–10										
Private consumer expenditure												
Advanced economies	**2.9**	**1.7**	**2.4**	**2.3**	**1.9**	**2.7**	**2.7**	**2.6**	**2.4**	**0.4**	**−1.0**	**0.7**
United States	3.6	2.0	2.7	2.7	2.8	3.5	3.4	2.9	2.7	−0.2	−0.9	0.9
Euro area	. . .	1.1	2.0	0.9	1.2	1.6	1.8	2.0	1.6	0.4	−0.9	−0.1
Germany	2.3	0.2	1.9	−0.8	0.1	0.1	0.3	1.3	−0.3	0.4	0.4	−1.0
France	1.7	1.9	2.5	2.3	2.1	2.3	2.5	2.6	2.4	1.0	0.7	0.8
Italy	1.7	0.4	0.7	0.2	1.0	0.7	1.1	1.2	1.2	−0.9	−1.7	0.7
Spain	2.7	1.8	3.4	2.8	2.9	4.2	4.2	3.8	3.6	−0.6	−5.1	−0.6
Japan	1.3	0.8	1.6	1.1	0.4	1.6	1.3	1.5	0.7	0.6	−1.1	0.5
United Kingdom	2.8	1.6	3.1	3.5	3.0	3.1	2.2	1.5	2.1	1.2	−3.1	−0.3
Canada	2.4	3.0	2.3	3.6	3.0	3.3	3.7	4.1	4.6	3.0	−0.1	2.2
Other advanced economies[1]	4.1	2.6	2.8	4.0	1.5	3.6	3.5	3.7	4.4	1.2	−0.4	2.0
Memorandum												
Major advanced economies	2.7	1.6	2.3	2.0	2.0	2.5	2.5	2.3	2.0	0.2	−0.8	0.6
Newly industrialized Asian economies	5.8	2.7	3.7	5.6	0.1	2.7	3.9	4.0	4.7	0.8	−0.5	2.4
Public consumption												
Advanced economies	**1.8**	**2.3**	**3.1**	**3.4**	**2.2**	**1.7**	**1.3**	**1.6**	**2.0**	**2.5**	**2.6**	**2.4**
United States	1.0	2.3	3.7	4.5	2.2	1.4	0.6	1.0	1.4	3.0	2.5	2.9
Euro area	. . .	2.0	2.1	2.4	1.7	1.6	1.5	1.9	2.2	2.0	2.4	1.9
Germany	1.7	1.4	0.5	1.5	0.4	−0.7	0.4	1.0	1.7	2.0	3.4	3.9
France	1.6	1.5	1.1	1.9	2.0	2.2	1.2	1.3	1.5	1.1	1.1	1.1
Italy	0.2	1.8	3.9	2.4	1.9	2.2	1.9	0.5	1.0	0.6	2.0	1.3
Spain	3.2	4.5	3.9	4.5	4.8	6.3	5.5	4.6	5.5	5.4	4.3	0.4
Japan	3.1	1.9	3.0	2.4	2.3	1.9	1.6	0.4	1.9	0.8	1.6	2.8
United Kingdom	1.3	2.4	2.4	3.5	3.4	3.0	2.0	1.6	1.2	2.8	2.9	1.4
Canada	0.8	2.9	3.9	2.5	3.1	2.0	1.4	3.0	3.3	3.7	2.7	3.3
Other advanced economies	2.9	2.7	3.2	3.5	2.5	1.7	2.3	3.0	2.7	3.0	3.4	2.0
Memorandum												
Major advanced economies	1.5	2.1	3.0	3.3	2.1	1.5	1.0	1.0	1.6	2.3	2.4	2.7
Newly industrialized Asian economies	4.4	3.3	3.8	4.0	2.7	1.9	2.7	3.8	3.5	3.4	4.6	2.4
Gross fixed capital formation												
Advanced economies	**3.6**	**0.0**	**−0.4**	**−1.2**	**2.1**	**4.6**	**4.3**	**4.0**	**2.5**	**−2.1**	**−12.4**	**−0.6**
United States	6.0	−0.9	−1.0	−2.7	3.1	6.2	5.3	2.5	−1.2	−3.6	−14.7	−1.2
Euro area	. . .	0.2	0.6	−1.4	1.3	2.3	3.3	5.5	4.8	0.0	−10.7	−2.4
Germany	2.2	−0.7	−3.7	−6.1	−0.3	−0.3	0.9	7.8	5.0	3.1	−10.1	−2.4
France	1.7	1.5	2.3	−1.7	2.2	3.3	4.4	4.4	6.5	0.6	−6.1	−0.7
Italy	1.3	−0.5	2.7	3.7	−1.2	2.3	0.8	2.9	2.0	−3.0	−13.3	−1.3
Spain	3.3	0.8	4.8	3.4	5.9	5.1	7.0	7.2	4.6	−4.4	−16.0	−6.8
Japan	−0.6	−1.8	−0.9	−4.9	−0.5	1.4	3.1	0.5	0.8	−5.0	−12.8	1.0
United Kingdom	2.8	0.7	2.6	3.6	1.1	5.7	2.4	6.5	7.8	−2.8	−15.3	−2.7
Canada	2.8	3.1	4.0	1.6	6.2	7.8	9.3	6.9	3.7	0.9	−9.8	1.5
Other advanced economies	4.8	2.2	−3.8	4.0	2.8	7.2	4.3	5.7	6.6	0.4	−7.9	3.6
Memorandum												
Major advanced economies	3.5	−0.5	−0.3	−2.2	1.8	4.4	4.1	3.4	1.4	−2.5	−13.1	−0.9
Newly industrialized Asian economies	6.5	1.0	−5.7	2.4	2.5	7.8	1.8	4.0	4.9	−2.7	−9.1	5.8

Table A3 *(concluded)*

	Ten-Year Averages		2001	2002	2003	2004	2005	2006	2007	2008	2009	2010
	1991–2000	2001–10										
Final domestic demand												
Advanced economies	**2.8**	**1.5**	**1.9**	**1.7**	**2.0**	**2.9**	**2.8**	**2.7**	**2.4**	**0.3**	**−2.7**	**0.9**
United States	3.7	1.6	2.1	1.9	2.8	3.6	3.3	2.5	1.7	−0.4	−2.8	1.1
Euro area	...	1.1	1.7	0.7	1.3	1.7	2.1	2.7	2.4	0.6	−2.4	−0.1
Germany	2.1	0.3	0.4	−1.4	0.1	−0.1	0.5	2.5	1.2	1.4	−1.3	−0.3
France	1.7	1.7	2.1	1.4	2.1	2.5	2.6	2.7	3.0	0.9	−0.6	0.6
Italy	1.3	0.5	1.7	1.3	0.7	1.4	1.2	1.4	1.3	−1.0	−3.4	0.5
Spain	2.9	2.1	3.9	3.2	4.0	4.8	5.2	4.9	4.2	−0.6	−6.3	−1.9
Japan	1.1	0.4	1.2	−0.2	0.5	1.6	1.9	1.1	1.0	−0.7	−3.2	1.1
United Kingdom	2.5	1.6	2.8	3.5	2.8	3.5	2.2	2.3	2.9	0.8	−3.9	−0.3
Canada	2.2	2.9	2.9	3.0	3.7	3.9	4.4	4.5	4.1	2.6	−1.7	2.3
Other advanced economies	4.2	2.5	1.1	3.8	1.8	4.1	3.4	4.0	4.6	1.4	−1.4	2.4
Memorandum												
Major advanced economies	2.6	1.3	1.9	1.3	2.0	2.7	2.6	2.3	1.8	0.0	−2.6	0.8
Newly industrialized Asian economies	5.7	2.4	1.1	4.4	1.1	3.7	3.1	4.0	4.7	0.4	−1.7	2.9
Stock building[2]												
Advanced economies	**0.0**	**−0.1**	**−0.6**	**0.1**	**0.1**	**0.3**	**−0.1**	**0.1**	**−0.1**	**−0.1**	**−0.9**	**0.4**
United States	0.1	−0.1	−0.9	0.5	0.1	0.4	−0.1	0.1	−0.3	−0.4	−1.0	0.6
Euro area	...	−0.1	−0.4	−0.3	0.1	0.2	−0.2	0.1	0.0	0.1	−0.8	−0.2
Germany	−0.1	−0.2	−0.9	−0.6	0.5	0.0	−0.4	−0.2	−0.1	0.1	−0.5	−0.6
France	0.1	−0.2	−0.4	−0.3	−0.3	0.5	0.2	0.0	0.2	−0.2	−1.5	0.1
Italy	0.0	−0.1	0.1	0.0	0.1	−0.1	−0.3	0.5	0.0	−0.3	−0.5	−0.3
Spain	−0.1	0.0	−0.1	0.0	−0.1	0.0	−0.1	0.3	−0.1	0.1	−0.2	−0.1
Japan	0.0	0.0	−0.2	−0.3	0.2	0.3	−0.1	0.2	0.3	−0.2	−0.2	0.1
United Kingdom	0.1	−0.1	0.1	−0.3	0.2	0.1	0.0	0.0	0.1	−0.4	−1.2	0.9
Canada	0.2	−0.1	−1.7	0.2	0.8	0.1	0.3	−0.1	0.2	−0.1	−0.9	0.1
Other advanced economies	0.0	0.0	−0.5	0.1	−0.1	0.6	0.0	0.0	−0.2	0.3	−1.4	1.0
Memorandum												
Major advanced economies	0.0	−0.1	−0.7	0.1	0.1	0.3	−0.1	0.1	−0.1	−0.3	−0.8	0.3
Newly industrialized Asian economies	0.0	0.0	−0.9	0.4	−0.4	1.0	−0.1	0.2	−0.3	1.1	−2.2	1.2
Foreign balance[2]												
Advanced economies	**0.0**	**0.1**	**0.1**	**−0.1**	**−0.3**	**−0.2**	**−0.1**	**0.2**	**0.5**	**0.4**	**0.2**	**0.2**
United States	−0.4	0.1	−0.2	−0.7	−0.5	−0.7	−0.3	−0.1	0.6	1.2	1.2	−0.2
Euro area	...	0.1	0.6	0.5	−0.6	0.3	−0.1	0.2	0.3	0.0	−0.8	0.6
Germany	0.0	0.5	1.7	2.0	−0.8	1.4	0.7	1.1	1.5	−0.3	−3.6	1.2
France	0.2	−0.4	0.1	0.0	−0.7	−0.7	−0.9	−0.4	−0.9	−0.4	−0.2	0.2
Italy	0.2	−0.2	0.2	−0.8	−0.8	0.2	−0.3	0.0	0.2	0.3	−1.0	0.4
Spain	−0.1	−0.2	−0.2	−0.6	−0.8	−1.7	−1.7	−1.4	−0.9	1.4	3.1	1.2
Japan	0.2	0.2	−0.8	0.7	0.7	0.8	0.3	0.8	1.1	0.2	−2.4	0.7
United Kingdom	−0.1	−0.1	−0.5	−1.1	−0.1	−0.7	0.0	0.4	−0.6	0.4	0.8	0.3
Canada	0.6	−1.0	0.7	−0.1	−2.5	−0.9	−1.7	−1.3	−1.6	−1.9	0.1	−0.4
Other advanced economies	0.5	0.5	0.8	−0.2	0.6	0.2	0.6	0.8	0.7	−0.1	1.0	0.0
Memorandum												
Major advanced economies	−0.1	0.0	0.0	−0.1	−0.4	−0.2	−0.2	0.2	0.5	0.5	−0.1	0.2
Newly industrialized Asian economies	0.4	1.2	1.3	0.6	2.2	1.2	1.6	1.6	2.0	0.2	0.8	0.3

[1]In this table, "other advanced economies" means advanced economies excluding the United States, euro area countries, and Japan.
[2]Changes expressed as percent of GDP in the preceding period.

Table A4. Emerging and Developing Economies, by Country: Real GDP[1]

(Annual percent change)

	Average 1991–2000	2001	2002	2003	2004	2005	2006	2007	2008	2009	2010	2014
Africa	**2.4**	**4.9**	**6.5**	**5.4**	**6.7**	**5.7**	**6.1**	**6.3**	**5.2**	**1.7**	**4.0**	**5.3**
Algeria	1.6	2.7	4.7	6.9	5.2	5.1	2.0	3.0	3.0	2.1	3.7	4.2
Angola	1.3	3.1	14.5	3.3	11.2	20.6	18.6	20.3	13.2	0.2	9.3	6.1
Benin	4.5	6.2	4.4	4.0	3.0	2.9	3.8	4.6	5.0	3.8	3.0	6.0
Botswana	6.4	3.5	9.0	6.3	6.0	1.6	5.1	4.4	2.9	−10.3	4.1	2.1
Burkina Faso	5.3	6.6	4.7	7.3	4.6	7.1	5.5	3.6	5.0	3.5	4.1	6.0
Burundi	−1.7	2.1	4.4	−1.2	4.8	0.9	5.1	3.6	4.5	3.2	3.6	5.0
Cameroon[2]	1.4	4.5	4.0	4.0	3.7	2.3	3.2	3.3	2.9	1.6	2.7	5.2
Cape Verde	6.8	6.1	5.3	4.7	4.3	6.5	10.8	7.8	5.9	3.5	4.0	6.4
Central African Republic	1.0	0.6	−0.6	−7.1	1.0	2.4	3.8	3.7	2.2	2.4	3.1	5.5
Chad	2.8	11.7	8.5	14.7	33.6	7.9	0.2	0.2	−0.2	1.6	4.6	2.3
Comoros	1.1	3.3	4.1	2.5	−0.2	4.2	1.2	0.5	1.0	1.0	1.5	4.0
Congo, Dem. Rep. of	−5.6	−2.1	3.5	5.8	6.6	7.9	5.6	6.3	6.2	2.7	5.4	6.8
Congo, Rep. of	1.4	3.8	4.6	0.8	3.5	7.8	6.2	−1.6	5.6	7.4	12.2	2.3
Côte d'Ivoire	3.1	0.0	−1.6	−1.7	1.6	1.9	0.7	1.6	2.3	3.7	4.0	6.0
Djibouti	−1.7	2.0	2.6	3.2	3.0	3.2	4.8	5.1	5.8	5.1	5.4	7.1
Equatorial Guinea	31.6	63.4	19.5	14.0	38.0	9.7	1.3	21.4	11.3	−5.4	−2.8	−1.9
Eritrea	. . .	8.8	3.0	−2.7	1.5	2.6	−1.0	1.3	1.0	0.3	1.4	3.7
Ethiopia	2.9	7.7	1.2	−3.5	9.8	12.6	11.5	11.5	11.6	7.5	7.0	7.7
Gabon	1.7	2.1	−0.3	2.4	1.1	3.0	1.2	5.6	2.3	−1.0	2.6	2.8
Gambia, The	4.2	5.8	−3.2	6.9	7.0	5.1	6.5	6.3	6.1	3.6	4.3	5.0
Ghana	4.5	4.2	4.5	5.2	5.6	5.9	6.4	5.7	7.3	4.5	5.0	5.1
Guinea	4.1	3.8	4.2	1.2	2.3	3.0	2.5	1.8	4.9	0.0	2.7	4.2
Guinea-Bissau	0.9	−0.6	−4.2	−0.6	2.2	3.5	0.6	2.7	3.3	1.9	2.5	4.0
Kenya	1.7	4.7	0.3	2.8	4.6	5.9	6.4	7.1	1.7	2.5	4.0	6.5
Lesotho	3.8	3.0	1.6	3.9	4.6	0.7	8.1	5.1	3.5	−1.0	3.1	4.3
Liberia	. . .	2.8	3.8	−31.3	2.6	5.3	7.8	9.4	7.1	4.9	6.3	12.9
Madagascar	1.7	6.0	−12.4	9.8	5.3	4.6	5.0	6.2	7.1	−0.4	0.9	5.3
Malawi	3.4	−4.1	1.7	5.7	5.4	3.3	6.7	8.6	9.7	5.9	4.6	3.3
Mali	3.6	12.1	4.3	7.2	1.2	6.1	5.3	4.3	5.1	4.1	4.5	5.3
Mauritania	2.9	2.9	1.1	5.6	5.2	5.4	11.4	1.0	2.2	2.3	4.7	5.9
Mauritius	6.0	4.1	2.2	4.1	4.3	3.4	3.5	4.2	6.6	2.1	2.0	4.2
Morocco	2.4	7.6	3.3	6.3	4.8	3.0	7.8	2.7	5.6	5.0	3.2	5.0
Mozambique	6.5	12.3	9.2	6.5	7.9	8.4	8.7	7.0	6.8	4.3	5.2	6.5
Namibia	3.9	1.2	4.8	4.3	12.3	2.5	7.1	5.5	2.9	−0.7	1.7	3.0
Niger	1.0	8.0	5.3	7.1	−0.8	8.4	5.8	3.3	9.5	1.0	5.2	5.8
Nigeria	1.9	8.2	21.2	10.3	10.6	5.4	6.2	7.0	6.0	2.9	5.0	6.3
Rwanda	0.7	8.5	11.0	0.3	5.3	7.2	7.3	7.9	11.2	5.3	5.2	6.0
São Tomé and Príncipe	1.5	3.1	11.6	5.4	6.6	5.7	6.7	6.0	5.8	4.0	4.5	7.0
Senegal	3.1	4.6	0.7	6.7	5.9	5.6	2.4	4.7	2.5	1.5	3.4	4.9
Seychelles	4.5	−2.3	1.2	−5.9	−2.9	7.5	8.3	7.3	−1.9	−8.7	4.0	5.0
Sierra Leone	−7.6	18.2	27.4	9.5	9.7	7.1	5.1	6.4	5.5	4.0	4.0	5.4
South Africa	1.8	2.7	3.7	3.1	4.9	5.0	5.3	5.1	3.1	−2.2	1.7	4.5
Sudan	3.5	6.2	5.4	7.1	5.1	6.3	11.3	10.2	6.8	4.0	5.5	4.9
Swaziland	2.9	1.0	1.8	3.9	2.5	2.2	2.9	3.5	2.4	0.4	2.6	2.5
Tanzania	2.9	6.0	7.2	6.9	7.8	7.4	6.7	7.1	7.4	5.0	5.6	7.5
Togo	0.9	−2.3	−0.3	5.2	2.4	1.2	3.9	1.9	1.1	2.4	2.6	4.0
Tunisia	4.7	5.0	1.7	5.6	6.0	4.1	5.3	6.3	4.6	3.0	4.0	6.0
Uganda	6.2	5.2	8.7	6.5	6.8	6.3	10.8	8.4	9.0	7.0	6.0	7.0
Zambia	−0.2	4.9	3.3	5.1	5.4	5.3	6.2	6.3	5.8	4.5	5.0	6.1
Zimbabwe[3]	0.6	−2.7	−4.4	−10.4	−3.6	−4.0	−6.3	−6.9	−14.1	3.7	6.0	6.0

Table A4 *(continued)*

	Average 1991–2000	2001	2002	2003	2004	2005	2006	2007	2008	2009	2010	2014
Central and eastern Europe[4]	**2.0**	**0.2**	**4.4**	**4.8**	**7.3**	**6.0**	**6.6**	**5.5**	**3.0**	**−5.0**	**1.8**	**4.0**
Albania	1.3	7.0	4.2	5.8	5.7	5.8	5.5	6.3	6.8	0.7	2.2	6.0
Bosnia and Herzegovina	...	3.6	5.0	3.5	6.3	3.9	6.9	6.8	5.5	−3.0	0.5	4.5
Bulgaria	−4.0	4.1	4.5	5.0	6.6	6.2	6.3	6.2	6.0	−6.5	−2.5	5.0
Croatia	...	3.8	5.4	5.0	4.2	4.2	4.7	5.5	2.4	−5.2	0.4	4.0
Estonia	...	7.5	7.9	7.6	7.2	9.4	10.0	7.2	−3.6	−14.0	−2.6	4.0
Hungary	1.0	4.1	4.1	4.2	4.8	4.0	3.9	1.2	0.6	−6.7	−0.9	3.5
Latvia	...	8.0	6.5	7.2	8.7	10.6	12.2	10.0	−4.6	−18.0	−4.0	4.0
Lithuania	...	6.7	6.9	10.2	7.4	7.8	7.8	8.9	3.0	−18.5	−4.0	4.0
Macedonia, FYR	...	−4.5	0.9	2.8	4.1	4.1	4.0	5.9	4.9	−2.5	2.0	4.0
Montenegro	...	1.1	1.9	2.5	4.4	4.2	8.6	10.7	7.5	−4.0	−2.0	4.0
Poland	3.8	1.2	1.4	3.9	5.3	3.6	6.2	6.8	4.9	1.0	2.2	4.0
Romania	−1.6	5.6	5.0	5.3	8.5	4.1	7.9	6.2	7.1	−8.5	0.5	5.0
Serbia	...	5.6	3.9	2.4	8.3	5.6	5.2	6.9	5.4	−4.0	1.5	5.5
Turkey	3.7	−5.7	6.2	5.3	9.4	8.4	6.9	4.7	0.9	−6.5	3.7	3.5
Commonwealth of Independent States[4],[5]	...	**6.1**	**5.2**	**7.8**	**8.2**	**6.7**	**8.4**	**8.6**	**5.5**	**−6.7**	**2.1**	**5.3**
Russia	...	5.1	4.7	7.3	7.2	6.4	7.7	8.1	5.6	−7.5	1.5	5.0
Excluding Russia	...	8.9	6.6	9.1	10.8	7.4	10.2	9.9	5.4	−4.7	3.6	5.9
Armenia	...	9.6	13.2	14.0	10.5	13.9	13.2	13.7	6.8	−15.6	1.2	4.5
Azerbaijan	...	6.5	8.1	10.5	10.4	24.3	30.5	23.4	11.6	7.5	7.4	0.9
Belarus	...	4.7	5.0	7.0	11.4	9.4	10.0	8.6	10.0	−1.2	1.8	6.9
Georgia	...	4.7	5.5	11.1	5.9	9.6	9.4	12.3	2.1	−4.0	2.0	5.0
Kazakhstan	...	13.5	9.8	9.3	9.6	9.7	10.7	8.9	3.2	−2.0	2.0	7.5
Kyrgyz Republic	...	5.3	0.0	7.0	7.0	−0.2	3.1	8.5	7.6	1.5	3.0	5.6
Moldova	...	6.1	7.8	6.6	7.4	7.5	4.8	3.0	7.2	−9.0	0.0	5.0
Mongolia	0.3	0.2	4.7	7.0	10.6	7.3	8.6	10.2	8.9	0.5	3.0	0.9
Tajikistan	...	10.2	9.1	10.2	10.6	6.7	7.0	7.8	7.9	2.0	3.0	6.0
Turkmenistan	...	20.4	15.8	17.1	14.7	13.0	11.4	11.6	10.5	4.0	15.3	8.0
Ukraine	...	9.2	5.2	9.6	12.1	2.7	7.3	7.9	2.1	−14.0	2.7	5.8
Uzbekistan	...	4.2	4.0	4.2	7.7	7.0	7.3	9.5	9.0	7.0	7.0	6.0

Table A4 *(continued)*

	Average 1991–2000	2001	2002	2003	2004	2005	2006	2007	2008	2009	2010	2014
Developing Asia	**7.4**	**5.8**	**6.9**	**8.2**	**8.6**	**9.0**	**9.8**	**10.6**	**7.6**	**6.2**	**7.3**	**8.5**
Afghanistan, I.R. of	...	...	...	15.1	8.8	16.1	8.2	12.1	3.4	15.7	8.6	8.9
Bangladesh	4.9	4.8	4.8	5.8	6.1	6.3	6.5	6.3	6.0	5.4	5.4	6.5
Bhutan	5.0	6.8	10.9	7.2	6.8	6.5	6.3	21.4	7.6	8.5	5.3	6.8
Brunei Darussalam	...	2.7	3.9	2.9	0.5	0.4	4.4	0.6	−1.5	0.2	0.6	1.7
Cambodia	...	8.1	6.6	8.5	10.3	13.3	10.8	10.2	6.7	−2.7	4.3	6.3
China	10.4	8.3	9.1	10.0	10.1	10.4	11.6	13.0	9.0	8.5	9.0	9.5
Fiji	5.0	2.0	3.2	1.0	5.5	0.7	3.3	−6.6	0.2	−2.5	1.2	3.0
India	5.6	3.9	4.6	6.9	7.9	9.2	9.8	9.4	7.3	5.4	6.4	8.1
Indonesia	4.0	3.6	4.5	4.8	5.0	5.7	5.5	6.3	6.1	4.0	4.8	6.3
Kiribati	5.2	−5.1	6.1	2.3	2.2	0.0	3.2	−0.5	3.4	1.5	1.1	1.1
Lao PDR	6.3	5.7	5.9	6.1	6.4	7.1	8.4	7.5	7.2	4.6	5.4	7.3
Malaysia	7.1	0.5	5.4	5.8	6.8	5.3	5.8	6.2	4.6	−3.6	2.5	6.0
Maldives	7.5	3.5	6.5	8.5	9.5	−4.6	18.0	7.2	5.8	−4.0	3.4	4.2
Myanmar	7.1	11.3	12.0	13.8	13.6	13.6	13.1	11.9	4.0	4.3	5.0	5.1
Nepal	5.0	5.6	0.1	3.9	4.7	3.1	3.7	3.2	4.7	4.0	4.1	5.5
Pakistan	3.9	1.9	3.2	4.9	7.4	7.7	6.1	5.6	2.0	2.0	3.0	5.5
Papua New Guinea	4.6	−0.1	−0.2	2.2	2.7	3.6	2.6	6.5	7.0	3.9	3.7	2.4
Philippines	3.0	1.8	4.4	4.9	6.4	5.0	5.3	7.1	3.8	1.0	3.2	4.5
Samoa	3.2	8.1	5.5	2.0	4.2	8.6	2.2	2.2	4.8	−5.5	−1.0	3.0
Solomon Islands	2.6	−8.0	−2.8	6.5	4.9	5.4	6.9	10.7	6.9	0.4	2.4	3.7
Sri Lanka	5.2	−1.5	4.0	5.9	5.4	6.2	7.7	6.8	6.0	3.0	5.0	5.4
Thailand	4.4	2.2	5.3	7.1	6.3	4.6	5.2	4.9	2.6	−3.5	3.7	6.0
Timor-Leste	...	18.9	2.4	0.1	4.2	6.2	−5.8	8.4	12.8	7.2	7.9	7.8
Tonga	1.6	2.6	3.0	3.2	1.4	5.4	0.6	−3.2	1.2	2.6	1.9	1.6
Vanuatu	2.8	−2.5	−7.4	3.2	5.5	6.5	7.4	6.8	6.6	3.0	3.5	4.5
Vietnam	7.6	6.9	7.1	7.3	7.8	8.4	8.2	8.5	6.2	4.6	5.3	7.0
Middle East	**4.0**	**2.5**	**3.8**	**6.9**	**5.9**	**5.5**	**5.8**	**6.2**	**5.4**	**2.0**	**4.2**	**4.8**
Bahrain	4.6	4.6	5.2	7.2	5.6	7.9	6.7	8.1	6.1	3.0	3.7	5.0
Egypt	4.4	3.5	3.2	3.2	4.1	4.5	6.8	7.1	7.2	4.7	4.5	6.0
Iran, I.R. of	3.7	3.7	7.5	7.2	5.1	4.7	5.8	7.8	2.5	1.5	2.2	3.2
Iraq	...	...	...	...	...	−0.7	6.2	1.5	9.5	4.3	5.8	6.8
Jordan	4.7	5.3	5.8	4.2	8.6	8.1	8.0	8.9	7.9	3.0	4.0	5.5
Kuwait	3.7	0.2	3.0	17.3	10.2	10.6	5.1	2.5	6.3	−1.5	3.3	4.7
Lebanon	7.1	4.5	3.3	4.1	7.5	2.5	0.6	7.5	8.5	7.0	4.0	4.5
Libya	0.2	−4.3	−1.3	13.0	4.4	10.3	6.7	7.5	3.4	1.8	5.2	7.1
Oman	4.5	5.6	2.1	0.4	3.4	4.9	6.0	7.7	7.8	4.1	3.8	4.1
Qatar	6.9	6.3	3.2	6.3	17.7	9.2	15.0	15.3	16.4	11.5	18.5	3.3
Saudi Arabia	2.7	0.5	0.1	7.7	5.3	5.6	3.2	3.3	4.4	−0.9	4.0	5.0
Syrian Arab Republic	4.8	3.7	5.9	−2.1	6.7	4.5	5.1	4.2	5.2	3.0	4.2	5.7
United Arab Emirates	4.4	1.7	2.6	11.9	9.7	8.2	9.4	6.3	7.4	−0.2	2.4	5.2
Yemen, Rep. of	5.7	3.8	3.9	3.7	4.0	5.6	3.2	3.3	3.6	4.2	7.3	4.7

Table A4 *(concluded)*

	Average 1991–2000	2001	2002	2003	2004	2005	2006	2007	2008	2009	2010	2014
Western Hemisphere	**3.3**	**0.7**	**0.6**	**2.2**	**6.0**	**4.7**	**5.7**	**5.7**	**4.2**	**−2.5**	**2.9**	**4.0**
Antigua and Barbuda	3.4	1.5	2.0	4.3	5.2	5.5	12.4	6.9	2.8	−6.5	−1.5	3.9
Argentina[6]	4.2	−4.4	−10.9	8.8	9.0	9.2	8.5	8.7	6.8	−2.5	1.5	3.0
Bahamas, The	2.1	0.8	2.6	−0.9	−0.8	5.7	4.3	0.7	−1.7	−3.9	−0.5	1.8
Barbados	1.0	−2.6	0.7	2.0	4.8	3.9	3.2	3.4	0.2	−3.0	0.0	2.5
Belize	6.0	5.0	5.1	9.3	4.6	3.0	4.7	1.2	3.8	1.0	2.0	2.5
Bolivia	3.8	1.7	2.5	2.7	4.2	4.4	4.8	4.6	6.1	2.8	3.4	3.7
Brazil	2.5	1.3	2.7	1.1	5.7	3.2	4.0	5.7	5.1	−0.7	3.5	3.7
Chile	6.5	3.5	2.2	4.0	6.0	5.6	4.6	4.7	3.2	−1.7	4.0	5.4
Colombia	2.7	2.2	2.5	4.6	4.7	5.7	6.9	7.5	2.5	−0.3	2.5	4.5
Costa Rica	5.2	1.1	2.9	6.4	4.3	5.9	8.8	7.8	2.6	−1.5	2.3	5.2
Dominica	2.1	−4.2	−5.1	0.1	3.0	3.3	3.8	1.8	3.2	1.1	2.0	3.0
Dominican Republic	6.1	1.8	5.8	−0.3	1.3	9.3	10.7	8.5	5.3	0.5	2.0	6.0
Ecuador	2.2	5.3	4.2	3.6	8.0	6.0	3.9	2.5	6.5	−1.0	1.5	3.0
El Salvador	4.6	1.7	2.3	2.3	1.9	3.1	4.2	4.7	2.5	−2.5	0.5	4.0
Grenada	4.5	−3.0	1.6	7.1	−5.7	11.0	−2.3	4.9	2.2	−4.0	0.0	3.5
Guatemala	3.7	2.4	3.9	2.5	3.2	3.3	5.4	6.3	4.0	0.4	1.3	3.5
Guyana	4.9	2.3	1.1	−0.7	1.6	−1.9	5.1	5.4	3.0	2.0	4.0	4.4
Haiti	0.3	−1.0	−0.3	0.4	−3.5	1.8	2.3	3.4	1.2	2.0	2.7	3.7
Honduras	3.3	2.7	3.8	4.5	6.2	6.1	6.6	6.3	4.0	−2.0	2.0	3.0
Jamaica	0.5	1.3	1.0	3.5	1.4	1.0	2.7	1.5	−1.0	−3.6	−0.2	2.1
Mexico	3.5	−0.2	0.8	1.7	4.0	3.2	5.1	3.3	1.3	−7.3	3.3	4.9
Nicaragua	3.6	3.0	0.8	2.5	5.3	4.4	3.9	3.2	3.2	−1.0	1.0	4.0
Panama	5.5	0.6	2.2	4.2	7.5	7.2	8.5	11.5	9.2	1.8	3.7	6.5
Paraguay	1.8	2.1	0.0	3.8	4.1	2.9	4.3	6.8	5.8	−4.5	3.9	5.5
Peru	4.0	0.2	5.0	4.0	5.0	6.8	7.7	8.9	9.8	1.5	5.8	5.5
St. Kitts and Nevis	4.1	2.0	1.0	0.5	7.6	5.6	5.3	0.9	2.4	−2.0	0.0	2.0
St. Lucia	2.2	−4.1	0.6	3.5	4.5	4.4	5.0	1.7	0.7	−2.5	−0.4	3.9
St. Vincent and the Grenadines	3.1	−0.1	3.2	2.8	6.8	2.6	7.6	7.0	0.9	−1.1	2.1	4.0
Suriname	0.7	4.5	2.8	6.3	8.0	3.9	4.5	5.4	6.0	1.5	3.5	5.5
Trinidad and Tobago	4.5	3.8	7.9	14.4	8.0	6.2	13.5	4.6	2.3	−0.8	2.0	2.4
Uruguay	2.9	−3.5	−7.1	2.3	4.6	6.8	4.6	7.6	8.9	0.6	3.5	3.9
Venezuela	2.1	3.4	−8.9	−7.8	18.3	10.3	10.3	8.4	4.8	−2.0	−0.4	0.4

[1]For many countries, figures for recent years are IMF staff estimates. Data for some countries are for fiscal years.

[2]The percent changes in 2002 are calculated over a period of 18 months, reflecting a change in the fiscal year cycle (from July–June to January–December).

[3]The Zimbabwe dollar ceased circulating in early 2009. Data are based on IMF staff estimates of price and exchange rate developments in U.S. dollars.

[4]Data for some countries refer to real net material product (NMP) or are estimates based on NMP. The figures should be interpreted only as indicative of broad orders of magnitude because reliable, comparable data are not generally available. In particular, the growth of output of new private enterprises of the informal economy is not fully reflected in the recent figures.

[5]Georgia and Mongolia, which are not members of the Commonwealth of Independent States, are included in this group for reasons of geography and similarities in economic structure.

[6]Private analysts are of the view that real GDP growth has been lower than the official reports since the last quarter of 2008.

Table A5. Summary of Inflation

(Percent)

	Average 1991–2000	2001	2002	2003	2004	2005	2006	2007	2008	2009	2010	2014
GDP deflators												
Advanced economies	**2.4**	**1.9**	**1.6**	**1.8**	**2.0**	**2.1**	**2.2**	**2.3**	**2.0**	**0.9**	**1.0**	**1.6**
United States	2.1	2.3	1.6	2.2	2.8	3.3	3.3	2.9	2.1	1.6	1.5	2.0
Euro area	...	2.4	2.6	2.2	1.9	2.0	2.0	2.4	2.4	0.6	0.6	1.4
Japan	0.1	−1.2	−1.5	−1.6	−1.1	−1.2	−0.9	−0.7	−0.9	−0.2	−0.8	0.1
Other advanced economies[1]	3.3	2.1	1.8	2.2	2.3	2.0	2.1	2.7	2.9	0.7	1.4	1.8
Consumer prices												
Advanced economies	**2.7**	**2.2**	**1.5**	**1.8**	**2.0**	**2.3**	**2.4**	**2.2**	**3.4**	**0.1**	**1.1**	**1.9**
United States	2.8	2.8	1.6	2.3	2.7	3.4	3.2	2.9	3.8	−0.4	1.7	2.2
Euro area[2]	...	2.4	2.3	2.1	2.2	2.2	2.2	2.1	3.3	0.3	0.8	1.5
Japan	0.8	−0.7	−0.9	−0.3	0.0	−0.3	0.3	0.0	1.4	−1.1	−0.8	0.8
Other advanced economies[1]	3.3	2.2	1.7	1.8	1.8	2.1	2.1	2.1	3.8	1.3	1.6	2.2
Emerging and developing economies	**44.5**	**7.9**	**6.9**	**6.7**	**5.9**	**5.9**	**5.6**	**6.4**	**9.3**	**5.5**	**4.9**	**4.0**
Regional groups												
Africa	24.5	10.8	9.0	8.7	6.7	7.1	6.4	6.0	10.3	9.0	6.5	4.7
Central and eastern Europe	59.5	25.9	18.6	11.2	6.6	5.9	5.9	6.0	8.1	4.8	4.2	3.3
Commonwealth of Independent States[3]	...	20.3	14.0	12.3	10.4	12.1	9.4	9.7	15.6	11.8	9.4	6.9
Developing Asia	8.1	2.8	2.1	2.6	4.1	3.8	4.2	5.4	7.5	3.0	3.4	2.8
Middle East	10.3	3.8	5.3	6.1	7.1	7.2	8.3	11.2	15.0	8.3	6.6	5.6
Western Hemisphere	64.8	6.5	8.6	10.4	6.6	6.3	5.3	5.4	7.9	6.1	5.2	5.2
Memorandum												
European Union	7.5	3.0	2.5	2.2	2.3	2.3	2.3	2.4	3.7	0.9	1.1	1.7
Analytical groups												
By source of export earnings												
Fuel	77.6	13.5	11.9	11.5	9.8	10.0	9.0	10.0	15.0	10.3	8.9	7.4
Nonfuel	35.8	6.5	5.7	5.6	5.0	4.9	4.8	5.6	7.9	4.3	3.9	3.2
of which, primary products	50.4	14.4	7.9	6.1	4.4	6.4	7.0	5.7	11.3	6.6	5.1	4.7
By external financing source												
Net debtor countries	42.6	8.6	8.1	7.4	5.5	5.8	5.8	5.9	8.7	6.6	5.6	4.0
of which, official financing	24.4	8.2	3.7	7.6	7.3	7.9	8.5	7.9	13.1	9.8	6.3	4.9
Net debtor countries by debt-servicing experience												
Countries with arrears and/or rescheduling during 2003–07	31.9	9.1	12.5	9.3	7.0	8.2	8.7	7.9	11.5	9.4	6.5	4.9
Memorandum												
Median inflation rate												
Advanced economies	2.6	2.6	2.3	2.1	2.0	2.1	2.2	2.2	3.8	0.5	1.3	2.0
Emerging and developing economies	8.7	4.7	3.6	4.4	4.5	6.0	6.1	6.4	10.4	4.9	4.4	4.0

[1]In this table, "other advanced economies" means advanced economies excluding the United States, euro area countries, and Japan.

[2]Based on Eurostat's harmonized index of consumer prices.

[3]Georgia and Mongolia, which are not members of the Commonwealth of Independent States, are included in this group for reasons of geography and similarities in economic structure.

Table A6. Advanced Economies: Consumer Prices

(Annual percent change)

	Average 1991–2000	2001	2002	2003	2004	2005	2006	2007	2008	2009	2010	2014	End of Period 2008	2009	2010
Consumer Prices															
Advanced economies	**2.7**	**2.2**	**1.5**	**1.8**	**2.0**	**2.3**	**2.4**	**2.2**	**3.4**	**0.1**	**1.1**	**1.9**	**1.6**	**0.7**	**1.1**
United States	2.8	2.8	1.6	2.3	2.7	3.4	3.2	2.9	3.8	−0.4	1.7	2.2	0.7	1.6	1.5
Euro area[1]	. . .	2.4	2.3	2.1	2.2	2.2	2.2	2.1	3.3	0.3	0.8	1.5	1.6	0.9	0.6
Germany	2.3	1.9	1.4	1.0	1.8	1.9	1.8	2.3	2.8	0.1	0.2	0.7	1.1	0.0	0.2
France	1.8	1.8	1.9	2.2	2.3	1.9	1.9	1.6	3.2	0.3	1.1	1.8	3.2	0.3	1.1
Italy	3.7	2.3	2.6	2.8	2.3	2.2	2.2	2.0	3.5	0.7	0.9	1.8	2.4	0.6	1.1
Spain	4.0	2.8	3.6	3.1	3.1	3.4	3.6	2.8	4.1	−0.3	0.9	1.7	1.5	0.4	0.8
Netherlands	2.3	5.1	3.8	2.2	1.4	1.5	1.7	1.6	2.2	0.9	1.0	1.5	2.2	0.9	1.0
Belgium	2.0	2.4	1.6	1.5	1.9	2.5	2.3	1.8	4.5	0.2	1.0	1.3	2.7	0.1	1.2
Greece	9.1	3.7	3.9	3.4	3.0	3.5	3.3	3.0	4.2	1.1	1.7	2.0	3.1	1.3	1.8
Austria	2.0	2.3	1.7	1.3	2.0	2.1	1.7	2.2	3.2	0.5	1.0	1.8	1.5	1.2	0.8
Portugal	4.7	4.4	3.7	3.3	2.5	2.1	3.0	2.4	2.7	−0.6	1.0	1.8	0.8	−0.5	1.1
Finland	1.9	2.7	2.0	1.3	0.1	0.8	1.3	1.6	3.9	1.0	1.1	1.7	3.4	1.0	1.1
Ireland	2.6	4.0	4.7	4.0	2.3	2.2	2.7	2.9	3.1	−1.6	−0.3	1.1	1.3	−1.3	0.1
Slovak Republic	. . .	7.1	3.3	8.6	7.5	2.7	4.5	2.7	4.6	1.5	2.3	2.3	4.4	2.0	2.3
Slovenia	. . .	8.4	7.5	5.6	3.6	2.5	2.5	3.6	5.7	0.5	1.5	3.0	2.1	0.5	2.1
Luxembourg	2.2	2.7	2.1	2.0	2.2	2.5	2.7	2.3	3.4	0.2	1.8	1.6	0.9	2.1	1.5
Cyprus	3.8	2.0	2.8	4.0	1.9	2.0	2.2	2.2	4.4	0.4	1.2	2.8	1.8	0.9	1.2
Malta	3.1	2.5	2.6	1.9	2.7	2.5	2.6	0.7	4.7	2.1	1.9	2.4	5.0	0.9	2.6
Japan	0.8	−0.7	−0.9	−0.3	0.0	−0.3	0.3	0.0	1.4	−1.1	−0.8	0.8	0.4	−1.5	−0.7
United Kingdom[1]	2.7	1.2	1.3	1.4	1.3	2.0	2.3	2.3	3.6	1.9	1.5	2.0	3.9	1.2	1.3
Canada	2.0	2.5	2.3	2.7	1.8	2.2	2.0	2.1	2.4	0.1	1.3	2.0	1.9	0.2	1.6
Korea	5.1	4.1	2.8	3.5	3.6	2.8	2.2	2.5	4.7	2.6	2.5	3.0	4.1	2.0	3.0
Australia	2.2	4.4	3.0	2.8	2.3	2.7	3.5	2.3	4.4	1.6	1.5	2.5	3.7	1.6	1.2
Taiwan Province of China	2.6	0.0	−0.2	−0.3	1.6	2.3	0.6	1.8	3.5	−0.5	1.5	2.0	3.8	−0.1	1.3
Sweden	2.7	2.7	1.9	2.3	1.0	0.8	1.5	1.7	3.3	2.2	2.4	2.0	2.1	3.1	2.2
Switzerland	1.9	1.0	0.6	0.6	0.8	1.2	1.0	0.7	2.4	−0.4	0.5	1.0	0.7	−0.4	0.5
Hong Kong SAR	5.3	−1.6	−3.0	−2.6	−0.4	0.9	2.0	2.0	4.3	−1.0	0.5	2.6	2.0	−2.8	0.5
Czech Republic	13.3	4.7	1.9	0.1	2.8	1.8	2.5	2.9	6.3	1.0	1.1	2.0	3.6	0.6	1.9
Norway	2.3	3.0	1.3	2.5	0.5	1.5	2.3	0.7	3.8	2.3	1.8	2.5	2.1	1.9	1.9
Singapore	1.7	1.0	−0.4	0.5	1.7	0.5	1.0	2.1	6.5	−0.2	1.6	1.8	5.4	−1.3	2.0
Denmark	2.1	2.4	2.4	2.1	1.2	1.8	1.9	1.7	3.4	1.7	2.0	2.0	2.9	2.3	1.7
Israel	9.5	1.1	5.7	0.7	−0.4	1.4	2.1	0.5	4.6	3.6	2.0	2.0	3.8	−0.5	1.8
New Zealand	1.8	2.6	2.6	1.7	2.3	3.0	3.4	2.4	4.0	1.5	1.0	2.1	3.4	0.9	1.4
Iceland	3.2	6.7	4.8	2.1	3.2	4.0	6.8	5.0	12.4	11.7	4.4	2.5	18.1	7.0	2.5
Memorandum															
Major advanced economies	2.4	1.9	1.3	1.7	2.0	2.3	2.3	2.1	3.2	−0.1	1.1	1.8	1.3	0.7	0.9
Newly industrialized Asian economies	4.1	1.9	1.0	1.4	2.4	2.2	1.6	2.2	4.5	1.0	1.9	2.6	3.9	0.5	2.1

[1]Based on Eurostat's harmonized index of consumer prices.

Table A7. Emerging and Developing Economies, by Country: Consumer Prices[1]

(Annual percent change)

	Average 1991–2000	2001	2002	2003	2004	2005	2006	2007	2008	2009	2010	2014	End of Period 2008	2009	2010
Africa	**24.5**	**10.8**	**9.0**	**8.7**	**6.7**	**7.1**	**6.4**	**6.0**	**10.3**	**9.0**	**6.5**	**4.7**	**11.7**	**6.7**	**6.3**
Algeria	16.3	4.2	1.4	2.6	3.6	1.6	2.5	3.6	4.5	4.6	3.4	3.0	5.8	3.5	3.3
Angola	549.4	152.6	108.9	98.3	43.6	23.0	13.3	12.2	12.5	14.0	15.4	0.0	13.2	14.0	16.0
Benin	7.6	4.0	2.4	1.5	0.9	5.4	3.8	1.3	8.0	4.0	2.8	2.8	9.9	3.5	3.3
Botswana	10.6	6.6	8.0	9.2	7.0	8.6	11.6	7.1	12.6	8.4	6.4	5.1	13.7	6.6	6.2
Burkina Faso	4.4	4.7	2.3	2.0	−0.4	6.4	2.4	−0.2	10.7	3.8	2.3	2.0	11.6	2.4	2.0
Burundi	15.2	9.3	−1.3	10.7	8.0	13.4	2.8	8.3	24.4	12.9	8.3	5.0	25.7	9.1	7.5
Cameroon[2]	4.9	2.8	6.3	0.6	0.3	2.0	4.9	1.1	5.3	2.9	2.0	2.0	5.3	0.1	2.0
Cape Verde	5.9	3.7	1.9	1.2	−1.9	0.4	4.8	4.4	6.8	1.5	2.0	2.0	6.7	1.0	2.0
Central African Republic	3.9	3.8	2.3	4.4	−2.2	2.9	6.7	0.9	9.3	4.6	2.8	2.5	14.5	1.1	2.5
Chad	4.5	12.4	5.2	−1.8	−4.8	3.7	7.7	−7.4	8.3	6.5	3.0	3.0	9.7	−9.0	3.0
Comoros	3.9	5.6	3.6	3.7	4.5	3.0	3.4	4.5	4.8	4.9	2.1	2.9	7.4	2.4	1.9
Congo, Dem. Rep. of	977.6	357.3	25.3	12.8	4.0	21.4	13.2	16.7	18.0	39.2	14.6	8.8	27.6	31.2	15.0
Congo, Rep. of	7.3	0.8	3.0	1.7	3.7	2.5	4.7	2.6	6.0	6.9	4.4	3.0	11.4	4.8	4.0
Côte d'Ivoire	6.0	4.4	3.1	3.3	1.5	3.9	2.5	1.9	6.3	5.9	3.2	2.5	9.0	3.4	3.0
Djibouti	3.6	1.8	0.6	2.0	3.1	3.1	3.5	5.0	12.0	5.5	5.0	3.0	12.0	5.5	5.0
Equatorial Guinea	6.5	8.8	7.6	7.3	4.2	5.7	4.5	2.8	5.9	4.1	6.1	4.1	6.0	5.7	4.9
Eritrea	. . .	14.6	16.9	22.7	25.1	12.5	15.1	9.3	12.6	14.0	14.5	14.0	14.0	14.0	15.0
Ethiopia	7.2	−5.2	−7.2	15.1	8.6	6.8	12.3	15.8	25.3	36.4	5.1	7.0	55.3	3.1	9.5
Gabon	4.0	2.1	0.2	2.1	0.4	1.2	−1.4	5.0	5.3	2.6	3.8	3.0	5.6	1.1	4.0
Gambia, The	4.2	4.5	8.6	17.0	14.3	5.0	2.1	5.4	4.5	6.4	5.7	5.0	6.8	6.0	5.5
Ghana	25.6	32.9	14.8	26.7	12.6	15.1	10.2	10.7	16.5	18.5	10.2	5.0	18.1	14.6	9.2
Guinea	7.3	5.4	3.0	11.0	17.5	31.4	34.7	22.9	18.4	4.9	9.4	5.0	13.5	8.5	7.0
Guinea-Bissau	32.8	3.3	3.3	−3.5	0.8	3.3	0.7	4.6	10.4	0.4	2.5	2.6	8.7	−3.1	2.9
Kenya	15.9	5.8	2.0	9.8	11.6	10.3	14.5	9.8	13.1	12.0	7.8	5.0	13.8	11.5	7.2
Lesotho	10.5	6.9	12.5	7.3	5.0	3.4	6.1	8.0	10.7	7.7	6.5	5.1	10.6	7.7	5.9
Liberia	. . .	12.1	14.2	10.3	3.6	6.9	7.2	13.7	17.5	7.3	5.0	5.0	9.4	10.5	4.5
Madagascar	16.2	6.9	16.2	−1.1	14.0	18.4	10.8	10.4	9.2	9.9	9.7	5.0	10.1	10.3	8.8
Malawi	30.9	27.2	17.4	9.6	11.4	15.5	13.9	7.9	8.7	8.6	8.2	13.0	9.9	7.8	8.3
Mali	3.6	5.2	4.9	−1.2	−3.1	6.4	1.5	1.5	9.1	2.5	2.1	2.3	7.4	2.9	2.2
Mauritania	5.1	7.7	5.4	5.3	10.4	12.1	6.2	7.3	7.3	4.9	5.8	5.0	3.9	6.0	5.5
Mauritius	7.5	5.4	6.5	3.9	4.7	4.9	8.9	9.1	8.8	6.4	4.0	5.0	9.7	3.1	5.0
Morocco	4.0	0.6	2.8	1.2	1.5	1.0	3.3	2.0	3.9	2.8	2.8	2.6	4.2	2.8	2.8
Mozambique	28.7	9.1	16.8	13.5	12.6	6.4	13.2	8.2	10.3	3.5	5.5	5.5	6.2	4.0	5.7
Namibia	9.9	9.3	11.3	7.2	4.1	2.3	5.1	6.7	7.1	9.1	6.8	4.5	10.9	7.3	6.2
Niger	5.0	4.0	2.7	−1.8	0.4	7.8	0.1	0.1	11.3	4.8	2.3	2.0	13.6	0.0	2.0
Nigeria	28.5	18.0	13.7	14.0	15.0	17.9	8.2	5.4	11.6	12.0	8.8	8.5	15.1	9.1	8.5
Rwanda	16.3	3.4	2.0	7.4	12.0	9.0	8.9	9.1	15.4	11.5	6.3	5.0	22.3	6.0	5.0
São Tomé and Príncipe	35.8	9.5	9.2	9.6	12.8	17.2	23.1	18.5	26.0	17.1	11.9	5.0	24.8	14.0	10.0
Senegal	4.1	3.0	2.3	0.0	0.5	1.7	2.1	5.9	5.8	−0.9	1.8	2.2	4.3	−0.3	2.2
Seychelles	2.3	6.0	0.2	3.3	3.9	0.6	−1.9	5.3	37.0	33.4	3.0	3.0	63.3	2.9	2.2
Sierra Leone	32.2	2.6	−3.7	7.5	14.2	12.1	9.5	11.7	14.8	10.6	8.5	5.7	12.2	9.0	8.0
South Africa	9.0	5.7	9.2	5.8	1.4	3.4	4.7	7.1	11.5	7.2	6.2	4.5	9.5	6.8	5.6
Sudan	67.9	4.9	8.3	7.7	8.4	8.5	7.2	8.0	14.3	11.0	9.0	5.5	14.9	10.0	8.0
Swaziland	8.9	7.5	11.7	7.4	3.4	4.8	5.3	8.2	13.1	7.8	6.9	5.3	12.9	7.4	6.4
Tanzania	19.6	5.1	4.6	4.4	4.1	4.4	7.3	7.0	10.3	10.6	4.9	5.0	13.5	6.5	5.0
Togo	6.1	3.9	3.1	−0.9	0.4	6.8	2.2	1.0	8.4	2.8	2.1	2.5	7.2	2.1	2.4
Tunisia	4.4	2.0	2.7	2.7	3.6	2.0	4.5	3.1	5.0	3.5	3.4	3.0	4.1	3.5	3.4
Uganda	12.6	4.5	−2.0	5.7	5.0	8.0	6.6	6.8	7.3	14.2	10.8	5.7	12.5	12.3	9.2
Zambia	60.0	21.7	22.2	21.4	18.0	18.3	9.0	10.7	12.4	14.0	10.2	5.0	16.6	12.0	8.0
Zimbabwe[3]	−4.3	−37.2	−34.4	−8.6	113.6	−31.5	33.0	−72.7	156.2	9.0	12.0	4.0	218.7	0.8	8.7

Table A7 *(continued)*

	Average 1991–2000	2001	2002	2003	2004	2005	2006	2007	2008	2009	2010	2014	End of Period 2008	2009	2010
Central and eastern Europe[4]	**59.5**	**25.9**	**18.6**	**11.2**	**6.6**	**5.9**	**5.9**	**6.0**	**8.1**	**4.8**	**4.2**	**3.3**	**6.7**	**4.3**	**3.9**
Albania	34.7	3.1	5.2	2.3	2.9	2.4	2.4	2.9	3.4	1.7	2.0	3.0	2.2	1.8	2.6
Bosnia and Herzegovina	...	4.5	0.3	0.5	0.3	3.6	6.1	1.5	7.4	0.9	1.6	2.5	3.8	0.8	1.8
Bulgaria	107.9	7.4	5.8	2.3	6.1	6.0	7.4	7.6	12.0	2.7	1.6	3.4	7.2	1.5	1.7
Croatia	...	3.8	1.7	1.8	2.0	3.3	3.2	2.9	6.1	2.8	2.8	3.0	2.8	3.0	2.8
Estonia	...	5.8	3.6	1.3	3.0	4.1	4.4	6.6	10.4	0.0	−0.2	2.5	7.0	−1.5	0.0
Hungary	20.0	9.2	5.3	4.6	6.8	3.6	3.9	7.9	6.1	4.5	4.1	3.0	3.5	6.1	2.4
Latvia	...	2.5	1.6	3.3	6.2	6.9	6.6	10.1	15.3	3.1	−3.5	1.1	10.4	−1.7	−2.6
Lithuania	...	1.6	0.3	−1.1	1.2	2.7	3.8	5.8	11.1	3.5	−2.9	1.6	8.5	−0.3	−1.8
Macedonia, FYR	...	5.5	2.2	1.2	−0.4	0.5	3.2	2.3	8.3	−0.5	2.0	3.0	4.1	−1.0	2.0
Montenegro	...	23.7	19.7	7.5	3.1	3.4	2.1	3.5	9.0	3.4	2.1	3.1	...	...	...
Poland	26.1	5.5	1.9	0.8	3.5	2.1	1.0	2.5	4.2	3.4	2.6	2.5	3.3	3.0	2.9
Romania	101.1	34.5	22.5	15.3	11.9	9.0	6.6	4.8	7.8	5.5	3.6	3.5	6.3	4.3	3.0
Serbia	...	91.8	19.5	11.7	10.1	17.3	12.7	6.5	11.7	9.9	7.3	4.7	8.6	10.0	7.0
Turkey	75.9	54.2	45.1	25.3	8.6	8.2	9.6	8.8	10.4	6.2	6.8	4.0	10.1	5.8	6.3
Commonwealth of Independent States[4,5]	...	**20.3**	**14.0**	**12.3**	**10.4**	**12.1**	**9.4**	**9.7**	**15.6**	**11.8**	**9.4**	**6.9**	**14.0**	**10.7**	**8.6**
Russia	...	21.5	15.8	13.7	10.9	12.7	9.7	9.0	14.1	12.3	9.9	7.5	13.3	11.0	9.0
Excluding Russia	...	17.1	9.2	8.6	9.1	10.7	8.8	11.5	19.6	10.6	8.0	5.6	15.7	9.8	7.4
Armenia	...	3.1	1.1	4.7	7.0	0.6	2.9	4.4	9.0	3.0	3.2	4.0	5.2	4.5	3.0
Azerbaijan	...	1.5	2.8	2.2	6.7	9.7	8.4	16.6	20.8	2.2	5.3	6.0	15.4	4.5	6.0
Belarus	...	61.1	42.6	28.4	18.1	10.3	7.0	8.4	14.8	13.0	8.3	6.0	13.3	11.0	8.0
Georgia	...	4.7	5.6	4.8	5.7	8.3	9.2	9.2	10.0	1.2	3.0	5.0	5.5	3.0	3.0
Kazakhstan	...	8.4	5.9	6.4	6.9	7.6	8.6	10.8	17.2	7.5	6.6	6.0	9.5	7.1	6.3
Kyrgyz Republic	...	6.9	2.1	3.1	4.1	4.3	5.6	10.2	24.5	8.0	6.7	4.5	20.1	5.0	7.0
Moldova	...	9.8	5.3	11.7	12.5	11.9	12.7	12.4	12.7	1.4	7.7	4.0	7.3	5.0	5.0
Mongolia	...	6.2	0.9	5.1	7.9	12.5	4.5	8.2	26.8	8.5	7.9	5.3	23.2	8.5	6.0
Tajikistan	...	38.6	12.2	16.4	7.2	7.3	10.0	13.2	20.4	8.0	10.9	6.5	11.8	11.8	10.0
Turkmenistan	...	11.6	8.8	5.6	5.9	10.7	8.2	6.3	14.5	0.4	3.5	4.5	8.9	4.1	2.8
Ukraine	...	11.9	0.7	5.2	9.0	13.5	9.1	12.8	25.2	16.3	10.3	5.0	22.3	14.0	9.0
Uzbekistan	...	27.3	27.3	11.6	6.6	10.0	14.2	12.3	12.7	12.5	9.5	8.0	14.4	10.2	9.0

Table A7 *(continued)*

	Average 1991–2000	2001	2002	2003	2004	2005	2006	2007	2008	2009	2010	2014	End of Period 2008	2009	2010
Developing Asia	**8.1**	**2.8**	**2.1**	**2.6**	**4.1**	**3.8**	**4.2**	**5.4**	**7.5**	**3.0**	**3.4**	**2.8**	**5.9**	**3.5**	**3.1**
Afghanistan, I.R. of	...	...	5.1	24.1	13.2	12.3	5.1	13.0	26.8	−9.3	7.6	4.0	3.2	6.0	5.0
Bangladesh	5.6	1.9	3.7	5.4	6.1	7.0	7.1	9.1	7.7	5.3	5.6	4.2	6.0	4.6	6.5
Bhutan	9.2	3.4	2.5	2.1	4.6	5.3	5.0	5.2	8.4	7.0	4.0	3.9	9.2	5.5	4.0
Brunei Darussalam	...	0.6	−2.3	0.3	0.9	1.1	0.2	0.3	2.7	1.2	1.2	1.2	...	...	...
Cambodia	...	0.2	3.3	−19.3	3.9	6.4	6.1	7.7	25.0	−0.6	4.1	3.1	12.5	5.0	4.6
China	7.2	0.7	−0.8	1.2	3.9	1.8	1.5	4.8	5.9	−0.1	0.6	1.9	2.8	0.8	0.6
Fiji	3.5	4.3	0.8	4.2	2.8	2.4	2.5	4.8	7.8	5.0	7.0	2.0	6.6	9.5	2.0
India	9.0	3.8	4.3	3.8	3.8	4.2	6.2	6.4	8.3	8.7	8.4	4.0	9.7	8.9	7.4
Indonesia	13.2	11.5	11.8	6.8	6.1	10.5	13.1	6.0	9.8	5.0	6.2	4.2	11.1	4.0	6.0
Kiribati	3.0	6.0	3.2	1.6	−0.7	−0.4	−1.5	4.2	11.0	9.1	2.8	2.8	18.6	2.8	2.8
Lao PDR	29.1	7.8	10.6	15.5	10.5	7.2	6.8	4.5	7.6	0.2	3.0	3.0	3.2	3.3	3.3
Malaysia	3.5	1.4	1.8	1.1	1.4	3.0	3.6	2.0	5.4	−0.1	1.2	2.5	4.3	1.2	1.2
Maldives	7.0	0.7	0.9	−2.8	6.3	2.5	3.6	7.6	11.9	5.5	4.5	3.0	8.6	6.7	4.7
Myanmar	24.1	34.5	58.1	24.9	3.8	10.7	26.3	32.9	22.5	6.9	4.7	6.0	9.2	4.5	5.0
Nepal	9.2	2.4	2.9	4.7	4.0	4.5	8.0	6.4	7.7	13.2	11.8	5.0	12.1	11.4	12.0
Pakistan	9.1	4.4	2.5	3.1	4.6	9.3	7.9	7.8	12.0	20.8	10.0	6.0	21.5	13.1	9.0
Papua New Guinea	9.5	9.3	11.8	14.7	2.1	1.8	2.4	0.9	10.7	8.2	5.0	3.7	11.2	5.3	4.8
Philippines	8.7	6.8	3.0	3.5	6.0	7.7	6.2	2.8	9.3	2.8	4.0	4.5	8.0	2.5	4.3
Samoa	3.5	1.9	7.4	4.3	7.8	7.8	3.2	4.5	6.2	14.2	6.5	4.0	8.8	9.2	6.0
Solomon Islands	10.4	7.4	9.5	10.5	6.9	7.1	11.1	7.7	17.2	8.0	7.0	5.9	17.5	5.5	8.4
Sri Lanka	9.7	14.2	9.6	9.0	9.0	11.0	10.0	15.8	22.6	4.6	13.0	7.0	14.4	8.0	10.7
Thailand	4.5	1.6	0.7	1.8	2.8	4.5	4.6	2.2	5.5	−1.2	2.1	1.8	0.4	2.4	1.2
Timor-Leste	...	3.6	4.7	7.2	3.2	1.8	4.1	8.9	7.6	4.0	4.0	4.0	5.7	4.0	4.0
Tonga	4.4	6.9	10.4	11.1	11.7	9.7	7.0	5.1	14.5	12.3	6.1	4.2	6.0	6.0	6.0
Vanuatu	3.0	3.7	2.0	3.0	1.4	1.2	2.0	3.9	4.8	4.3	3.0	3.0	5.8	3.5	3.0
Vietnam	15.4	−0.3	4.1	3.3	7.9	8.4	7.5	8.3	23.1	7.0	11.0	5.0	19.9	7.0	10.0
Middle East	**10.3**	**3.8**	**5.3**	**6.1**	**7.1**	**7.2**	**8.3**	**11.2**	**15.0**	**8.3**	**6.6**	**5.6**	**13.7**	**6.8**	**6.6**
Bahrain	−0.3	−1.2	−0.5	1.7	2.2	2.6	2.0	3.3	3.5	3.0	2.5	2.0	5.1	3.0	2.5
Egypt	8.9	2.4	2.4	3.2	8.1	8.8	4.2	11.0	11.7	16.2	8.5	6.5	20.2	10.0	8.0
Iran, I.R. of	23.9	11.3	15.7	15.6	15.3	10.4	11.9	18.4	25.4	12.0	10.0	10.0	17.8	10.0	10.0
Iraq	...	...	...	...	...	37.0	53.2	30.8	2.7	6.9	6.0	4.0	6.8	6.0	6.0
Jordan	3.5	1.8	1.8	1.6	3.4	3.5	6.3	5.4	14.9	0.2	4.0	1.7	9.6	3.5	3.3
Kuwait	2.2	1.4	0.8	1.0	1.3	4.1	3.1	5.5	10.5	4.6	4.4	3.0	10.5	4.6	4.4
Lebanon	18.5	−0.4	1.8	1.3	1.7	−0.7	5.6	4.1	10.8	2.5	3.5	2.0	6.4	2.9	3.0
Libya	5.8	−8.8	−9.9	−2.1	1.0	2.9	1.4	6.2	10.4	5.0	4.5	3.0	10.4	5.0	4.5
Oman	0.5	−0.8	−0.3	0.2	0.7	1.9	3.4	5.9	12.6	3.3	3.0	2.0	7.7	3.1	2.9
Qatar	2.7	1.4	0.2	2.3	6.8	8.8	11.8	13.8	15.0	0.0	4.0	3.0	15.0	0.0	4.0
Saudi Arabia	0.8	−1.1	0.2	0.6	0.4	0.6	2.3	4.1	9.9	4.5	4.0	3.0	7.8	3.7	3.5
Syrian Arab Republic	5.6	3.4	−0.5	5.8	4.4	7.2	10.4	4.7	15.2	7.5	6.0	5.0	15.4	7.5	6.0
United Arab Emirates	3.6	2.7	2.9	3.2	5.0	6.2	9.3	11.1	12.3	2.5	3.3	3.9	...	...	...
Yemen, Rep. of	34.6	11.9	12.2	10.8	12.5	9.9	10.8	7.9	19.0	8.4	8.9	8.4	10.8	6.1	11.7

Table A7 *(concluded)*

	Average 1991–2000	2001	2002	2003	2004	2005	2006	2007	2008	2009	2010	2014	End of Period 2008	2009	2010
Western Hemisphere	**64.8**	**6.5**	**8.6**	**10.4**	**6.6**	**6.3**	**5.3**	**5.4**	**7.9**	**6.1**	**5.2**	**5.2**	**8.1**	**5.1**	**5.3**
Antigua and Barbuda	2.7	1.7	2.4	2.0	2.0	2.1	1.8	1.4	5.3	−0.8	2.5	2.5	0.7	−1.4	2.5
Argentina[6]	15.7	−1.1	25.9	13.4	4.4	9.6	10.9	8.8	8.6	5.6	5.0	5.0	7.2	5.0	5.0
Bahamas, The	2.5	2.0	2.2	3.0	1.0	2.2	1.8	2.5	4.5	1.8	0.6	1.5	4.5	1.0	0.2
Barbados	2.9	2.6	−1.2	1.6	1.4	6.1	7.3	4.0	8.1	3.5	5.2	2.1	7.2	3.2	7.2
Belize	1.8	1.2	2.2	2.6	3.1	3.7	4.2	2.3	6.4	2.7	1.8	2.5	4.4	1.0	2.5
Bolivia	9.1	1.6	0.9	3.3	4.4	5.4	4.3	8.7	14.0	4.3	4.5	3.5	11.8	3.0	4.0
Brazil	204.4	6.8	8.4	14.8	6.6	6.9	4.2	3.6	5.7	4.8	4.1	4.5	5.9	4.2	4.4
Chile	9.4	3.6	2.5	2.8	1.1	3.1	3.4	4.4	8.7	2.0	2.3	3.0	7.6	−0.5	2.5
Colombia	20.0	8.0	6.3	7.1	5.9	5.0	4.3	5.5	7.0	4.6	3.8	3.1	7.7	3.8	3.6
Costa Rica	15.9	11.3	9.2	9.4	12.3	13.8	11.5	9.4	13.4	8.4	5.0	4.2	13.9	5.0	5.0
Dominica	2.1	1.6	0.1	1.6	2.4	1.6	2.6	3.2	6.3	1.8	1.6	1.5	1.9	1.8	1.5
Dominican Republic	10.4	8.9	5.2	27.4	51.5	4.2	7.6	6.1	10.6	0.9	5.4	3.0	4.5	5.0	5.0
Ecuador	42.5	37.7	12.6	7.9	2.7	2.1	3.3	2.3	8.4	5.0	3.0	2.5	8.8	3.0	2.5
El Salvador	7.9	3.8	1.9	2.1	4.5	4.7	4.0	4.6	7.3	1.0	1.8	2.8	5.5	1.0	2.5
Grenada	2.2	1.7	1.1	2.2	2.3	3.5	4.2	3.9	8.0	1.4	3.2	2.0	5.2	1.7	1.8
Guatemala	11.5	7.3	8.1	5.6	7.6	9.1	6.6	6.8	11.4	2.2	3.9	4.0	9.4	1.5	3.8
Guyana	16.6	2.6	5.4	6.0	4.7	6.9	6.7	12.2	8.1	2.9	3.5	5.0	6.4	3.3	4.0
Haiti	19.7	16.5	9.3	26.7	28.3	16.8	14.2	9.0	14.4	3.5	3.9	5.7	19.8	−4.0	5.0
Honduras	18.2	9.7	7.7	7.7	8.1	8.8	5.6	6.9	11.4	5.9	6.0	5.8	10.8	4.5	6.0
Jamaica	24.9	6.9	7.0	10.1	13.5	15.1	8.5	9.3	22.0	9.4	8.7	6.2	16.8	8.7	8.7
Mexico	18.3	6.4	5.0	4.5	4.7	4.0	3.6	4.0	5.1	5.4	3.5	3.0	6.5	4.3	3.2
Nicaragua	19.2	4.7	4.0	6.5	8.5	9.6	9.1	11.1	19.9	4.3	4.2	6.5	13.8	2.5	4.0
Panama	1.2	0.3	1.0	0.6	0.5	2.9	2.5	4.2	8.8	2.3	2.6	2.5	6.8	2.6	2.5
Paraguay	13.4	7.3	10.5	14.2	4.3	6.8	9.6	8.1	10.2	2.8	3.6	3.1	7.5	2.5	5.0
Peru	38.0	2.0	0.2	2.3	3.7	1.6	2.0	1.8	5.8	3.2	2.0	2.0	6.7	1.2	2.0
St. Kitts and Nevis	3.3	2.1	2.1	2.3	2.2	3.4	8.5	4.5	5.4	3.4	2.1	2.2	7.6	2.0	2.2
St. Lucia	3.2	5.4	−0.3	1.0	1.5	3.9	4.1	2.2	7.2	2.2	2.8	2.2	3.8	3.1	2.2
St. Vincent and the Grenadines	2.5	0.8	1.3	0.2	3.0	3.7	3.0	6.9	10.1	4.2	2.9	2.9	8.7	2.9	2.9
Suriname	75.5	39.8	15.5	23.0	9.1	9.9	11.3	6.4	14.6	7.5	6.0	7.5	9.3	5.5	4.3
Trinidad and Tobago	5.2	5.5	4.2	3.8	3.7	6.9	8.3	7.9	12.1	7.2	5.0	5.0	14.5	4.0	6.0
Uruguay	35.2	4.4	14.0	19.4	9.2	4.7	6.4	8.1	7.9	7.5	7.4	5.0	9.2	7.5	6.5
Venezuela	43.3	12.5	22.4	31.1	21.7	16.0	13.7	18.7	30.4	29.5	30.0	33.8	30.9	28.0	32.0

[1]In accordance with standard practice in the *World Economic Outlook*, movements in consumer prices are indicated as annual averages rather than as December–December changes during the year, as is the practice in some countries. For many countries, figures for recent years are IMF staff estimates. Data for some countries are for fiscal years.

[2]The percent changes in 2002 are calculated over a period of 18 months, reflecting a change in the fiscal year cycle (from July–June to January–December).

[3]The Zimbabwe dollar ceased circulating in early 2009. Data are based on IMF staff estimates of price and exchange rate developments in U.S. dollars.

[4]For many countries, inflation for the earlier years is measured on the basis of a retail price index. Consumer price index (CPI) inflation data with broader and more up-to-date coverage are typically used for more recent years.

[5]Georgia and Mongolia, which are not members of the Commonwealth of Independent States, are included in this group for reasons of geography and similarities in economic structure.

[6]Private analysts estimate that CPI inflation has been considerably higher. The authorities have created a board of academic advisors to assess these issues.

Table A8. Major Advanced Economies: General Government Fiscal Balances and Debt[1]

(Percent of GDP unless noted otherwise)

	Average 1993–2002	2003	2004	2005	2006	2007	2008	2009	2010	2014
Major advanced economies										
Actual balance	−2.7	−4.7	−4.1	−3.3	−2.3	−2.2	−4.6	−10.1	−9.0	−5.7
Output gap[2]	−0.4	−1.1	−0.3	0.0	0.5	0.7	−0.6	−4.6	−4.1	0.0
Structural balance[2]	−2.3	−3.3	−2.9	−2.5	−2.0	−1.7	−3.3	−5.2	−5.4	−3.9
United States										
Actual balance	−1.6	−4.8	−4.3	−3.2	−2.2	−2.8	−5.9	−12.5	−10.0	−6.7
Output gap[2]	−0.6	−1.2	0.1	0.8	0.9	0.7	−0.8	−4.5	−3.9	0.0
Structural balance[2]	−1.0	−2.4	−2.2	−1.7	−1.4	−1.4	−3.4	−5.1	−5.3	−3.1
Net debt	45.9	40.8	42.4	42.7	41.8	42.3	47.9	58.2	66.8	84.9
Gross debt	64.4	60.2	61.2	61.4	60.9	61.9	70.4	84.8	93.6	108.2
Euro area										
Actual balance	−2.9	−3.0	−2.9	−2.5	−1.2	−0.6	−1.8	−6.2	−6.6	−3.5
Output gap[2]	−0.2	−0.8	−0.6	−0.6	0.7	1.8	1.2	−2.9	−3.1	0.0
Structural balance[2]	−2.7	−2.8	−2.7	−2.6	−2.0	−1.8	−2.5	−4.0	−4.2	−3.2
Net debt	59.4	59.7	60.3	60.5	58.6	56.2	59.0	68.6	74.6	83.7
Gross debt	68.6	68.7	69.1	69.6	67.8	65.7	69.2	80.0	86.3	95.6
Germany[3]										
Actual balance	−2.4	−4.0	−3.8	−3.3	−1.5	−0.5	−0.1	−4.2	−4.6	0.0
Output gap[2]	0.0	−1.7	−1.9	−2.3	−0.4	0.9	1.0	−3.6	−3.3	0.0
Structural balance[2,4]	−2.0	−3.2	−2.8	−2.3	−1.4	−0.7	−0.6	−2.2	−2.7	0.0
Net debt	48.9	57.7	60.0	61.8	60.1	56.9	60.5	70.3	76.2	81.6
Gross debt	56.1	62.8	64.7	66.4	65.9	63.4	67.1	78.7	84.5	89.3
France										
Actual balance	−3.5	−4.1	−3.6	−2.9	−2.3	−2.7	−3.4	−7.0	−7.1	−4.7
Output gap[2]	−0.2	0.1	0.4	0.3	0.8	1.0	0.0	−3.2	−3.2	0.3
Structural balance[2,4]	−3.3	−4.0	−3.6	−3.4	−2.6	−3.1	−3.3	−4.0	−4.1	−4.7
Net debt	46.6	53.2	55.3	56.7	53.9	54.1	57.8	67.0	72.9	82.9
Gross debt	56.0	62.9	65.0	66.4	63.6	63.8	67.5	76.7	82.6	92.6
Italy										
Actual balance	−4.7	−3.5	−3.5	−4.3	−3.3	−1.5	−2.7	−5.6	−5.6	−5.3
Output gap[2]	−0.3	−0.3	0.0	−0.4	0.8	1.6	−0.1	−3.4	−3.5	0.0
Structural balance[2,4]	−4.8	−3.5	−3.8	−4.3	−3.8	−2.4	−2.7	−3.7	−3.8	−5.3
Net debt	111.1	102.5	102.0	103.8	104.4	101.3	103.6	112.8	117.0	125.7
Gross debt	115.0	104.4	103.8	105.8	106.5	103.5	105.7	115.8	120.1	128.5
Japan										
Actual balance	−5.5	−8.0	−6.2	−5.0	−4.0	−2.5	−5.8	−10.5	−10.2	−8.0
Excluding social security	−6.8	−8.1	−6.6	−5.4	−4.1	−2.4	−4.8	−9.1	−8.9	−6.6
Output gap[2]	−0.8	−2.2	−1.1	−0.8	−0.4	0.2	−1.7	−7.0	−5.5	−0.4
Structural balance[2]	−5.2	−7.1	−5.7	−4.7	−3.8	−2.6	−5.2	−7.6	−8.0	−8.0
Excluding social security	−6.8	−7.6	−6.4	−5.2	−4.0	−2.4	−4.5	−7.6	−7.7	−6.6
Net debt	42.7	76.5	82.7	84.6	84.3	80.4	88.1	104.6	115.0	143.5
Gross debt	117.2	167.2	178.1	191.6	191.3	187.7	196.6	218.6	227.0	245.6
United Kingdom										
Actual balance	−2.5	−3.3	−3.3	−3.3	−2.6	−2.6	−5.1	−11.6	−13.2	−6.8
Output gap[2]	−0.3	−0.4	0.1	−0.3	0.0	0.4	−0.1	−4.9	−4.7	0.0
Structural balance[2]	−2.2	−2.8	−3.3	−3.0	−2.6	−2.9	−5.5	−9.0	−9.6	−6.2
Net debt	37.6	33.7	35.5	37.3	38.0	38.3	45.6	62.1	75.1	91.8
Gross debt	43.1	38.5	40.2	42.1	43.2	44.1	52.0	68.7	81.7	98.3
Canada										
Actual balance	−1.8	−0.1	0.9	1.5	1.6	1.6	0.1	−4.9	−4.1	0.0
Output gap[2]	0.0	−0.7	−0.1	0.5	1.0	1.2	−0.5	−4.6	−4.1	0.0
Structural balance[2]	−1.6	0.3	0.9	1.3	1.1	1.0	0.4	−2.2	−1.6	0.0
Net debt	58.7	38.7	35.2	30.6	26.5	23.5	22.2	28.2	31.3	29.4
Gross debt	92.6	76.6	72.6	71.0	68.0	64.2	62.7	78.2	79.3	68.9

Note: The methodology and specific assumptions for each country are discussed in Box A1 in this Statistical Appendix.

[1]Debt data refer to the end of the year. Debt data are not always comparable across countries.

[2]Percent of potential GDP.

[3]Beginning in 1995, the debt and debt-service obligations of the Treuhandanstalt (and of various other agencies) were taken over by the general government. This debt is equivalent to 8 percent of GDP, and the associated debt service to ½ to 1 percent of GDP.

[4]Excludes sizable one-off receipts from the sale of assets, including licenses.

Table A9. Summary of World Trade Volumes and Prices

(Annual percent change)

	Ten-Year Averages		2001	2002	2003	2004	2005	2006	2007	2008	2009	2010
	1991–2000	2001–10										
Trade in goods and services												
World trade[1]												
Volume	7.1	3.6	0.2	3.6	5.5	10.7	7.8	9.1	7.3	3.0	−11.9	2.5
Price deflator												
In U.S. dollars	−0.8	3.8	−3.4	1.1	10.3	9.6	5.3	5.2	8.1	11.2	−12.2	5.4
In SDRs	−0.6	2.1	0.0	−0.6	2.0	3.7	5.6	5.7	3.9	7.7	−9.4	3.7
Volume of trade												
Exports												
Advanced economies	7.0	2.4	−0.4	2.4	3.4	9.1	6.1	8.6	6.3	1.9	−13.6	2.0
Emerging and developing economies	8.4	6.7	2.2	7.2	11.0	14.8	11.7	11.0	9.8	4.6	−7.2	3.6
Imports												
Advanced economies	7.0	2.1	−0.4	2.7	4.2	9.2	6.5	7.6	4.7	0.5	−13.7	1.2
Emerging and developing economies	7.1	7.6	2.8	6.4	10.3	15.9	12.2	12.4	13.8	9.4	−9.5	4.6
Terms of trade												
Advanced economies	−0.1	0.0	0.4	0.9	1.0	−0.2	−1.4	−1.1	0.3	−1.8	2.0	−0.2
Emerging and developing economies	−0.3	1.3	−2.4	0.3	0.8	2.4	5.3	3.6	0.7	4.1	−6.3	4.6
Trade in goods												
World trade[1]												
Volume	7.5	3.4	−0.4	3.7	6.3	10.9	7.5	9.0	6.6	2.7	−13.0	2.7
Price deflator												
In U.S. dollars	−1.0	3.9	−3.8	0.6	9.9	9.8	6.2	5.9	8.3	12.0	−13.2	5.7
In SDRs	−0.7	2.2	−0.3	−1.2	1.6	3.9	6.4	6.4	4.1	8.5	−10.5	4.1
World trade prices in U.S. dollars[2]												
Manufactures	−1.3	3.9	−3.3	2.1	14.3	8.7	3.6	3.8	9.0	8.6	−9.1	3.1
Oil	2.1	10.5	−13.8	2.5	15.8	30.7	41.3	20.5	10.7	36.4	−36.6	24.3
Nonfuel primary commodities	−1.7	4.5	−4.8	1.9	5.9	15.2	6.1	23.2	14.1	7.5	−20.3	2.4
Food	−2.3	5.1	−2.0	3.5	6.3	14.0	−0.9	10.5	15.2	23.4	−14.9	1.2
Beverages	−1.3	6.2	−13.3	24.3	4.8	−0.9	18.1	8.4	13.8	23.3	−4.1	−5.5
Agricultural raw materials	−0.4	−0.7	−3.4	−0.2	0.6	4.1	0.5	8.8	5.0	−0.8	−20.7	2.3
Metals	−1.7	7.1	−10.3	−3.5	11.8	34.6	22.4	56.2	17.4	−8.0	−30.5	6.2
World trade prices in SDRs[2]												
Manufactures	−1.0	2.2	0.2	0.3	5.7	2.8	3.8	4.2	4.8	5.2	−6.3	1.5
Oil	2.4	8.7	−10.7	0.8	7.1	23.6	41.6	21.0	6.4	32.1	−34.6	22.4
Nonfuel primary commodities	−1.4	2.8	−1.3	0.2	−2.1	9.0	6.3	23.8	9.6	4.1	−17.7	0.8
Food	−2.0	3.4	1.5	1.8	−1.7	7.8	−0.7	11.0	10.7	19.5	−12.2	−0.4
Beverages	−1.0	4.4	−10.2	22.2	−3.1	−6.3	18.3	8.8	9.4	19.4	−1.1	−7.0
Agricultural raw materials	−0.1	−2.3	0.1	−1.9	−7.0	−1.6	0.8	9.3	0.9	−3.9	−18.1	0.7
Metals	−1.4	5.3	−7.0	−5.1	3.3	27.3	22.7	56.9	12.8	−10.9	−28.2	4.5
World trade prices in euros[2]												
Manufactures	1.9	−0.4	−0.3	−3.2	−4.5	−1.1	3.4	3.0	−0.1	1.1	−2.6	0.5
Oil	5.4	5.9	−11.1	−2.8	−3.3	18.9	41.0	19.5	1.4	27.1	−32.0	21.2
Nonfuel primary commodities	1.6	0.2	−1.8	−3.3	−11.6	4.8	5.9	22.3	4.5	0.1	−14.6	−0.2
Food	0.9	0.8	1.1	−1.8	−11.2	3.7	−1.1	9.6	5.6	14.9	−8.8	−1.3
Beverages	1.9	1.8	−10.5	17.9	−12.5	−9.9	17.8	7.5	4.2	14.8	2.8	−7.9
Agricultural raw materials	2.9	−4.8	−0.4	−5.4	−16.0	−5.3	0.3	8.0	−3.8	−7.6	−15.0	−0.3
Metals	1.5	2.7	−7.4	−8.4	−6.7	22.4	22.2	55.0	7.5	−14.3	−25.5	3.5

Table A9 (concluded)

	Ten-Year Averages		2001	2002	2003	2004	2005	2006	2007	2008	2009	2010
	1991–2000	2001–10										
Trade in goods												
Volume of trade												
Exports												
Advanced economies	7.2	1.9	−1.2	2.4	4.0	8.9	5.6	8.5	5.2	1.6	−15.6	2.3
Emerging and developing economies	8.3	6.3	1.7	6.9	11.4	14.2	10.9	10.4	8.8	4.4	−7.9	3.7
Fuel exporters	3.4	4.0	0.4	2.5	11.7	8.9	5.6	4.0	3.7	4.0	−5.3	4.8
Nonfuel exporters	10.4	7.2	2.3	8.5	11.3	16.0	12.9	13.2	11.0	4.6	−9.1	3.3
Imports												
Advanced economies	7.6	1.9	−1.2	3.1	5.0	9.6	6.3	7.9	4.2	0.0	−14.9	1.5
Emerging and developing economies	7.2	7.7	2.7	6.3	11.6	16.8	12.3	11.8	13.4	9.2	−9.7	4.7
Fuel exporters	−0.4	11.1	16.2	9.0	8.9	15.2	16.6	12.6	19.8	18.4	−7.3	4.8
Nonfuel exporters	9.5	6.9	0.4	5.8	12.1	17.1	11.4	11.6	12.1	7.0	−10.2	4.7
Price deflators in SDRs												
Exports												
Advanced economies	−1.3	1.6	−0.1	−0.9	2.6	3.0	3.7	4.3	3.9	5.7	−8.0	2.7
Emerging and developing economies	1.4	4.2	−1.1	−0.2	1.3	7.4	14.1	11.4	5.3	13.8	−15.4	8.8
Fuel exporters	3.1	7.3	−7.3	0.7	4.6	17.4	32.7	18.7	8.0	26.0	−28.9	15.9
Nonfuel exporters	1.0	2.9	1.4	−0.4	0.1	3.9	7.1	8.2	4.1	8.7	−8.8	6.0
Imports												
Advanced economies	−1.3	1.6	−0.7	−1.9	1.4	3.3	5.6	5.7	3.5	8.1	−10.4	2.8
Emerging and developing economies	1.7	2.5	1.3	−0.7	0.0	4.1	7.0	7.2	4.4	9.1	−9.6	3.9
Fuel exporters	1.6	2.7	0.5	0.5	0.9	4.6	7.7	8.0	5.1	6.9	−8.3	1.9
Nonfuel exporters	1.5	2.5	1.4	−0.9	−0.1	4.1	6.9	7.0	4.2	9.7	−9.9	4.4
Terms of trade												
Advanced economies	0.1	0.0	0.5	1.0	1.2	−0.3	−1.8	−1.3	0.4	−2.2	2.6	0.0
Emerging and developing economies	−0.3	1.6	−2.3	0.5	1.2	3.1	6.6	3.9	0.8	4.3	−6.4	4.8
Regional groups												
Africa	0.1	2.5	−3.3	−0.2	2.8	3.0	13.6	9.0	−0.3	11.3	−17.1	9.4
Central and eastern Europe	−0.7	0.3	2.4	0.4	0.8	1.1	−0.3	−1.7	1.4	−2.1	3.8	−2.3
Commonwealth of Independent States[3]	0.0	4.4	−2.5	−1.9	8.7	12.1	14.8	9.3	2.6	18.2	−20.5	8.8
Developing Asia	−0.6	0.1	1.0	0.8	−0.7	−1.9	−0.9	−0.3	−0.4	−2.0	2.3	3.4
Middle East	2.1	3.7	−8.5	1.2	0.6	10.3	23.9	6.0	1.5	14.4	−18.9	13.2
Western Hemisphere	−0.2	1.7	−3.9	1.1	2.4	5.5	5.1	8.4	2.0	3.1	−6.8	0.4
Analytical groups												
By source of export earnings												
Fuel exporters	1.5	4.5	−7.7	0.1	3.7	12.3	23.2	9.9	2.7	17.9	−22.4	13.7
Nonfuel exporters	−0.5	0.4	0.0	0.5	0.3	−0.2	0.2	1.1	−0.1	−0.9	1.2	1.5
Memorandum												
World exports in billions of U.S. dollars												
Goods and services	6,106	13,276	7,626	8,007	9,329	11,322	12,889	14,840	17,258	19,731	15,218	16,542
Goods	4,869	10,588	6,087	6,366	7,442	9,036	10,334	11,952	13,806	15,880	11,919	13,056
Average oil price[4]	2.1	10.5	−13.8	2.5	15.8	30.7	41.3	20.5	10.7	36.4	−36.6	24.3
In U.S. dollars a barrel	18.73	53.98	24.3	25.0	28.9	37.8	53.4	64.3	71.1	97.0	61.5	76.5
Export unit value of manufactures[5]	−1.3	3.9	−3.3	2.1	14.3	8.7	3.6	3.8	9.0	8.6	−9.1	3.1

[1]Average of annual percent change for world exports and imports.

[2]As represented, respectively, by the export unit value index for manufactures of the advanced economies; the average of U.K. Brent, Dubai, and West Texas Intermediate crude oil prices; and the average of world market prices for nonfuel primary commodities weighted by their 2002–04 shares in world commodity exports.

[3]Georgia and Mongolia, which are not members of the Commonwealth of Independent States, are included in this group for reasons of geography and similarities in economic structure.

[4]Average of U.K. Brent, Dubai, and West Texas Intermediate crude oil prices.

[5]For manufactures exported by the advanced economies.

Table A10. Summary of Balances on Current Account

(Billions of U.S. dollars)

	2001	2002	2003	2004	2005	2006	2007	2008	2009	2010	2014
Advanced economies	**−223.4**	**−219.2**	**−219.1**	**−220.3**	**−408.5**	**−458.9**	**−365.3**	**−533.1**	**−261.7**	**−166.2**	**−154.9**
United States	−398.3	−459.1	−521.5	−631.1	−748.7	−803.5	−726.6	−706.1	−369.8	−324.7	−475.2
Euro area[1]	5.2	46.1	42.9	116.8	46.8	41.0	34.4	−92.7	−82.1	−36.4	62.3
Japan	87.8	112.6	136.2	172.1	165.7	170.4	211.0	157.1	96.9	105.6	89.4
Other advanced economies[2]	81.9	81.3	123.3	122.0	127.7	133.3	116.0	108.5	93.3	89.3	168.6
Memorandum											
Newly industrialized Asian economies	48.0	55.7	81.0	83.5	80.2	90.0	103.6	76.1	98.0	96.0	116.5
Emerging and developing economies	**48.0**	**80.7**	**149.6**	**223.8**	**448.3**	**659.7**	**664.5**	**724.6**	**355.6**	**548.1**	**968.3**
Regional groups											
Africa	1.4	−8.4	−3.8	1.8	14.5	52.4	31.7	32.4	−37.1	−22.3	−4.3
Central and eastern Europe	−11.5	−19.4	−32.2	−53.2	−59.1	−87.3	−130.8	−155.2	−48.4	−62.5	−76.0
Commonwealth of Independent States[3]	33.0	30.3	35.7	63.5	87.5	96.3	71.7	108.1	48.0	79.6	94.1
Developing Asia	39.3	66.9	85.1	92.9	167.5	288.0	413.8	423.9	381.5	438.6	676.6
Middle East	40.0	27.8	55.9	96.8	202.9	262.6	264.9	345.3	42.8	151.6	306.6
Western Hemisphere	−54.2	−16.5	8.9	22.0	34.9	47.8	13.1	−29.9	−31.3	−36.8	−28.7
Memorandum											
European Union	−26.7	16.9	17.7	65.5	−7.4	−48.7	−83.1	−196.7	−127.3	−87.0	−9.5
Analytical groups											
By source of export earnings											
Fuel	84.4	60.7	108.1	189.0	357.1	481.6	450.7	621.9	126.6	314.5	507.0
Nonfuel	−36.4	20.0	41.5	34.9	91.2	178.1	213.8	102.7	228.9	233.6	461.3
of which, primary products	−3.6	−2.9	−2.5	0.3	−2.4	7.6	5.4	−8.8	−4.5	−8.4	−7.1
By external financing source											
Net debtor countries	−74.4	−40.0	−34.2	−62.7	−99.9	−119.7	−211.1	−352.8	−190.5	−248.5	−258.4
of which, official financing	−2.1	−4.5	−6.2	−4.3	−6.3	−6.7	−9.6	−18.8	−17.2	−21.9	−18.3
Net debtor countries by debt-servicing experience											
Countries with arrears and/or rescheduling during 2003–07	−13.5	4.0	5.1	−4.4	−12.0	−13.7	−27.3	−47.9	−30.9	−35.1	−42.0
World[1]	**−175.4**	**−138.5**	**−69.5**	**3.5**	**39.8**	**200.8**	**299.2**	**191.5**	**93.9**	**381.9**	**813.4**
Memorandum											
In percent of total world current account transactions	−1.1	−0.9	−0.4	0.0	0.2	0.7	0.9	0.5	0.3	1.2	1.8
In percent of world GDP	−0.5	−0.4	−0.2	0.0	0.1	0.4	0.5	0.3	0.2	0.6	1.1

[1]Reflects errors, omissions, and asymmetries in balance of payments statistics on current account, as well as the exclusion of data for international organizations and a limited number of countries. Calculated as the sum of the balance of individual euro area countries. See "Classification of Countries" in the introduction to this Statistical Appendix.

[2]In this table, "other advanced economies" means advanced economies excluding the United States, euro area countries, and Japan.

[3]Georgia and Mongolia, which are not members of the Commonwealth of Independent States, are included in this group for reasons of geography and similarities in economic structure.

Table A11. Advanced Economies: Balance on Current Account

(Percent of GDP)

	2001	2002	2003	2004	2005	2006	2007	2008	2009	2010	2014
Advanced economies	**−0.9**	**−0.8**	**−0.7**	**−0.7**	**−1.2**	**−1.3**	**−0.9**	**−1.3**	**−0.7**	**−0.4**	**−0.3**
United States	−3.9	−4.3	−4.7	−5.3	−5.9	−6.0	−5.2	−4.9	−2.6	−2.2	−2.7
Euro area[1]	0.1	0.7	0.5	1.2	0.5	0.4	0.3	−0.7	−0.7	−0.3	0.5
Germany	0.0	2.0	1.9	4.7	5.1	6.1	7.5	6.4	2.9	3.6	5.1
France	1.8	1.2	0.8	0.6	−0.4	−0.5	−1.0	−2.3	−1.2	−1.4	−0.7
Italy	−0.1	−0.8	−1.3	−0.9	−1.7	−2.6	−2.4	−3.4	−2.5	−2.3	−2.5
Spain	−3.9	−3.3	−3.5	−5.3	−7.4	−9.0	−10.0	−9.6	−6.0	−4.7	−4.0
Netherlands	2.4	2.5	5.5	7.5	7.3	9.3	7.6	7.5	7.0	6.8	6.7
Belgium	3.4	4.6	4.1	3.5	2.6	2.6	1.7	−2.5	−1.0	−0.9	1.0
Greece	−7.2	−6.5	−6.6	−5.8	−7.3	−11.1	−14.2	−14.4	−10.0	−9.0	−6.8
Austria	−0.8	2.7	1.7	2.1	2.0	2.8	3.1	3.5	2.1	2.0	1.7
Portugal	−9.9	−8.1	−6.1	−7.6	−9.5	−10.0	−9.4	−12.1	−9.9	−9.7	−8.7
Finland	8.6	8.8	5.2	6.6	3.6	4.5	4.1	2.4	0.5	2.0	3.6
Ireland	−0.6	−1.0	0.0	−0.6	−3.5	−3.6	−5.3	−5.2	−1.7	0.6	−1.2
Slovak Republic	−8.3	−7.9	−5.9	−7.8	−8.5	−7.0	−5.3	−6.5	−8.0	−7.8	−3.8
Slovenia	0.2	1.1	−0.8	−2.7	−1.7	−2.5	−4.2	−5.5	−3.0	−4.7	−4.8
Luxembourg	8.8	10.5	8.1	11.8	11.0	10.4	9.8	9.1	7.6	7.0	6.3
Cyprus	−3.3	−3.7	−2.2	−5.0	−5.8	−7.0	−11.7	−18.3	−10.0	−9.8	−9.4
Malta	−3.8	2.5	−3.1	−6.0	−8.8	−9.2	−7.0	−5.6	−6.1	−6.1	−4.3
Japan	2.1	2.9	3.2	3.7	3.6	3.9	4.8	3.2	1.9	2.0	1.5
United Kingdom	−2.1	−1.7	−1.6	−2.1	−2.6	−3.3	−2.7	−1.7	−2.0	−1.9	−2.0
Canada	2.3	1.7	1.2	2.3	1.9	1.4	1.0	0.5	−2.6	−1.8	0.9
Korea	1.6	0.9	1.9	3.9	1.8	0.6	0.6	−0.7	3.4	2.2	2.1
Australia	−2.0	−3.7	−5.3	−6.1	−5.8	−5.3	−6.3	−4.6	−3.2	−5.6	−5.0
Taiwan Province of China	6.5	8.9	10.0	6.0	4.9	7.2	8.6	6.4	7.9	8.0	9.3
Sweden	4.3	5.0	7.2	6.7	7.0	8.6	8.6	7.8	6.4	5.4	6.0
Switzerland	7.8	8.3	12.8	12.9	13.6	14.4	9.9	2.4	6.1	7.1	10.9
Hong Kong SAR	5.9	7.6	10.4	9.5	11.4	12.1	12.3	14.2	10.7	10.8	7.6
Czech Republic	−5.3	−5.7	−6.3	−5.3	−1.3	−2.6	−3.1	−3.1	−2.1	−2.2	−2.5
Norway	16.1	12.6	12.3	12.7	16.3	17.2	15.9	19.5	13.9	15.6	14.4
Singapore	13.1	13.1	23.7	18.1	22.7	25.4	23.5	14.8	12.6	12.5	11.9
Denmark	3.1	2.5	3.4	3.1	4.3	2.9	0.7	1.0	1.1	1.5	1.0
Israel	−1.6	−1.1	0.5	1.7	3.1	5.0	2.8	1.0	3.2	2.4	2.8
New Zealand	−2.8	−3.9	−4.3	−6.4	−8.5	−8.7	−8.2	−8.9	−7.1	−6.7	−6.2
Iceland	−4.3	1.6	−4.8	−9.8	−16.1	−25.3	−19.9	−40.6	−5.3	0.7	0.2
Memorandum											
Major advanced economies	−1.4	−1.4	−1.5	−1.4	−1.9	−2.0	−1.3	−1.5	−1.1	−0.8	−0.9
Euro area[2]	−0.4	0.6	0.3	0.8	0.1	−0.1	0.1	−0.5	−1.0	−1.0	−0.2
Newly industrialized Asian economies	4.6	4.9	6.7	6.3	5.3	5.5	5.7	4.4	6.4	5.9	5.4

[1]Calculated as the sum of the balances of individual euro area countries.

[2]Corrected for reporting discrepancies in intra-area transactions.

Table A12. Emerging and Developing Economies, by Country: Balance on Current Account

(Percent of GDP)

	2001	2002	2003	2004	2005	2006	2007	2008	2009	2010	2014
Africa	**0.3**	**−1.8**	**−0.6**	**0.3**	**1.7**	**5.4**	**2.9**	**2.5**	**−3.1**	**−1.7**	**−0.2**
Algeria	12.9	7.7	13.0	13.1	20.6	24.8	22.6	23.2	2.7	7.3	8.2
Angola	−16.0	−1.3	−5.2	3.5	16.8	25.2	15.9	7.5	−3.4	2.2	4.1
Benin	−6.4	−8.4	−8.3	−7.2	−5.5	−5.7	−9.9	−8.2	−9.7	−9.1	−6.6
Botswana	9.9	3.2	5.7	3.5	15.2	17.2	14.3	7.0	−7.6	−16.3	3.3
Burkina Faso	−11.2	−10.0	−8.7	−10.6	−11.7	−9.6	−8.3	−10.9	−10.8	−11.6	−9.0
Burundi	−4.6	−3.5	−4.6	−8.4	−1.2	−14.5	−15.7	−14.2	−10.9	−8.3	−9.7
Cameroon	−3.6	−5.1	−1.8	−3.4	−3.4	0.6	−0.8	−1.0	−7.2	−4.6	−2.7
Cape Verde	−10.7	−11.2	−11.2	−14.4	−3.4	−5.0	−8.7	−12.4	−18.5	−15.4	−11.2
Central African Republic	−1.8	−1.6	−2.2	−1.7	−6.5	−3.0	−6.2	−9.8	−9.5	−9.7	−9.2
Chad	−31.8	−94.7	−48.8	−17.4	2.4	−9.0	−10.6	−12.2	−20.8	−7.5	−5.3
Comoros	3.0	−1.7	−3.2	−4.6	−7.2	−6.1	−6.7	−11.3	−8.0	−10.4	−10.1
Congo, Dem. Rep. of	−4.0	−1.6	1.0	−2.4	−10.4	−2.1	−1.5	−15.3	−14.6	−23.7	−16.6
Congo, Rep. of	−4.6	0.6	2.5	−7.3	2.2	1.5	−9.4	−1.9	−11.2	2.1	2.5
Côte d'Ivoire	−0.6	6.7	2.1	1.6	0.2	2.8	−0.7	2.4	24.6	1.1	−4.0
Djibouti	−2.9	−1.6	3.4	−1.3	−3.2	−14.7	−25.6	−39.2	−17.1	−17.5	−19.9
Equatorial Guinea	−41.2	0.9	−33.3	−21.6	−6.2	7.1	4.3	9.9	−5.3	0.0	5.6
Eritrea	−4.6	6.8	9.7	−0.7	0.3	−3.6	−0.7	0.8	−3.7	−3.3	−2.1
Ethiopia	−3.0	−4.7	−1.4	−4.0	−6.3	−9.1	−4.5	−5.6	−5.6	−9.3	−4.2
Gabon	11.0	6.8	9.5	11.2	22.9	10.4	13.7	17.1	2.8	6.8	4.1
Gambia, The	−2.6	−2.8	−4.9	−13.4	−20.1	−14.6	−13.4	−16.7	−17.1	−17.6	−14.2
Ghana	−5.3	−0.5	−1.6	−4.0	−8.3	−9.9	−12.0	−18.7	−12.7	−15.4	−6.5
Guinea	−2.7	−2.5	−0.8	−2.8	−0.4	−2.2	−8.8	−12.0	−1.7	−4.4	−3.8
Guinea-Bissau	−13.2	−5.3	−5.0	6.6	−0.4	−10.2	9.5	−3.3	−3.1	−4.5	−6.4
Kenya	−3.1	2.2	−0.2	0.1	−0.8	−2.5	−4.1	−6.8	−8.1	−6.3	−4.0
Lesotho	−13.2	−20.7	−12.8	−5.7	−7.5	4.3	12.7	−4.0	−15.1	−21.2	−20.5
Liberia	−18.7	−6.5	−26.4	−21.1	−38.4	−13.8	−27.9	−25.9	−41.8	−60.7	−14.6
Madagascar	−1.3	−6.0	−4.9	−9.1	−10.9	−8.8	−14.6	−24.2	−18.7	−17.3	−8.7
Malawi	−6.8	−8.6	−5.8	−7.3	−11.7	−7.2	−1.6	−7.8	−4.1	−5.5	−3.2
Mali	−10.4	−3.1	−6.3	−8.5	−8.6	−4.2	−7.8	−8.4	−7.3	−7.6	−7.9
Mauritania	−11.7	3.0	−13.6	−34.6	−47.2	−1.3	−11.4	−15.7	−9.0	−16.4	6.8
Mauritius	3.2	5.7	2.4	0.8	−3.5	−5.3	−8.0	−8.7	−9.3	−10.6	−7.0
Morocco	4.3	3.7	3.2	1.7	1.8	2.2	−0.1	−5.4	−5.5	−4.7	−1.0
Mozambique	−3.0	−12.7	−6.6	1.7	−10.7	−8.3	−12.2	−11.8	−12.1	−12.2	−11.2
Namibia	1.7	3.4	6.1	7.0	4.7	13.8	9.1	1.8	−1.0	−2.1	−0.8
Niger	−5.1	−9.7	−7.5	−7.3	−8.9	−8.6	−7.8	−13.3	−21.2	−22.0	−6.6
Nigeria	4.7	−12.6	−5.7	5.8	6.5	26.5	18.8	20.4	6.9	13.8	14.5
Rwanda	−3.5	−7.5	−9.6	1.9	2.3	−4.7	−2.4	−5.5	−6.8	−9.6	−7.0
São Tomé and Príncipe	−22.7	−17.0	−14.5	−16.8	−10.3	−28.8	−29.9	−29.0	−31.1	−28.0	−30.4
Senegal	−4.3	−5.6	−6.1	−6.1	−7.7	−9.5	−11.8	−12.3	−11.7	−10.8	−10.4
Seychelles	−19.5	−13.6	0.2	−6.0	−19.7	−13.9	−23.4	−50.2	−24.2	−32.5	−25.2
Sierra Leone	−6.3	−2.0	−4.8	−5.7	−7.0	−3.5	−3.4	−9.0	−9.1	−8.6	−5.5
South Africa	0.3	0.8	−1.1	−3.2	−4.0	−6.3	−7.3	−7.4	−5.0	−6.5	−7.5
Sudan	−12.7	−10.3	−7.9	−6.5	−11.1	−15.2	−12.5	−9.0	−11.2	−9.1	−8.3
Swaziland	−4.2	4.7	6.7	3.1	−4.0	−7.2	−4.7	−5.4	−6.6	−7.1	−3.6
Tanzania	−4.5	−6.2	−4.2	−3.6	−4.1	−7.7	−9.0	−9.7	−9.9	−9.1	−9.1
Togo	−9.3	−5.5	−4.2	−3.0	7.8	−2.9	−3.9	−6.6	−6.9	−8.2	0.2
Tunisia	−5.1	−3.6	−2.9	−2.7	−1.0	−2.0	−2.5	−4.2	−3.8	−2.9	−3.1
Uganda	−3.5	−4.6	−4.7	0.1	−1.4	−3.4	−3.1	−3.2	−5.5	−5.7	−4.5
Zambia	−19.9	−13.8	−14.7	−11.7	−8.3	1.2	−6.6	−7.2	−3.9	−2.9	−2.1
Zimbabwe[1]	−2.2	−9.1	−20.1	−12.6	−16.2	−12.6	−10.7	−29.5	−21.4	−19.9	−17.9

Table A12 *(continued)*

	2001	2002	2003	2004	2005	2006	2007	2008	2009	2010	2014
Central and eastern Europe	**−2.0**	**−3.0**	**−4.0**	**−5.4**	**−5.0**	**−6.6**	**−7.9**	**−8.0**	**−3.1**	**−3.9**	**−3.7**
Albania	−3.1	−7.2	−5.0	−4.0	−6.1	−5.6	−9.1	−14.1	−11.5	−8.0	−3.1
Bosnia and Herzegovina	−12.5	−17.8	−19.4	−16.3	−18.0	−8.4	−12.7	−14.7	−8.8	−9.1	−7.0
Bulgaria	−5.6	−2.4	−5.5	−6.6	−12.4	−18.5	−25.2	−25.5	−11.4	−8.3	−5.6
Croatia	−3.2	−7.3	−5.4	−4.6	−5.7	−6.7	−7.6	−9.4	−6.1	−5.4	−6.3
Estonia	−5.2	−10.6	−11.3	−11.3	−10.0	−16.9	−17.8	−9.3	1.9	2.0	−3.2
Hungary	−6.0	−7.0	−7.9	−8.4	−7.5	−7.5	−6.5	−8.4	−2.9	−3.3	−3.4
Latvia	−7.5	−6.7	−8.2	−12.8	−12.4	−22.7	−21.6	−12.6	4.5	6.4	4.1
Lithuania	−4.7	−5.2	−6.9	−7.6	−7.1	−10.7	−14.6	−11.6	1.0	0.5	−2.5
Macedonia, FYR	−7.2	−9.4	−4.1	−8.4	−2.6	−0.9	−7.2	−13.1	−10.6	−9.7	−6.2
Montenegro	...	...	−6.8	−7.2	−8.5	−24.1	−29.4	−29.6	−16.0	−11.0	−9.0
Poland	−2.8	−2.5	−2.1	−4.0	−1.2	−2.7	−4.7	−5.5	−2.2	−3.1	−3.1
Romania	−5.5	−3.3	−5.8	−8.4	−8.9	−10.4	−13.5	−12.4	−5.5	−5.6	−6.0
Serbia	−2.5	−8.3	−7.2	−12.1	−8.7	−10.1	−15.6	−17.3	−9.1	−10.6	−4.2
Turkey	1.9	−0.3	−2.5	−3.7	−4.6	−6.0	−5.8	−5.7	−1.9	−3.7	−3.1
Commonwealth of Independent States²	**8.0**	**6.5**	**6.2**	**8.2**	**8.7**	**7.4**	**4.2**	**4.9**	**2.9**	**4.4**	**3.3**
Russia	11.1	8.4	8.2	10.1	11.0	9.5	5.9	6.1	3.6	4.5	2.9
Excluding Russia	−0.8	1.0	0.2	2.2	1.3	0.6	−1.3	1.1	0.6	4.0	4.6
Armenia	−9.5	−6.2	−6.8	−0.5	−1.0	−1.8	−6.4	−11.5	−13.7	−13.7	−7.5
Azerbaijan	−0.9	−12.3	−27.8	−29.8	1.3	17.6	28.8	35.5	19.6	23.1	15.8
Belarus	−3.3	−2.2	−2.4	−5.3	1.4	−3.9	−6.8	−8.4	−9.6	−7.1	−3.2
Georgia	−6.4	−6.4	−9.6	−6.9	−11.1	−15.1	−19.7	−22.7	−16.3	−17.6	−14.9
Kazakhstan	−5.4	−4.2	−0.9	0.8	−1.8	−2.5	−7.8	5.1	−2.0	3.9	4.1
Kyrgyz Republic	−1.5	−4.0	1.7	4.9	2.8	−3.1	−0.2	−8.2	−7.8	−12.4	−5.1
Moldova	−2.5	−1.5	−6.6	−1.8	−8.3	−11.3	−17.0	−17.7	−11.8	−11.9	−13.0
Mongolia	−12.0	−8.6	−7.1	1.3	1.3	7.0	6.7	−13.1	−6.9	−10.3	44.6
Tajikistan	−4.9	−3.5	−1.3	−3.9	−2.7	−2.8	−8.6	−7.9	−13.7	−13.3	−7.8
Turkmenistan	1.7	6.7	2.7	0.6	5.1	15.7	15.5	18.7	17.8	29.1	39.0
Ukraine	3.7	7.5	5.8	10.6	2.9	−1.5	−3.7	−7.2	0.4	0.2	−2.8
Uzbekistan	−1.0	1.2	5.8	7.2	7.7	9.1	7.3	12.8	7.2	6.7	5.1

Table A12 *(continued)*

	2001	2002	2003	2004	2005	2006	2007	2008	2009	2010	2014
Developing Asia	**1.6**	**2.5**	**2.8**	**2.7**	**4.2**	**6.1**	**7.0**	**5.9**	**5.0**	**5.2**	**5.4**
Afghanistan, I.R. of	. . .	−3.7	−17.0	−4.6	−2.5	−4.9	0.9	−1.6	−0.9	−0.9	−3.2
Bangladesh	−0.9	0.3	0.3	−0.3	0.0	1.2	1.1	1.9	2.1	1.0	0.4
Bhutan	−12.3	−20.0	−20.5	−24.6	−16.7	5.6	8.1	0.6	−3.1	−8.5	−21.3
Brunei Darussalam	48.4	41.2	47.7	48.6	52.8	56.3	50.7	50.6	35.2	36.8	38.6
Cambodia	−1.1	−2.4	−3.6	−2.2	−3.8	−0.6	−2.7	−11.1	−5.5	−7.2	−5.4
China	1.3	2.4	2.8	3.6	7.2	9.5	11.0	9.8	7.8	8.6	8.4
Fiji	−6.7	2.5	−6.6	−12.9	−11.4	−25.1	−17.4	−25.0	−25.9	−27.9	−17.5
India	0.3	1.4	1.5	0.1	−1.3	−1.1	−1.0	−2.2	−2.2	−2.5	−1.8
Indonesia	4.3	4.0	3.5	0.6	0.1	3.0	2.4	0.1	0.9	0.5	−1.0
Kiribati	16.1	7.6	−19.5	−11.1	−19.1	−2.6	−1.0	−0.9	−3.1	−6.3	−11.4
Lao PDR	−10.7	−9.4	−12.4	−16.9	−17.8	−10.3	−15.4	−16.5	−15.4	−8.1	−20.1
Malaysia	7.9	8.0	12.0	12.1	15.0	16.0	15.4	17.9	13.4	11.0	10.8
Maldives	−9.8	−5.6	−4.5	−15.8	−36.4	−33.0	−41.5	−51.7	−29.0	−22.9	−16.1
Myanmar	−2.4	0.2	−1.0	2.4	3.7	7.1	9.2	4.0	1.5	−1.8	−6.2
Nepal	4.5	4.2	2.4	2.7	2.0	2.2	0.5	3.1	4.2	1.0	0.0
Pakistan	0.4	3.9	4.9	1.8	−1.4	−3.9	−4.8	−8.3	−5.1	−4.8	−3.4
Papua New Guinea	6.5	−1.0	4.5	2.2	4.2	2.3	1.8	2.8	−6.7	−4.7	−3.1
Philippines	−2.4	−0.4	0.4	1.9	2.0	4.5	4.9	2.5	3.2	1.2	0.9
Samoa	0.1	−1.1	5.8	−8.5	−9.6	−11.1	−16.1	−6.2	−2.1	−5.2	−2.2
Solomon Islands	−6.4	−4.4	6.3	16.3	−7.0	−6.4	−12.4	−18.7	−11.1	−18.2	−24.2
Sri Lanka	−1.1	−1.4	−0.4	−3.1	−2.5	−5.3	−4.3	−9.4	−1.2	−1.3	−0.7
Thailand	4.4	3.7	3.4	1.7	−4.3	1.1	5.7	−0.1	4.9	2.7	1.6
Timor-Leste	−12.6	−15.9	−15.4	20.7	78.4	165.2	296.1	408.3	66.2	49.4	−50.8
Tonga	−9.5	5.1	−3.1	4.2	−2.6	−9.7	−10.4	−10.4	−8.8	−8.7	−7.6
Vanuatu	2.0	−5.4	−6.6	−5.0	−7.4	−4.1	−5.9	−6.2	−5.3	−4.8	−6.5
Vietnam	2.1	−1.7	−4.9	−3.5	−1.1	−0.3	−9.8	−11.9	−9.7	−9.4	−4.9
Middle East	**6.3**	**4.4**	**7.9**	**11.6**	**19.3**	**20.9**	**18.1**	**18.3**	**2.6**	**7.9**	**11.7**
Bahrain	2.8	−0.7	2.0	4.2	11.0	13.8	15.8	10.6	3.7	6.2	19.7
Egypt	0.0	0.7	2.4	4.3	3.2	1.6	1.9	0.5	−2.4	−2.8	−1.5
Iran, I.R. of	5.2	3.1	0.6	0.6	8.8	9.2	11.9	6.7	3.0	3.6	2.8
Iraq	. . .	. . .	. . .	. . .	6.1	16.3	10.1	13.3	−28.4	−15.2	4.8
Jordan	0.1	5.7	12.2	0.8	−17.4	−10.8	−17.2	−11.3	−10.0	−8.8	−7.0
Kuwait	23.9	11.2	19.7	30.6	42.5	49.8	44.7	44.7	29.4	35.3	48.5
Lebanon	−19.3	−14.1	−13.2	−15.5	−13.4	−5.3	−6.8	−11.6	−11.3	−10.5	−9.3
Libya	12.3	3.0	19.9	21.4	38.9	44.6	40.7	40.7	16.7	24.0	28.3
Oman	10.0	6.8	2.4	3.6	16.8	15.4	8.3	9.1	−0.5	4.8	3.6
Qatar	27.3	21.9	25.3	22.4	33.2	28.3	30.4	28.0	10.8	25.3	26.7
Saudi Arabia	5.1	6.3	13.1	20.8	28.5	27.8	24.3	28.6	4.1	11.4	14.4
Syrian Arab Republic	6.3	−3.6	−12.6	−1.6	−2.2	−2.8	−3.3	−4.0	−3.2	−4.3	−3.8
United Arab Emirates	9.5	4.9	8.5	9.1	18.0	22.6	16.1	15.7	−1.6	5.2	12.7
Yemen, Rep. of	6.8	4.1	1.5	1.6	3.8	1.1	−7.0	−4.3	−5.2	−2.3	−2.8

Table A12 *(concluded)*

	2001	2002	2003	2004	2005	2006	2007	2008	2009	2010	2014
Western Hemisphere	**−2.7**	**−0.9**	**0.5**	**1.0**	**1.3**	**1.5**	**0.4**	**−0.7**	**−0.8**	**−0.9**	**−0.5**
Antigua and Barbuda	−8.0	−11.5	−12.9	−8.3	−12.3	−30.8	−32.9	−31.3	−29.4	−27.9	−28.5
Argentina	−1.4	8.9	6.3	2.1	1.7	2.3	1.6	1.4	4.4	4.9	2.0
Bahamas, The	−11.6	−7.8	−8.6	−5.4	−9.6	−19.3	−17.5	−13.2	−9.4	−10.3	−9.9
Barbados	−4.1	−6.5	−6.3	−12.0	−13.1	−8.4	−5.4	−10.5	−5.2	−5.9	−5.3
Belize	−21.9	−17.7	−18.2	−14.7	−13.6	−2.1	−4.0	−10.2	−6.7	−5.6	−5.8
Bolivia	−3.4	−4.1	1.0	3.8	6.5	11.3	12.0	12.1	1.1	1.3	1.0
Brazil	−4.2	−1.5	0.8	1.8	1.6	1.3	0.1	−1.8	−1.3	−1.9	−0.8
Chile	−1.6	−0.9	−1.1	2.2	1.2	4.9	4.4	−2.0	0.7	−0.4	−2.2
Colombia	−1.2	−1.5	−1.1	−0.8	−1.3	−1.8	−2.8	−2.8	−2.9	−3.1	−2.1
Costa Rica	−3.7	−4.9	−4.8	−4.3	−4.9	−5.1	−6.3	−9.2	−3.6	−4.8	−4.8
Dominica	−18.4	−13.6	−12.8	−16.5	−28.0	−18.3	−28.7	−32.3	−32.4	−28.6	−22.3
Dominican Republic	−3.0	−3.6	5.9	3.5	−1.6	−3.7	−5.3	−10.0	−6.1	−6.1	−3.4
Ecuador	−3.2	−4.8	−1.4	−1.6	0.3	3.9	3.5	2.3	−3.1	−3.0	−3.2
El Salvador	−1.1	−2.8	−4.7	−4.0	−3.3	−3.6	−5.5	−7.2	−1.8	−2.6	−2.7
Grenada	−19.7	−26.6	−25.3	−9.0	−31.3	−33.4	−41.7	−40.9	−28.0	−26.9	−28.6
Guatemala	−6.5	−6.1	−4.6	−4.9	−4.6	−5.0	−5.2	−4.8	−1.7	−3.3	−4.4
Guyana	−18.5	−14.7	−11.6	−9.3	−14.8	−20.9	−18.0	−21.5	−19.1	−21.3	−12.9
Haiti	−2.0	−0.9	−1.6	−1.6	2.6	−1.4	−0.3	−4.3	−2.6	−2.8	−2.9
Honduras	−6.3	−3.6	−6.8	−7.7	−3.0	−3.7	−10.3	−14.0	−9.1	−9.2	−8.0
Jamaica	−10.6	−11.8	−8.2	−5.2	−9.9	−9.6	−15.7	−19.8	−14.4	−11.5	−6.2
Mexico	−2.6	−2.0	−1.0	−0.7	−0.5	−0.5	−0.8	−1.4	−1.2	−1.3	−1.4
Nicaragua	−19.4	−17.7	−16.2	−14.5	−14.6	−13.5	−17.6	−23.8	−15.3	−18.3	−15.3
Panama	−1.5	−0.8	−4.5	−7.5	−4.9	−3.1	−7.3	−12.4	−9.4	−12.4	−6.0
Paraguay	−4.2	1.8	2.3	2.1	0.3	0.5	0.7	−2.1	0.5	−1.6	−0.8
Peru	−2.1	−1.9	−1.5	0.0	1.4	3.1	1.1	−3.3	−2.1	−2.3	−1.6
St. Kitts and Nevis	−32.0	−39.1	−34.8	−20.1	−18.2	−20.4	−24.2	−28.1	−22.8	−23.8	−21.2
St. Lucia	−15.6	−15.0	−14.7	−10.9	−17.1	−30.2	−40.6	−34.5	−16.0	−17.1	−21.0
St. Vincent and the Grenadines	−10.4	−11.5	−20.8	−24.8	−22.3	−24.1	−35.1	−33.7	−29.5	−31.6	−21.9
Suriname	−14.4	−14.4	−18.0	−11.0	−14.2	5.2	−0.5	−0.3	−0.7	−2.4	1.0
Trinidad and Tobago	5.0	0.9	8.7	12.5	22.5	39.6	25.7	25.5	11.2	16.9	16.0
Uruguay	−2.6	2.9	−0.5	0.3	0.0	−2.3	−0.3	−4.6	−1.6	−2.0	−0.1
Venezuela	1.6	8.2	14.1	13.8	17.7	14.7	8.8	12.3	1.8	5.4	5.7

[1]The Zimbabwe dollar ceased circulating in early 2009. Data are based on IMF staff estimates of price and exchange rate developments in U.S. dollars.

[2]Georgia and Mongolia, which are not members of the Commonwealth of Independent States, are included in this group for reasons of geography and similarities in economic structure.

Table A13. Emerging and Developing Economies: Net Financial Flows[1]

(Billions of U.S. dollars)

	Average 1998–2000	2001	2002	2003	2004	2005	2006	2007	2008	2009	2010
Emerging and developing economies											
Private financial flows, net	77.9	78.2	53.0	177.5	226.5	285.7	262.0	696.5	129.5	−52.5	28.3
Private direct investment, net	152.0	170.7	151.6	150.0	191.6	251.7	254.4	411.2	425.0	279.0	269.5
Private portfolio flows, net	−2.7	−47.1	−45.9	1.8	17.7	32.7	−32.4	88.1	−85.4	−99.8	−110.4
Other private financial flows, net	−71.3	−45.4	−52.8	25.7	17.2	1.2	39.9	197.1	−210.1	−231.6	−130.8
Official financial flows, net[2]	−4.7	16.6	25.6	−48.9	−46.1	−83.4	−140.2	−69.5	−105.7	50.3	−14.2
Change in reserves[3]	−38.2	−89.4	−153.3	−302.6	−425.2	−541.6	−719.1	−1,227.3	−676.9	−360.2	−569.2
Memorandum											
Current account[4]	−9.7	48.0	80.7	149.6	223.8	448.3	659.7	664.5	724.6	355.6	548.1
Africa											
Private financial flows, net	6.3	1.9	0.5	3.8	17.5	16.9	6.9	30.0	28.5	21.0	45.9
Private direct investment, net	7.6	23.1	13.6	17.4	15.9	23.4	20.3	31.5	41.9	26.4	32.2
Private portfolio flows, net	2.5	−6.4	−1.4	−0.5	10.5	5.9	17.1	9.8	−20.8	5.2	8.5
Other private financial flows, net	−3.8	−14.8	−11.7	−13.1	−8.9	−12.5	−30.5	−11.3	7.5	−10.6	5.2
Official flows, net[2]	0.9	5.6	5.2	4.2	2.4	8.3	6.6	6.6	6.0	15.6	16.4
Change in reserves[3]	−3.9	−10.4	−5.7	−10.9	−31.6	−43.2	−54.5	−61.1	−53.6	13.9	−22.4
Central and eastern Europe											
Private financial flows, net	28.8	16.1	16.5	39.0	52.3	103.4	118.8	185.5	154.7	6.4	47.1
Private direct investment, net	15.6	17.7	13.0	15.1	31.7	40.0	64.4	77.1	69.3	31.8	37.4
Private portfolio flows, net	2.3	2.2	0.6	5.6	17.0	18.9	−0.4	−2.9	−9.9	−7.5	4.7
Other private financial flows, net	10.9	−3.7	3.0	18.3	3.5	44.5	54.7	111.3	95.3	−18.0	5.0
Official flows, net[2]	1.0	−4.2	15.5	5.1	9.8	3.1	3.8	−6.4	21.1	34.5	14.7
Change in reserves[3]	−7.2	−1.7	−8.0	−10.8	−12.8	−44.1	−32.7	−36.3	−5.7	−1.9	−0.6
Commonwealth of Independent States[5]											
Private financial flows, net	−5.9	−0.8	−1.6	22.9	1.6	22.9	56.2	124.9	−97.4	−98.5	−17.8
Private direct investment, net	4.2	4.9	5.1	5.4	13.2	11.7	21.4	28.3	49.1	16.6	25.7
Private portfolio flows, net	0.1	0.9	0.6	0.8	−0.2	−3.7	12.7	15.8	−31.3	2.6	6.3
Other private financial flows, net	−10.2	−6.6	−7.4	16.7	−11.4	14.9	22.1	80.9	−115.2	−117.8	−49.9
Official flows, net[2]	−12.7	2.6	6.6	−13.2	−6.2	−11.9	−30.2	−1.6	−25.7	20.8	17.8
Change in reserves[3]	−4.8	−14.4	−15.1	−32.7	−54.9	−77.1	−127.8	−168.1	33.2	20.8	−78.3
Developing Asia											
Private financial flows, net	−12.9	30.5	51.0	81.1	143.1	90.2	54.9	200.6	35.7	−54.3	−113.0
Private direct investment, net	53.0	46.3	60.1	58.6	68.0	93.7	84.7	153.1	139.8	93.4	65.6
Private portfolio flows, net	−10.1	−18.5	−12.1	23.9	38.9	15.4	−50.9	63.2	7.9	−85.2	−127.5
Other private financial flows, net	−55.8	2.7	2.9	−1.4	36.2	−18.9	21.0	−15.6	−112.1	−62.5	−51.1
Official flows, net[2]	8.9	−2.7	−10.2	−17.8	0.8	0.5	−2.4	6.2	−0.3	3.6	5.4
Change in reserves[3]	−21.2	−58.8	−110.8	−166.8	−258.8	−235.2	−322.6	−629.5	−437.5	−329.3	−344.3
Middle East											
Private financial flows, net	3.7	−8.1	−19.7	9.9	−3.7	2.0	−11.6	43.3	−58.9	48.0	25.8
Private direct investment, net	4.8	9.4	8.5	15.4	12.7	29.3	34.1	34.7	34.5	39.5	38.5
Private portfolio flows, net	−5.4	−11.5	−18.3	−15.5	−24.3	−9.0	−22.5	−36.1	−10.7	1.5	−7.4
Other private financial flows, net	4.3	−6.0	−9.8	10.0	7.8	−18.4	−23.2	44.7	−82.8	7.0	−5.3
Official flows, net[2]	−11.4	−12.4	−7.8	−30.7	−43.8	−42.2	−74.4	−73.4	−110.2	−51.6	−76.1
Change in reserves[3]	−3.7	−5.9	−15.0	−47.8	−44.9	−108.5	−131.3	−199.3	−161.9	−44.4	−105.4
Western Hemisphere											
Private financial flows, net	57.9	38.5	6.4	20.9	15.7	50.3	36.9	112.2	67.0	24.8	40.4
Private direct investment, net	66.6	69.3	51.3	38.1	50.1	53.7	29.5	86.6	90.4	71.1	70.1
Private portfolio flows, net	8.0	−13.8	−15.2	−12.5	−24.3	5.1	11.5	38.4	−20.6	−16.5	4.9
Other private financial flows, net	−16.7	−16.9	−29.7	−4.8	−10.2	−8.5	−4.1	−12.8	−2.9	−29.7	−34.6
Official flows, net[2]	8.6	27.7	16.4	3.5	−9.2	−41.1	−43.6	−0.9	3.6	27.5	7.6
Change in reserves[3]	2.5	1.8	1.5	−33.6	−22.2	−33.5	−50.3	−133.1	−51.5	−19.3	−18.1
Memorandum											
Fuel exporting countries											
Private financial flows, net	−6.8	−13.9	−30.0	21.8	−9.0	2.8	8.1	117.9	−223.1	−88.1	−22.3
Other countries											
Private financial flows, net	84.7	92.1	82.9	155.7	235.5	282.9	253.9	578.7	352.7	35.6	50.6

[1]Net financial flows comprise net direct investment, net portfolio investment, and other net official and private financial flows, and changes in reserves.

[2]Excludes grants and includes transactions in external asets and liabilities of official agencies.

[3]A minus sign indicates an increase.

[4]The sum of the current account balance, net private financial flows, net official flows, and the change in reserves equals, with the opposite sign, the sum of the capital account and errors and omissions.

[5]Georgia and Mongolia, which are not members of the Commonwealth of Independent States, are included in this group for reasons of geography and similarities in economic structure.

Table A14. Emerging and Developing Economies: Private Financial Flows[1]

(Billions of U.S. dollars)

	Average 1998–2000	2001	2002	2003	2004	2005	2006	2007	2008	2009	2010
Emerging and developing economies											
Private financial flows, net	77.9	78.2	53.0	177.5	226.5	285.7	262.0	696.5	129.5	−52.5	28.3
Assets	−135.1	−86.3	−100.0	−134.4	−237.0	−393.7	−739.7	−963.6	−576.4	−489.3	−588.9
Liabilities	213.1	164.5	153.0	311.9	463.5	679.3	1,001.7	1,660.1	705.9	436.8	617.2
Africa											
Private financial flows, net	6.3	1.9	0.5	3.8	17.5	16.9	6.9	30.0	28.5	21.0	45.9
Assets	−9.7	−11.6	−11.5	−13.3	−12.0	−19.2	−32.3	−28.3	−10.6	−16.6	−17.7
Liabilities	16.0	13.5	12.0	17.1	29.5	36.1	39.2	58.3	39.1	37.6	63.6
Central and eastern Europe											
Private financial flows, net	28.8	16.1	16.5	39.0	52.3	103.4	118.8	185.5	154.7	6.4	47.1
Assets	−6.8	−8.6	−2.6	−10.4	−31.0	−17.5	−55.3	−44.5	−28.4	−11.4	−11.7
Liabilities	35.6	24.7	19.0	49.4	83.3	120.9	174.0	230.0	183.1	17.8	58.9
Commonwealth of Independent States											
Private financial flows, net	−5.9	−0.8	−1.6	22.9	1.6	22.9	56.2	124.9	−97.4	−98.5	−17.8
Assets	−11.5	−13.6	−25.7	−23.7	−57.7	−85.8	−97.3	−162.0	−264.4	−93.8	−98.6
Liabilities	5.6	12.8	24.1	46.6	59.3	108.8	153.5	286.9	167.0	−4.7	80.8
Developing Asia											
Private financial flows, net	−12.9	30.5	51.0	81.1	143.1	90.2	54.9	200.6	35.7	−54.3	−113.0
Assets	−65.5	−20.3	−34.1	−37.5	−27.7	−141.2	−230.6	−266.2	−210.6	−311.9	−369.3
Liabilities	52.6	50.8	85.0	118.6	170.9	231.4	285.5	466.8	246.3	257.7	256.2
Middle East											
Private financial flows, net	3.7	−8.1	−19.7	9.9	−3.7	2.0	−11.6	43.3	−58.9	48.0	25.8
Assets	−7.3	2.7	−1.4	−17.4	−63.6	−85.4	−234.0	−353.9	18.2	9.5	−34.1
Liabilities	11.0	−10.7	−18.3	27.3	59.9	87.4	222.4	397.2	−77.2	38.5	59.8
Western Hemisphere											
Private financial flows, net	57.9	38.5	6.4	20.9	15.7	50.3	36.9	112.2	67.0	24.8	40.4
Assets	−34.2	−35.0	−24.8	−32.1	−45.0	−44.6	−90.2	−108.7	−80.6	−65.1	−57.5
Liabilities	92.1	73.5	31.2	52.9	60.6	94.9	127.1	220.9	147.6	89.9	97.9

[1]Private financial flows comprise direct investment, portfolio investment, and other long- and short-term investment flows.

Table A15. Emerging and Developing Economies: Reserves[1]

	2001	2002	2003	2004	2005	2006	2007	2008	2009	2010
					Billions of U.S. dollars					
Emerging and developing economies	**857.1**	**1,032.8**	**1,363.7**	**1,815.4**	**2,311.2**	**3,081.8**	**4,378.4**	**4,962.5**	**5,322.7**	**5,891.9**
Regional groups										
Africa	64.2	71.6	89.9	125.9	159.9	221.0	289.2	332.0	318.1	340.6
Sub-Sahara	35.4	35.7	39.6	62.0	82.6	115.7	146.6	157.5	141.7	152.2
Excluding Nigeria and South Africa	18.6	22.1	25.7	31.7	35.5	50.1	65.4	73.6	68.1	76.1
Central and eastern Europe	75.0	92.8	115.9	135.8	166.2	211.7	268.1	265.5	267.4	267.9
Commonwealth of Independent States[2]	43.9	58.1	92.3	148.8	214.4	356.1	548.7	504.0	483.1	561.5
Russia	33.1	44.6	73.8	121.5	176.5	296.2	467.6	413.4	380.7	434.3
Excluding Russia	10.8	13.5	18.5	27.3	37.9	59.8	81.2	90.5	102.4	127.2
Developing Asia	380.2	497.1	671.1	935.8	1,157.8	1,491.5	2,131.6	2,537.7	2,867.0	3,211.3
China	216.3	292.0	409.2	615.5	822.5	1,069.5	1,531.3	1,950.3	2,240.0	2,528.6
India	46.4	68.2	99.5	127.2	132.5	171.3	267.6	248.0	263.1	284.8
Excluding China and India	117.5	136.9	162.4	193.1	202.8	250.7	332.6	339.3	363.8	397.9
Middle East	135.1	152.6	199.3	248.5	357.7	491.1	695.6	825.9	870.3	975.7
Western Hemisphere	158.6	160.5	195.4	220.6	255.3	310.3	445.1	497.5	516.8	534.9
Brazil	35.6	37.5	48.9	52.5	53.3	85.2	179.5	192.9	219.8	240.2
Mexico	44.8	50.6	59.0	64.1	74.1	76.3	87.1	95.1	93.5	93.5
Analytical groups										
By source of export earnings										
Fuel	188.0	214.9	291.7	419.1	612.9	927.2	1,343.1	1,474.2	1,460.7	1,652.1
Nonfuel	669.1	817.9	1,072.0	1,396.3	1,698.3	2,154.6	3,035.3	3,488.3	3,862.0	4,239.8
of which, primary products	19.2	21.1	22.5	23.8	25.7	31.0	33.0	43.0	49.0	51.6
By external financing source										
Net debtor countries	392.0	458.0	580.4	679.2	762.3	960.3	1,332.8	1,385.7	1,458.8	1,545.9
of which, official financing	15.5	18.2	34.7	38.4	39.1	44.7	54.6	58.2	64.2	70.3
Net debtor countries by debt-servicing experience										
Countries with arrears and/or rescheduling during 2003–07	36.6	40.7	50.3	60.3	74.9	90.5	123.5	121.5	124.5	134.9
Other groups										
Heavily indebted poor countries	12.2	15.4	18.0	22.3	23.1	30.5	41.0	45.0	47.1	51.8
Middle East and north Africa	164.1	188.9	250.2	313.8	437.0	598.5	840.0	1,002.2	1,048.0	1,166.0

Table A15 *(concluded)*

	2001	2002	2003	2004	2005	2006	2007	2008	2009	2010
	Ratio of reserves to imports of goods and services[3]									
Emerging and developing economies	**48.8**	**54.7**	**60.7**	**63.4**	**67.1**	**75.3**	**87.1**	**80.4**	**107.0**	**107.9**
Regional groups										
Africa	45.2	45.9	47.2	53.3	56.8	70.0	72.8	67.3	76.6	74.8
Sub-Sahara	33.0	30.2	27.0	34.4	37.6	46.7	47.4	42.1	45.7	44.5
Excluding Nigeria and South Africa	30.7	34.6	33.7	33.2	30.4	38.1	38.9	34.0	37.0	36.9
Central and eastern Europe	36.5	39.5	37.9	33.9	35.6	37.4	37.3	30.8	44.8	41.4
Commonwealth of Independent States[2]	34.3	40.9	52.5	65.3	76.8	101.2	115.6	81.3	115.9	123.2
Russia	44.6	52.9	71.5	93.0	107.4	141.7	165.5	112.3	163.2	172.0
Excluding Russia	20.0	23.3	25.4	28.1	33.0	41.9	42.3	36.0	55.8	62.5
Developing Asia	58.2	67.7	74.0	79.1	81.4	89.2	106.8	106.6	144.4	144.8
China	79.7	89.0	91.1	101.5	115.5	125.4	148.0	158.2	227.8	221.8
India	65.0	90.0	107.1	97.0	72.8	75.5	95.1	73.6	81.1	83.3
Excluding China and India	37.8	41.4	44.5	43.3	38.4	42.3	49.0	41.8	53.6	54.1
Middle East	67.4	69.1	78.2	77.9	87.4	99.3	112.8	101.1	113.0	118.7
Western Hemisphere	37.1	40.2	47.2	44.4	43.4	44.8	53.8	49.9	65.4	62.1
Brazil	49.0	60.8	76.8	65.6	54.4	70.7	113.8	87.6	129.6	126.9
Mexico	24.2	27.3	31.4	29.8	30.5	27.4	28.5	28.5	36.3	33.5
Analytical groups										
By source of export earnings										
Fuel	57.9	59.3	68.7	78.5	89.8	112.6	125.6	106.1	125.0	130.7
Nonfuel	46.7	53.6	58.8	59.9	61.5	65.9	76.7	73.0	101.5	101.1
of which, primary products	47.1	51.3	48.3	41.1	35.6	38.0	31.7	32.7	45.5	42.8
By external financing source										
Net debtor countries	38.3	43.4	47.6	44.4	41.6	44.0	50.3	43.2	57.0	55.8
of which, official financing	36.5	38.1	60.2	55.4	46.6	45.7	45.6	39.4	46.2	46.8
Net debtor countries by debt-servicing experience										
Countries with arrears and/or rescheduling during 2003–07	29.6	35.3	36.7	34.8	35.0	35.6	39.9	31.1	39.0	39.5
Other groups										
Heavily indebted poor countries	28.5	31.2	30.9	31.1	27.0	31.3	33.8	30.3	34.8	35.5
Middle East and north Africa	68.7	71.9	82.5	82.4	90.9	104.4	116.9	105.2	118.1	122.9

[1]In this table, official holdings of gold are valued at SDR 35 an ounce. This convention results in a marked underestimation of reserves for countries that have substantial gold holdings.

[2]Georgia and Mongolia, which are not members of the Commonwealth of Independent States, are included in this group for reasons of geography and similarities in economic structure.

[3]Reserves at year-end in percent of imports of goods and services for the year indicated.

Table A16. Summary of Sources and Uses of World Savings

(Percent of GDP)

	Averages 1987–94	Averages 1995–2002	2003	2004	2005	2006	2007	2008	2009	2010	Average 2011–14
World											
Savings	22.5	22.1	21.0	22.1	22.9	24.1	24.5	24.2	21.7	22.6	24.5
Investment	22.4	22.2	21.2	22.1	22.6	23.3	23.9	24.0	21.9	22.0	23.6
Advanced economies											
Savings	22.1	21.5	19.3	20.0	20.2	20.9	20.7	19.5	16.9	17.5	19.1
Investment	22.8	21.6	20.0	20.6	21.1	21.6	21.5	21.0	18.0	17.9	19.5
Net lending	−0.7	−0.1	−0.7	−0.6	−0.9	−0.6	−0.9	−1.5	−1.2	−0.4	−0.4
Current transfers	−0.4	−0.5	−0.6	−0.7	−0.7	−0.7	−0.8	−0.8	−0.8	−0.7	−0.7
Factor income	−0.5	0.3	0.2	0.5	0.7	1.1	0.5	0.1	−0.3	0.3	0.2
Resource balance	0.2	0.1	−0.3	−0.5	−0.9	−1.0	−0.6	−0.8	−0.1	0.0	0.0
United States											
Savings	15.9	17.3	13.9	14.5	15.1	16.2	14.5	12.6	11.0	12.6	15.6
Investment	18.6	19.6	18.7	19.7	20.3	20.5	19.5	18.2	15.0	15.0	18.4
Net lending	−2.7	−2.3	−4.8	−5.2	−5.2	−4.3	−5.0	−5.6	−4.0	−2.3	−2.7
Current transfers	−0.4	−0.6	−0.6	−0.7	−0.8	−0.7	−0.8	−0.9	−0.8	−0.7	−0.7
Factor income	−0.7	0.7	0.3	0.7	1.3	2.0	0.8	0.1	−0.8	0.7	0.4
Resource balance	−1.5	−2.5	−4.4	−5.1	−5.7	−5.7	−5.0	−4.8	−2.4	−2.3	−2.4
Euro area											
Savings	...	21.5	20.8	21.6	21.2	22.1	22.5	21.4	18.6	18.3	19.0
Investment	...	20.8	20.1	20.4	20.8	21.6	22.2	22.2	19.4	18.7	19.1
Net lending	...	0.6	0.7	1.2	0.5	0.5	0.4	−0.7	−0.8	−0.4	−0.1
Current transfers[1]	−0.5	−0.7	−0.8	−0.8	−0.9	−1.0	−1.0	−1.1	−1.0	−1.0	−1.0
Factor income[1]	−0.9	−0.4	−0.7	−0.1	−0.2	0.0	−0.4	−0.7	−0.6	−0.6	−0.6
Resource balance[1]	1.0	1.7	2.1	2.2	1.6	1.3	1.7	1.1	1.0	1.3	1.7
Germany											
Savings	23.4	20.3	19.3	21.8	22.0	23.8	25.9	25.6	19.8	19.3	20.0
Investment	23.7	20.8	17.4	17.1	16.9	17.6	18.3	19.2	16.9	15.6	15.3
Net lending	−0.3	−0.5	1.9	4.7	5.1	6.1	7.5	6.4	2.9	3.6	4.7
Current transfers	−1.6	−1.4	−1.3	−1.3	−1.3	−1.2	−1.3	−1.3	−1.3	−1.3	−1.2
Factor income	−0.9	−0.4	−0.7	0.9	1.1	1.6	1.7	1.1	1.0	1.0	1.2
Resource balance	2.2	1.2	3.9	5.0	5.3	5.7	7.1	6.6	3.2	3.9	4.7
France											
Savings	20.3	20.9	20.3	20.1	19.9	20.6	21.2	19.9	18.9	18.4	19.0
Investment	20.6	18.9	18.9	19.5	20.3	21.1	22.2	22.2	19.9	19.8	20.6
Net lending	−0.3	2.0	1.4	0.6	−0.4	−0.5	−1.0	−2.3	−1.0	−1.4	−1.6
Current transfers	−0.6	−0.8	−1.1	−1.1	−1.3	−1.2	−1.2	−1.2	−1.3	−1.3	−1.3
Factor income	−0.5	0.8	1.4	1.1	1.4	1.6	1.5	1.3	1.5	1.4	0.9
Resource balance	0.9	2.1	1.1	0.6	−0.5	−0.9	−1.3	−2.3	−1.3	−1.5	−1.2
Italy											
Savings	20.2	21.2	19.4	19.9	19.0	19.0	19.4	17.8	15.6	15.0	15.2
Investment	21.3	20.1	20.7	20.8	20.7	21.6	21.8	21.2	18.1	17.4	17.9
Net lending	−1.1	1.1	−1.3	−0.9	−1.7	−2.6	−2.4	−3.4	−2.5	−2.3	−2.7
Current transfers	−0.4	−0.5	−0.5	−0.6	−0.7	−0.9	−0.9	−1.0	−0.8	−0.8	−0.8
Factor income	−1.6	−1.1	−1.3	−1.1	−1.0	−0.9	−1.3	−1.9	−1.8	−1.7	−1.5
Resource balance	0.9	2.7	0.6	0.7	0.0	−0.8	−0.3	−0.5	0.1	0.2	−0.3
Japan											
Savings	33.1	28.6	26.1	26.8	27.2	27.7	28.8	26.6	23.2	23.4	24.0
Investment	30.6	26.2	22.8	23.0	23.6	23.8	24.1	23.5	21.2	21.3	22.0
Net lending	2.5	2.4	3.2	3.7	3.6	3.9	4.7	3.1	2.0	2.0	2.0
Current transfers	−0.1	−0.2	−0.2	−0.2	−0.2	−0.2	−0.3	−0.3	−0.2	−0.2	−0.2
Factor income	0.7	1.3	1.7	1.8	2.3	2.7	3.1	3.0	2.7	2.4	2.7
Resource balance	1.9	1.2	1.7	2.0	1.5	1.4	1.9	0.4	−0.5	−0.2	−0.5
United Kingdom											
Savings	16.0	16.1	15.1	15.0	14.5	14.2	15.6	15.3	11.6	12.2	14.0
Investment	18.6	17.5	16.7	17.1	17.1	17.5	18.3	17.0	13.7	14.1	16.0
Net lending	−2.7	−1.4	−1.6	−2.1	−2.6	−3.3	−2.7	−1.7	−2.0	−1.9	−2.0
Current transfers	−0.7	−0.8	−0.9	−0.9	−0.9	−0.9	−1.0	−0.9	−1.1	−1.1	−1.1
Factor income	−0.4	0.5	1.5	1.5	1.7	0.7	1.5	1.9	1.1	1.0	1.2
Resource balance	−1.6	−1.1	−2.3	−2.7	−3.4	−3.1	−3.2	−2.7	−2.0	−1.9	−2.1
Canada											
Savings	16.9	20.4	21.2	23.0	24.0	24.4	24.4	23.7	18.6	19.0	21.1
Investment	20.3	19.6	20.0	20.7	22.1	23.0	23.4	23.2	21.2	20.9	21.1
Net lending	−3.4	0.8	1.2	2.3	1.9	1.4	1.0	0.5	−2.6	−1.8	0.0
Current transfers	−0.2	0.1	0.0	−0.1	−0.1	−0.1	−0.1	−0.1	−0.1	−0.2	−0.2
Factor income	−3.5	−3.1	−2.5	−1.9	−1.7	−1.0	−0.7	−0.9	−0.7	−0.4	−0.5
Resource balance	0.2	3.8	3.7	4.2	3.7	2.5	1.9	1.5	−1.8	−1.3	0.6

Table A16 *(continued)*

	Averages		2003	2004	2005	2006	2007	2008	2009	2010	Average 2011–14
	1987–94	1995–2002									
Newly industrialized Asian economies											
Savings	34.9	31.9	31.5	32.6	31.4	31.6	31.8	32.1	28.4	29.2	30.0
Investment	30.2	28.6	24.8	26.4	25.9	26.1	26.0	27.6	22.0	23.3	24.3
Net lending	4.7	3.4	6.6	6.2	5.5	5.5	5.8	4.5	6.4	5.9	5.7
Current transfers	0.0	−0.4	−0.7	−0.7	−0.7	−0.7	−0.7	−0.6	−0.7	−0.6	−0.6
Factor income	1.2	0.4	0.8	0.6	0.3	0.5	0.4	1.2	−0.3	−0.2	0.5
Resource balance	3.4	3.3	6.5	6.4	5.9	5.7	6.1	3.8	7.4	6.7	5.7
Emerging and developing economies											
Savings	24.1	24.4	27.9	29.7	31.5	33.3	34.3	34.8	32.6	33.5	34.7
Investment	25.3	24.9	25.9	27.2	27.3	28.2	30.0	30.9	30.6	30.6	31.2
Net lending	−2.1	−0.5	2.0	2.5	4.2	5.2	4.2	3.9	2.0	2.9	3.5
Current transfers	0.5	1.0	1.7	1.7	1.7	1.8	1.7	1.5	1.5	1.4	1.3
Factor income	−1.3	−1.9	−2.0	−2.0	−1.8	−1.7	−1.6	−1.6	−1.4	−1.5	−0.5
Resource balance	−0.8	0.4	2.3	2.8	4.3	5.1	4.2	3.9	1.9	3.0	2.7
Memorandum											
Acquisition of foreign assets	1.5	3.6	5.7	6.8	9.6	11.6	14.0	6.7	4.5	5.7	6.2
Change in reserves	0.5	1.2	4.0	4.7	5.0	5.7	7.9	3.6	2.0	3.0	2.9
Regional groups											
Africa											
Savings	18.1	18.5	21.2	22.5	23.9	28.4	27.5	27.9	22.1	23.7	25.3
Investment	19.2	20.1	21.5	22.4	22.1	22.9	24.5	25.0	25.1	25.3	25.9
Net lending	−1.2	−1.5	−0.3	0.1	1.7	5.5	2.9	2.8	−3.0	−1.6	−0.6
Current transfers	2.5	2.6	3.2	3.3	3.2	4.4	4.3	4.2	4.7	3.8	3.5
Factor income	−3.4	−4.0	−4.4	−5.0	−5.3	−4.5	−5.0	−4.8	−4.3	−4.3	−3.8
Resource balance	−0.3	−0.1	0.8	1.8	3.9	5.5	3.6	3.4	−3.5	−1.2	−0.2
Memorandum											
Acquisition of foreign assets	0.1	2.7	3.0	4.1	6.2	9.6	8.7	5.9	1.4	4.4	5.3
Change in reserves	0.4	1.4	1.9	4.4	5.2	5.7	5.5	4.2	−1.2	1.7	2.8
Central and eastern Europe											
Savings	23.0	18.6	16.1	16.4	16.5	16.9	16.8	16.9	16.6	17.3	18.6
Investment	25.9	21.9	20.2	21.8	21.6	23.5	25.0	24.9	19.7	21.2	22.5
Net lending	−2.9	−3.3	−4.0	−5.4	−5.1	−6.6	−8.2	−8.0	−3.1	−3.9	−4.0
Current transfers	1.7	2.1	2.2	2.0	1.9	2.0	1.8	1.6	1.8	1.9	2.0
Factor income	−3.5	−1.5	−2.0	−2.5	−2.1	−2.4	−3.1	−2.8	−2.2	−2.3	−2.4
Resource balance	−1.1	−3.9	−4.2	−4.9	−4.9	−6.2	−6.9	−6.8	−2.7	−3.6	−3.6
Memorandum											
Acquisition of foreign assets	0.9	2.0	2.6	4.0	5.1	6.1	5.2	2.0	0.1	1.0	2.2
Change in reserves	−0.6	1.5	1.3	1.3	3.7	2.5	2.2	0.3	0.1	0.0	0.5
Commonwealth of Independent States[2]											
Savings	. . .	24.7	27.3	29.8	30.0	30.1	30.3	30.9	24.9	26.6	27.7
Investment	. . .	20.9	21.2	21.7	21.4	23.0	26.4	26.2	22.2	22.7	24.1
Net lending	. . .	3.8	6.1	8.2	8.6	7.1	3.9	4.7	2.6	3.9	3.5
Current transfers	. . .	0.5	0.6	0.5	0.5	0.4	0.3	0.5	0.7	0.6	0.5
Factor income	. . .	−2.6	−2.9	−2.2	−2.9	−3.7	−3.3	−3.7	−3.9	−5.1	−3.1
Resource balance	. . .	6.0	8.4	9.9	10.9	10.3	6.8	7.9	5.9	8.4	6.1
Memorandum											
Acquisition of foreign assets	. . .	5.4	11.6	14.0	15.4	14.9	17.5	9.6	2.4	8.3	8.1
Change in reserves	. . .	1.6	5.7	7.1	7.7	9.8	9.9	−1.5	−1.3	4.3	3.3

Table A16 *(continued)*

	Averages		2003	2004	2005	2006	2007	2008	2009	2010	Average 2011–14
	1987–94	1995–2002									
Developing Asia											
Savings	29.5	32.7	36.4	38.3	41.3	43.9	46.8	47.7	47.1	46.9	46.8
Investment	34.2	31.9	33.6	35.8	37.2	37.9	39.8	41.9	42.1	41.7	41.3
Net lending	−2.0	0.8	2.7	2.6	4.1	6.0	7.0	5.8	4.9	5.2	5.5
Current transfers	0.9	1.4	2.2	2.1	2.2	2.2	2.2	2.1	2.0	1.8	1.6
Factor income	−1.5	−1.5	−1.2	−1.1	−0.8	−0.6	−0.3	−0.3	−0.4	−0.4	0.4
Resource balance	−1.5	0.9	1.7	1.6	2.6	4.3	5.0	4.0	3.3	3.8	3.4
Memorandum											
Acquisition of foreign assets	3.7	5.4	6.1	7.3	9.6	11.4	14.1	8.3	7.3	7.4	7.0
Change in reserves	1.3	1.8	5.5	7.4	5.8	6.8	10.7	6.1	4.3	4.1	3.5
Middle East											
Savings	18.3	26.2	32.1	35.6	42.0	43.1	42.7	41.9	28.9	33.3	36.7
Investment	23.8	22.7	24.2	24.0	22.0	21.7	23.9	22.8	25.5	24.4	24.4
Net lending	−5.5	3.6	7.8	11.6	20.1	21.4	18.8	19.1	3.5	8.9	12.3
Current transfers	−3.8	−2.7	−2.2	−2.0	−1.0	−1.3	−1.5	−1.6	−2.0	−2.0	−1.8
Factor income	2.1	2.2	0.2	0.4	1.1	2.2	2.6	2.0	1.2	1.4	4.7
Resource balance	−3.8	4.1	9.9	13.2	19.9	20.5	17.7	18.7	4.3	9.6	9.5
Memorandum											
Acquisition of foreign assets	2.5	4.0	10.9	14.4	27.9	37.3	43.3	12.8	5.3	10.2	14.2
Change in reserves	0.0	1.2	6.7	5.4	10.3	10.4	13.6	8.6	2.7	5.5	6.7
Western Hemisphere											
Savings	18.6	17.9	19.8	22.0	22.0	23.2	22.4	22.1	18.9	19.2	20.0
Investment	18.8	20.7	19.2	20.8	20.6	21.7	22.2	22.9	19.8	20.1	20.8
Net lending	−1.4	−2.8	0.6	1.2	1.4	1.5	0.2	−0.8	−0.9	−0.9	−0.8
Current transfers	0.8	1.1	2.0	2.1	2.0	2.1	1.8	1.6	1.5	1.4	1.5
Factor income	−2.0	−2.8	−3.0	−3.0	−3.0	−3.2	−2.9	−2.7	−2.2	−2.1	−1.9
Resource balance	0.6	−1.0	1.6	2.1	2.4	2.6	1.3	0.3	−0.2	−0.2	−0.4
Memorandum											
Acquisition of foreign assets	0.1	1.8	3.3	2.8	3.0	3.1	6.0	2.2	2.0	1.4	1.5
Change in reserves	0.6	0.2	1.8	1.0	1.3	1.6	3.7	1.2	0.5	0.4	0.5
Analytical groups											
By source of export earnings											
Fuel											
Savings	26.1	26.8	30.9	34.0	37.9	39.3	38.0	38.1	27.5	31.0	32.9
Investment	25.7	22.5	23.1	23.3	21.9	22.4	25.2	24.2	23.8	23.3	23.9
Net lending	−3.2	4.3	7.8	10.7	16.0	16.9	12.8	13.9	3.7	7.7	9.0
Current transfers	−1.9	−1.9	−1.4	−1.1	−0.6	−0.3	−0.5	−0.6	−0.7	−0.7	−0.7
Factor income	−0.7	−1.0	−2.5	−2.3	−2.4	−2.1	−1.9	−2.2	−2.2	−2.5	0.1
Resource balance	0.0	7.2	11.7	14.2	18.9	19.2	15.2	16.7	6.6	11.0	9.6
Memorandum											
Acquisition of foreign assets	1.6	4.9	11.2	13.5	21.4	25.4	28.0	12.1	3.9	9.4	11.2
Change in reserves	−0.3	1.1	5.2	6.9	9.2	10.5	11.1	3.8	−0.4	4.6	4.9
Nonfuel											
Savings	23.2	24.0	27.2	28.7	29.8	31.6	33.2	33.8	34.0	34.1	35.2
Investment	25.2	25.4	26.5	28.2	28.7	29.8	31.4	33.0	32.4	32.6	33.3
Net lending	−1.9	−1.4	0.7	0.5	1.1	1.8	1.8	0.7	1.6	1.5	2.0
Current transfers	1.2	1.6	2.4	2.3	2.4	2.4	2.3	2.2	2.1	1.9	1.9
Factor income	−1.5	−2.0	−1.9	−1.9	−1.7	−1.6	−1.5	−1.4	−1.2	−1.2	−0.6
Resource balance	−1.0	−1.0	0.2	0.0	0.4	1.1	1.0	−0.1	0.6	0.7	0.8
Memorandum											
Acquisition of foreign assets	1.5	3.3	4.5	5.2	6.4	7.6	9.9	5.0	4.6	4.7	4.8
Change in reserves	0.7	1.2	3.7	4.2	3.9	4.3	7.0	3.6	2.7	2.5	2.3

Table A16 (concluded)

	Averages		2003	2004	2005	2006	2007	2008	2009	2010	Average 2011–14
	1987–94	1995–2002									
By external financing source											
Net debtor countries											
Savings	19.8	18.8	20.2	21.4	21.6	22.7	23.0	22.3	21.9	21.2	22.8
Investment	20.8	21.5	20.9	22.7	23.3	24.4	25.6	26.0	24.2	23.9	25.2
Net lending	–2.2	–2.7	–0.7	–1.3	–1.7	–1.7	–2.6	–3.8	–2.3	–2.7	–2.4
Current transfers	1.7	2.1	3.1	3.0	3.0	3.0	2.9	2.8	2.9	2.7	2.7
Factor income	–1.5	–1.5	–2.4	–2.6	–2.6	–2.6	–2.6	–2.6	–2.2	–2.2	–2.2
Resource balance	–1.5	–2.6	–1.4	–1.7	–2.1	–2.1	–2.9	–4.0	–3.0	–3.2	–3.0
Memorandum											
Acquisition of foreign assets	0.4	1.8	3.1	3.0	3.0	4.3	6.1	1.5	1.2	1.5	2.0
Change in reserves	0.5	0.7	2.3	1.6	1.9	2.5	4.2	1.1	0.9	0.9	1.2
Official financing											
Savings	14.4	16.4	18.4	20.6	21.2	22.1	22.7	21.5	20.1	20.6	23.0
Investment	19.7	20.2	21.6	22.3	23.3	23.9	24.9	25.8	24.8	25.9	26.7
Net lending	–5.2	–3.7	–3.2	–1.7	–2.1	–1.7	–2.2	–4.2	–4.6	–5.2	–3.7
Current transfers	4.4	5.7	8.6	9.5	10.4	10.3	10.7	10.3	10.3	9.4	9.1
Factor income	–3.7	–2.5	–1.7	–1.6	–1.7	–1.1	–0.6	–0.8	–1.3	–1.6	–1.9
Resource balance	–5.9	–6.9	–10.1	–9.6	–10.9	–10.9	–12.3	–13.8	–13.6	–13.0	–10.8
Memorandum											
Acquisition of foreign assets	1.0	0.5	0.3	1.8	1.6	2.8	2.8	1.6	1.0	1.0	2.2
Change in reserves	1.3	0.4	9.2	1.4	0.9	2.1	2.7	1.3	1.7	1.5	2.1
Net debtor countries by debt-servicing experience											
Countries with arrears and/or rescheduling during 2003–07											
Savings	16.1	14.5	19.5	19.3	20.1	21.6	21.2	19.9	19.5	19.0	19.5
Investment	19.4	18.6	17.9	19.8	21.6	23.0	24.1	24.5	22.7	22.3	22.9
Net lending	–3.3	–4.2	1.7	–0.5	–1.4	–1.4	–3.0	–4.6	–3.2	–3.3	–3.4
Current transfers	1.8	2.9	5.7	5.6	5.8	5.7	5.2	4.6	5.1	4.3	4.2
Factor income	–2.8	–4.3	–3.8	–4.1	–3.8	–3.6	–3.8	–3.8	–2.9	–3.0	–2.9
Resource balance	–2.4	–2.8	–0.3	–1.9	–3.5	–3.5	–4.4	–5.4	–5.4	–4.6	–4.7
Memorandum											
Acquisition of foreign assets	1.1	2.2	4.1	2.8	2.3	3.0	5.0	0.9	0.3	1.0	1.2
Change in reserves	0.2	0.3	2.4	2.0	2.6	1.9	3.5	0.2	0.3	1.0	0.8

Note: The estimates in this table are based on individual countries' national accounts and balance of payments statistics. Country group composites are calculated as the sum of the U.S dollar values for the relevant individual countries. This differs from the calculations in the April 2005 and earlier issues of the *World Economic Outlook*, where the composites were weighted by GDP valued at purchasing power parities as a share of total world GDP. For many countries, the estimates of national savings are built up from national accounts data on gross domestic investment and from balance-of-payments-based data on net foreign investment. The latter, which is equivalent to the current account balance, comprises three components: current transfers, net factor income, and the resource balance. The mixing of data source, which is dictated by availability, implies that the estimates for national savings that are derived incorporate the statistical discrepancies. Furthermore, errors, omissions, and asymmetries in balance of payments statistics affect the estimates for net lending; at the global level, net lending, which in theory would be zero, equals the world current account discrepancy. Despite these statistical shortcomings, flow of funds estimates, such as those presented in these tables, provide a useful framework for analyzing development in savings and investment, both over time and across regions and countries.

[1]Calculated from the data of individual euro area countries.

[2]Georgia and Mongolia, which are not members of the Commonwealth of Independent States, are included in this group for reasons of geography and similarities in economic structure.

Table A17. Summary of World Medium-Term Baseline Scenario

	Eight-Year Averages		Four-Year Average 2007–10	2007	2008	2009	2010	Four-Year Average 2011–14
	1991–98	1999–2006						
	Annual percent change unless otherwise noted							
World real GDP	**2.8**	**4.0**	**2.5**	**5.2**	**3.0**	**−1.1**	**3.1**	**4.4**
Advanced economies	2.5	2.7	0.3	2.7	0.6	−3.4	1.3	2.5
Emerging and developing economies	3.3	5.8	5.2	8.3	6.0	1.7	5.1	6.4
Memorandum								
Potential output								
Major advanced economies	2.5	2.3	1.2	2.0	1.6	0.5	0.7	1.3
World trade, volume[1]	**6.6**	**6.8**	**−0.1**	**7.3**	**3.0**	**−11.9**	**2.5**	**6.4**
Imports								
Advanced economies	6.3	6.2	−2.1	4.7	0.5	−13.7	1.2	5.3
Emerging and developing economies	7.1	9.3	4.2	13.8	9.4	−9.5	4.6	8.1
Exports								
Advanced economies	6.6	5.7	−1.2	6.3	1.9	−13.6	2.0	5.7
Emerging and developing economies	8.2	9.6	2.5	9.8	4.6	−7.2	3.6	7.7
Terms of trade								
Advanced economies	0.2	−0.4	0.1	0.3	−1.8	2.0	−0.2	−0.3
Emerging and developing economies	−1.6	2.5	0.7	0.7	4.1	−6.3	4.6	−0.1
World prices in U.S. dollars								
Manufactures	−0.6	2.5	2.6	9.0	8.6	−9.1	3.1	1.7
Oil	−6.8	22.0	4.4	10.7	36.4	−36.6	24.3	2.6
Nonfuel primary commodities	−1.5	5.0	0.0	14.1	7.5	−20.3	2.4	0.9
Consumer prices								
Advanced economies	2.9	2.0	1.7	2.2	3.4	0.1	1.1	1.6
Emerging and developing economies	54.4	7.5	6.5	6.4	9.3	5.5	4.9	4.2
Interest rates (in percent)								
Real six-month LIBOR[2]	3.1	1.3	0.7	2.4	0.9	−0.4	−0.1	2.7
World real long-term interest rate[3]	3.8	2.3	2.0	2.0	0.4	2.9	2.5	3.4
	Percent of GDP							
Balances on current account								
Advanced economies	0.1	−0.9	−0.8	−0.9	−1.3	−0.7	−0.4	−0.4
Emerging and developing economies	−1.8	2.1	3.3	4.3	3.9	2.0	2.8	3.5
Total external debt								
Emerging and developing economies	35.9	34.5	25.7	27.9	24.2	26.0	24.6	22.8
Debt service								
Emerging and developing economies	6.0	8.6	6.9	7.0	6.9	7.4	6.4	5.9

[1]Data refer to trade in goods and services.

[2]London interbank offered rate on U.S. dollar deposits minus percent change in U.S. GDP deflator.

[3]GDP-weighted average of 10-year (or nearest maturity) government bond rates for United States, Japan, Germany, France, Italy, United Kingdom, and Canada.

WORLD ECONOMIC OUTLOOK
SELECTED TOPICS

I. Methodology—Aggregation, Modeling, and Forecasting

II. Historical Surveys

III. Economic Growth—Sources and Patterns

IV. Inflation and Deflation, and Commodity Markets

V. Fiscal Policy

VI. Monetary Policy, Financial Markets, and Flow of Funds

VII. Labor Markets, Poverty, and Inequality

VIII. Exchange Rate Issues

IX. External Payments, Trade, Capital Movements, and Foreign Debt

X. Regional Issues

XI. Country-Specific Analyses

XII. Special Topics

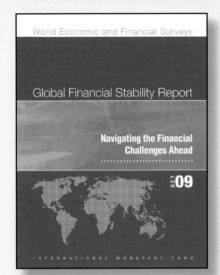
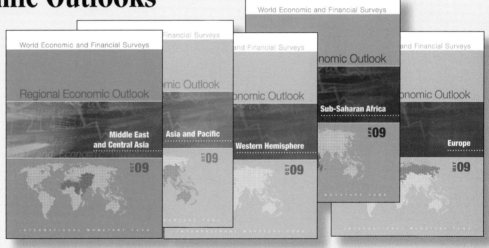

1-2010

1-2010